National Parks Australia

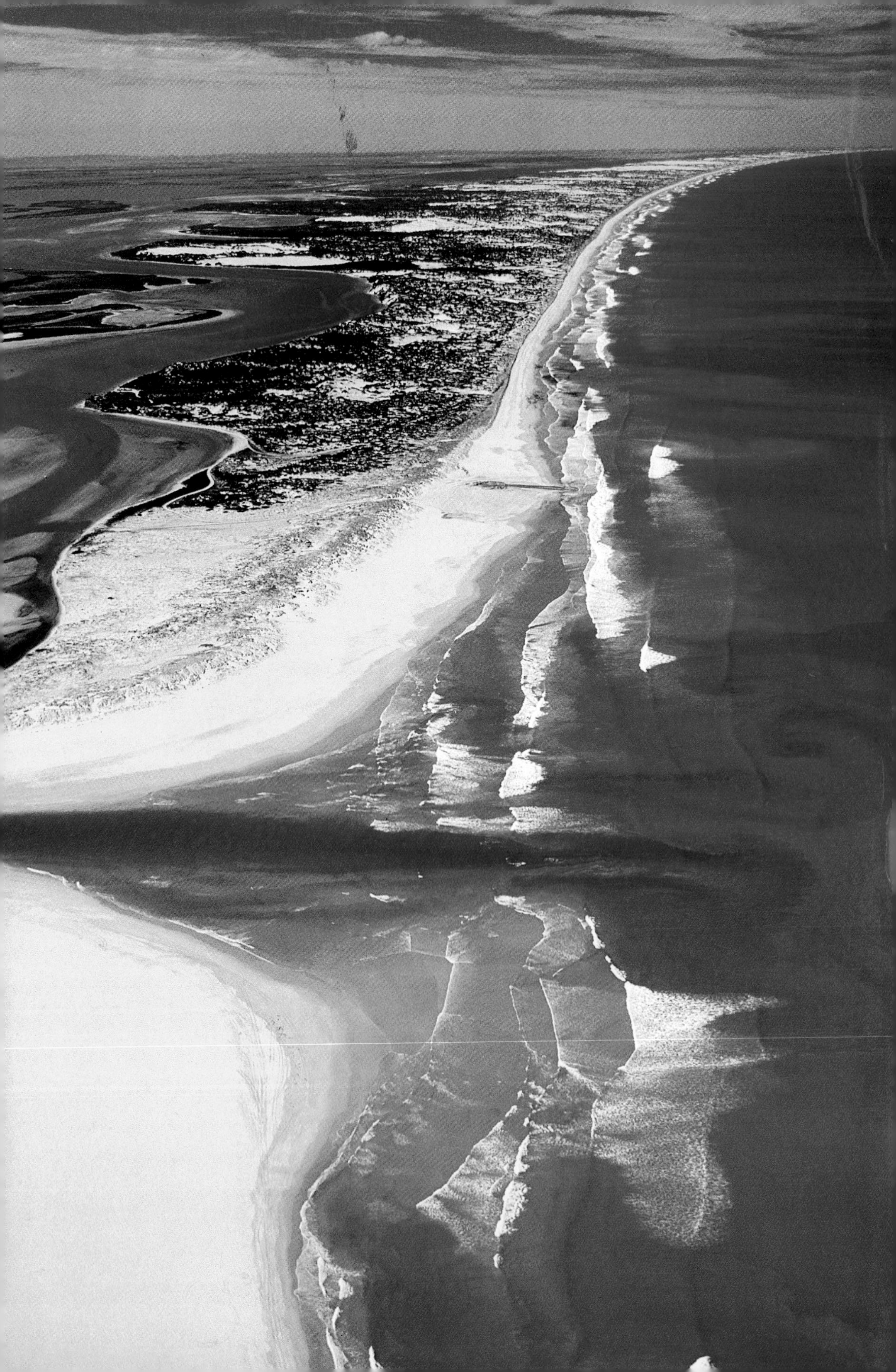

National Parks Australia

Ron & Viv Moon

Enjoy the beauty of
Australia's natural heritage

Managing Director	Cheryl Perry
Publishing Manager	Sarah Anderson
Art Director	Stan Lamond
Managing Editor	Kate Etherington
Senior Editor	Dannielle Doggett
Editor	Denise Imwold
Captions	Margaret McPhee Susan Page
Cover Design	Stan Lamond
Cartographer	John Frith
Map Editors	Louise Buchanan Heather McNamara Dee Rogers
Picture Research	Gordon Cheers
Photo Library	Alan Edwards
Typesetting	Dee Rogers
Index	Heather McNamara
Publishing Assistant	Cara Codemo
Production	Bernard Roberts

Photographers

Fred Adler, Chris Bell, Rob Blakers, Lorraine Blyth, Ken Brass, Claver Carroll, Kevin Deacon, Grant Dixon, Mike Edmondson, Bruce Elder, Stuart Owen Fox, Peter Gill, Denise Greig, Ivy Hansen, Richard I'Anson, Ionas Kaltenbach, Judith Kempen, Colin Kerr, Stan Lamond, Mike Langford, Gary Lewis, John McCann, David McGonigal, Richard McKenna, Shane Mensforth, Ron Moon, Peter O'Reilly, Nick Rains, Jamie Robertson, Tony Rodd, Don Skirrow, Raoul Slater, Steve Starling, Ken Stepnell, Oliver Strewe, Glenn Tempest, Sharyn Vanderhorst, Colleen Vigar, Neil Wehlack, Murray White, Vic Widman, Geoff Woods, Grant Young, James Young

Captions for preliminary pages and state opening spreads

Page 1: Maits Rest Rainforest Walk in Otway National Park, Victoria.

Page 2: The Murray Mouth in Coorong National Park, Limestone Coast, South Australia.

Page 3: View from the top of the sandstone cliffs of Hanging Rock in the Grose Valley in Blue Mountains National Park, New South Wales.

Page 6: Dove Lake, Cradle Mountain-Lake St Clair National Park, Tasmania.

Pages 12–13: Mount Mooloolong, in the KaKa Mundi Section of Queensland's Carnarvon National Park, at sunset.

Pages 52–53: Seven Mile Beach National Park, on the New South Wales south coast.

Pages 96–97: Looking towards Buffalo Plateau, Alpine National Park, Victoria.

Pages 140–141: Walls of Jerusalem National Park, Tasmania.

Pages 162–163: Aerial view of Lake Eyre, Lake Eyre National Park, South Australia.

Pages 192–193: The Pinnacles at Nambung National Park, Western Australia.

Pages 228–229: View of Kata Tjuta (the Olgas) from the top of Uluru (Ayers Rock), Northern Territory.

Gregory's

Published by
Gregory's Publishing Company
(A division of Universal Publishers Pty Ltd)
ACN 000 087 132

Marketed and distributed by Universal Publishers Pty Ltd
New South Wales: 1 Waterloo Road, Macquarie Park 2113
Ph: (02) 9857 3700 Fax: (02) 9888 9850
Queensland: 1 Manning Street, South Brisbane 4101
Ph: (07) 3844 1051 Fax: (07) 3844 4637
South Australia: Freecall: 1800 021 987
Victoria: 585 Burwood Road, Hawthorn 3122
Ph: (03) 9818 4455 Fax: (03) 9818 6123
Western Australia: 38a Walters Drive, Osborne Park 6017
Ph: (08) 9244 2488 Fax: (08) 9244 2554

Produced by Global Book Publishing Pty Ltd
Level 8, 15 Orion Road, Lane Cove, NSW Australia 2066
Phone 61 2 9425 5800 fax 61 2 9425 5804

ISBN 0 7319 1970 X

Second edition published in 2006

National Library of Australia Cataloguing-in-Publication
Moon, Ron.
National Parks Australia.
ISBN 0 7319 1970 X.
1. National parks and reserves - Australia - Guidebooks. 2. Australia - Guidebooks. I. Moon, Viv. II. Title.
(Series : See Australia (Sydney)).
919.4047

Printed in China by C&C Offset Printing Co. Ltd.,
Film separation Pica Digital Pte Ltd, Singapore

Global Book Publishing would be pleased to hear from photographers interested in supplying photographs.

Key to Road Maps

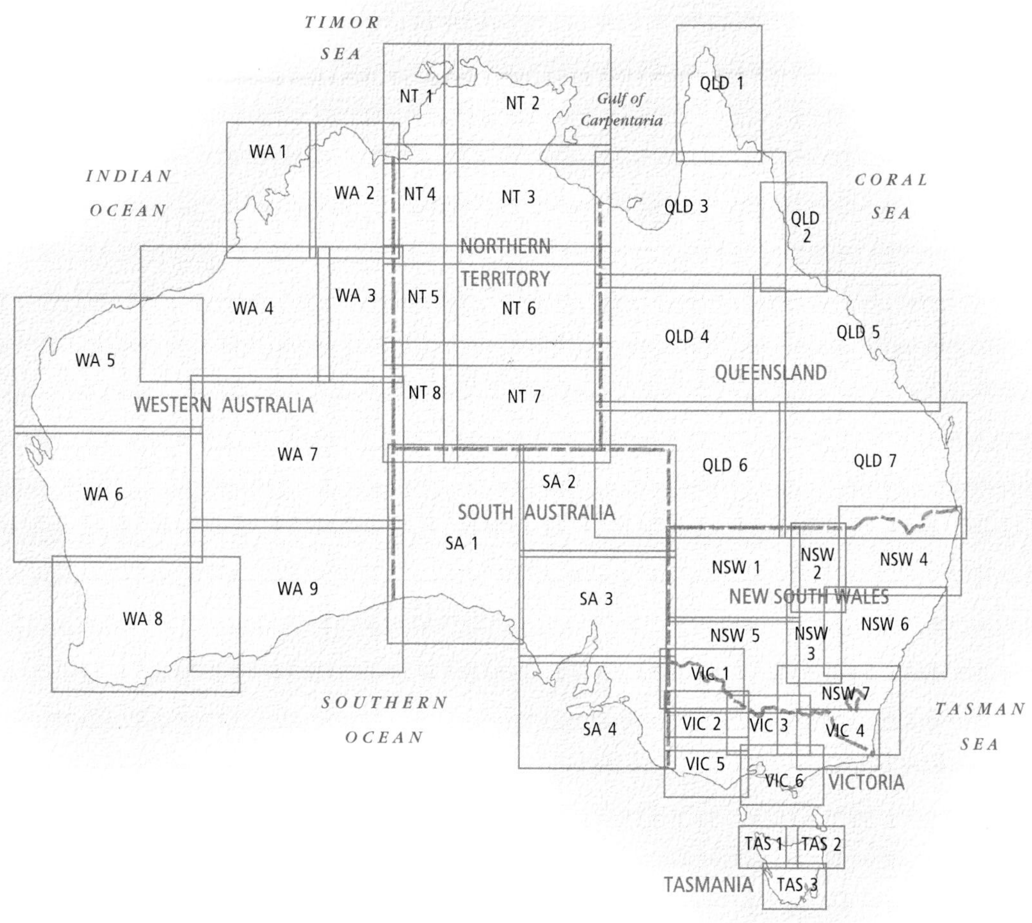

Legend to Road Maps

Freeway or motorway with national or federal route number	66 A8 1	Major linear feature (as noted)	Dog Fence
Freeway or motorway tunnel	M1	International airport	
Highway with state route numbers	69 A20	Major built up area, state or territory capital	
Major sealed road with metroad route number	5	Major city or town, other towns	
Minor sealed road, bridge		Homestead, ruin, mine,	
Major unsealed road, gate, grid		Landmark or tourist feature, mountain peak	
Minor unsealed road or track, 4WD where indicated	4WD	Bore, well or waterhole, tank or dam	
Walking track		Major river, other watercourse	
Road distances in kilometres, major and intermediate	12 18 30	Perennial lake, dry or intermittent lake	
Railway line with station	Watson	Boundary of prohibited area or military reserve	
Underground railway (city maps only)		State ot territory border	
Tramline with station (city maps only)		Marine park or reserve, coral reef	
Railway line, dismantled or abandoned (regional maps)		Aboriginal land	
Ferry route		National park, reserve, conservation area or state forest	

Contents

See and Experience Australia's National Parks

Australia is an ancient land. The country we see today, and the plants and animals that inhabit it, are the result of eons of upheavals, weathering and dramatic climatic change. Some of the most ancient rocks on earth, dated to about 4500 million years old, are found in Western Australia. More recently, the invasion of the continent by humans has shaped the landscape.

It was, however, when Australia separated from the supercontinent of Gondwanaland, which started to break up about 180 million years ago, that the chain of events that really shaped this continent began. By around 55 million years ago, Australia was a single landmass floating north through the Indian Ocean. The animals that remained on this great, isolated raft began to develop into the monotremes and marsupials we know so well today.

Right: *The mist-shrouded valleys of Lamington National Park are a refuge for many different species of plants, birds and animals in south-east Queensland.*

Over the last 40 million years our continent has seen waves of invaders come and settle. First on the scene were probably bats flying in from the ever-closer continent of Asia and the island of Papua New Guinea. Rodents followed and as the ice ages waxed and waned more and more animals made it to our shores.

Finally, some 50 000 to 100 000 years ago, humans floated on primitive rafts across the relatively narrow watery gaps that remained in the island chain that linked Australia with Asia. These settlers came via Indonesia and Papua New Guinea in a number of waves and, as traditional hunters and gatherers, spread out right across the continent.

Twenty million years ago the ancestors of today's lizards were crawling along the rainforest floor. Today's lizards have adapted to a wide range of habitats.

The last group of settlers came from a faraway shore just a couple of hundred years ago and today their descendants, and those of the plants and animals they introduced, dominate much of the land and its flora and fauna.

A Rich Tapestry of Parks

This rich and varied heritage of our continent—its plants, animals and human history—is protected in the parks and reserves dotted across the vast Australian landscape, so that it can be seen and experienced.

Alpine meadows in the high country of New South Wales and Victoria; rich verdant rainforests in Queensland; the floodplains and escarpments of the Northern Territory; impenetrable temperate forests and untouched rivers in Tasmania; towering gums in the south-west of Western Australia; and the untracked desert country and outback

Below: *Nigli Gap in Keep River National Park in the Northern Territory. The rugged cliffs are a legacy of volcanic and glacial activity that shaped the landforms in this area.*

mountain ranges in South Australia: these are just some of the landscapes in our parks. All offer not only a safe habitat for our unique flora and fauna, but also places where we can seek solace, enjoyment and adventure as we get back to nature.

Australia is fortunate that it has the landmass and the lack of population pressure to incorporate much of its natural treasures in parks and reserves of significant size. In the last 25 years, with a growing awareness of our natural heritage, each state and territory has vastly increased the amount of land protected in national parks and reserves, with some of those parks in excess of one million hectares. Some parks are bigger than European countries!

Picturesque Cephissus Falls, in Tasmania's Cradle Mountain–Lake St Clair National Park is one of many scenic spots that reward bushwalkers prepared to spend some time trekking through the park.

Experiencing Our Wonderland of Parks and Reserves

Many national parks, forest scenic reserves, state parks and conservation parks have easy access and facilities such as developed camping grounds, picnic areas, toilets, and walking tracks with wheelchair access; other parks can only be reached by 4WD, and have remote area camping with few, if any, facilities.

Right: *Litchfield National Park is an easy 2 hours' drive from Darwin, in the Northern Territory. The park has bush camping areas as well as areas with BBQ and toilet facilities, but visitors must be totally self-sufficient.*

While bushwalking is permitted in most of our parks, with many parks having designated tracks and day walking trails, other activities may have restrictions placed on them. Wheeled transport such as mountain-bike riding, trail-bike riding and four-wheel driving are limited, or banned completely, in some of our parks.

A few parks and reserves in Australia have no access and no facilities at all, closed for very strong and compelling environmental reasons, the exception being for scientific research.

Parklands are costly to maintain and most charge an entry fee. Charges vary from state to state and from park to park. Some have an entrance fee and others just a camping fee, while some parks have no fees at all.

Most states have a pass system of some sort where for the payment of an annual fee, you can camp in many of the parks and reserves in that state, or in certain areas of the state, for a considerable saving over the daily rate.

Then there is the matter of rules and regulations. These too vary from state to state and from park to park, and especially between a state's national parks, state parks, conservation parks and forest reserves.

It is worth contacting each state's national parks' organisation for information on facilities, access, charges, regulations, and to find out if they operate any park pass systems. A good place to start is on the web, at each state's national park site.

The Whitsunday Islands National Park, off Queensland's coast. Whitsunday Island is the largest island in the group, and has the best camping facilities.

Left: *A cross-country skier in Victoria's Alpine National Park. Although the northern half of Australia is tropical, there are plenty of opportunities for snow sports in parks in New South Wales, Tasmania and Victoria.*

Far left: *Visitors to Drovers Cave National Park in Western Australia. This park caters mainly to experienced cavers, but bushwalkers will also find the area of interest.*

Where to Go, What to See

The choice is endless and really only limited by your imagination and your experience. The lists that follow are just to get you started—they are by no means comprehensive.

Bushwalkers can stretch their legs in so many parks around the country it is almost impossible to name them all. For starters there's Blue Mountains National Park in New South Wales; Alpine National Park in Victoria; Flinders Ranges National Park in South Australia; Cradle Mountain–Lake St Clair National Park in Tasmania; Stirling Ranges National Park in Western Australia; Lamington National Park in Queensland; and West MacDonnell National Park in the Northern Territory. Each offers a unique and vastly different walking experience.

For skiers the choice might not be so great, but there are the vast Kosciuszko and Alpine National Parks along with the smaller but no less unique Baw Baw National Park and Mount Buffalo National Park, both in Victoria, while Tasmania has Ben Lomond and Mount Field National Parks.

For those who love to spend their days afloat there are the waters around Wilsons Promontory National Park in Victoria; Myall Lakes National Park in New South Wales; Whitsunday Islands National Park in Queensland; Gurig National Park in the Northern Territory; Cape Range National Park in Western Australia; Coorong National Park in South Australia; and Franklin–Gordon Wild Rivers National Park in Tasmania.

Rock climbers, four-wheel drivers, history lovers, photographers and nature watchers all can claim their piece of paradise in Australia's national parks. There are adventures and experiences to last (and to take) a lifetime. You'd better start now!

Bird-watching is a popular activity in many national parks. Australia has about 700 bird species, with many, such as the emu (Dromaius novaehollandiae) *unique to this country.*

on the net

AUSTRALIA
Australian Government Department of the Environment and Heritage Parks and Reserves
www.deh.gov.au/parks

QUEENSLAND
Environmental Protection Agency
www.epa.qld.gov.au

NEW SOUTH WALES
National Parks and Wildlife Service
www.npws.nsw.gov.au/parks

VICTORIA
Parks Victoria
www.parkweb.vic.gov.au

TASMANIA
Parks and Wildlife Service Tasmania
www.parks.tas.gov.au

NORTHERN TERRITORY
Natural Resources, Environment and the Arts Parks and Wildlife Service
www.nt.gov.au/nreta/parks

SOUTH AUSTRALIA
Department for Environment and Heritage
www.dehaa.sa.gov.au/parks

WESTERN AUSTRALIA
Department of Conservation and Land Management
www.calm.wa.gov.au

Queensland

Queensland's national parks system is the most diverse in the nation, encompassing tropical rainforests, deserts, melaleuca heathland, granite country, mangrove-lined estuaries, eucalypt forests and beautiful islands bordered by coral reefs. The state's 220 national parks provide homes and protection for many varieties of wildlife, including some of Australia's rarest and most endangered creatures and plants, as well as Australian Aboriginal artworks and artefacts. Apart from providing a protected habitat for wildlife, Queensland's national parks offer visitors numerous opportunities to enjoy the great outdoors. The coastal and island parks are the most popular, but the inland parks also offer visitors a variety of experiences and delights.

Daintree National Park

Stretching along the coast from the Daintree River in the south to the Bloomfield River in the north, the Daintree National Park is divided into two parts, the larger centred around the Mossman River and Gorge, and the other spread along the coast between the Daintree River and the Bloomfield River, further north.

fact file

WHERE: The Mossman Gorge section is located 80 km north of Cairns; the Cape Tribulation section starts another 25 km further north
Map: Qld 3 N3

WHEN: End of April until October

WHY: Bushwalking, bird-watching, 4WD

SIZE: 73 600 ha

RANGER: Cape Tribulation (07) 4098 0052; Mossman Gorge (07) 4098 2188

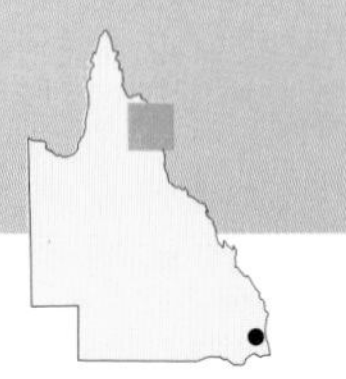

The park is a spectacular wilderness of rugged mountain ranges, fast-flowing streams, towering rainforest trees and lush, tangled undergrowth in myriad shades of green. At Cape Tribulation the visitor can experience the splendour of north Queensland's tropical rainforests while being only a stone's throw from the World Heritage listed Great Barrier Reef.

In the Past

The 56 500 hectare Mossman Gorge section of the Daintree National Park is 80 km north of Cairns, while the 17 100 hectare Cape Tribulation section is 104 km north of the city. These two sections of park were combined in 1988 to become an important component in the Wet Tropics World Heritage Area that takes in much of the surrounding range country.

Captain James Cook named Cape Tribulation itself when his ship, the *Endeavour*, was holed on a reef just north of the cape in 1770. The Aboriginal word for the cape—'Kurranji', which means cassowary—was the name used by the Kuku Yalanji people who had lived in this piece of coastal paradise for thousands of years.

A female yellow-bellied sunbird (Nectarina jugularis), *using her long curved beak to extract food from a spider's web.*

Wildlife

Because of its wide range in elevation from sea level to more than 1300 metres above that, the Cape Tribulation area is home to some of Australia's rarest types of mammals. The largest and most spectacular of these is the Bennett's tree-

kangaroo. Confined almost entirely to the rainforests of Cape Tribulation and nearby Cedar Bay to the north, this little-known marsupial is more often heard than seen as it crashes through the forest canopy.

The smallest member of the kangaroo family, the musky rat-kangaroo, is also only found here. In many ways it is more particularly like a possum, not only in looks, but also in its ability to climb trees.

Another rarely encountered rainforest resident is the Herbert River ringtail possum. Found only at altitudes of 300 metres above sea level, this beautiful black and white possum is sometimes seen at night with the aid of a torch.

Bird life in both the Mossman Gorge and Cape Tribulation sections is varied and prolific. The large flightless cassowary, which often stands up to 2 metres tall, is occasionally sighted by bushwalkers on rainforest tracks. Never try and get too close to these stocky, helmeted birds as they can inflict serious injuries with their powerful legs.

Unfortunately, cassowaries have become rare due to land clearing, and even in protected places like the Daintree they are threatened by feral pigs that destroy their nests.

Light scratching sounds in the leaf litter on the forest floor usually indicate the presence of chowchillas nearby. These conspicuous 28 cm long birds, with their dark brown backs and white and orange neck and chest markings, are confined to the Wet Tropics region. The large brush-turkey and the slightly smaller orange-footed scrubfowl are other ground dwellers regularly seen in the park.

Above: *The coastal lowland rainforest of Cape Tribulation reaches right to the shoreline, giving the cape the label of 'where the rainforest meets the reef'.*

Left: *The southern cassowary* (Casuorius casuorius) *has a bony 'helmet' to protect its head. This flightless bird lives in the dense undergrowth of the rainforest.*

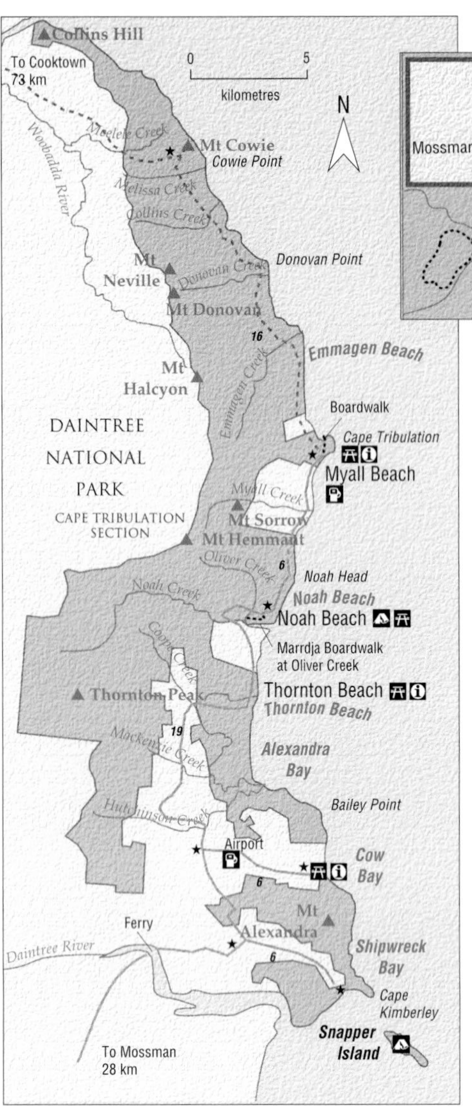

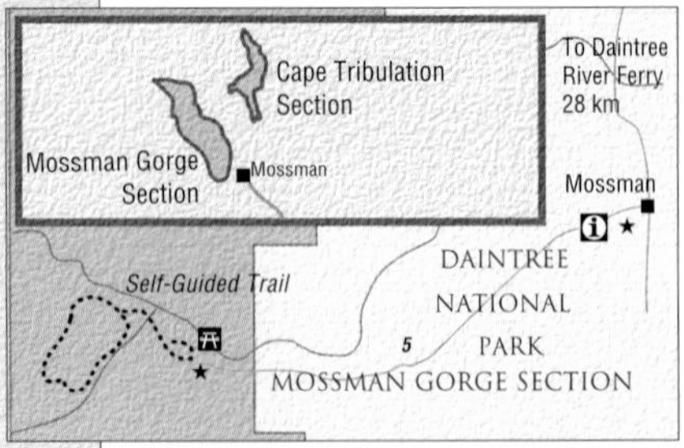

Below: *The dense canopy of the tropical rainforest trees blocks out much of the sunlight, but there are still plenty of plants growing alongside the creeks.*

The white-lipped tree frog (Litoria infrafrenata), *like all Australia's tree frogs, is a descendant of ancestors existing before the Australian continent separated from Gondwana. It is about 13 cm long, one of the largest frogs in the world.*

At least six species of rainforest pigeons inhabit the Daintree. The largest and most impressive of these is the colourful wompoo fruit-dove which spends most of its time in the upper canopy. Other pigeons include the superb fruit dove and the Torresian imperial pigeon.

Another impressive bird of this area is the brilliantly plumed buff-breasted paradise kingfisher, which breeds in this region but migrates to New Guinea for the cooler months of the year.

Activities

A short track from the car park leads along the edge of the Mossman River to a popular swimming and cooling-off spot. But beware, the fast current flow can be dangerous and the slippery rocks can trap the unwary. The river is also subject to flash flooding and a number of drownings have occurred here.

A walking track continues over the swinging bridge across Rex Creek and takes you along a self-guided walk through the rainforest. This 2.7 km loop trail follows Rex Creek for a section and brings you back to the swing bridge.

There are no easily accessible waterfalls, despite some maps showing them. In fact, most of the Mossman Gorge section of the Daintree is wilderness that is virtually inaccessible. Anyone trying to hike in this beautiful region should be a fully experienced and equipped bushwalker. Those intending to hike in the park need to discuss their plans with park staff and complete a bushwalking registration form. Bushwalkers also require a permit if they plan to camp overnight in the remote areas of the park. Permits can be obtained before setting out from the Queensland Parks and Wildlife Service office in Mossman.

Roaring Meg Falls are in the north of the park, on the upper Bloomfield River. These falls can only be reached by 4WD vehicles; the 2-hour drive goes past some spectacular scenery.

There are some beautiful walks in the Cape Tribulation section, including the 4 hour return trip from Myall Beach, just south of Cape Tribulation, to Emmagen Creek. Walkers should start this hike on the outgoing tide so they can skirt around the rocks at Emmagen Beach.

At the Kulki picnic area at Cape Tribulation, a 400 m boardwalk leads from the car park to a viewing platform overlooking the sea and the beach. From Dubuji there is a 1200 m boardwalk through rainforest, swamp and mangrove areas.

At Oliver Creek, near Noah Beach, the very interesting Marrdja Boardwalk winds its way for 800 metres through mangroves and rainforest.

South of Cow Bay village, the Jindalba picnic area is the starting point for two walking trails, a short one providing good views over the rainforest and a longer hiking trail.

did you know?

Many of the rainforest plants in this park are relict species that have grown in these forests for tens of millions of years. This area has the highest concentration of primitive flowering plants in the world.

The rock orchid (Dendrobium speciosum) *is one of many epiphytic plants growing on the rainforest trees, which may play host to ferns, fungi and mosses as well as orchids.*

The beautiful beaches north and south of Cape Tribulation are great for swimming from late April until the end of September when bluebottles and other marine stingers are absent. Never swim anywhere near the mouth of a saltwater creek or in the Daintree and Bloomfield Rivers, as estuarine crocodiles inhabit these places.

You can also enjoy snorkelling and sea kayaking along this coast.

The beach, reefs and coastal waters are protected in the Great Barrier Reef Marine Park and fishing and spearfishing, as well as any collecting, are prohibited within the designated National Park zone north of, and including Cape Tribulation. South of Cape Tribulation limited line fishing and bait netting are allowed.

The drive north from Cape Tribulation to the Bloomfield River is only suitable for 4WD vehicles but is a highlight of a trip to this park. Numerous steep, slippery climbs mean that this trip is generally reserved for the dry season, and it is closed after heavy rain. Check with the RACQ by phoning 1300 130 595 or (07) 3361 2406, for current road conditions.

Access

The best way to the Mossman Gorge section of the park is to drive north along the Cook Highway for 76 km until you reach Mossman. A 5 km bitumen road connects the town to the picnic ground at Mossman Gorge.

To reach Cape Tribulation, go north from Mossman for 28 km until you reach the Daintree River ferry, which operates 6 am to midnight, 7 days a week except Good Friday and Christmas Day. It is free to use!

From the northern side of the Daintree River the bitumen road winds for about 40 km through private land and segments of the national park until it reaches Cape Tribulation.

Motorists who want to continue on to the Bloomfield River from Cape Tribulation must do so in a 4WD vehicle. This road is graded dirt, and is often impassable after heavy rain. Drive slowly to avoid hitting wildlife. It makes an enjoyable way to go to Cooktown.

Camping

Apart from bush camping, there are no facilities for camping in the Mossman Gorge section of the park.

The main camping ground in the Cape Tribulation section is at Noah Beach, 8 km south of Cape Tribulation. Toilets, showers and drinking water are provided. Camp fires are prohibited in the park, and only fuel stoves should be used. The camping area is closed during the wet season.

don't miss

The Kuku Yalanji people used the rainforest plants for food, medicine, tools and building materials. Rainforest plant tours led by Australian Aboriginal guides show visitors the plants and their uses.

Snapper Island, south of Cape Kimberley, has four camping sites with toilet and barbecue facilities. A permit from the Queensland Parks and Wildlife Service in Cairns or Mossman is essential.

Private camping areas, hostels, resorts and holiday units can be found adjacent to the Cape Tribulation section of the park and there is some accommodation in Mossman township.

Although most of the Mossman Gorge Section is undeveloped, part of the gorge itself is easily accessible. In some places there are quiet pools; in others the water swirls through rocks.

Below: *Perhaps the most luxurious of the accommodation options for Daintree visitors, Silky Oaks Lodge is surrounded by trees and overlooks a natural lagoon.*

Great Sandy National Park (Fraser Island and Cooloola)

The Great Sandy National Park has two sections: one is the whole of Fraser Island and the other is further south on the Queensland mainland at Cooloola. Although quite different, both feature beautiful perched lakes and striking coloured sands.

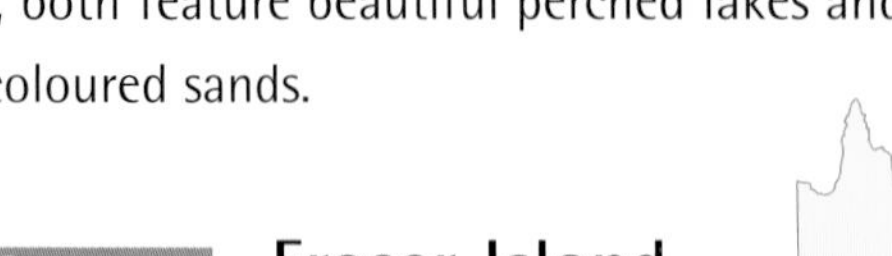

fact file

FRASER ISLAND

WHERE: 190 km north of Brisbane
Map: Qld 7 N2

WHEN: All year

WHY: Fishing, lakes, rainforest, wildlife, 4WD only

SIZE: 165 280 ha

RANGER: Tewantin (07) 5449 7792; Rainbow Beach (07) 5486 3160; Waddy Point (07) 4127 9190

COOLOOLA

WHERE: 200 km north of Brisbane via the Bruce Highway
Map: Qld 7 N4

WHEN: All year

WHY: Water sports, bushwalks, 4WD

SIZE: 56 600 ha

RANGER: Tewantin (07) 5449 7792; Rainbow Beach (07) 5486 3160

Fraser Island

First-time visitors to Fraser Island are often left speechless when asked to describe the beauty and variety of life on this spectacular sand island off the Queensland coast. Here you can find luxuriant subtropical rainforests growing out of the sand and melaleuca swamps, along with perched dune lakes, fantastic fishing (in both the surf and calm water) and over 230 species of birds. This World Heritage listed island has become one of Australia's most visited and best known national parks.

Fraser Island is also famous for its coloured sands that are similar to those found in the southern section of the Great Sandy National Park at Cooloola on the mainland. One of the most striking examples of these coloured sands can be seen at the 'Cathedrals' on the eastern beach, which is also known as the Teewah Sands.

Fraser Island's sand dunes are constantly being changed by wind, although some parts have been stabilised by a layer of plant growth.

The Aquarium Pools, at low tide; these pools of bubbling water are also known as the Champagne Pools. They are located between Indian Head and Waddy Point.

In the Past

The Butchalla people are thought to have inhabited Fraser Island for more than 5000 years. The rapid decline of the indigenous population began in the 1840s when the timber-getters arrived, bringing diseases that almost wiped out the tribes.

Fraser Island got its name with the rescue of Eliza Fraser. The drama began on 13 May 1836 when a ship carrying Eliza struck a coral reef off the northern tip of Cape York Peninsula. The crew and passengers managed to make their way to Fraser Island, then called Great Sandy Island, but they were quickly rounded up by the local indigenous people. Some died, but others escaped, and Mrs Fraser was rescued after nearly 7 weeks. Within 10 years Great Sandy Island was being called Fraser Island.

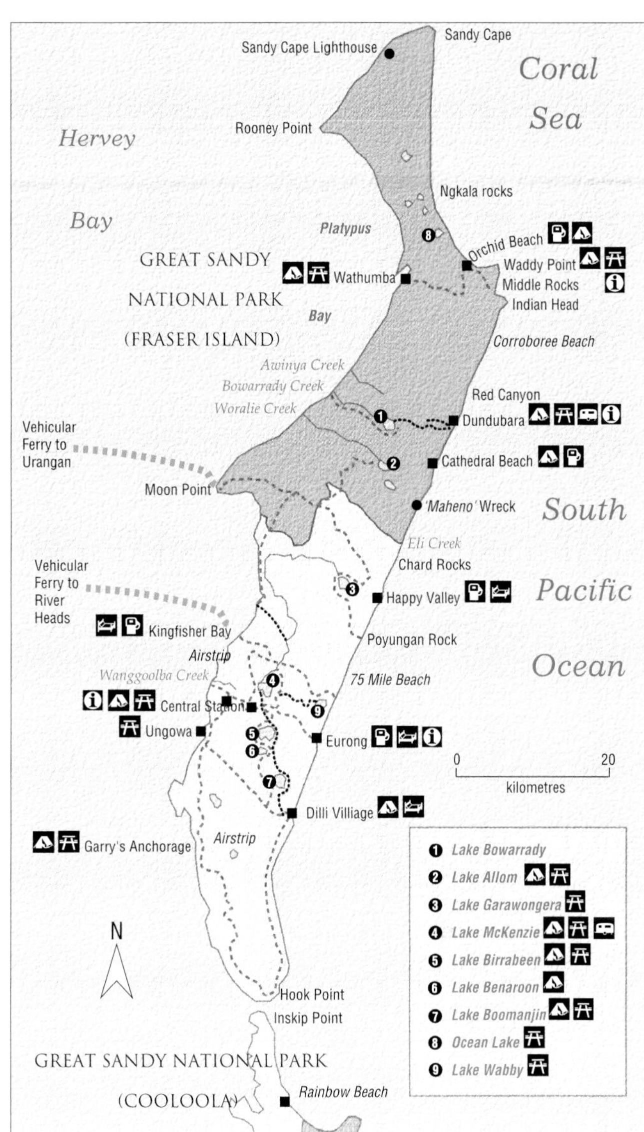

The logging of Fraser Island's beautiful forests began in the early 1860s and continued until all commercial cutting ceased in 1992.

During World War II, Fraser Island became a base for the famous 'Z Force' commando units.

Perched Lakes, Flowing Streams

There are more than 40 perched dune lakes on Fraser Island, including the world's largest, the 200 hectare Lake Boomanjin. These lakes have some of the purest drinking water found anywhere in the world, and while some

don't miss

Central Station camping and picnic area is also good for birdwatching, with rainforest birds like rufous fantails and eastern yellow robins as well as less common species such as the noisy pitta and wompoo pigeon.

dingoes

The dingoes on Fraser are the purest strain of dingoes in Australia and in many ways the island is probably the best place to see the wild dogs at close quarters.

However, because people have fed the dogs, many attacks on humans, especially young children, have occurred. Feeding the dingoes is now completely banned and fines apply for people found doing so. Children should not be left alone.

are crystal clear with white sandy bottoms, others have a reddish colour which comes from tea-trees growing near the lake. The water is so pure in the lakes that only three species of small fish live in them.

Apart from the dune lakes the island has a number of freshwater streams which flow consistently throughout the year. Eli Creek is the biggest of these.

The biggest stream on the island is Eli Creek, which flows onto the eastern beach a few kilometres south of the *Maheno* shipwreck. At numerous other places along the beach fresh water bubbles out of the sand, providing easy access to good drinking water. None of this water has to be boiled as the sand filters out any impurities.

Activities

For more than 70 years visitors have been travelling to Fraser Island to enjoy its fantastic fishing. At the height of the season, between July and October, hundreds of anglers from around Australia gather on the surf beaches of the island's east coast to try their luck and skills against the huge schools of taylor which migrate up the coast.

Other fish found on the east coast beaches include silver bream, jewfish and golden trevally. In the calm waters on the western side of the island flathead, whiting, bream and a few other species of fish can be caught throughout the year. Mud crabs are also present in good numbers around the mangrove-lined estuaries on the western side of the island, although you will probably need a small boat to get to the places where you can drop your crab pots.

Since there are no formed roads on Fraser Island, a 4WD vehicle is necessary if you want to explore the island. Some of the inland tracks are difficult to negotiate due to the soft sand; you should try to keep your beach driving within 2 hours either side of low tide. It is best to keep tyres deflated to around 140 kPa (20 psi).

As visitor numbers increase, accidents on the inland sandy tracks are becoming all too common, so take care.

Apart from walks along Fraser Island's beautiful coastline, there are numerous forest hiking trails in the central and southern parts of the island. One excellent track to start out on is the 6 km Lake Birrabeen to Central Station walk, which would take about 2 hours one way. Birdwatchers will love this track as it meanders through a wide variety of the park's vegetation. A short walking track at Central Station (25 minutes one way) follows the crystal clear Wanggoolba Creek past towering brush box, hoop pine, white beech, ribbon wood and strangler figs.

Access

Fraser Island is approximately 190 km north of Brisbane. The island can be reached by a number of methods including vehicular barges, passenger launches, aircraft or private boats.

A 4WD vehicle is essential for driving on the island. If you don't have your own, they can be hired at Hervey Bay, Rainbow Beach, the Sunshine Coast and Brisbane.

People bringing a vehicle to Fraser Island must get a RAM vehicle permit

The beach at Waddy Point is a good launching spot for the fantastic reef fishing on the Gardner Banks east of Waddy Point and Indian Head.

An aerial view of Fraser Island shows the blanket of sand-adapted vegetation that covers most of the inland area. The plant types include grasses, eucalypt and banksia woodland and sub-tropical rainforest.

did you know?

Fraser Island is the largest sand island in the world. It is 123 km from north to south and 25 km across at its widest point. It was formed from the sediments carried by rivers to the coast over hundreds of thousands of years.

and attach it to their car windscreen. The permit is valid for one month. Normal road rules apply for beach driving.

There are five vehicular barges that service Fraser Island. On the southern end of the island two barges operate between Hook Point and Inskip Point just north of Rainbow Beach, phone (07) 5486 3227.

From Hervey Bay, barges to Wanggoolba Creek and Kingfisher Bay depart from River Heads. The barge to Moon Point leaves from Urangan boat harbour. Bookings are required for the three Hervey Bay barges, phone (07) 4125 4444.

Visitors who arrive by light aircraft will land either at Toby's Gap, which is managed by the Queensland Parks and Wildlife Service, or at Wanggoolba Creek, which is managed by the Eurong Beach Resort. Landing permission and entry permits are needed for private aircraft before arrival. Contact airstrip managers or Queensland Parks and Wildlife Service, Maryborough, phone (07) 4121 1800.

Camping and Accommodation

The Queensland Parks and Wildlife Service has camping grounds at Lake Boomanjin, Central Station, Lake Allom, Waddy Point, Wathumba, Dundubara and Lake McKenzie. Facilities in these places include toilets, picnic tables, barbecues and showers (except for Lake Allom). Lake McKenzie and Dundubara are the only places that are suitable for camper trailers.

Beach camping is permitted at undeveloped sites along the east coast and at some spots on the west coast. Always select existing formed beach camp sites.

Private camp grounds, suitable for caravans, exist at Cathedral Beach Resort, phone (07) 4127 9177 and Dilli Village, phone (07) 4127 9130.

Motel type accommodation is available at Eurong, phone (07) 4127 9122; Dilli Village, phone (07) 4127 9130; Happy Valley, phone (07) 4127 9144; and Kingfisher Bay Resort, phone 1800 072 555.

The Australian pelican (Pelecanus conspicillatus) *is found near the water (seasides, lakes and rivers) throughout most of Australia, as well as on islands like Fraser.*

Cooloola

The Cooloola section of the Great Sandy National Park protects the largest tract of natural land on Queensland's southern coast. Spectacular sand dunes and the tranquil headwaters of the Noosa River are the main highlights.

Lakes are also a major feature of this section of the park and Poona, nestled high in the dunes, is one of the five main perched lakes found in Cooloola. Apart from a few little grebes and musk ducks, Poona is almost devoid of waterfowl. In contrast, other larger lakes such as Cootharaba are slightly brackish and teem with marine life that provide food for many species of birds such as pelicans and sea-eagles.

One of the many other features of Cooloola is its rainforests. An excellent way to experience the tranquillity of these forests is to do the 4.4 km, 2 hour return walk to Lake Poona.

Flaked stone tools like these ones found in Cooloola were used by Australian Aboriginals in many areas of Queensland. Tools made from bone, teeth and wood were also used.

In the Past

The Kabi people were the original inhabitants of this area, but, as on Fraser Island, when the timber-getters arrived in the 1840s the local people were almost wiped out by the diseases that came with the new arrivals.

Opposite page: *Tall rainforest trees near Lake Poona grow in sand. Open forests of blackbutt and tallowwood as well as coastal heaths are also found in Cooloola.*

Activities

Surf fishing is a favourite pastime at Cooloola, with whiting, bream and flathead among the frequent catches. River fishing is also popular, as is swimming, though marine stingers can be a problem when northeasterlies blow.

Canoeing is the best way to explore the Noosa River. Canoes can be hired from Elanda Point. The park has a number of 4WD tracks leading through it or onto the beach. There are many walks in the area to enjoy.

Access and Camping

There are two approaches to the park. Coming from the south you turn off the Bruce Highway near Eumundi and continue to Tewantin and catch the ferry across the Noosa River. From there a gravel track a few kilometres long brings you to the track which leads to the beach. The second approach is from the north: take the Tin Can Bay turn-off at Gympie and continue for about 47 km until the turn-off to Rainbow Beach. Five km before you reach this small town you will see a national parks sign to the Freshwater camping area.

The Freshwater camping area is the most developed, but there are other sites on the banks of Noosa River, at Poverty Point and on the Cooloola Wilderness Trail. You can also camp on the beach between the Noosa Shire boundary and Little Freshwater Creek. Sites should be booked in advance with the ranger.

tourist info

Kinaba Information Centre, Elanda Point
(07) 5449 7364

Carnarvon National Park

The area comprising Carnarvon National Park is only a part of the massive Consuelo Tableland. This predominantly sandstone region rises to 900 metres and is home to four of eastern Australia's major river systems.

fact file

WHERE: 720 km north-west of Brisbane
Map: Qld 7 D1

WHEN: June to November (summer can be very hot)

WHY: Breathtaking scenery, good walking tracks, 4WD

SIZE: 298 000 ha

RANGER: (07) 4984 4505

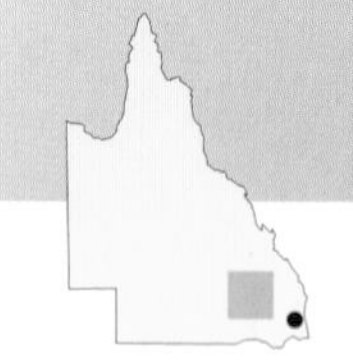

The park is made up of a number of different sections: Carnarvon Gorge, Buckland Tableland, Ka Ka Mundi, Goodliffe, Salvator Rosa, Mount Moffat and Moolayember. Although Carnarvon Gorge occupies only a fraction of the park, it is by far the most scenic and easily accessible section.

The main 30 km long gorge was created by Carnarvon Creek. Vertical sandstone cliffs, some up to 200 metres high, rise up from the gorge floor, their colours varying from brilliant whites through to yellow, orange and brown.

A wide variety of wildlife can be observed while walking through the gorge. The diversity of plant life found in the park provides many ideal habitats for the area's numerous bird species.

Magnificent Aboriginal Rock Art

The original Australian Aboriginals have long since vanished from the area, leaving only their unique artistry behind them. For thousands of years they depicted their way of life on the undersides of many of the large rock overhangs found throughout the gorge.

Cathedral Cave, one of the largest rock art sites so far discovered, is about 10 km from the day-use area. Boomerangs, spears, emus' feet and goannas are pictured on one side of this large sandstone wall, while on another section human hands, which signify a person's relationship to one particular place, are found.

The 'Art Gallery' is another stone-age masterpiece–which has been carbon-dated at over 4000 years–and is found 500 metres off the main track.

Australian Aboriginal rock art at the 'Art Gallery' which is one of the largest and most interesting of the fifty-odd rock art sites in the park.

Activities

At least 3 or 4 days should be set aside to visit Carnarvon just to explore the beauty of the main gorge.

The best way to do this is to follow the well-defined trail which begins near the ranger's headquarters at Carnarvon Gorge, tracing the contours of Carnarvon Creek until it reaches Cathedral Cave 10 km upstream. This will take about 8 hours for the return walk.

QLD

Access and Camping

The park is generally accessible to conventional vehicles, except perhaps after heavy rain. From Brisbane, the best route is probably via Roma and Injune. The road is good bitumen except for the last 43 km or so, which is dirt.

The main camping area has been closed, and only a day-use area is located near the ranger base and visitor information centre at Carnarvon Gorge Section. Bushwalkers can pitch their tent at Big Bend camping area, which is 10 km into the gorge. The only facility is a toilet.

Campers and those looking for accommodation are catered for at the Carnarvon Gorge Wilderness Lodge, phone (07) 4984 4503, and the Takarakka Bush Resort, phone (07) 4984 4535, both located just outside the park. Both facilities also have convenience stores.

Bush camping is allowed in the sections of Ka Ka Mundi, Mount Moffat and Salvator Rosa.

Left: *Cabbage tree palms, fine-needled casuarinas and weeping bottlebrush grow along Carnarvon Creek; up higher, ironbark, flooded gums and swamp mahogany predominate.*

don't miss

The clear shallow waters of Carnarvon Creek are home to the elusive platypus. Sightings of this intriguing creature can occasionally be made from some of the higher banks along the creek.

Adventurous hikers can travel a further 15 km into the more remote parts of the gorge. There are also a number of side gorges to be explored such as Hellhole Gorge and Violet Gorge.

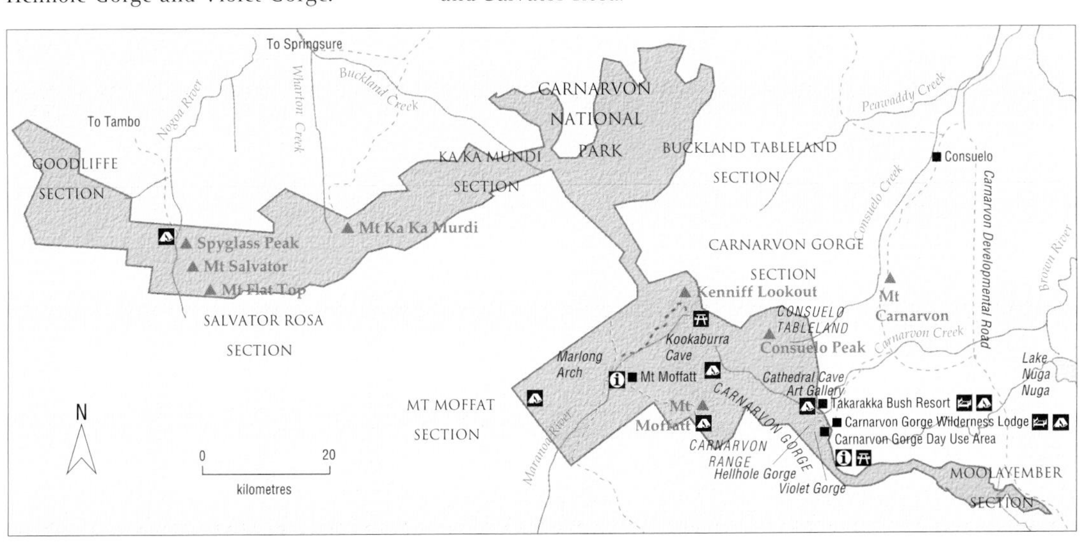

Lamington National Park

The lush rainforest-covered ridges and misty valleys of Lamington National Park have been silently beckoning nature-lovers and travellers for nearly 90 years. Apart from being the most popular national park in Queensland, Lamington is also one of the oldest, gazetted in 1915.

fact file

WHERE: 85 km south-west of Surfers Paradise
Map: Qld 7 N8

WHEN: All year

WHY: Rainforest walks, wildlife, waterfalls

SIZE: 20 600 ha

RANGER: Green Mountains (07) 5544 0634; Binna Burra (07) 5533 3584

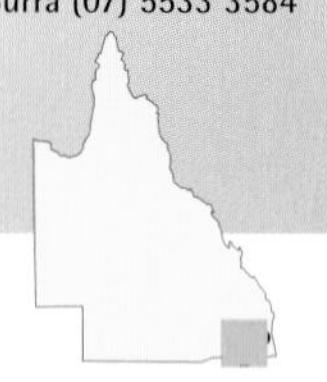

The park owes much of its existence to the dedication of Robert Collins, who campaigned tirelessly throughout the early 1900s to have the area protected from logging. When Collins died it was Romeo Lahey, whose family owned one of Queensland's largest timber mills at the time, who led the final push to have the 20 600 hectare wilderness declared a national park.

Rich Flora, Abundant Wildlife

A wide range of vegetation can be found within the park. Huge brush box, tulip oak, giant stinging trees and buttress-rooted Moreton Bay figs are just a few of the many plant species which thrive here.

Gnarled Antarctic beech trees thrive in the higher parts of the park that are more than 1000 metres above sea level. Eucalypt woodlands, grass-trees and other dry vegetation dominate the lower sections of the park.

The male regent bowerbird (Sericulus chrysocephalus) *builds his bower on the ground like other bowerbirds, but otherwise lives in the trees.*

Having such a wide range of vegetation, it is little wonder that Lamington is regarded as one of the most important refuges for wildlife in south-east Queensland. Red-necked wallabies and whiptail wallabies are often seen while other common mammals found include the brush-tail possum, sugar glider, greater glider, the rare brush-tailed phascogale, the red-necked pademelon, mountain brush-tail possum, ringtail possum, both the short- and long-nosed bandicoots and the endangered tiger quoll. Reptiles are also abundant, among them large rainforest skinks and beautifully patterned snakes such as the carpet python.

Lamington is renowned as a bird-watcher's paradise. Some of Australia's rarest and most colourful species are found here, including the noisy pitta, crimson rosella, king parrot, Albert's lyrebird and regent bowerbird.

Wonderful Walks

The well-marked system of trails in Lamington provides hikers with some of the best walks in Australia. These can vary from pleasant, 2 hour jaunts

to 3 day hikes over parts of Queensland's roughest terrain.

One interesting way of viewing the park's many wonders from above is via the rainforest canopy walk. Here visitors can stroll across a suspension bridge dangling 15 metres above the forest floor.

Access and Camping

Lamington is situated 120 km south of Brisbane and 85 km southwest of Southport on the Gold Coast and can be accessed by conventional vehicles. The park is made up of two sections, Binna Burra and Green Mountains–Binna Burra is 35 km by bitumen road from Nerang, while Green Mountain is 115 km from Brisbane and can be accessed via Canungra. Caravans are not recommended.

Camping in the Binna Burra section is only available in the private camping area, part of Binna Burra Lodge, while a national park camp ground is situated near the ranger station at Green Mountain. Showers, toilets, picnic tables and drinking water are provided. Fires are banned within the park. Camping permits need to be booked well in advance, phone the ranger on (07) 5544 0634.

Accommodation is available at O'Reilly's Rainforest Guesthouse (Green Mountain), phone (07) 5544 0644, or Binna Burra Mountain Lodge, phone (07) 5533 3622.

Left: *The tall straight hoop pine* (Araucaria cunninghamii) *thrives on this exposed slope. The park's rich volcanic soils allow a wide range of vegetation to flourish.*

did you know?

Lamington National Park was named for Lord Lamington, Governor of Queensland from 1896–1902. Unfortunately, he will not be remembered as one of Queensland's early nature-lovers; he marked his only visit to the region by shooting a koala.

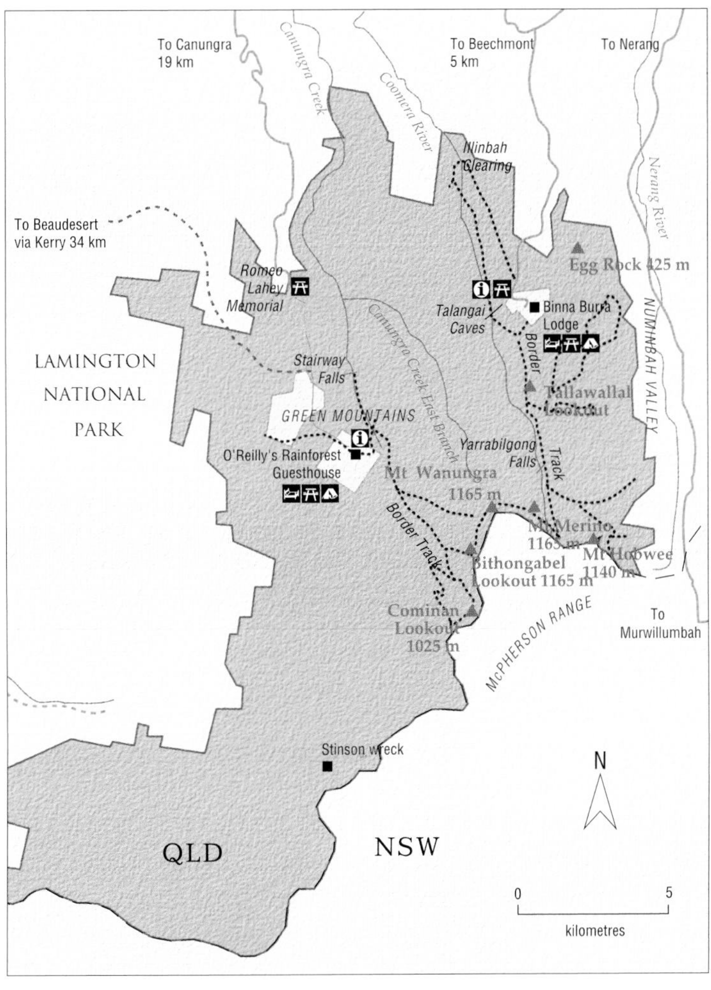

Boodjamulla (Lawn Hill) National Park

Located 400 km northwest of Mount Isa, Boodjamulla National Park is becoming a favoured spot for nature-lovers from all over Australia. The dominant feature of this sprawling wilderness is Lawn Hill Gorge, which cuts its way through the sandstone plateaus of the Constance Range. The 60 metre walls of the gorge protect the warm, clear waters of one of Australia's most pristine waterways.

fact file

WHERE: 400 km north-west of Mount Isa, on the Queensland/Northern Territory border
Map: Qld 3 A8

WHEN: June to September

WHY: Wildlife, canoeing, bushwalks, 4WD

SIZE: 262 000 ha

RANGER: (07) 4748 5572

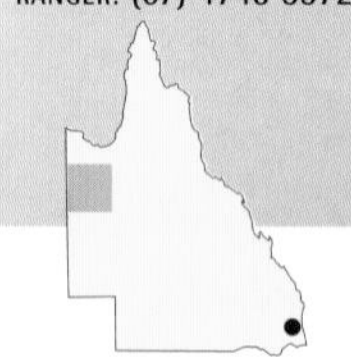

Above right: *Lawn Hill Creek is a permanent watercourse, fed from many springs.*

Although freshwater crocodiles (Crocodylus johnstoni) *look dangerous, they are not a threat to people.*

Australian Aboriginal habitation at Lawn Hill goes back some 17 000 years. The Waanyi people hunted and fished there until the 1930s when missionaries 'removed them' to Mornington Island. Their ancient art can be seen at the Rainbow Dreaming and Wild Dog Dreaming art sites.

The more remote Riversleigh section of the park, which the Gregory River flows through, has a World Heritage listed fossil deposit of the remains of prehistoric mammals and reptiles.

North-west of Lawn Hill Gorge is the Highlands Plains area. This is a designated wilderness region with no access to vehicles.

Wildlife

Besides harmless freshwater crocodiles, the park is a haven for an amazing variety of wildlife, including more than 135 species of birds and 36 different types of mammals. Snakes and lizards are also plentiful.

Early mornings in Boodjamulla are particularly beautiful, with the calls of countless parrots, kookaburras and magpies filling the air.

Nights in Boodjamulla often have a magical touch—the sound of croaking frogs mingling with the high-pitched shrills of little bats. Dingoes are common throughout the park as well, and their long, drawn-out howling can provide that extra-special touch to a night in the great outdoors.

Activities

At least 3 or 4 days should be spent in Lawn Hill to fully appreciate it.

There are 20 km of walking tracks in the park. The 7 km return walk (about 3 hours) to the upper gorge is a good one as it passes through a wide variety of diverse habitats.

Take your canoe or inflatable boat (or hire one from the camping ground or from Adels Grove), as many peaceful hours can be spent paddling along the creek.

Access

Reaching Boodjamulla is an adventure in itself. The gravel roads in this region can be hard on conventional vehicles and a 4WD is recommended.

Visitors should be self-sufficient in food, fuel, camping supplies and vehicle spare parts. The nearest place to buy fuel is Gregory Downs Hotel, phone (07) 4748 5566, 100 km east of the park. Mount Isa,

400 km to the south-east, is the best spot to buy food and other essentials.

During the wet season, access can be cut for weeks at a time and the roads closed. Contact the RACQ, phone 1300 130 595, for the latest reports.

Camping

The camp sites have toilets, showers and fireplaces, but collecting firewood within the park is strictly prohibited. Gas fires are preferred. There is also a private and popular camp site 10 km away at Adels Grove, phone (07) 4748 5502.

For more information and permits, contact the ranger.

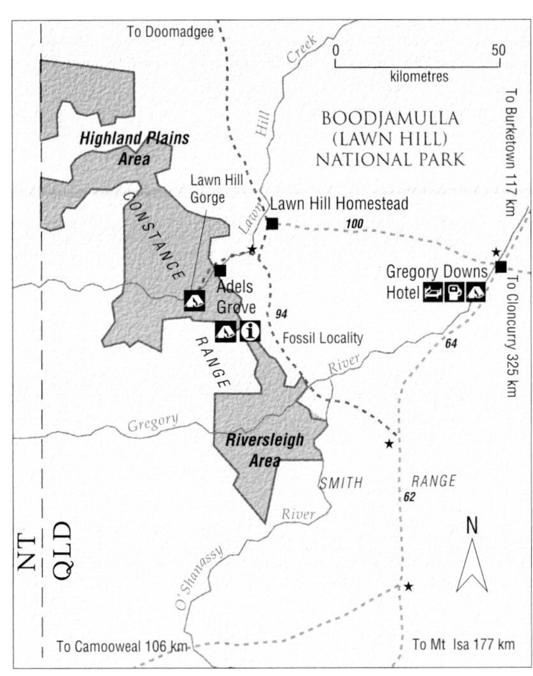

While much of the park is grassland and open forest, the red cliffs around Lawn Hill Gorge are covered by rainforest plants.

Whitsunday Islands National Park

White sandy beaches, azure blue seas, forest-covered slopes, abundant wildlife and isolated camping spots are just some of the more inviting aspects of a trip to the Whitsunday Islands National Park. These sparkling isles are part of the Cumberland and Northumberland Island groups that lie off the Queensland coast between Bowen and Mackay.

The islands visible today were once the peaks of a large coastal mountain range. About 6000 years ago the valleys were flooded when sea levels rose.

WHERE: Off the Queensland coast between Bowen and Mackay
Map: Qld 5 G3

WHEN: March to November

WHY: Snorkelling, swimming, relaxing

SIZE: 20 500 ha

RANGER: (07) 4946 7022

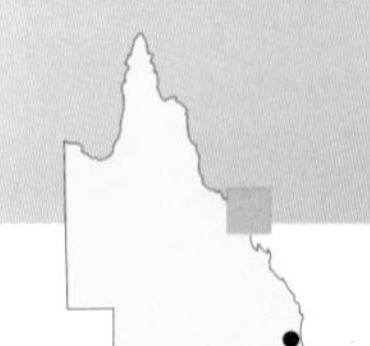

There are 70-odd islands in the Whitsundays, and all are protected by various national parks. The Whitsunday Islands National Park covers 32 islands, including Whitsunday Island, the largest in the group.

Australian Aboriginals lived on many of the larger islands, such as Lindeman, Whitsunday and Hook, and traded with other tribes on the mainland.

Captain James Cook sailed through the islands in 1770, noting that they abounded in good, safe anchorages and naming them the 'Whitsundays' after the day on which they were first sighted.

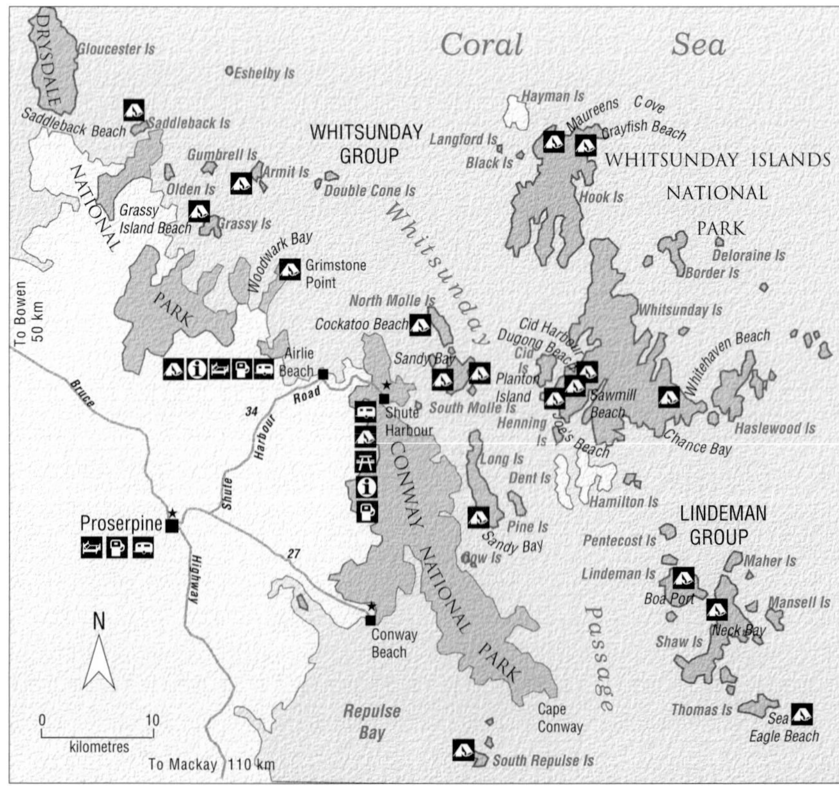

don't miss

There are spectacular views to be had from the higher, forested areas of some of the islands. For example, a marked bushwalking track on Whitsunday Island leads up to an impressive lookout at Tongue Point.

The Great Barrier Reef is made up of approximately 2900 individual reefs. Thousands of tropical fish, coral, mollusc, seaweed and bird species live in this beautiful habitat.

Diving and Snorkelling

The lure of swimming among the colourful coral and fish in the Great Barrier Reef Marine Park is one of the main attractions that entice thousands of people every year to the Whitsundays. Visitors can either go out with one of the many professional diving outfits based at Airlie Beach (ProDive Whitsundays, phone 07 4948 1888), or bring their own snorkel, mask and fins.

Access and Camping

Unless you arrive in your own boat, the best way to visit the Whitsunday Islands is to book with one of the many travel agencies operating in the region. Various types of power and sail boats operating out of Airlie Beach transport visitors to and from the different island camp sites. Contact the Airlie Beach Tourist Information Centre, phone (07) 4946 6665.

Visitors to the Whitsundays have a wide choice of islands to camp on, although many of them are isolated and difficult to reach.

Covering an area of 10 930 hectares, Whitsunday Island is by far the largest, and offers the best camping facilities in the Whitsunday group. Whitehaven Beach on the east of the island is a spectacular white, sandy beach stretching for 6 km along the coast. The largest camping ground on Whitsunday Island is located at Dugong Beach, on the western side, where up to 40 people can stay at any one time.

Other islands with facilities include North Molle (Cockatoo Beach) and Thomas Island (Sea Eagle Beach).

If you prefer solitude and wilderness, you could try Crayfish Beach on Hook Island. This camping spot is for a maximum of two people. Other great places for bush camping include Geographers Beach on Henning Island—great for views and forest walks—and Princess Alexandria Bay on Lindeman Island.

Rainbow lorikeets (Trichoglossus haematodus) *are very sociable birds, flying and feeding in groups of up to fifty, and gathering in even larger groups to roost at night.*

Apart from Whitsunday Island and North Molle, drinking water must be taken with you. Adequate food supplies for your stay, plus 2 extra days' emergency rations in case the weather delays your departure, should also be taken.

A medical kit that has vinegar to treat marine stings should be included with your camping gear.

Camping permits and more information can be obtained from the Queensland Parks and Wildlife Service Whitsunday Information Centre, Airlie Beach, on (07) 4946 7022.

Lakefield National Park

Lakefield is Queensland's second-largest national park, covering 537 000 hectares north of Laura and taking in much of the Normanby, Bizant, Morehead, Hann, North Kennedy and Kennedy Rivers.

fact file

WHERE: 300 km north-west of Cairns
Map: Qld 1 E10, Qld 3 L1

WHEN: May to October

WHY: Fishing, camping, nature watching

SIZE: 537 000 ha

RANGER: New Laura (07) 4060 3260; Lakefield (07) 4060 3271; Cooktown (07) 4069 5777

This rich region of flat grassy plains and flood plains attracts thousands of birds, making the area a birdwatcher's delight. As well as the 180-odd species of birds recorded, there are 18 species of mammals and 38 species of reptiles. Lakefield is one of the few parks in Queensland where fishing is allowed, and the prize fish is the mighty barramundi. There are some top spots to catch fish, with a number of places suitable to launch a boat. No fishing is allowed between 1 November and 31 January; at other times a bag limit applies.

Access and Camping

Access is restricted to the dry season, with the best access via Laura on the main road north from Cairns. Contact the RACQ, phone 1300 130 595, for the latest road reports.

The carefully restored Old Laura homestead is one of a few historic sites in the park.

The main route through the park runs north from Laura past the ranger stations of New Laura and Lakefield, and then west to the small tourist stop of Musgrave. All the roads and the country here demand a 4WD vehicle.

There are many camp sites available in Lakefield with most of them located on the larger waterholes. An excellent camp with toilets, fireplaces and tables is located at Kalpowar.

The Hann River Crossing is a popular camping spot for 4WD enthusiasts during the dry season, but the low-lying area becomes flooded in the wet season.

More National Parks of Importance

Currawinya National Park

SIZE: 151 300 ha
MAP: Qld 6 L9

Currawinya, in the south-west of the state, was gazetted a national park in 1991. The semi-arid park was established to protect the area's freshwater lakes, which are an important refuge for inland birds in times of drought. Lake Wyara abounds with black swans, pelicans and many duck species, while Lake Numalla, in the north-west of the park, is a 2200 hectare body of fresh water.

There are no designated walking tracks in the park but birdwatching is popular. Fishing is allowed (no permit required) in the Paroo River but not in the freshwater lakes.

Access to the park is via Cunnamulla and Eulo, Bourke or Thargomindah. 4WD vehicles are recommended. You should check road conditions with the ranger before setting out.

Because it is such a remote park with no real facilities, visitors should come well supplied with food and water. There are numerous bush camping sites, and camping permits and fees apply.

For more details, contact the ranger on (07) 4655 4001.

Eungella National Park

SIZE: 51 700 ha
MAP: Qld 5 F3

Towering mountain peaks, deep gorges, tumbling waterfalls and crystal clear streams all combine to make Eungella one of the treasures of Queensland. Much of the park is trackless wilderness but the southern part is easily accessible and popular.

A number of reasonably easy walking trails have been constructed around Broken River but the main drawcard for many people is the plentiful number of platypus that can be seen here. Early morning or sunset is best. The 2 hours after dusk are the best time to see the nocturnal animals of the rainforest (ringtail possums, short-nosed bandicoots, bush rats are some), as this is when they move to new feeding areas.

This brown tree snake (Boiga irregularis) *in Eungella National Park is mildly venomous to humans. It is found in tropical northern Australia and down along the eastern coast to Sydney.*

Above: *The black swan* (Cygnus atratus) *is Australia's only native swan. Currawinya provides a refuge for these birds in the dry season.*

The park is also a paradise for birdwatchers, with over 100 species being recorded.

From Mackay, a good bitumen road leads all the way to the park, with the park's camping ground located at Fern Flat. It can be popular with visitors, so book ahead for a site.

Camping permits are required. Contact the ranger, phone (07) 4958 4552.

The lotusbird (Irediparra gallinacea) *can be found along Australia's north and north-east coasts. It is one of the many bird species in Eungella.*

Girraween National Park

SIZE: 11 700 ha
MAP: Qld 7 L9

Girraween National Park, situated in rugged granite country 260 km south-west of Brisbane on the Queensland–New South Wales border, is a spectacular paradise for wildlife, wildflowers, and wilderness seekers.

There are some easy-to-follow walking tracks, ranging from the 900 metre link circuit to the 10.4 km trail that weaves its way through the forest to Mount Norman.

A large waterhole in Bald Rock Creek near the picnic area is a great place to go swimming.

The park is accessible to conventional vehicles throughout the year. There are two large camping grounds, one at Bald Rock Creek, the other across the road at Castle Rock Camping Area. Both are well equipped. Due to the park's popularity, visitors should book with the ranger, phone (07) 4684 5157.

The granite landscape of Girraween has eroded over millions of years to form enormous granite boulders and domes.

Green Island National Park

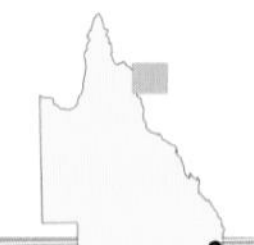

SIZE: 12 ha
MAP: Qld 2 B2

Situated 27 km north-east of Cairns in the waters of the Great Barrier Reef Marine Park, Green Island is a coral cay with its own surrounding reef.

This tiny island is almost covered by rainforest, courtesy of the wind and birds that carried seeds there. Hikers can enjoy walking through the lush vegetation, but the island's small size (300 metres by 650 metres) ensures the walks are brief.

The main attraction is the reef: the clear waters around the island make conditions excellent for diving and snorkelling, as the reef abounds with countless varieties of colourful fish and other sea life.

Camping is not permitted on Green Island, although visitors can stay at the small luxury resort. Many visitors come just for the day, to swim and snorkel. There is an underwater observatory too.

For further information, contact Queensland Parks and Wildlife Service, Cairns, on (07) 4046 6600, or Green Island Resort, on (07) 4031 3300.

Hinchinbrook Island National Park

SIZE: 39 000 ha
MAP: Qld 2 C6

Nature lovers and wilderness seekers are drawn to the pristine rainforests, isolated sandy coves, mountain peaks and mangrove-lined estuaries which are just a few of the facets of Hinchinbrook Island, Australia's largest island national park and a refuge for many endangered plants and animals.

Right: *The waters around Green Island are paradise for snorkellers, with starfish, sea urchins, turtles and giant clams as well as beautifully coloured fish and coral to be seen.*

QLD

Hinchinbrook Island's picturesque eastern coast. The island was part of the Australian mainland until the end of the last ice age, when sea levels rose.

Below: *Cunninghams Gap in Main Range National Park is named for Allan Cunningham, who explored this area while searching for a pass across the mountains.*

The island has some of the best walking trails in Queensland, including the tough 32 km Thorsbone Trail that runs from Ramsay Bay to George Point.

Most visitors to the island travel by boat from the small town of Cardwell. Hinchinbrook Ferries runs a return service to the island for day visitors as well as campers; phone (07) 4066 8270.

Campers should be well prepared and bring everything they need. Only fuel stoves are permitted.

For camping permits, contact the ranger at the Rainforest and Reef Centre, Cardwell on (07) 4066 8601.

Main Range National Park

SIZE: 18 400 ha
MAP: Qld 7 M8

Main Range National Park has long been known as one of the finest bush-walking areas in south-east Queensland.

Situated 116 km west of Brisbane, the park straddles the Great Dividing Range from Kangaroo Mountain in the north to Wilsons Peak on the border. An extensive range of vegetation, including rainforest, eucalypts and grass-trees, can be found, while its fauna is also extremely varied.

One of the best places to take in the grandeur of Main Range is from Governors Chair lookout, a 150 metre walk up from the car park in the Spicers Gap section of the park.

The park headquarters is located just off the Cunningham Highway. The main camping area is at Cunninghams Gap on the banks of West Gap Creek, located near the ranger station. The quieter Spicers Gap camping area can be reached via the Moogerah Dam road.

For more details contact the ranger on (07) 4666 1133.

Cunningham's skink (Egernia cunninghami) *grows to about 30 centimetres long. It usually lives in rock crevices or under large rock slabs, and can be seen in Main Range National Park.*

Moreton Island National Park

SIZE: 17 000 ha
MAP: Qld 7 N6

Moreton Island National Park is only 40 km east of Brisbane and a short barge trip from the mainland. The island is made up almost entirely of sand, and there are several freshwater lakes, including beautiful Blue Lagoon.

The rocky headland of Cape Moreton in the north of Moreton Island is the site of Queensland's oldest lighthouse, built in 1857.

Many visitors come to Moreton for the great fishing. Once on the ocean beach you can either head north to Cape Moreton or south to Reeders Point.

A number of barges cross to Moreton, including The Combie Trader, phone (07) 3203 6399, and the Moreton Venture, phone (07) 3909 3333.

The island is suitable for 4WD vehicles only. There is a fee for vehicles and passengers and also a landing fee, valid for one month. Contact the ranger on (07) 3408 2710, for details.

There are five Queensland Parks and Wildlife Service camping grounds on Moreton. You can also bush camp at most other places around the coast. Food, fuel and ice can be purchased at the small township of Bulwer and at Kooringal.

Simpson Desert National Park

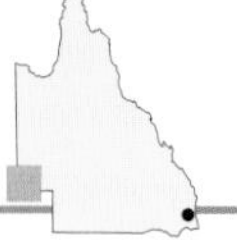

SIZE: 550 000 ha
MAP: Qld 6 A3

The Simpson Desert National Park is the biggest national park in the state. This remote desert country was one of the last areas in Australia to be explored by Europeans, with the route taken by travellers from Birdsville being established in the late 1950s. Glistening salt lakes are found in the park's west.

A 4WD vehicle is essential for this area. A permit is needed to enter and camp in the park, which is available from the Queensland Parks and Wildlife Service in Birdsville, phone (07) 4656 3249, or Longreach, phone (07) 4652 7333.

Access is only via the main road from Birdsville, then onto the QAA Line to the border and then south to Poeppel Corner.

Camping is only allowed beside the track. The most popular camp sites are at the eastern boundary of the park or at Poeppel Corner itself. Wood is scarce, so a gas stove is recommended.

Right: *Even the desolate sand dunes of the Simpson Desert support some plant life, and the plants give cover to a large number of small reptiles. Dingoes are also often seen.*

QLD

Popular Parks at a Glance

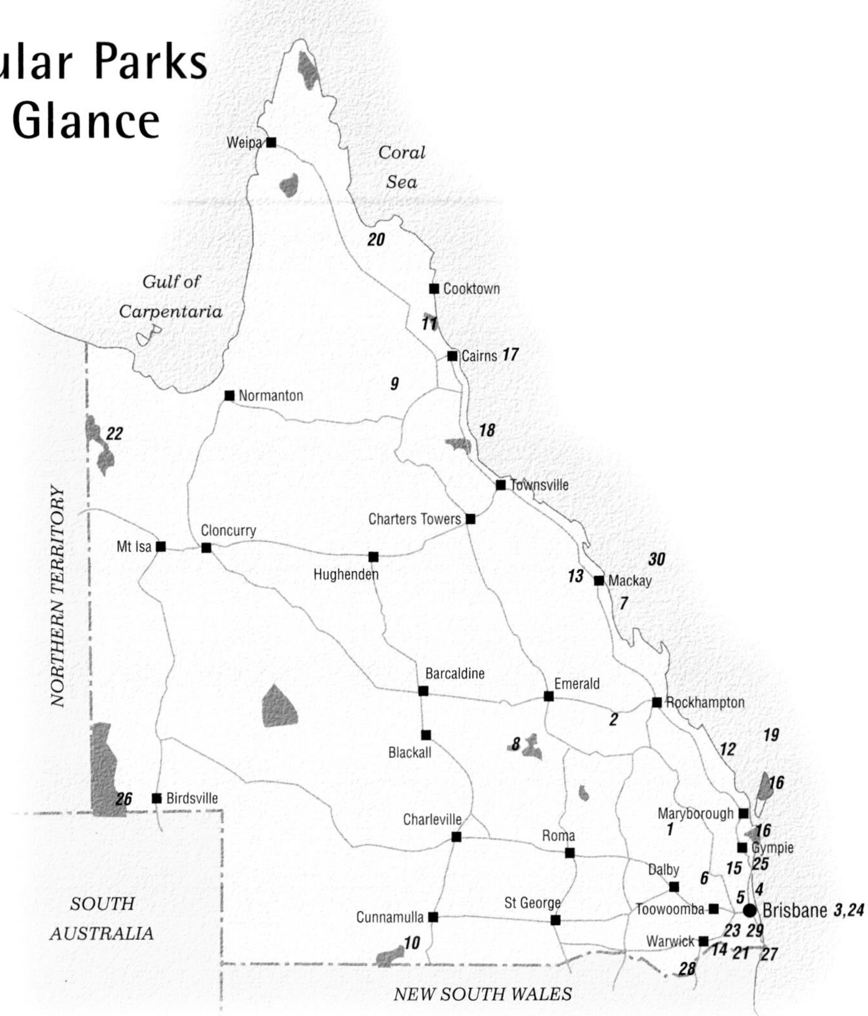

	Park	Camping	Caravan Access	Disabled Access	4WD Access	Picnic Areas	Toilets	Walking Tracks	Kiosk	Information
1	Auburn River NP	●			●	●		●		
2	Blackdown Tableland NP	●		●		●	●	●		
3	Blue Lake NP (Stradbroke Is)				●			●		
4	Bribie Island Recreation Area	●			●	●	●	●		
5	Brisbane FP	●		●		●	●	●	●	●
6	Bunya Mountains NP	●		●	●	●	●	●		●
7	Cape Palmerston NP	●			●	●	●	●		
8	Carnarvon NP	●		●	●	●	●	●		●
9	Chillagoe–Mungana Caves NP							●		
10	Currawinya NP	●			●	●	●			●
11	Daintree NP	●		●		●	●	●		
12	Deepwater NP	●			●	●	●			
13	Eungella NP	●		●		●	●	●		●
14	Girraween NP	●	●			●	●	●		●
15	Glass House Mountains NP			●		●	●	●		
16	Great Sandy NP	●	●	●	●	●	●	●		●
17	Green Island NP			●			●	●		
18	Hinchinbrook NP	●				●	●	●		
19	Capricornia Cays NP	●					●	●		●
20	Lakefield NP	●			●		●	●		
21	Lamington NP	●				●	●	●		●
22	Boodjamulla (Lawn Hill) NP	●			●	●	●	●		●
23	Main Range NP	●				●	●	●		
24	Moreton Island NP	●			●	●	●			●
25	Noosa NP					●	●	●		●
26	Simpson Desert NP	●			●					
27	Springbrook NP	●		●		●	●	●		●
28	Sundown NP	●			●	●	●	●		
29	Tamborine NP			●		●	●	●		●
30	Whitsunday Islands NP	●				●	●	●		

Map 1

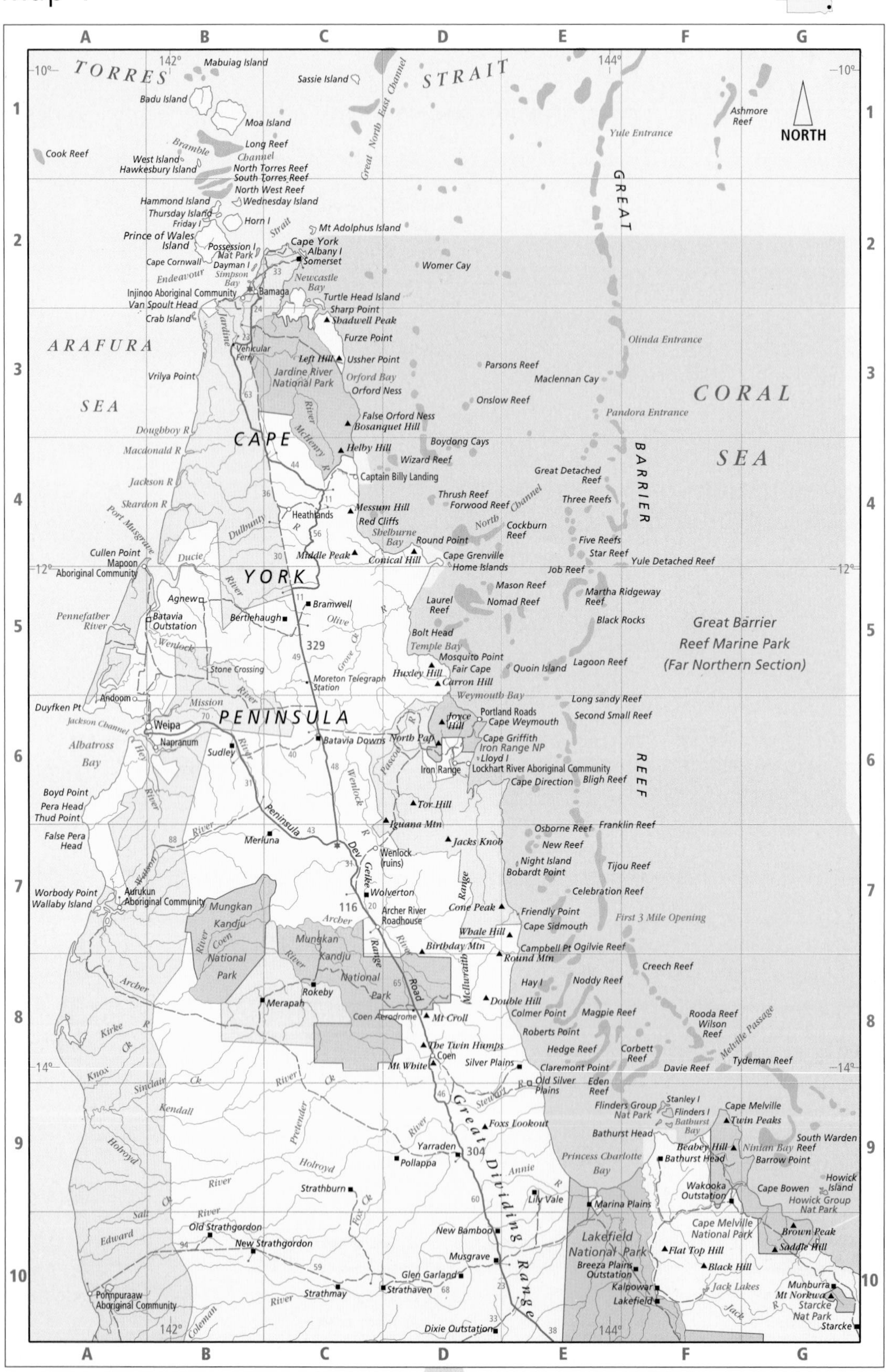
TORRES STRAIT
CORAL SEA
ARAFURA SEA
CAPE YORK PENINSULA
GREAT BARRIER REEF
Great Barrier Reef Marine Park (Far Northern Section)
NORTH
kilometres
Mabuiag Island
Sassie Island
Badu Island
Moa Island
Cook Reef
West Island
Hawkesbury Island
Long Reef
North Torres Reef
South Torres Reef
North West Reef
Hammond Island
Wednesday Island
Thursday Island
Friday I
Horn I
Prince of Wales Island
Mt Adolphus Island
Cape York
Albany I
Somerset
Possession I Nat Park
Dayman I
Cape Cornwall
Injinoo Aboriginal Community
Bamaga
Van Spoult Head
Crab Island
Turtle Head Island
Sharp Point
Shadwell Peak
Furze Point
Womer Cay
Yule Entrance
Ashmore Reef
Olinda Entrance
Vrilya Point
Jardine River National Park
Left Hill
Ussher Point
Orford Bay
Orford Ness
Parsons Reef
Maclennan Cay
Onslow Reef
Pandora Entrance
False Orford Ness
Bosanquet Hill
Helby Hill
Boydong Cays
Wizard Reef
Captain Billy Landing
Great Detached Reef
Thrush Reef
Forwood Reef
Three Reefs
Heathlands
Messum Hill
Red Cliffs
Shelburne Bay
Round Point
Cockburn Reef
Five Reefs
Star Reef
Yule Detached Reef
Middle Peak
Conical Hill
Cape Grenville
Home Islands
Job Reef
Cullen Point
Mapoon Aboriginal Community
Mason Reef
Nomad Reef
Laurel Reef
Martha Ridgeway Reef
Black Rocks
Agnew
Bramwell
Bertiehaugh
Batavia Outstation
Bolt Head
Temple Bay
Mosquito Point
Fair Cape
Quoin Island
Lagoon Reef
Huxley Hill
Carron Hill
Stone Crossing
Moreton Telegraph Station
Weymouth Bay
Long sandy Reef
Andoom
Portland Roads
Cape Weymouth
Second Small Reef
Duyfken Pt
Weipa
Napranum
Joyce Hill
Batavia Downs
North Pap
Cape Griffith
Iron Range NP
Lloyd I
Sudley
Albatross Bay
Iron Range
Lockhart River Aboriginal Community
Cape Direction
Bligh Reef
Boyd Point
Pera Head
Thud Point
Tor Hill
Iguana Mtn
False Pera Head
Merluna
Jacks Knob
Osborne Reef
Franklin Reef
New Reef
Wenlock (ruins)
Night Island
Bobardt Point
Tijou Reef
Worbody Point
Wallaby Island
Aurukun Aboriginal Community
Wolverton
Celebration Reef
Mungkan Kandju National Park
Archer River Roadhouse
Cone Peak
Friendly Point
Cape Sidmouth
First 3 Mile Opening
Whale Hill
Birthday Mtn
Campbell Pt
Ogilvie Reef
Round Mtn
Creech Reef
Hay I
Noddy Reef
Rokeby
Merapah
Double Hill
Colmer Point
Magpie Reef
Rooda Reef
Wilson Reef
Coen Aerodrome
Mt Croll
Roberts Point
Melville Passage
The Twin Humps
Hedge Reef
Corbett Reef
Coen
Mt White
Silver Plains
Claremont Point
Davie Reef
Tydeman Reef
Old Silver Plains
Eden Reef
Flinders Group Nat Park
Stanley I
Flinders I
Bathurst Bay
Cape Melville
Twin Peaks
Foxs Lookout
Bathurst Head
South Warden Reef
Yarraden
Pollappa
Princess Charlotte Bay
Beabey Hill
Ninian Bay
Barrow Point
Howick Island
Strathburn
Wakooka Outstation
Cape Bowen
Howick Group Nat Park
Lily Vale
Marina Plains
Cape Melville National Park
Old Strathgordon
New Strathgordon
New Bamboo
Lakefield National Park
Brown Peak
Saddle Hill
Flat Top Hill
Musgrave
Breeza Plains Outstation
Black Hill
Glen Garland
Strathaven
Strathmay
Kalpowar
Lakefield
Jack Lakes
Munburra
Mt Norkwa
Starcke Nat Park
Pormpuraaw Aboriginal Community
Dixie Outstation
Starcke
Great Dividing Range
Peninsula Road
Endeavour Strait
Simpson Bay
Newcastle Bay
Great North East Channel
Bramble Channel
North Channel
Jackson Channel
Jardine
Doughboy R
Macdonald R
Jackson R
Skardon R
Port Musgrave
Ducie
Dulbunty R
McHenry R
Pennefather River
Wenlock
Mission River
Olive R
Hey River
Pascoe R
Watson River
Archer
Coen River
Kirke R
Knox Ck
Sinclair Ck
Kendall
Holroyd
Pretender
Stewart R
Annie R
Salt Ck
Edward River
Fox Ck
Coleman River
Jack R
McIlwraith Range
Geikie Range
Dev
142°
144°
10°
12°
14°
A B C D E F G
1 2 3 4 5 6 7 8 9 10

Map 2

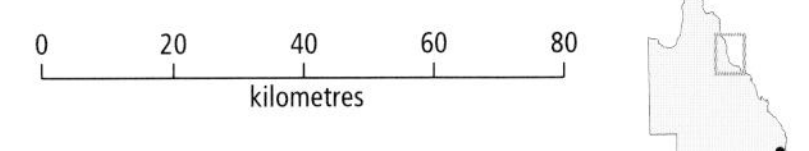

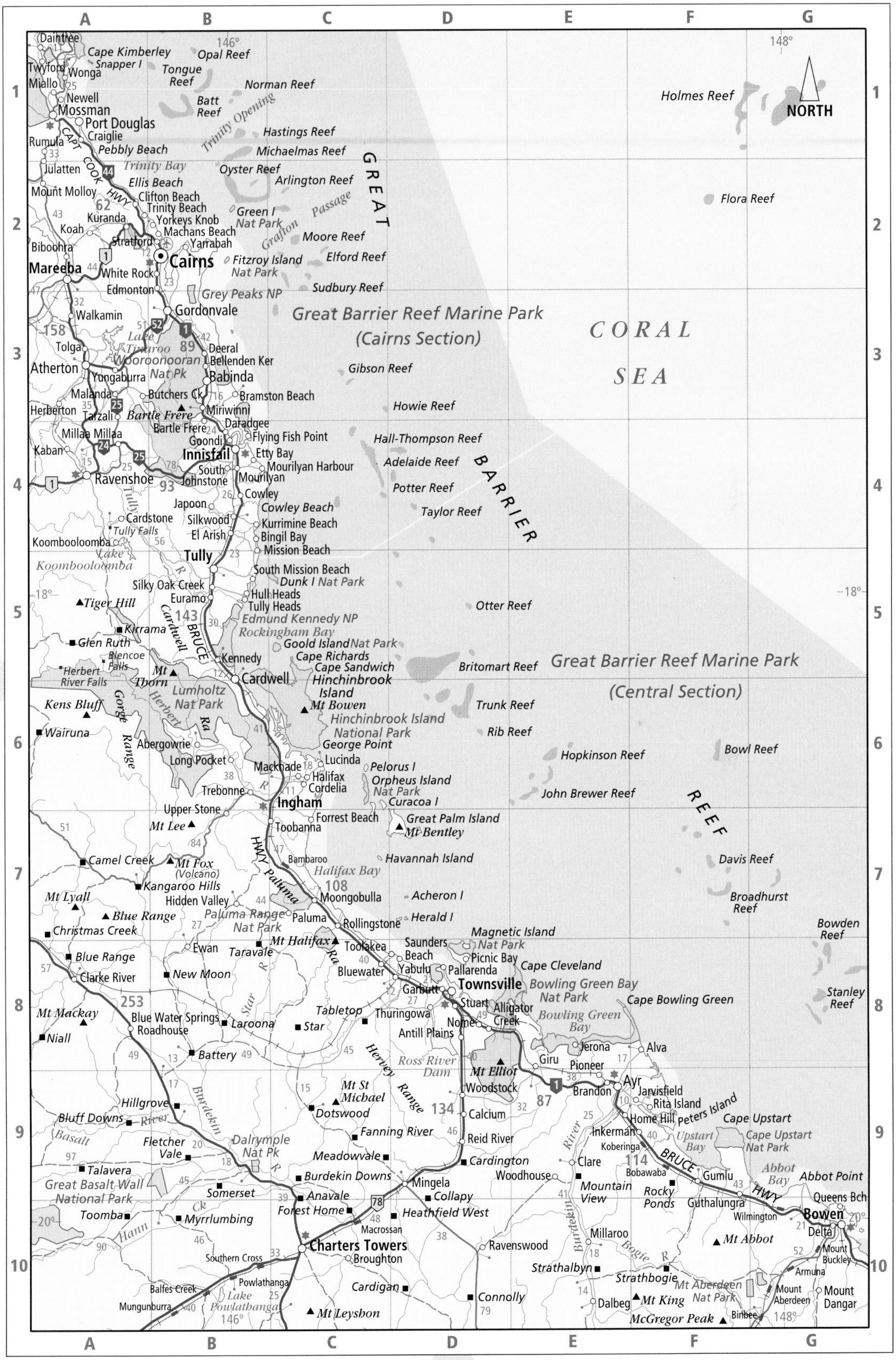

A B C D E F G

1 2 3 4 5 6 7 8 9 10

NORTH

Daintree
Cape Kimberley
Snapper I
Opal Reef
Twyford
Wonga
Tongue Reef
Miallo
Norman Reef
Newell
Batt Reef
Mossman
Trinity Opening
Port Douglas
Rumula
Craiglie
Hastings Reef
CAPT COOK HWY
Pebbly Beach
Michaelmas Reef
Trinity Bay
Julatten
Oyster Reef
Ellis Beach
Arlington Reef
Mount Molloy
Clifton Beach
Trinity Beach
Green I
Nat Park
Kuranda
Yorkeys Knob
Grafton Passage
Koah
Machans Beach
Moore Reef
Biboohra
Stratford
Yarrabah
Cairns
Fitzroy Island
Nat Park
Elford Reef
Mareeba
White Rock
Edmonton
Sudbury Reef
Grey Peaks NP
Walkamin
Gordonvale
Great Barrier Reef Marine Park
(Cairns Section)
Lake Tinaroo
Deeral
Tolga
Wooroonooran
Bellenden Ker
Atherton
Yungaburra
Nat Pk
Babinda
Gibson Reef
Malanda
Butchers Ck
Bramston Beach
Herberton
Tarzali
Bartle Frere
Miriwinni
Howie Reef
Millaa Millaa
Bartle Frere
Daradgee
Goondi
Flying Fish Point
Hall-Thompson Reef
Kaban
Innisfail
Etty Bay
Adelaide Reef
Ravenshoe
South Johnstone
Mourilyan Harbour
Mourilyan
Potter Reef
Cowley
Japoon
Cowley Beach
Taylor Reef
Cardstone
Silkwood
Kurrimine Beach
Tully Falls
El Arish
Bingil Bay
Koombooloomba
Mission Beach
Lake Koombooloomba
Tully
South Mission Beach
Dunk I Nat Park
Silky Oak Creek
Hull Heads
Euramo
Tully Heads
Tiger Hill
Otter Reef
Edmund Kennedy NP
Rockingham Bay
Kirrama
BRUCE
Cardwell R
Glen Ruth
Goold Island Nat Park
Blencoe Falls
Kennedy
Cape Richards
Britomart Reef
Herbert River Falls
Mt Thorn
Cardwell
Cape Sandwich
Hinchinbrook Island
Lumholtz Nat Park
Kens Bluff
Gorge Range
Herbert Ra
Mt Bowen
Hinchinbrook Island
National Park
Trunk Reef
Wairuna
Rib Reef
Abergowrie
George Point
Long Pocket
Lucinda
Macknade
Halifax
Pelorus I
Orpheus Island
Nat Park
Trebonne
Cordelia
Curacoa I
Upper Stone
Ingham
Forrest Beach
Great Palm Island
Mt Lee
Toobanna
Mt Bentley
Hopkinson Reef
Bowl Reef
John Brewer Reef
GREAT BARRIER REEF
CORAL SEA
Great Barrier Reef Marine Park
(Central Section)
Holmes Reef
Flora Reef
Camel Creek
Mt Fox
(Volcano)
HWY
Bambaroo
Havannah Island
Kangaroo Hills
Halifax Bay
Davis Reef
Mt Lyall
Hidden Valley
Paluma
Moongobulla
Acheron I
Broadhurst Reef
Blue Range
Paluma Range
Nat Park
Paluma
Rollingstone
Herald I
Christmas Creek
Bowden Reef
Mt Halifax
Magnetic Island
Nat Park
Ewan
Taravale
Toolakea
Saunders Beach
Picnic Bay
Blue Range
Bluewater
Yabulu
Pallarenda
Cape Cleveland
Clarke River
New Moon
Star R
Garbutt
Townsville
Bowling Green Bay
Nat Park
Stanley Reef
Stuart
Alligator Creek
Cape Bowling Green
Mt Mackay
Blue Water Springs Roadhouse
Laroona
Star
Tabletop
Thuringowa
Nome
Bowling Green Bay
Niall
Antill Plains
Jerona
Alva
Battery
Ross River Dam
Hervey Range
Giru
Pioneer
Mt Elliot
Ayr
Hillgrove
Burdekin
Mt St Michael
Woodstock
Brandon
Jarvisfield
Rita Island
Bluff Downs
River
Dotswood
Calcium
Home Hill
Peters Island
Cape Upstart
Basalt
Fanning River
Inkerman
Upstart Bay
Cape Upstart
Nat Park
Fletcher Vale
Dalrymple Nat Pk
Reid River
Koberinga
Meadowvale
BRUCE
Talavera
Cardington
Clare
River
Bobawaba
Great Basalt Wall
National Park
Somerset
Burdekin Downs
Woodhouse
Gumlu
Abbot Bay
Abbot Point
Mingela
Mountain View
Rocky Ponds
HWY
Anavale
Collapy
Guthalungra
Queens Bch
Toomba
Myrrlumbing
Forest Home
Heathfield West
Wilmington
Bowen
Hann
Ck
Macrossan
Millaroo
Delta
Charters Towers
Ravenswood
Bogie
Mt Abbot
Southern Cross
Broughton
R
Mount Buckley
Balfes Creek
Powlathanga
Strathalbyn
Strathbogie
Armuna
Lake Powlathanga
Cardigan
Mt Aberdeen
Nat Park
Mount Aberdeen
Mount Dangar
Mungunburra
Connolly
Dalbeg
Mt King
Mt Leysbon
McGregor Peak
Binbee

QLD 3

Map 3

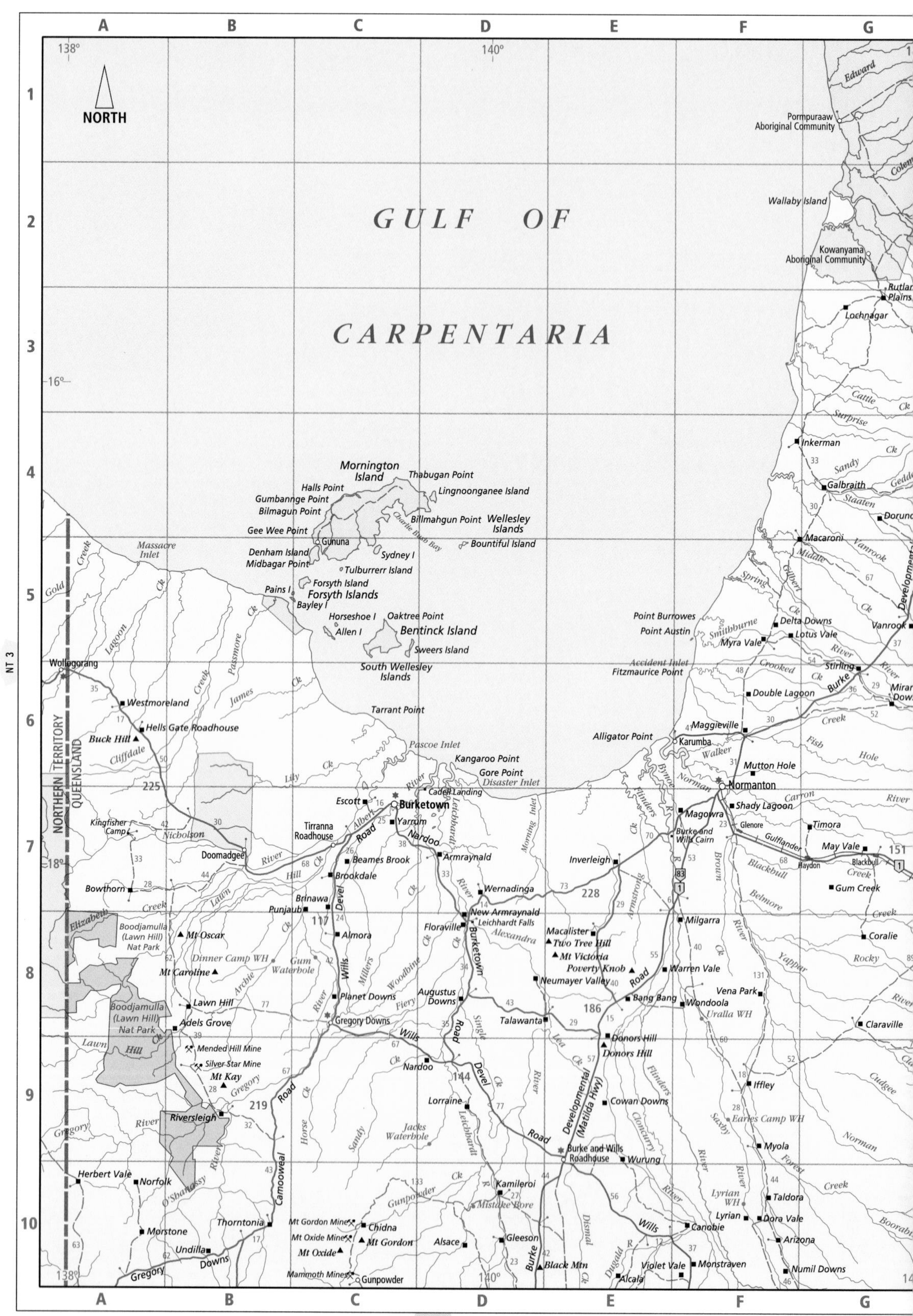
NORTH
GULF OF CARPENTARIA
Mornington Island
Thabugan Point
Lingnoonganee Island
Halls Point
Gumbannge Point
Bilmagun Point
Billmahgun Point
Wellesley Islands
Gee Wee Point
Gununa
Bountiful Island
Denham Island
Midbagar Point
Sydney I
Tulburrerr Island
Forsyth Island
Forsyth Islands
Pains I
Bayley I
Horseshoe I
Allen I
Oaktree Point
Bentinck Island
Sweers Island
South Wellesley Islands
Tarrant Point
Pascoe Inlet
Kangaroo Point
Gore Point
Disaster Inlet
Cadell Landing
Burketown
Escott
Yarrum
Tirranna Roadhouse
Doomadgee
Wollogorang
Westmoreland
Hells Gate Roadhouse
Buck Hill
Massacre Inlet
Kingfisher Camp
Bowthorn
Boodjamulla (Lawn Hill) Nat Park
Mt Oscar
Mt Caroline
Lawn Hill
Adels Grove
Mended Hill Mine
Silver Star Mine
Mt Kay
Riversleigh
Herbert Vale
Norfolk
Morstone
Undilla
Thorntonia
Gregory Downs
Beames Brook
Brookdale
Brinawa
Punjaub
Almora
Planet Downs
Armraynald
Wernadinga
New Armraynald
Leichhardt Falls
Floraville
Augustus Downs
Talawanta
Nardoo
Lorraine
Jacks Waterbole
Kamileroi
Mistake Bore
Gleeson
Alsace
Mt Gordon Mine
Mt Oxide Mine
Mt Oxide
Mt Gordon
Chidna
Mammoth Mines
Gunpowder
Black Mtn
Burke and Wills Roadhouse
Wurung
Cowan Downs
Donors Hill
Macalister
Two Tree Hill
Mt Victoria
Poverty Knob
Neumayer Valley
Bang Bang
Wondoola
Warren Vale
Milgarra
Inverleigh
Magowra
Burke and Wills Cairn
Normanton
Shady Lagoon
Glenore
Timora
May Vale
Haydon
Blackbull
Gum Creek
Coralie
Vena Park
Claraville
Uralla WH
Iffley
Eales Camp WH
Myola
Taldora
Lyrian WH
Lyrian
Dora Vale
Arizona
Numil Downs
Canobie
Monstraven
Violet Vale
Alcala
Alligator Point
Karumba
Maggieville
Mutton Hole
Point Burrowes
Point Austin
Accident Inlet
Fitzmaurice Point
Myra Vale
Delta Downs
Lotus Vale
Stirling
Double Lagoon
Inkerman
Galbraith
Macaroni
Lochnagar
Rutland Plains
Wallaby Island
Kowanyama Aboriginal Community
Pormpuraaw Aboriginal Community
Developmental Road
(Matilda Hwy)
Wills Road
Devel Road
Burketown Road
Nardoo Road
Camooweal Road
Gregory Downs
Burke
NORTHERN TERRITORY
QUEENSLAND
NT 3
QLD 4

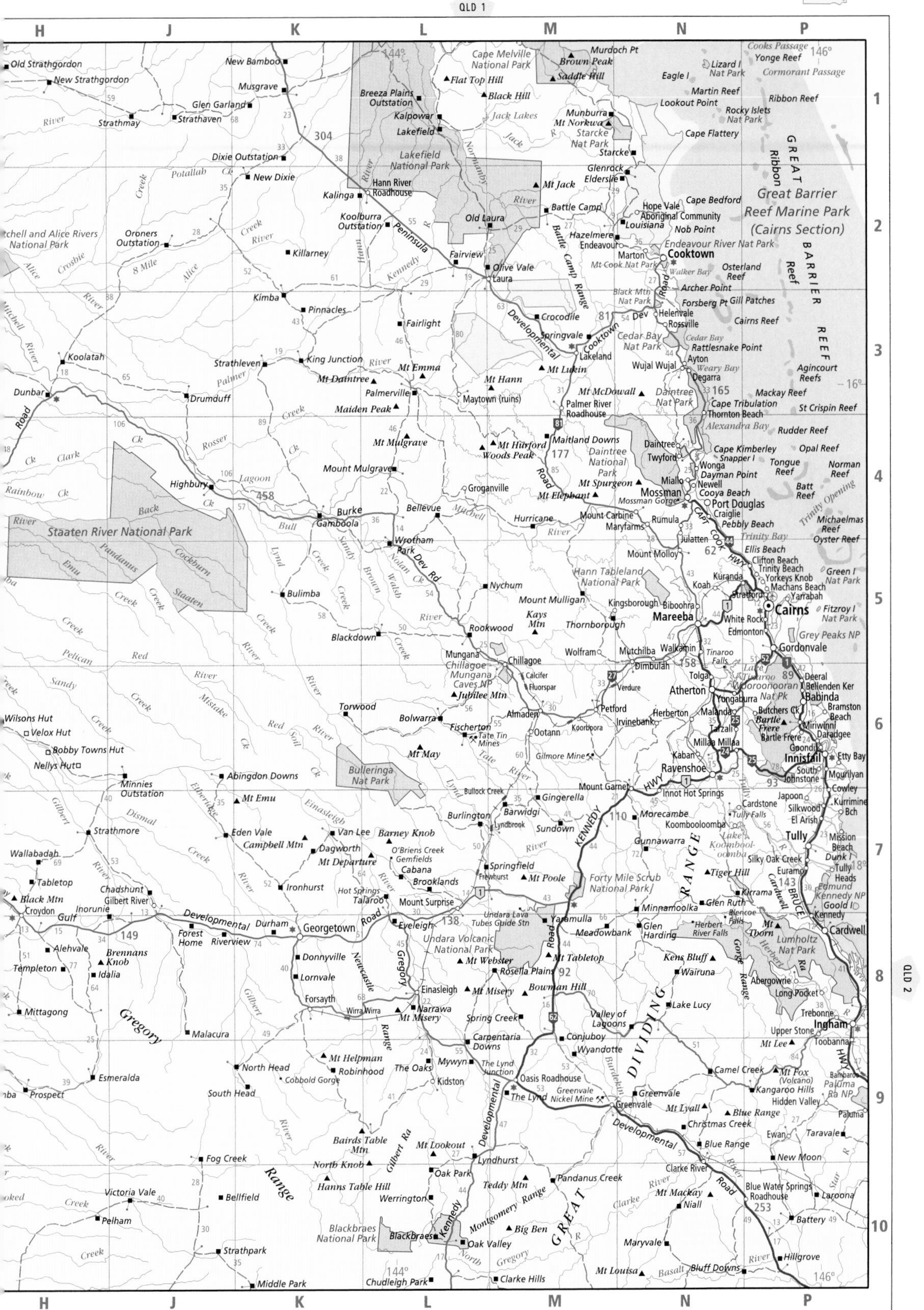

0 20 40 60 80
kilometres
QLD 1
H J K L M N P
1 2 3 4 5 6 7 8 9 10
QLD
Old Strathgordon
New Strathgordon
Strathmay
Strathaven
New Bamboo
Musgrave
Glen Garland
304
Dixie Outstation
New Dixie
Potallah Ck
Oroners Outstation
Mitchell and Alice Rivers National Park
8 Mile
Killarney
Kimba
Pinnacles
Koolatah
Dunbar
Road
Strathleven
King Junction
Palmer River
Drumduff
Highbury
Lagoon
458
Rosser Ck
Staaten River National Park
Clark Ck
Rainbow Ck
Burke
Gamboola
Bull
Lynd
Bulimba
Blackdown
Wilsons Hut
Velox Hut
Bobby Towns Hut
Nellys Hut
Minnies Outstation
Abingdon Downs
Mt Emu
Strathmore
Eden Vale
Campbell Mtn
Wallabadah
Tabletop
Chadshunt
Gilbert River
Black Mtn
Croydon
Gulf
Inorunie
149
Developmental
Durham
Forest Home
Riverview
Georgetown
Alehvale
Brennans Knob
Idalia
Templeton
Mittagong
Gregory
Malacura
North Head
Esmeralda
Prospect
South Head
Fog Creek
Victoria Vale
Bellfield
Pelham
Strathpark
Middle Park
Range
Cape Melville National Park
Flat Top Hill
Black Hill
Breeza Plains Outstation
Kalpowar
Lakefield
Lakefield National Park
Hann River Roadhouse
Kalinga
Koolburra Outstation
Peninsula
Kennedy
Fairview
Olive Vale
Laura
Old Laura
Mt Jack
Battle Camp
Battle Camp Range
Crocodile
Springvale
Lakeland
Developmental
Fairlight
Mt Emma
Mt Daintree
Palmerville
Maiden Peak
Maytown (ruins)
Mt Hann
Mt Lukin
Mt Mulgrave
Mount Mulgrave
Mt Harford
Woods Peak
Groganville
Bellevue
Wrotham Park
Dev Rd
Nychum
Rookwood
Mungana
Chillagoe
Chillagoe Mungana Caves NP
Jubilee Mtn
Torwood
Bolwarra
Fischerton
Tate Tin Mines
Mt May
Bulleringa Nat Park
Burlington
Barwidgi
Sundown
Van Lee
Barney Knob
Dagworth
O'Briens Creek Gemfields
Mt Departure
Cabana
Brooklands
Ironhurst
Hot Springs
Talaroo
Mount Surprise
Eveleigh
138
Undara Volcanic National Park
Undara Lava Tubes Guide Stn
Mt Webster
Rosella Plains
Donnyville
Lornvale
Forsayth
Wirra Wirra
Einasleigh
Narrawa
Mt Misery
Newcastle Range
Gregory
Mt Helpman
Robinhood
The Oaks
Mywyn
Kidston
Cobbold Gorge
Bairds Table Mtn
Gilbert Ra
Mt Lookout
North Knob
Hanns Table Hill
Oak Park
Werrington
Blackbraes National Park
Blackbraes
Kennedy
Oak Valley
Montgomery Range
Chudleigh Park
Clarke Hills
Murdoch Pt
Brown Peak
Saddle Hill
Munburra
Mt Norkwa
Starcke Nat Park
Starcke
Glenrock
Eldersile
Hazelmere
Endeavour
Marton
Mt Cook Nat Park
Cooktown
Black Mtn Nat Park
Dev
Helenvale
Rossville
Cedar Bay Nat Park
Wujal Wujal
Mt McDowall
Palmer River Roadhouse
81
177
Maitland Downs
Daintree National Park
Mt Spurgeon
Mt Elephant
Mossman Gorge
Hurricane
Mount Carbine
Maryfarms
Mount Molloy
Hann Tableland National Park
Mount Mulligan
Kays Mtn
Thornborough
Kingsborough
Wolfram
Mutchilba
Dimbulah
Verdure
Chillagoe
Calcifer
Fluorspar
Almaden
Petford
Ootann
Koorboora
Irvinebank
Gilmore Mine
Gingerella
Mount Garnet
Kennedy
HWY
110
Morecambe
Koombooloomba
Gunnawarra
Forty Mile Scrub National Park
Yamamulla
Meadowbank
Minnamoolka
Glen Harding
Mt Tabletop
Bowman Hill
Spring Creek
Valley of Lagoons
Carpentaria Downs
Conjuboy
Wyandotte
The Lynd Junction
Oasis Roadhouse
The Lynd
Greenvale Nickel Mine
Greenvale
Lyndhurst
Teddy Mtn
Pandanus Creek
Big Ben
Great
Maryvale
Mt Louisa
Basalt
Bluff Downs
Kens Bluff
Wairuna
Lake Lucy
Dividing Range
Tiger Hill
Glen Ruth
Mt Lyall
Blue Range
Christmas Creek
Clarke River
Mt Mackay
Niall
Road
Lizard I Nat Park
Eagle I
Martin Reef
Lookout Point
Cape Flattery
Hope Vale Aboriginal Community
Louisiana
Cape Bedford
Nob Point
Endeavour River Nat Park
Walker Bay
Osterland Reef
Archer Point
Forsberg Pt
Gill Patches
Cedar Bay
Rattlesnake Point
Ayton
Weary Bay
Degarra
165
Daintree Nat Park
Cape Tribulation
Thornton Beach
Alexandra Bay
Daintree
Twyford
Cape Kimberley
Snapper I
Wonga
Dayman Point
Miallo
Newell
Cooya Beach
Mossman
Port Douglas
Craiglie
Pebbly Beach
Rumula
Julatten
62
Capt Cook Hwy
Trinity Bay
Ellis Beach
Clifton Beach
Trinity Beach
Yorkeys Knob
Machans Beach
Yarrabah
Kuranda
Koah
Biboohra
Mareeba
Stratford
Cairns
White Rock
Edmonton
Gordonvale
Walkamin
Tinaroo Falls
158
Lake Tinaroo
Tolga
Atherton
Yungaburra
Wooroonooran Nat Pk
Herberton
Malanda
Tarzali
Millaa Millaa
Butchers Ck
Bartle Frere
Bartle Frere
Kaban
Ravenshoe
Innot Hot Springs
Cardstone
Tully Falls
Lake Koombooloomba
Tully
Cardwell
Silky Oak Creek
Euramo
143
Kirrama
Blencoe Falls
Herbert River Falls
Mt Thorn
Gorge Range
Lumholtz Nat Park
Abergowrie
Long Pocket
Trebonne
Ingham
Upper Stone
Mt Lee
Toobanna
Camel Creek
Mt Fox (Volcano)
Kangaroo Hills
Hidden Valley
Bambaroo
Paluma Ra NP
Paluma
Ewan
Taravale
New Moon
Blue Water Springs Roadhouse
253
Laroona
Battery
Hillgrove
Cooks Passage
Yonge Reef
Cormorant Passage
Ribbon Reef
Rocky Islets Nat Park
Great Barrier Reef Marine Park (Cairns Section)
Great Barrier Reef
Ribbon Reef
Cairns Reef
Agincourt Reefs
Mackay Reef
St Crispin Reef
Rudder Reef
Opal Reef
Tongue Reef
Norman Reef
Batt Reef
Trinity Opening
Michaelmas Reef
Oyster Reef
Green I Nat Park
Fitzroy I Nat Park
Grey Peaks NP
Deeral
Bellenden Ker
Babinda
Bramston Beach
Miriwinni
Daradgee
Goondi
Innisfail
Etty Bay
South Johnstone
Mourilyan
Japoon
Cowley
Silkwood
Kurrimine Bch
El Arish
Mission Beach
Dunk I
Tully Heads
Edmund Kennedy NP
Gould I
Kennedy
Bruce Hwy
144°
146°
16°
18°
QLD 2
QLD 4

Map 4

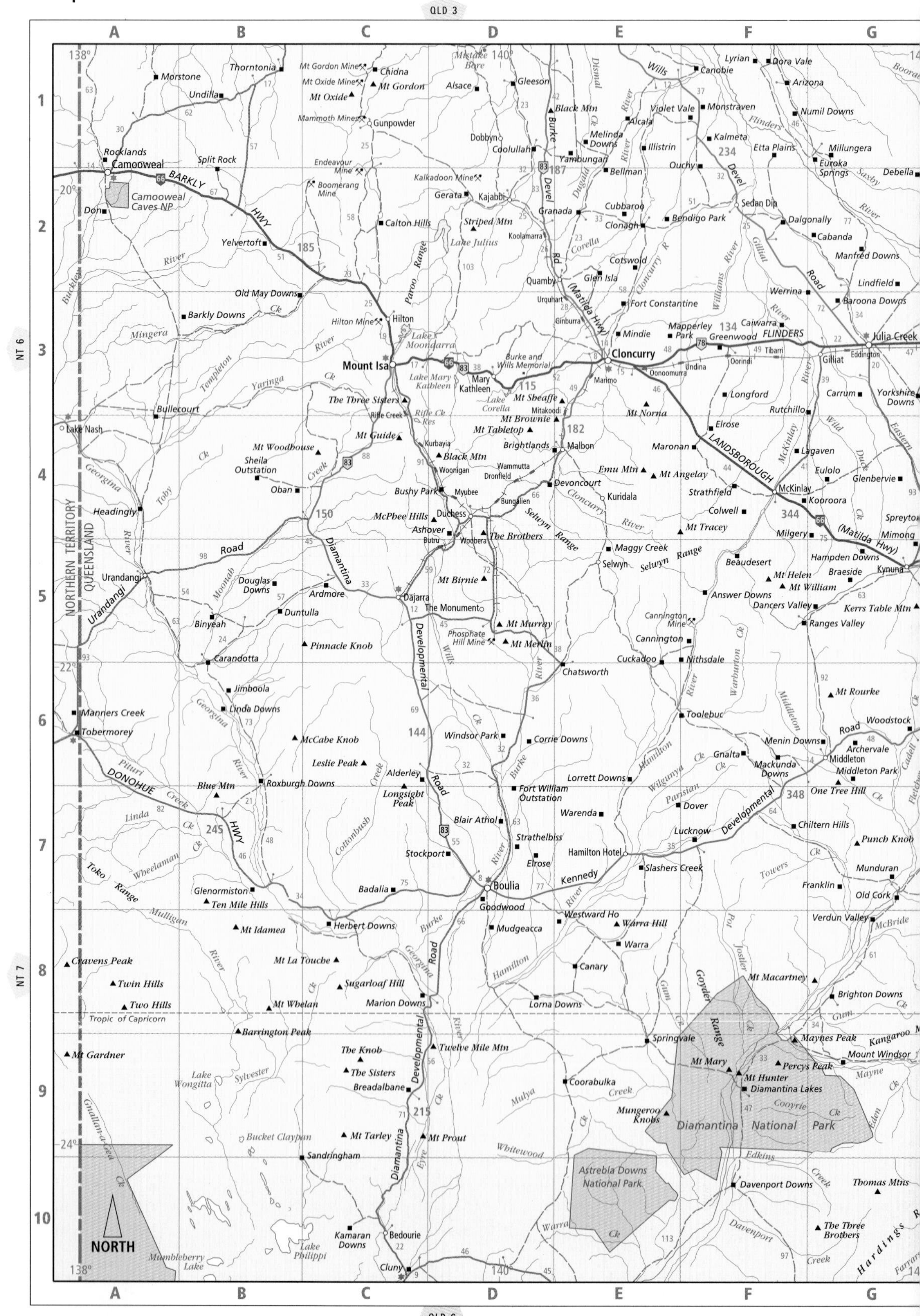
QLD 3
A
B
C
D
E
F
G
NT 6
NT 7
QLD 6
1
2
3
4
5
6
7
8
9
10
138°
140°
20°
22°
24°
Morstone
Thorntonia
Undilla
Rocklands
Camooweal
Split Rock
BARKLY
HWY
Camooweal Caves NP
Don
Yelvertoft
Old May Downs
Barkly Downs
Mingera
Templeton
Yaringa
River
Ck
Bullecourt
Lake Nash
Georgina
Toby
Headingly
Urandangi
Road
NORTHERN TERRITORY
QUEENSLAND
Douglas Downs
Binyeah
Duntulla
Carandotta
Jimboola
Linda Downs
Manners Creek
Tobermorey
DONOHUE
HWY
Pituri
Creek
Blue Mtn
Roxburgh Downs
Linda
Wheeleman
Toko Range
Glenormiston
Ten Mile Hills
Mulligan
Mt Idamea
Cravens Peak
Twin Hills
Two Hills
Tropic of Capricorn
Barrington Peak
Mt Gardner
Lake Wongitta
Sylvester
Bucket Claypan
Mumbleberry Lake
NORTH
Mt Gordon Mine
Chidna
Mt Oxide Mine
Mt Gordon
Mt Oxide
Mammoth Mines
Gunpowder
Endeavour Mine
Boomerang Mine
Kalkadoon Mine
Calton Hills
Paroo Range
Hilton Mine
Hilton
Lake Moondarra
Mount Isa
Lake Mary Kathleen
Mary Kathleen
The Three Sisters
Rifle Creek
Rifle Ck Res
Mt Guide
Mt Woodhouse
Sheila Outstation
Oban
Kurbayia
Black Mtn
Woonigan
Bushy Park
Myubee
McPhee Hills
Duchess
Ashover
Butru
Woobera
The Brothers
Diamantina
Ardmore
Dajarra
Mt Birnie
The Monument
Mt Murray
Phosphate Hill Mine
Mt Merlin
Pinnacle Knob
Developmental
Wills
McCabe Knob
Leslie Peak
Alderley
Longsight Peak
Cottonbush
Windsor Park
Corrie Downs
Blair Athol
Stockport
Badalia
Herbert Downs
Boulia
Goodwood
Mudgeacca
Mt La Touche
Sugarloaf Hill
Marion Downs
Twelve Mile Mtn
The Knob
The Sisters
Breadalbane
Mt Tarley
Mt Prout
Sandringham
Kamaran Downs
Bedourie
Lake Philippi
Cluny
Eyre
Mistake Bore
Alsace
Gleeson
Dobbyn
Coolullah
Gerata
Kajabbi
Striped Mtn
Koolamarra
Lake Julius
Quamby
Urquhart
Ginburra
Burke and Wills Memorial
Lake Corella
Mt Sheaffe
Mitakoodi
Mt Brownie
Mt Tabletop
Brightlands
Malbon
Wammutta
Dronfield
Devoncourt
Bungalien
Selwyn Range
Black Mtn
Burke
Devel
Rd
Melinda Downs
Yambungan
Bellman
Granada
Cubbaroo
Clonagh
Corella
Cotswold
Glen Isla
(Matilda Hwy)
Fort Constantine
Mindie
Cloncurry
Marimo
Mt Norna
Emu Mtn
Mt Angelay
Kuridala
Cloncurry River
Maggy Creek
Selwyn
Cannington Mine
Cannington
Cuckadoo
Nithsdale
Chatsworth
Toolebuc
Lorrett Downs
Fort William Outstation
Warenda
Strathelbiss
Elrose
Hamilton Hotel
Kennedy
Westward Ho
Warra Hill
Warra
Canary
Hamilton
Lorna Downs
Springvale
Coorabulka
Mungeroo Knobs
Mulya
Whitewood
Astrebla Downs National Park
Warra
Dismal
Dugald
Wills
Canobie
Lyrian
Dora Vale
Arizona
Violet Vale
Alcala
Monstraven
Numil Downs
Illistrin
Kalmeta
Flinders
Etta Plains
Millungera
Euroka Springs
Ouchy
Devel
Sedan Dip
Bendigo Park
Dalgonally
Cabanda
Manfred Downs
Lindfield
Werrina
Baroona Downs
Williams
Gilliat
Mapperley Park
Greenwood
Caiwarra
FLINDERS
Julia Creek
Tibarri
Eddington
Oonoomurra
Undina
Oorindi
Gilliat
Longford
Carrum
Yorkshire Downs
Rutchillo
Elrose
Maronan
LANDSBOROUGH
Lagaven
McKinlay
Eulolo
Glenbervie
Strathfield
Kooroora
Colwell
Mt Tracey
Milgery
(Matilda Hwy)
Mimong
Spreyton
Beaudesert
Hampden Downs
Kynuna
Mt Helen
Braeside
Mt William
Answer Downs
Dancers Valley
Kerrs Table Mtn
Ranges Valley
Warburton
Middleton
Mt Rourke
Woodstock
Menin Downs
Archervale
Middleton
Gnalta
Mackunda Downs
Middleton Park
One Tree Hill
Dover
Wilgunya
Parisian
Lucknow
Developmental
Chiltern Hills
Punch Knob
Slashers Creek
Towers
Munduran
Franklin
Old Cork
Verdun Valley
McBride
Mt Macartney
Brighton Downs
Goyder Range
Maynes Peak
Kangaroo
Mount Windsor
Percys Peak
Mt Mary
Mt Hunter
Diamantina Lakes
Cooryie
Diamantina National Park
Edkins
Davenport Downs
Thomas Mtns
The Three Brothers
Davenport
Hardings Range

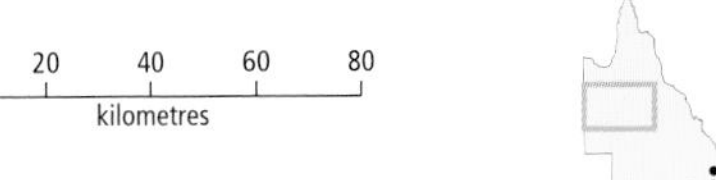

QLD 3

QLD 5

QLD 6

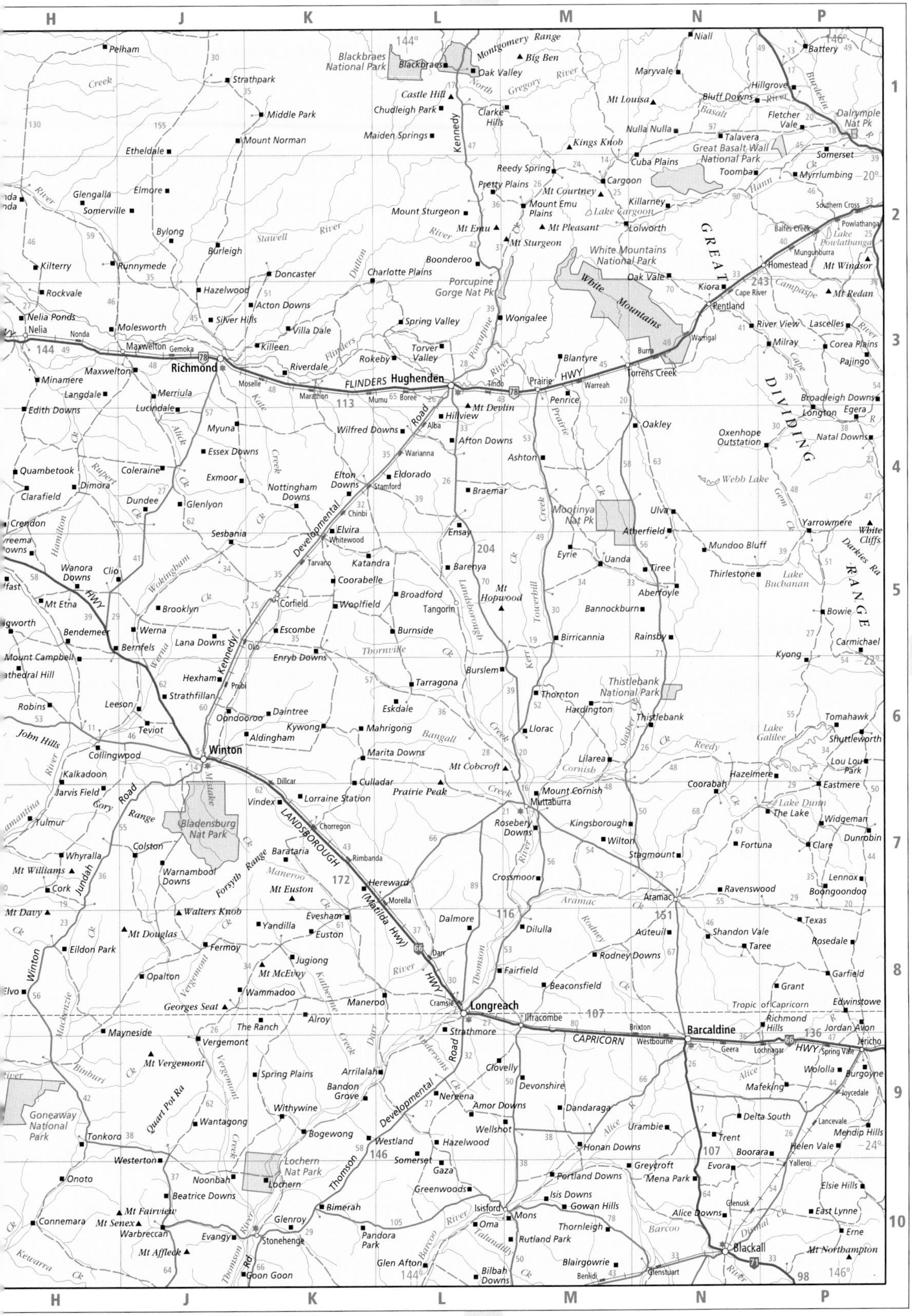

Map 5

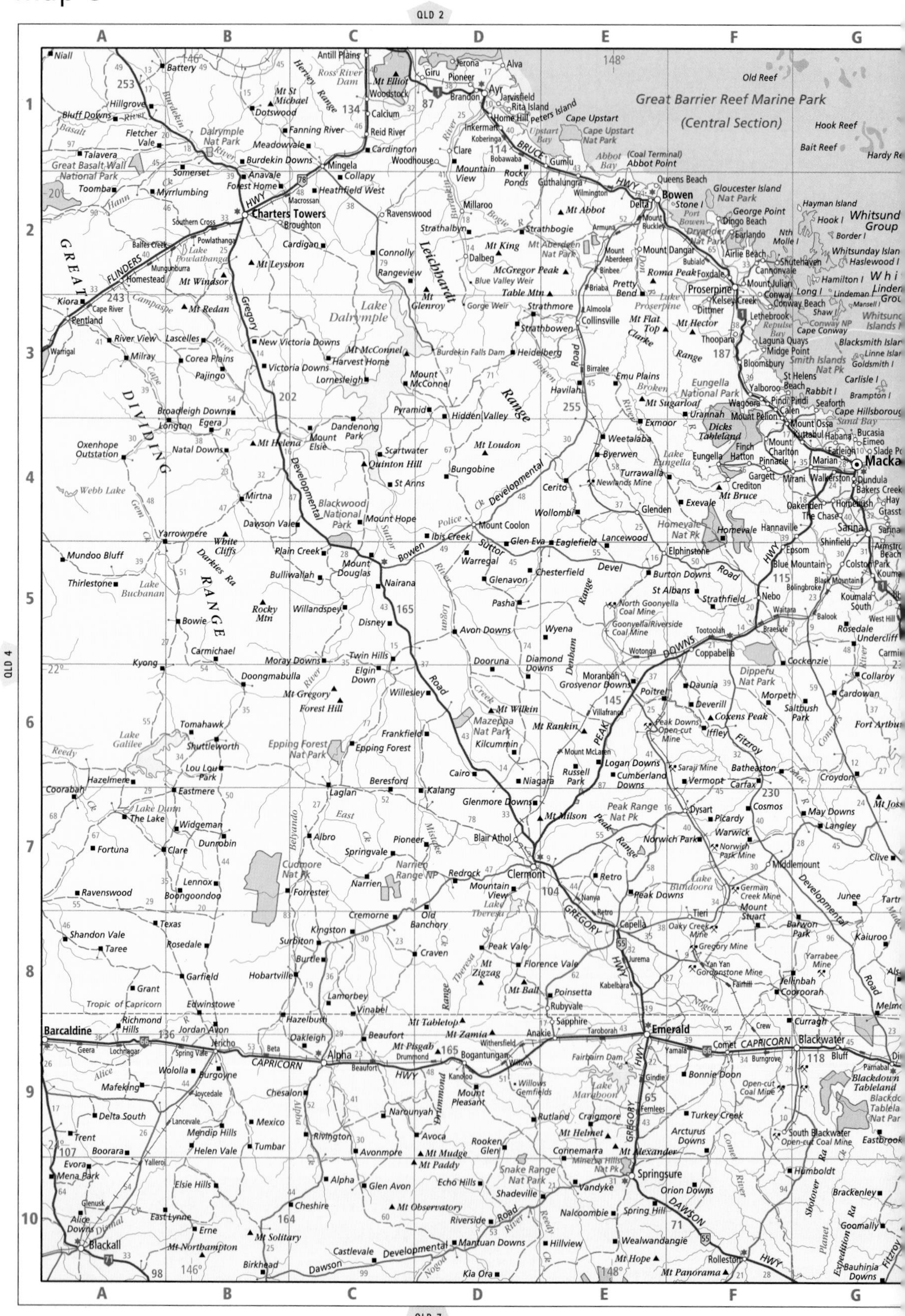
QLD 2
QLD 4
QLD 7
A
B
C
D
E
F
G
1
2
3
4
5
6
7
8
9
10
146°
148°
22°
Niall
Battery
Hillgrove
Bluff Downs
Basalt
Fletcher Vale
Talavera
Great Basalt Wall National Park
Toomba
Somerset
Myrrlumbing
Dalrymple Nat Park
Burdekin River
Antill Plains
Ross River Dam
Mt St Michael
Dotswood
Hervey Range
Mt Elliot
Woodstock
Calcium
Reid River
Fanning River
Meadowvale
Cardington
Burdekin Downs
Mingela
Anavale
Forest Home
Collapy
Heathfield West
Macrossan
Charters Towers
Broughton
Southern Cross
Balfes Creek
Powlathanga
Lake Powlathanga
Mungunburra
Homestead
FLINDERS HWY
Mt Windsor
Mt Leyshon
Cardigan
Ravenswood
Giru
Jerona
Alva
Pioneer
Ayr
Brandon
Jarvisfield
Rita Island
Home Hill
Peters Island
Inkerman
Kobernga
Clare
Bobawaba
Woodhouse
Mountain View
Rocky Ponds
BRUCE HWY
Gumlu
Guthalungra
Upstart Bay
Cape Upstart
Cape Upstart Nat Park
Abbot Bay
(Coal Terminal)
Abbot Point
Great Barrier Reef Marine Park
(Central Section)
Old Reef
Hook Reef
Bait Reef
Hardy Reef
Queens Beach
Bowen
Gloucester Island Nat Park
Stone I
Port Bowen
Delta
Mount Buckley
George Point
Dingo Beach
Earlando
Hayman Island
Hook I
Whitsunday Group
Border I
Whitsunday Island
Haslewood I
Hamilton I
Lindeman I
Shutehaven
Airlie Beach
Cannonvale
Mount Julian
Conway
Conway Beach
Proserpine
Kelsey Creek
Dittmer
Lethebrook
Cape Conway
Laguna Quays
Midge Point
Thoopara
Bloomsbury
Blacksmith Island
Smith Islands Nat Pk
Goldsmith I
Carlisle I
Brampton I
St Helens Beach
Yalboroo
Pindi Pindi
Seaforth
Cape Hillsborough
Sand Bay
Millaroo
Mt Abbot
Strathalbyn
Strathbogie
Mt Aberdeen Nat Park
Mount Aberdeen
Binbee
Armuna
Mount Dangar
Bubialo
Roma Peak
Foxdale
Briaba
Pretty Bend
Mt King
Dalbeg
McGregor Peak
Blue Valley Weir
Table Mtn
Connolly
Rangeview
Leichhardt
Mt Glenroy
Gorge Weir
Strathmore
Almoola
Collinsville
Mt Flat Top
Mt Hector
Strathbowen
Heidelberg
Burdekin Falls Dam
Lake Dalrymple
Pentland
Kiora
Cape River
River View
Lascelles
Milray
Corea Plains
Pajingo
Warrigal
Mt Redan
Gregory
New Victoria Downs
Victoria Downs
Mt McConnel
Harvest Home
Lornesleigh
Mount McConnel
Birralee
Havilah
Emu Plains
Eungella National Park
Mt Sugarloaf
Urannah
Dicks Tableland
Wagoora
Mount Pelion
Mount Ossa
Kuttabul
Habana
Bucasia
Eimeo
Mount Charlton
Finch Hatton
Pinnacle
Eungella
Gargett
Marian
Walkerston
Mackay
Dundula
Bakers Creek
Mirani
Broadleigh Downs
Longton
Egera
Oxenhope Outstation
Natal Downs
DIVIDING
Webb Lake
Mirtna
Mt Helena
Mount Elsie
Dandenong Park
Pyramid
Hidden Valley
Mt Loudon
Scartwater
Quinton Hill
St Anns
Bungobine
Weetalaba
Byerwen
Lake Eungella
Turrawalla
Newlands Mine
Crediton
Mt Bruce
Exevale
Glenden
Cerito
Wollombi
Developmental Rd
Blackwood National Park
Mount Hope
Dawson Vale
Mount Coolon
Ibis Creek
Yarrowmere
White Cliffs
Mundoo Bluff
Thirlestone
Lake Buchanan
Darkies Ra
Plain Creek
Mount Douglas
Bulliwallah
Nairana
Warregal
Glen Eva
Eaglefield
Lancewood
Glenavon
Chesterfield
Elphinstone
Homevale Nat Pk
Homevale
Burton Downs
St Albans
Strathfield
Nebo
Hannaville
Oakenden
Homebush
The Chase
Sarina
Shinfield
Epsom
Blue Mountain
Koumala
Bolingbroke
Black Mountain
Koumala South
Balook
Rosedale
West Hill
Undercliff
Bowie
RANGE
Rocky Mtn
Willandspey
Disney
Pasha
Wyena
Avon Downs
North Goonyella Coal Mine
Goonyella Riverside Coal Mine
Tootoolah
Waitara
Braeside
Carmichael
Kyong
Doongmabulla
Moray Downs
Twin Hills
Elgin Down
Dooruna
Diamond Downs
Wotonga
Coppabella
Cockenzie
Collaroy
Cardowan
Moranbah
Grosvenor Downs
Poitrel
Daunia
Dipperu Nat Park
Morpeth
Saltbush Park
Fort Arthur
Mt Gregory
Forest Hill
Willesley
Mt Wilkin
Mazeppa Nat Park
Kilcummin
Mt Rankin
Villafranca
Deverill
Coxens Peak
Iffley
Peak Downs Open-cut Mine
Fitzroy
Lake Galilee
Tomahawk
Shuttleworth
Reedy
Epping Forest Nat Park
Epping Forest
Frankfield
Lou Lou Park
Hazelmere
Coorabah
Eastmere
Beresford
Cairo
Niagara
Russell Park
Mount McLaren
Logan Downs
Cumberland Downs
Saraji Mine
Vermont
Batheaston
Carfax
Croydon
Laglan
Kalang
Glenmore Downs
Lake Dunn
The Lake
Widgeman
Dunrobin
Fortuna
Clare
Albro
Springvale
Pioneer
Mt Milson
Peak Range Nat Pk
Dysart
Picardy
Warwick
Norwich Park
Norwich Park Mine
Cosmos
May Downs
Langley
Blair Athol
Clermont
Middlemount
Clive
Cudmore Nat Pk
Narrien
Narrien Range NP
Redrock
Mountain View
Lake Theresa
Retro
Lake Blundoora
German Creek Mine
Peak Downs
Nanya
Tieri
Mount Stuart
Junee
Ravenswood
Lennox
Boongoondoo
Forrester
Cremorne
Old Banchory
Capella
Oaky Creek Mine
Barwon Park
Kaiuroo
Texas
Shandon Vale
Taree
Rosedale
Kingston
Surbiton
Craven
Peak Vale
Gregory Mine
Yarrabee Mine
Garfield
Hobartville
Burtle
Mt Zigzag
Florence Vale
Jurema
Yan Yan
Gordonstone Mine
Fairhill
Yellinbah
Grant
Tropic of Capricorn
Edwinstowe
Lamorbey
Vinabel
Mt Ball
Poinsetta
Rubyvale
Kabelbara
Cooroorah
Barcaldine
Richmond Hills
Jordan Avon
Hazelbush
Oakleigh
Beaufort
Mt Tabletop
Mt Zamia
Anakie
Sapphire
Taroborah
Emerald
Crew
Curragh
Geera
Lochnagar
Spring Vale
Jericho
Beta
Alpha
Mt Pisgah
Drummond
Bogantungan
Withersfield
Willows
Fairbairn Dam
Yamala
Comet
CAPRICORN HWY
Blackwater
Bluff
Burngrove
Pamabal
Alice
Wololla
Burgoyne
Mafeking
Joycedale
Chesalon
Kanoloo
Mount Pleasant
Willows Gemfields
Lake Maraboon
Gindie
Bonnie Doon
Open-cut Coal Mine
Blackdown Tableland
Delta South
Lancevale
Mendip Hills
Mexico
Narounyah
Rutland
Craigmore
Fernlees
Turkey Creek
South Blackwater Open-cut Coal Mine
Eastbrook
Trent
Boorara
Helen Vale
Tumbar
Rivington
Avoca
Mt Helmet
Arcturus Downs
Evora
Mena Park
Yalleroi
Avonmore
Mt Mudge
Mt Paddy
Rooken Glen
Connemarra
Minerva Hills Nat Pk
Mt Alexander
Springsure
Humboldt
Brackenley
Elsie Hills
Alpha
Glen Avon
Echo Hills
Snake Range Nat Park
Shadeville
Vandyke
Orion Downs
Glenusk
Cheshire
Mt Observatory
Alice Downs
East Lynne
Erne
Mt Solitary
Riverside
Nalcoombie
Spring Hill
DAWSON HWY
Goomally
Blackall
Mt Northampton
Castlevale
Mantuan Downs
Hillview
Wealwandangie
Expedition Ra
Shotover Ra
Mt Hope
Rolleston
Birkhead
Dawson
Developmental Road
Kia Ora
Mt Panorama
Bauhinia Downs

0 20 40 60 80
kilometres

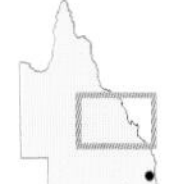

H J K L M N P

150° 152°

NORTH

1 2 3 4 5 6 7 8 9 10

-20° -22° -24°

GREAT BARRIER REEF

Hewitt Reef
Black Reef
Round Reef
Bugatti Reef
Square Reef
Hunt Reefs
Edgell Reefs
Bax Reef
Robertson Reefs
Packer Reefs
Boulton Reef
Stevens Reef
Credlin Reefs
Creal Reef
Warland Reef
Cumberland Islands
Cole Reefs
Calder Island
South Cumberland Island National Park
Gable Reefs
Chauvel Reefs
Bees
Scawfell Island
Hibiscus Coast
Penrith Island
Prince Reef
Pompey Reef
Prudhoe Island
Double I
Knight I
Minster Island
Beverley Group Nat Park
Heralds Reef Prong
Cape Palmerston
Digby Island
Heralds Prong No. 3
Cape Palmerston NP
Curlew I
Middle Island
North East Island Nat Park
Thomas Cay
Heralds Prong No. 2
Percy Isles
South Island Nat Park
Yarrawonga Point
Swain Reefs
West Hill Island
West Hill Nat Pk
Northumberland Isles
Duke Islands
Bamborough Island
Wild Duck I NP
Aquila I
Marble Island
High Peak Island
Gannett Cay
West Point
Long Island
Quail Island
Broad Sound Channel
Cheviot Island
Clairview
Stanage
Kalarka
Price Mtn
Leicester I
Cape Townshend
Broad Sound
Collins I
Townshend Island
St Lawrence
Reef Point
Newport
Torilla Pen
Shoalwater Bay
Pearl Bay
Rosewood Island
Perforated Point
Warginburra Peninsula
Great Barrier Reef Marine Park
(Mackay-Capricorn Section)
Wumalgi
Double Mtn
Cape Clinton
Styx
Glenprairie
Military Training Area
Freshwater Bay
Ogmore
Banksia
Cliff Point
Mt O'Connell Nat Pk
Mt Phipps
Cape Manifold
BRUCE HWY
Kooltandra
Mt O'Connell
Mt Atherton
Conical Mtn
Marlborough
Byfield
Stockyard Point
Princhester
Kunwarara
Byfield National Park
The Oaks
Water Park Point
Balmoral
Corio Bay
Goodedulla Nat Pk
Canoona
Rossmoya
Capricorn Coast
Curtis Channel
Nth Keppel I Nat Park
Leura
Boomer Range
Fitzroy River
Yaamba
Milman
Cooberrie
Yeppoon
Mt Etna Caves
Rosslyn Bay
The Caves
Great Keppel Island
Ridgelands
Tanby
Broomfield Reef
Waroula
Cawarral
Emu Park
North West I
Wilson Island
Parkhurst
Dalma
Mt Archer NP
Keppel Sands
Black Mtn
Gracemere
Rockhampton
Hummocky Island
Heron Island
Capricorn Group
Foleyvale
Stanwell
Kabra
Gavial
Broadmount
Cape Keppel
Cape Capricorn
Curtis Is Nat Park
Mast Head Island
One Tree Island
Sorrel Hills
Wycarbah
Midgee
Bouldercombe
Port Alma
Mt Barker
Curtis Island
Fitzroy Reef
Westwood
Black Head
Polmaise Reef
Gogango
Windah
Bajool
Rundle Range Nat Park
Llewellyn Reef
Wallaroo
Duaringa
Mount Morgan
Raglan
South End
Boult Reef
Grantleigh
Epala
Facing Island
Hoskyn Islands
Mt Helen
Mount Larcom
Bunker Group
Fairfax Islands
Ambrose
Gladstone
Lady Musgrave Island
Coomooboolaroo
Dululu
Yarwun
East End
Boyne Island
Wowan
Cedric Mtn
Tannum Sands
Richards Point
Cooneel
Mt Alma
Stirrat
Bustard Point
Vimy
Lancefield
Calliope
Benaraby
Middle Island
Awoonga Lake
Turkey Beach
Perch Creek
Mt Redshirt
Rannes
Jooro
Fry
Castle Tower Nat Pk
Eurimbula Nat Park
Bustard Bay
Lady Elliot Island
Kokotungo
Goovigen
Barmundu
Seventeen Seventy
Agnes Water
Baralaba
Koorngba
Jambin
Bindawalla
Bororen
Round Hill
Mimosa Park
Mt Ramsay
Koonkool
Callide Coal Mine and Power Stn
Wietalaba
Deepwater Nat Park
Redcliffe
Blue Hills
Callide
Amys Peak
Nagoorin
Miriam Vale
Hinemoa
Biloela
Callide Dam
Ubobo
Colosseum
Taunton
Walba
Banana
Thangool
Kroombit Tops National Park
Littlemore
Rosevale
Rules Beach
Oombabeer
Scoria
Many Peaks
Kolonan
Lowmead

H J K L M N P

Map 6

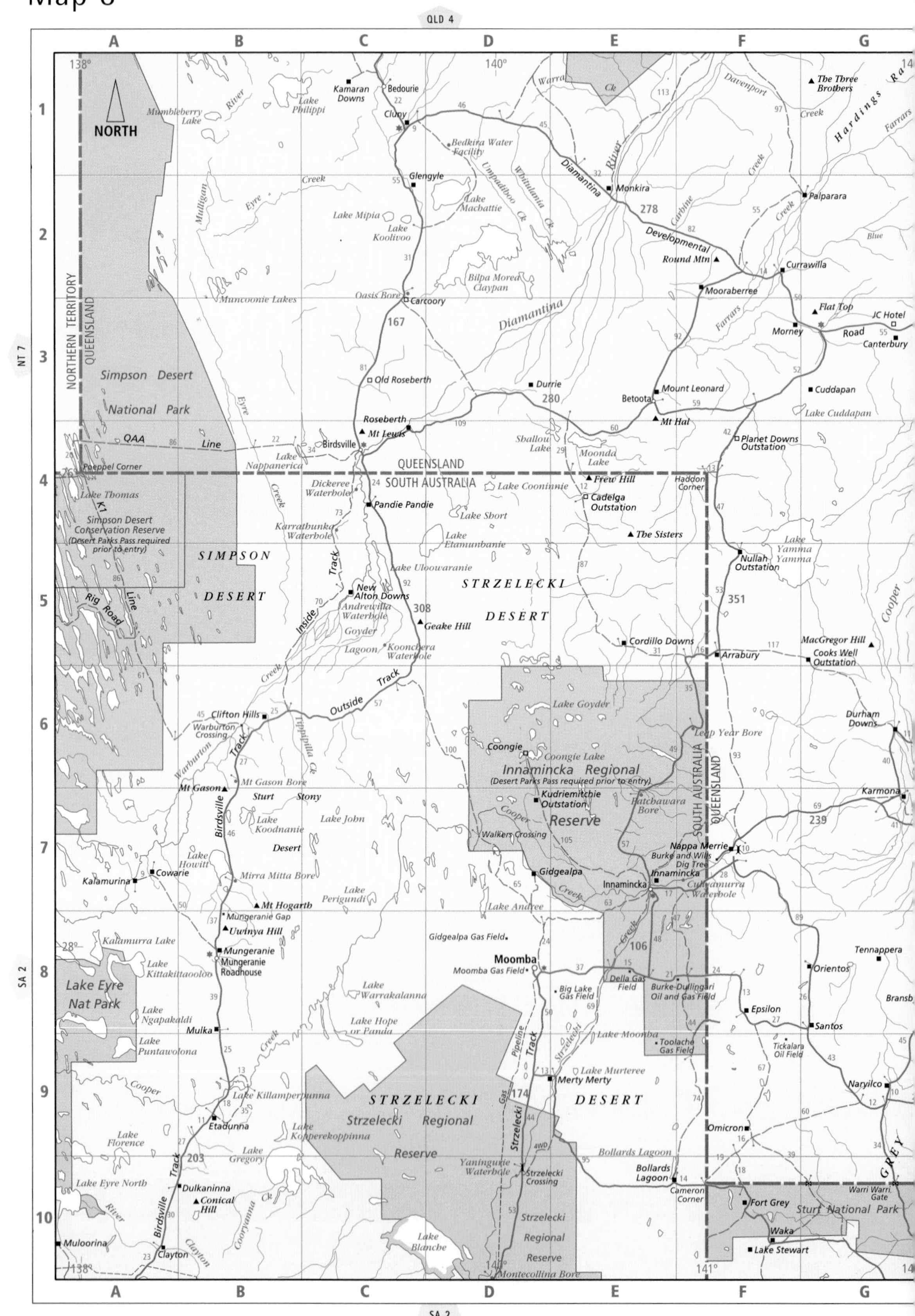
QLD 4
NT 7
SA 2
NORTH
NORTHERN TERRITORY
QUEENSLAND
SOUTH AUSTRALIA
138°
140°
141°
28°
Mumbleberry Lake
Lake Philippi
Kamaran Downs
Bedourie
Cluny
Bedkira Water Facility
Glengyle
Lake Machattie
Lake Mipia
Lake Koolivoo
Muncoonie Lakes
Oasis Bore
Carcoory
Bilpa Morea Claypan
Diamantina
Diamantina Developmental
Monkira
Round Mtn
Mooraberree
Currawilla
Palparara
The Three Brothers
Hardings Ra
Davenport
Flat Top
Morney
JC Hotel
Road
Canterbury
Cuddapan
Lake Cuddapan
Simpson Desert National Park
Old Roseberth
Durrie
Betoota
Mount Leonard
Mt Hal
Roseberth
Mt Lewis
Birdsville
QAA Line
Poeppel Corner
Lake Nappanerica
Shallow Lake
Moonda Lake
Planet Downs Outstation
QUEENSLAND
SOUTH AUSTRALIA
Lake Thomas
K1
Simpson Desert Conservation Reserve
(Desert Parks Pass required prior to entry)
Dickeree Waterhole
Pandie Pandie
Lake Cooninnie
Frew Hill
Cadelga Outstation
Haddon Corner
Karrathunka Waterhole
Lake Short
Lake Etamunbanie
The Sisters
Lake Yamma Yamma
Nullah Outstation
SIMPSON DESERT
Rig Road
Inside Track
New Alton Downs
Andrewilla Waterhole
Goyder Lagoon
Koonchera Waterhole
Lake Uloowaranie
Geake Hill
STRZELECKI DESERT
Cordillo Downs
Arrabury
MacGregor Hill
Cooks Well Outstation
Cooper
Outside Track
Clifton Hills
Warburton Crossing
Lake Goyder
Leap Year Bore
Durham Downs
Coongie
Coongie Lake
Innamincka Regional Reserve
(Desert Parks Pass required prior to entry)
Kudriemitchie Outstation
Patchawara Bore
Mt Gason
Mt Gason Bore
Sturt Stony Desert
Lake Koodnanie
Lake John
Karmona
Walkers Crossing
Nappa Merrie
Burke and Wills Dig Tree
Innamincka
Cullyamurra Waterhole
Lake Howitt
Kalamurina
Cowarie
Mirra Mitta Bore
Gidgealpa
Lake Perigundi
Mt Hogarth
Mungeranie Gap
Uwinya Hill
Lake Andree
Kalamurra Lake
Gidgealpa Gas Field
Moomba
Moomba Gas Field
Della Gas Field
Burke-Dullingari Oil and Gas Field
Tennappera
Orientos
Mungeranie
Mungeranie Roadhouse
Lake Kittakittaooloo
Lake Eyre Nat Park
Lake Ngapakaldi
Lake Warrakalanna
Big Lake Gas Field
Epsilon
Santos
Bransby
Mulka
Lake Puntawolona
Lake Hope or Panda
Lake Moomba
Toolache Gas Field
Tickalara Oil Field
Lake Killamperpunna
Lake Murteree
Merty Merty
Naryilco
STRZELECKI DESERT
Strzelecki Regional Reserve
Etadunna
Lake Florence
Lake Kopperekoppinna
Lake Gregory
Bollards Lagoon
Omicron
Pipeline Track
Strzelecki Track
Yaningurie Waterhole
Strzelecki Crossing
Lake Eyre North
Dulkaninna
Conical Hill
Cameron Corner
Fort Grey
Warri Warri Gate
Sturt National Park
Waka
Lake Stewart
GREY
Birdsville Track
Lake Blanche
Muloorina
Clayton
Montecollina Bore
Strzelecki Regional Reserve
Cooryanna Ck
River

0 20 40 60 80
kilometres

QLD 4

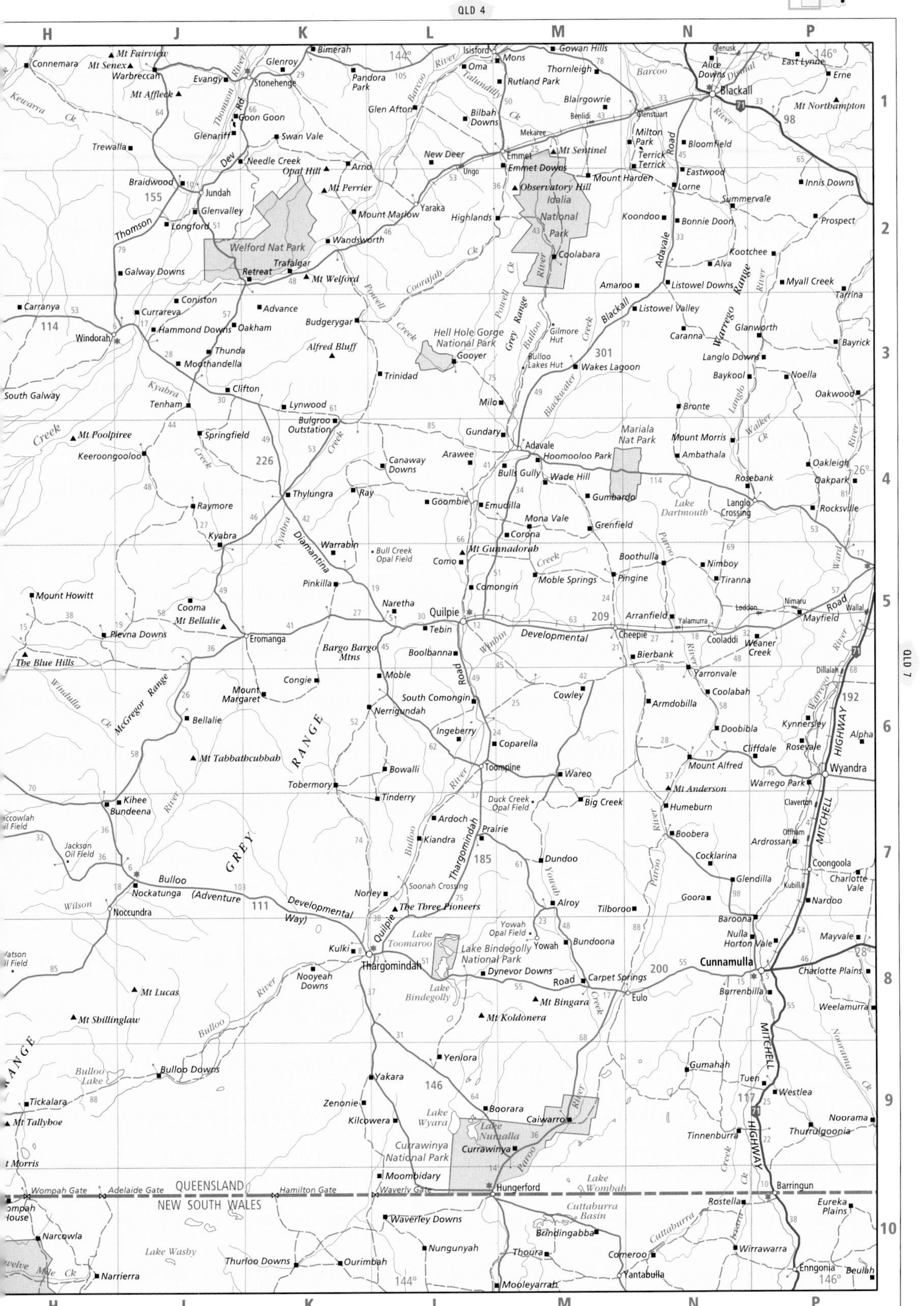

QLD 7

NSW 1

Map 7

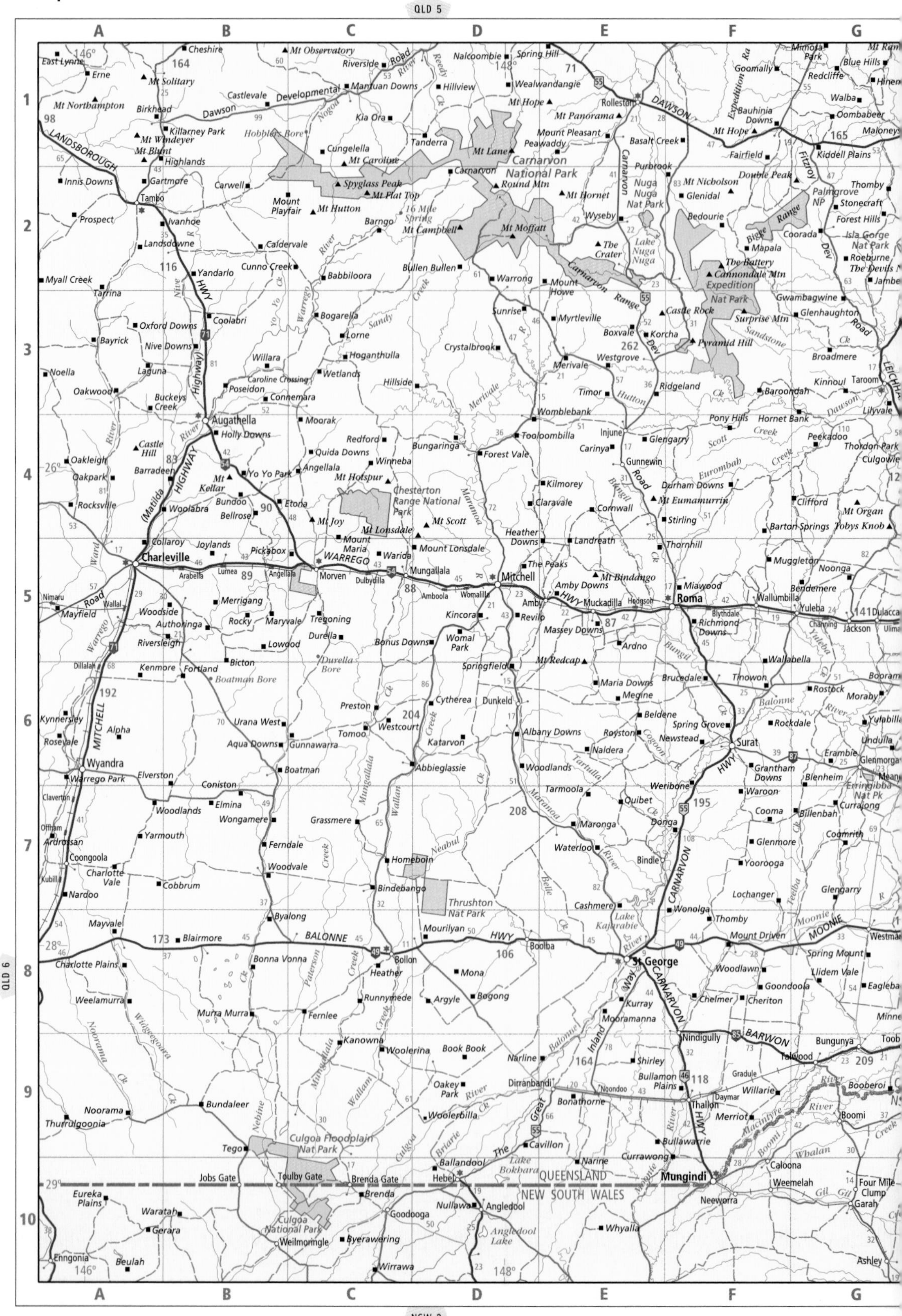
QLD 5
NSW 2
QLD 6
A
B
C
D
E
F
G
1
2
3
4
5
6
7
8
9
10
146°
148°
26°
28°
29°
East Lynne
Erne
Cheshire
Mt Solitary
Mt Northampton
Birkhead
Castlevale
Dawson
Developmental
Road
Mt Observatory
Riverside
Mantuan Downs
Nalcoombie
Spring Hill
Hillview
Wealwandangie
Mt Hope
Rollesto
Dawson
Goomally
Mimosa Park
Blue Hills
Redcliffe
Walba
Oombabeer
Maloneys
Bauhinia Downs
Mt Hope
Killarney Park
Mt Windeyer
Mt Blunt
Highlands
Landsborough
Innis Downs
Gartmore
Tambo
Prospect
Ivanhoe
Landsdowne
Yandarlo
Myall Creek
Tarrina
Hobblers Bore
Kia Ora
Cungelella
Mt Caroline
Spyglass Peak
Mt Flat Top
Tanderra
Mt Lane
Carnarvon National Park
Carnarvon
Round Mtn
Mt Panorama
Mount Pleasant
Peawaddy
Basalt Creek
Purbrook
Mt Nicholson
Glenidal
Nuga Nuga Nat Park
Mt Hornet
Wyseby
Fairfield
Kiddell Plains
Double Peak
Palmgrove NP
Thomby
Stonecraft
Forest Hills
Bedourie
Coorada
Isla Gorge Nat Park
Roeburne
The Devils
Jambe
Mapala
Carwell
Mount Playfair
Mt Hutton
Barngo
16 Mile Spring
Mt Campbell
Mt Moffatt
Caldervale
Cunno Creek
Babbiloora
Bullen Bullen
Warrong
Mount Howe
The Crater
Lake Nuga Nuga
The Battery
Cannondale Mtn
Expedition Nat Park
Gwambagwine
Glenhaughton
Coolabri
Oxford Downs
Bayrick
Nive Downs
Laguna
Noella
Oakwood
Buckeys Creek
Bogarella
Lorne
Hoganthulla
Willara
Caroline Crossing
Wetlands
Poseidon
Connemara
Hillside
Crystalbrook
Sunrise
Myrtleville
Castle Rock
Korcha
Boxvale
Pyramid Hill
Surprise Mtn
Broadmere
Westgrove
Merivale
Timor
Ridgeland
Baroondah
Kinnoul
Taroom
Leichhardt
Lilyvale
Augathella
Holly Downs
Moorak
Womblebank
Tooloombilla
Injune
Glengarry
Pony Hills
Hornet Bank
Peekadoo
Thordon Park
Culgowie
Castle Hill
Oakleigh
Oakpark
Barradeen
Redford
Quida Downs
Winneba
Bungaringa
Forest Vale
Carinya
Gunnewin
Yo Yo Park
Angellala
Mt Hotspur
Mt Kellar
Bundoo
Chesterton Range National Park
Kilmorey
Durham Downs
Mt Eumamurrin
Clifford
Mt Organ
Tobys Knob
Rocksville
Woolabra
Bellrose
Etona
Mt Joy
Mt Scott
Mt Lonsdale
Claravale
Cornwall
Stirling
Barton Springs
Collaroy
Joylands
Pickabox
Mount Maria
Mount Lonsdale
Heather Downs
Landreath
Thornhill
Charleville
Warrego
Warida
The Peaks
Muggleton
Noonga
Arabella
Lumea
Angellala
Morven
Dulbydilla
Mungallala
Amboola
Womalilla
Mitchell
Mt Bindango
Amby Downs
Miawood
Bendemere
Nimaru
Mayfield
Wallal
Woodside
Merrigang
Rocky
Maryvale
Tregoning
Kincora
Amby
Revilo
Muckadilla
Hodgson
Roma
Wallumbilla
Yuleba
Dulacca
Jackson
Blythdale
Richmond Downs
Authoringa
Riversleigh
Lowood
Durella
Bonus Downs
Womal Park
Massey Downs
Ardno
Wallabella
Dillalah
Kenmore
Fortland
Bicton
Boatman Bore
Durella Bore
Springfield
Mt Redcap
Bruce Dale
Tinowon
Booram
Maria Downs
Megine
Rostock
Moraby
Kynnersley
Roseyale
Alpha
Mitchell
Urana West
Aqua Downs
Gunnawarra
Preston
Tomoo
Westcourt
Cytherea
Dunkeld
Katarvon
Albany Downs
Beldene
Royston
Spring Grove
Newstead
Naldera
Rockdale
Yulabilla
Surat
Undulla
Erambie
Glenmorgan
Wyandra
Warrego Park
Elverston
Coniston
Boatman
Abbieglassie
Woodlands
Tarmoola
Grantham Downs
Blenheim
Erringibba Nat Pk
Claverton
Elmina
Woodlands
Wongamere
Grassmere
Quibet
Weribone
Waroon
Currajong
Yarmouth
Maronga
Donga
Cooma
Billenbah
Offham
Ardrossan
Coongoola
Ferndale
Homeboin
Waterloo
Bindle
Glenmore
Coomrith
Charlotte Vale
Kubilla
Nardoo
Cobbrum
Woodvale
Bindebango
Thrushton Nat Park
Yoorooga
Lochanger
Glengarry
Cashmere
Wonolga
Thomby
Mayvale
Byalong
Mourilyan
Lake Kajarabie
Mount Driven
Moonie
Westmar
Blairmore
Balonne
Hwy
Boolba
Spring Mount
Charlotte Plains
Bonna Vonna
Bollon
Heather
St George
Woodlawn
Llidem Vale
Mona
Goondoola
Eaglebar
Weelamurra
Runnymede
Argyle
Bogong
Kurray
Chelmer
Cheriton
Murra Murra
Fernlee
Mooramanna
Nindigully
Barwon
Bungunya
Kanowna
Woolerina
Book Book
Narline
Shirley
Talwood
Bullamon Plains
Gradule
Willarie
Booberoi
Oakey Park
Dirranbandi
Noondoo
Thallon
Daymar
Merriot
Boomi
Noorama
Thurrulgoonia
Bundaleer
Woolerbilla
Bonathorne
Cavillon
Bullawarrie
Tego
Culgoa Floodplain Nat Park
Ballandool
Lake Bokhara
Narine
Currawong
Caloona
Whalan
Jobs Gate
Toulby Gate
Brenda Gate
Hebel
Queensland
Mungindi
Weemelah
Four Mile Clump
Eureka Plains
Brenda
New South Wales
Neewarra
Garah
Waratah
Goodooga
Nullawa
Angledool
Gerara
Culgoa National Park
Whyalla
Weilmoringle
Byerawering
Angledool Lake
Enngonia
Beulah
Wirrawa
Ashley
Carnarvon
Hwy
Inland Way
The Great

0 20 40 60 80
kilometres

QLD 5

H J K L M N P
1 2 3 4 5 6 7 8 9 10
NORTH
152°
154°
26°
28°
Great Barrier Reef Marine Park
(Mackay-Capricorn Section)
Hervey Bay Marine Park
SOUTH
PACIFIC
OCEAN
Sunshine Coast
Gold Coast
Biloela
Banana
Callide
Thangool
Kroombit Tops National Park
Cania Gorge Nat Park
Monto
Mundubbera
Eidsvold
Gayndah
Biggenden
Childers
Bundaberg
Gin Gin
Hervey Bay
Fraser Island
Great Sandy National Park
Maryborough
Gympie
Murgon
Kingaroy
Nanango
Noosa Heads
Nambour
Maroochydore
Caloundra
Bribie Island
Cape Moreton
Moreton Island
Tangalooma
Caboolture
BRISBANE
Ipswich
Toowoomba
Dalby
Chinchilla
Miles
Condamine
Gatton
Esk
North Stradbroke Island
South Stradbroke Island
Southport
Surfers Paradise
Burleigh Heads
Coolangatta
Tweed Heads
Murwillumbah
Brunswick Heads
Byron Bay
Ballina
Lismore
Casino
Kyogle
Warwick
Stanthorpe
Tenterfield
Inglewood
Goondiwindi
Boggabilla
Texas
Yetman
Moonie
Millmerran
Allora
Killarney
Beaudesert
Evans Head
Bundjalung National Park
Moreton Bay
Deception Bay
Redcliffe
Tin Can Bay
Rainbow Beach
Double Island Point
Sandy Cape
Woodgate
Torrington SRA
Girraween Nat Pk
Sundown Nat Pk

NSW 4

New South Wales

Of all the states in Australia, New South Wales' national parks provide the greatest variety of scenic wonders, diversity of vegetation and opportunities for recreational pursuits. There are coastal parks that include some of the world's best beaches, and remote areas with breathtaking scenery. The parks also link us to Australian Aboriginal heritage with excellent art sites and middens to be found. Almost every park has access by conventional vehicles to superb picnic areas, camping grounds and walking trails. Many of the parks also provide opportunities for 4WD devotees. Like the 1994 bushfires, the fires of December 2001 and January 2002 left some parks blackened and temporarily closed. The Australian bush, however, is resilient and quick to regain its natural beauty.

Blue Mountains National Park

Part of the Greater Blue Mountains World Heritage Area, the Blue Mountains National Park attracts over 3 million visitors a year. It's little wonder really, considering it is virtually in sight of Sydney, being only 100 km west of the Harbour Bridge, and it has some of the most spectacular scenery of any of the national parks in Australia.

fact file

WHERE: 100 km west of Sydney via the Great Western Highway
Map: NSW 6 G8

WHEN: September to May

WHY: Superb lookouts, walking trails, waterfalls, wildflowers in spring, abseiling, rock climbing and canyoning

SIZE: 248 148 ha

RANGER: National Parks and Wildlife Service—Blue Mountains Heritage Centre, Blackheath (02) 4787 8877, or Glenbrook Tourist Information Centre (02) 4739 6266

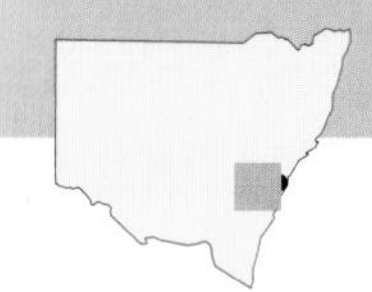

don't miss

For a heart-stopping thrill, ride the Scenic Railway with its near-vertical drop. Originally used by coal miners, this is the steepest inclined funicular railway in the world. For a more sublime experience take in the breathtaking views of Katoomba Falls and Jamison Valley from the Skyway cable car.

The visitor to Blue Mountains National Park will be astounded at the raw beauty of the sandstone cliffs and the deep gorges. There is a variety of activities to pursue in the mountains, from sitting around a campfire listening to bird calls and watching a fiery sunset reflect off the giant cliff faces, to dangling precariously on the end of a rope as you abseil down a waterfall into a valley that dates from the Jurassic era.

In the Past

The sandstone, which forms the dramatic scenery, was originally deposited by river systems that drained into a coastal plain more than 275 million years ago. Then 50 million years ago the area was uplifted, forming the Great Dividing Range. Volcanoes added to the dramatic scene before the weathering process began to etch the landscape. The deep gorges and towering cliffs of today are the result of continual weathering.

Australian Aboriginals once inhabited this area and there is a great deal of evidence of their occupation, dating back 14 000 years, in the form of art sites and grinding-stone marks in the sandstone cliffs.

The mountains formed a natural barrier to the early settlers in Sydney. A route over the mountains was not found until 1813 when Blaxland, Wentworth and Lawson stumbled across the only possible route. The rich plains to the west ensured that a rough road was quickly cut, and the present-day Great

Western Highway follows closely the route of the first coach trail.

The mountains remained sparsely populated until 1868 when the Great Western Railway opened, which brought the scenic beauty of the mountains within reach of the growing Sydney population. In the 1890s reserves were established to protect the natural areas within the mountains, while Blue Mountains National Park itself was proclaimed in 1959.

Activities

Tourism is big in the mountains and there are plenty of places to stay, as well as unusual ways to enjoy the natural wonders. A good example is the Scenic Railway, with its near-vertical

Pulpit Rock Lookout is so-called because it stands out from the main cliff face. The lookout provides magnificent views of Mount Banks, the Grose Valley and the cliffs where Govetts Leap is situated.

Below left: *Katoomba Falls has two drops separated by a small ledge. The water falls 200 metres into the Jamison Valley below.*

Below: *The turpentine tree* (Syncarpia glomulifera) *was given this name because the smell of its sap reminded early explorers of turpentine.*

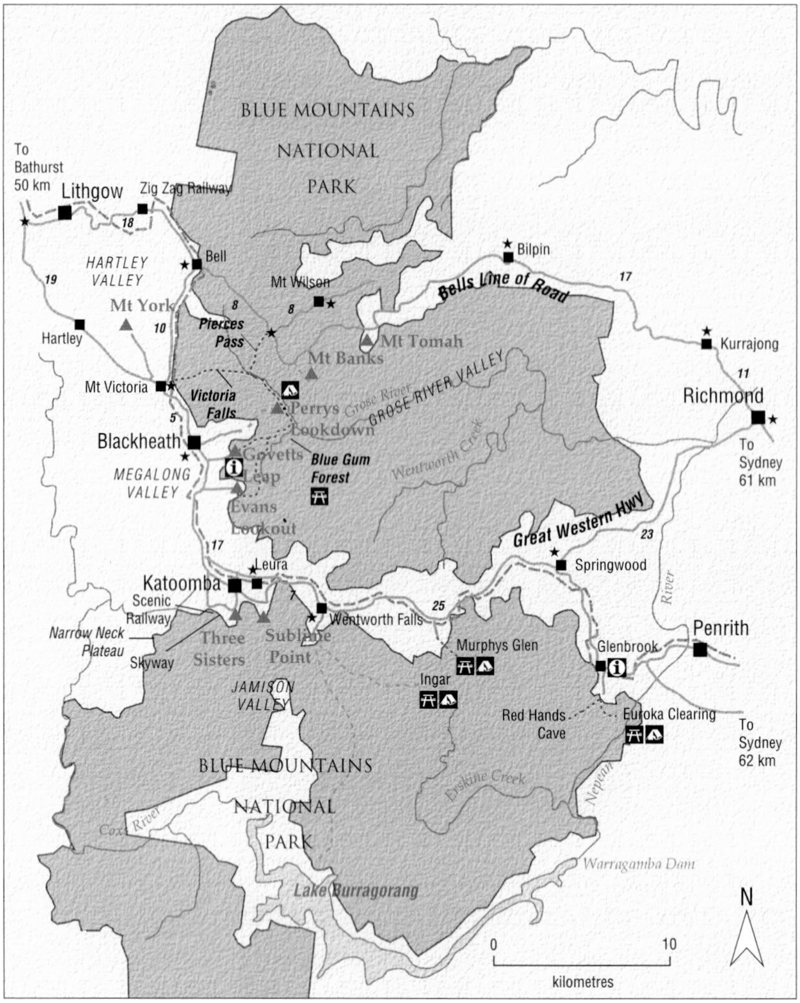

drop, and the Skyway cable car that stretches across deep, fern-filled gullies.

The most famous attraction in the mountains is the Three Sisters rock formation. Situated within the confines of the town of Katoomba, there is very easy access, parking being the only problem due to the huge number of tourists that flock to the area. For something completely different you could try rock climbing or abseiling on one of the Three Sisters and there are plenty of adventure companies based in the mountains that can assist you in this pursuit.

Bushwalking is another great activity and the park has many wonderful trails. Some are quite easy and include the scenic lookouts, while others require a degree of fitness and an overnight camp, as they extend into deep river valleys. The National Parks and Wildlife Service has excellent publications detailing the many walks and giving their degree of difficulty and the time they take.

Around the major towns of Katoomba, Leura and Blackheath there are impressive lookouts accessible to everyone. The already mentioned Three Sisters has viewing platforms, walks to the base of the rock formations and a well-stocked information and souvenir shop.

From Katoomba it is possible to follow the cliff drive which passes several other lookouts over the Jamison Valley, as well as some great picnic locations both east and west of Katoomba. Along this route you will also find the Skyway and the Scenic Railway.

At Leura there are several splendid lookouts over Sublime Point. These are among the best in the park and are within an easy five minute walk from the car park.

In the Glenbrook area there are good walks with views over the Nepean River

Protected, moist gullies of the Blue Mountains National Park contain pockets of warm temperate rainforest in which plants such as tree ferns, epiphytes and coachwood and sassafras trees thrive.

as well as Aboriginal hand stencils to view at Red Hands Cave. Abseiling off the cliffs in this part of the park is also popular and every weekend you will find groups of people enjoying this exhilarating sport.

There are a number of adventure tour companies who can safely take you on abseiling trips off huge cliffs, rock-climbing expeditions, or canyoning through narrow gorges where waterfalls plunge into deep pools of icy cold water. Or you could try the Grand Canyon Track, which lets you have the thrill of canyoning without getting wet.

West of Katoomba, around Blackheath, there are several roads out to lookouts above the Grose Valley. This is one of the most spectacular regions as the rock faces of the cliffs are several hundred metres high. The better known lookouts include Evans, Govetts Leap, Perrys Lookdown and Victoria Falls. There are several easy walking trails along the top of the escarpment that will take no longer than 2 hours.

The most renowned walks in the Blue Mountains are those that descend into the Grose Valley from Govetts Leap and Perrys Lookdown. You will need to be fit to tackle the steep trails and you must always be prepared for dramatic changes in the weather. Because the mountains are at a high altitude, sudden temperature drops and even snowfalls are common. Heavy rain can cut tracks in the valleys and the area should be avoided in this type of weather.

There are several walks in the Grose Valley, with the famous Blue Gum Forest being one of the better known attractions. This beautiful forest was saved from destruction back in the 1930s by keen bushwalkers.

If you are planning a walking trip into the Grose Valley it is suggested that you contact the Heritage Centre at Blackheath to obtain maps and advice about your intended walk. It is very wise to let someone reliable know of

The striking, bright red, wax-like waratah (Telopea speciosissima) *glows like a jewel in the shrub understorey of the Blue Mountains. The best time to see them is September to November.*

The Three Sisters, hard sandstone rock pinnacles, are the most famous feature in the park and are best viewed from the lookout at Echo Point in Katoomba.

Dramatic Narrow Neck is best seen from Cahills Lookout off the western end of Cliff Drive in Katoomba. Spectacular views of Boars Head Rock and the Megalong Valley are also provided from this lookout.

Coachwood (Ceratopetalum apetalum) *are tall slender trees noted for the mossy circles on their trunks. They are common in the park's rainforest areas.*

your intended route and time of return in order to avoid unnecessary searching.

There are some good lookouts off the Bells Line of Road and these are found a few minutes off the main road at Pierces Pass, Mount Banks and Mount Tomah, where you'll find the excellent high country botanical gardens.

Access

The park takes in some 248 148 hectares of rugged country west of Sydney and is best accessed along the Great Western Highway. It stretches in the east from Glenbrook, almost at the foot of the mountains, to west of Katoomba near Mount Victoria where the road descends onto the western plains. Its northern boundary is the Bells Line of Road where the Wollemi National Park continues northwards and its southern section stretches all the way to Wombeyan Caves, west of Mittagong.

The park has three distinct regions: the Glenbrook section covering the lower Blue Mountains down to Lake Burragorang and west to Wentworth Falls; the southwestern section which includes the Jamison Valley and the Three Sisters, and is the most remote area extending south towards Kanangra-Boyd National Park and on to Wombeyan Caves; and the northern section between the Great Western Highway and the Bells Line of Road, which includes the Grose Valley and contains some of the best lookouts and walking trails.

You can even visit the park by train or bus. Check out the CityRail website to plan your railway journey or the local bus network website for the town nearest the places you would like to visit.

The agile, arboreal ring-tail possum (Pseudocheirus peregrinus) *is so-called because the tip of its long prehensile tail can be coiled into a ring and acts as a fifth limb.*

Camping

Entry is free to all areas of the park except those areas south of Glenbrook. Camping fees apply throughout the park. You need to take drinking water with you to most areas.

In the Glenbrook section there is a camping ground at Euroka Clearing, however, unless you have a New South Wales Parks Annual Pass, you'll need to buy a vehicle day pass as well as pay a camping fee. It is necessary to book and pay for your site at the Glenbrook Tourist Information Centre, phone (02) 4739 6266.

There are also camping locations at Ingar and Murphys Glen, both south of Woodford, which are accessed off the highway at Wentworth Falls.

In the northern section, or the Grose Valley, there is one official camp site at Perrys Lookdown. This is accessed off the Great Western Highway at Blackheath. This section of the park is very popular with bushwalkers, however, bush camping is permitted in only two places in the Grose Valley: Acacia Flat and Burra Korain Flat. In other areas outside the Grose Valley it is possible to bush camp away from roads, walking trails and picnic areas.

The southern section is much more remote, and camping within 3 km of Lake Burragorang is not permitted as this is part of the catchment area for Sydney's water supply.

tourist info

The National Parks and Wildlife Service conducts guided tours under its Discovery programme. These include interpretive walks, night-time tours, trips for the kids and campfire talks. For details, contact the Blue Mountains Heritage Centre on (02) 4787 8877. The National Parks and Wildlife Service also has extensive information on all walking trails.

Abseiling, rock climbing and canyoning tours: contact Blue Mountains Adventure Company (02) 4782 1271

Horse trail rides in the Megalong Valley: Werriberri Trail Rides (02) 4787 9171 and Packsaddlers (02) 4787 9150

Tours of the mountains: Blue Mountains Guides, (02) 4782 6109

Kosciuszko National Park

Kosciuszko National Park is the leader in New South Wales in terms of size, attractions, activities and grandeur. At 690 000 hectares it is the largest park in the state, taking up nearly 1 per cent of the state's landmass. It stretches from the Victorian border all the way to the Brindabella Range west of Canberra and sprawls across the highest peaks of the Great Dividing Range. It protects Australia's tallest mountain, Mount Kosciuszko, which reaches a height of 2228 metres. The park includes more than 300 000 hectares of wilderness area.

Mount Kosciuszko National Park provides excellent winter skiing conditions for both downhill and cross-country skiers.

fact file

WHERE: About halfway between Melbourne and Sydney; 2 hours' drive from Canberra
Map: NSW 7 G8

WHEN: June to September for skiing; November to February for bushwalking and camping

WHY: Ski fields, excellent walks with mountain scenery, 4WD

SIZE: 690 000 ha

RANGER: National Parks and Wildlife Service, Jindabyne (02) 6450 5555

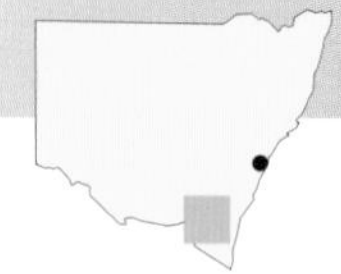

Right: *Fishing, in season, is a major attraction in the park. Rivers and lakes are regularly stocked from trout hatcheries.*

The Snowy Mountains, over which the park spreads its protective mantle, are the home of Australia's largest power generating scheme, the Snowy Mountains Hydro-Electric Scheme. Only in the far south and the north-east of the park are you totally free from the signs of this huge development, but the man-made lakes do add another dimension to the scene.

The park is known primarily for its sensational snow-skiing over the winter months. During summer it becomes an idyllic escape for many hundreds of visitors who savour the crisp mountain air and expansive mountain views. During this time many of the fabulous camp sites beside the rivers and lakes of the mountains are filled to overflowing with campers enjoying the bright blue skies and fresh air. The walking tracks across the main range are visited by numerous walkers, awestruck by the uninterrupted views and carpets of wildflowers. Below, in the deep valleys, the lakes created by the hydro-electric scheme and the rivers are full of boats, canoes and anglers.

Bushwalkers can explore the wilderness areas, while historians will enjoy discovering the huts and homesteads of the high country left by the pioneers.

In the Past

It is known that the Australian Aboriginals visited the mountains at times during the year, the harsh winter making them unsuitable for permanent human habitation. Europeans ventured into the mountains in the early 1800s as graziers searched for better grasslands to feed their stock. The Polish explorer Count Strzelecki supposedly climbed the highest peak in 1840 and named it for Polish patriot Tadeusz Kosciuszko; however, some say that he was, in fact, on Mount Townsend.

In 1859 there was a minor gold rush at Kiandra and during the late 1800s and early 1900s timber-getters worked the giant stands of timber in the lower valleys.

In 1944 the Kosciuszko State Park was established and

five years later the Snowy Mountains Scheme began. This was indeed an engineering feat of epic proportions. Five rivers were diverted from an easterly flow to a westerly flow; 145 km of tunnels were bored through solid rock; 17 dams were constructed; 7 power stations established and over 1600 km of roads blazed through some of the most rugged country in the land. This brought enormous economic development to Australia in the form of power generation and irrigation for the Western Plains. However, some are now arguing that the changes to nature will ultimately wreak havoc over our land.

The Kosciuszko National Park was proclaimed in 1967 and more recently it has been recognised by UNESCO as an International Biosphere Reserve.

Carpets of cheerful alpine buttercups (Ranunculus anemoneus), *which are found in the wild only on the slopes of Mount Kosciuszko, are a feature of the park in spring and early summer.*

Activities

Right: *In emergencies snow caves can be constructed for shelter from bad weather. The temperature inside is just above a constant 0°C. Adequate ventilation is essential.*

In winter there is primarily one pastime in the park: skiing. The whole of the mountains can be blanketed in metre-deep snow for up to 4 months. There are tremendous opportunities for downhill and cross-country skiing as well as snowboarding, and thousands flock to the ski fields each winter to enjoy the slopes and the night life in the resorts.

At higher altitudes, some parts of the park are covered with snow for much of the year. Vegetated areas may be scattered or follow the contours of the slopes.

The park lends itself to a much greater variety of activities during the warmer months. Although the nights can still be extremely cold, the days are usually clear and sunny. The scenery at this time is excellent and many bushwalkers prefer this time of year to tackle the many hundreds of kilometres of walking trails that are available.

It would be impossible to list all of the tracks that can be walked—details of these trails can be obtained from the National Parks and Wildlife Service office in Jindabyne. The tracks vary from short walks of as little as one hour duration to overnight camp-outs which cover up to 20 km of the mountaintop ranges. If you are planning a long overnight walk ensure that you are totally self-sufficient and ready for the worst blizzard-style, weather conditions. You will also need to carry your own cooking stoves and fuel with you, as the lighting of fires in higher altitudes is severely restricted.

There are excellent opportunities for boating, canoeing and swimming in the rivers and lakes of the valleys during

summer. Trout fishing in season is another major attraction as the rivers and dams are regularly stocked from trout hatcheries. Make sure you are aware of any local regulations (many rivers are open only to fly fishing) and wherever you fish in New South Wales you require a fishing licence.

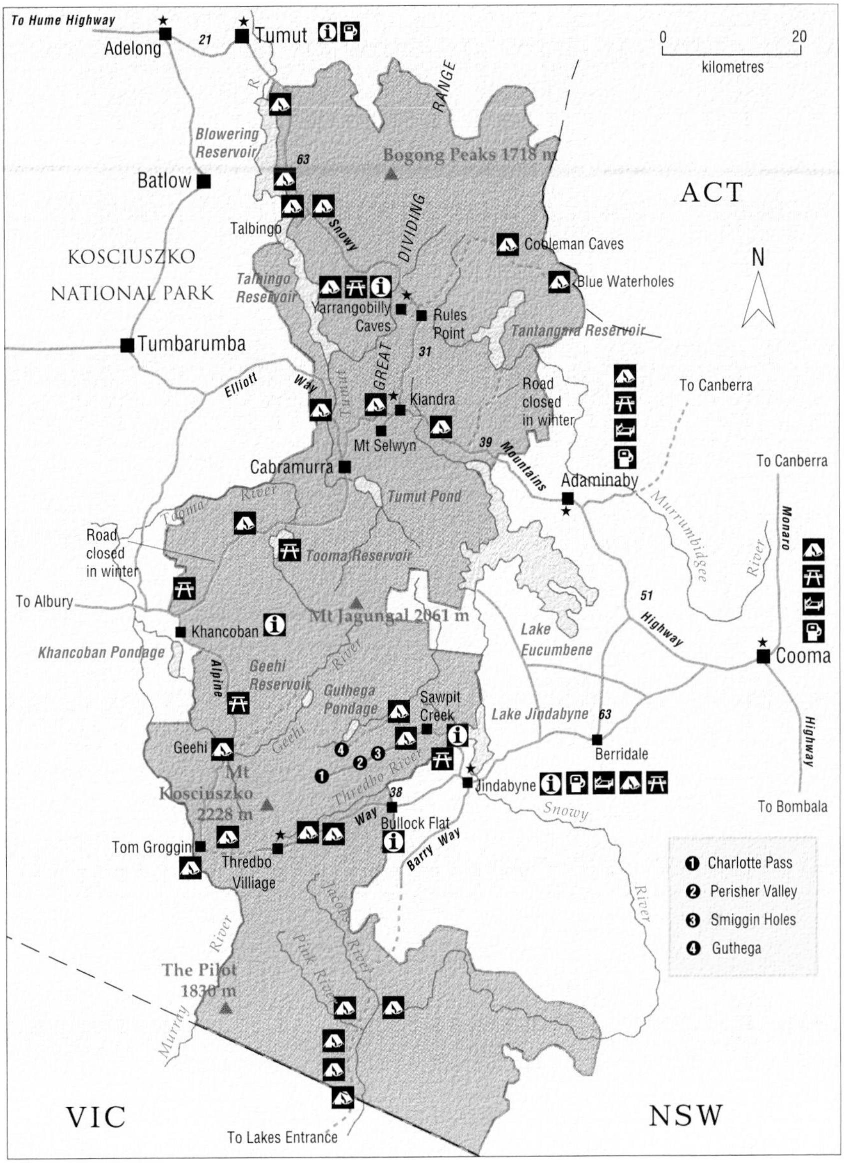

Horseriding is a popular activity but is only permitted in approved areas. Check before setting out or use an approved trail-riding operator. Mountain bike riding is allowed on management trails but not on designated walking tracks, and the bikes are not to be taken off the trails. There are a number of bike hire and tour operators in the area.

Whitewater rafting on the Snowy River, the Geehi River and the Murray River, as well as other similar adventure sports, are readily catered for.

Other visitors to the park will have an interest in the mighty hydro-electric scheme that reshaped the mountains and there are tours conducted to the power stations and dams.

The Yarrangobilly and Cooleman Caves are another feature of the Snowy

did you know?

Blue Lake in Mount Kosciuszko National Park is one of only four glacial lakes in mainland Australia. The lake was created by glaciation wearing down the granite bedrock, and is frozen over in winter.

Upper Pond Dam is one of the 17 dams built during the construction of the massive Snowy Mountains Hydro-Electric Scheme (1949–1972).

Mountains. The underground majesty of these caves is difficult to rival and there are self-guided tours as well as professional tours. There is even a natural hot spa at Yarrangobilly that can be enjoyed throughout the year.

The resort town of Thredbo, in the southern part of the park, offers a multitude of activities all year round.

The National Parks and Wildlife Service provides discovery tours and talks during the summer and there are commercial tour operators that can also meet your needs.

Access

It takes about 6 hours to drive to the park from Sydney or 2 hours from Canberra. The major entry into the park is via the Monaro Highway from Canberra, driving through Cooma and then on to Jindabyne.

You can also fly to Cooma and then drive to Jindabyne, but most people come by car or by coach.

There are alternative access routes into the park and each of them is spectacular. For those living in the western parts of the state it would be easiest to follow the Snowy Mountains Highway through Tumut before climbing the mountains past Lake Blowering up to Kiandra. From there it's onto Adaminaby and Cooma, from where the major ski resorts of Perisher and Thredbo are easily accessed via Jindabyne.

As an alternative, from Kiandra follow the Alpine Way to Cabramurra and then along the mountains on their western side to Khancoban. This marks the third possible entry point into the Snowies. For those travelling from Albury or Melbourne this would be an ideal route to follow as it traces the shoreline of the Hume Weir. Khancoban nestles at the foot of the towering mountains and from here you can follow the Alpine Way past Geehi and Tom Groggin to Thredbo, eventually emerging at Jindabyne.

It is possible to virtually circumnavigate the Snowy Mountains on a good road. However, some sections are closed in winter as the road is subject to heavy snowfalls.

During winter (1 June to 10 October) all vehicles travelling to and through the park must carry properly fitting snow chains and fit them when advised.

Camping

There are many opportunities for camping within the park, but be aware that sudden and severe weather changes are always possible.

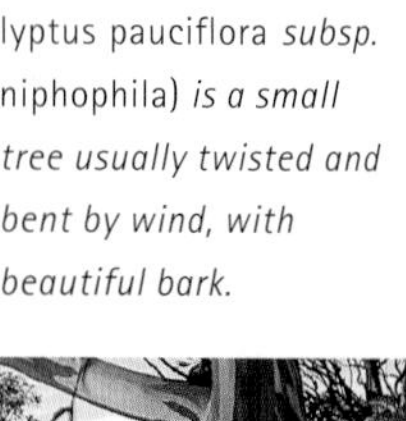

The snow gum (Eucalyptus pauciflora *subsp.* niphophila) *is a small tree usually twisted and bent by wind, with beautiful bark.*

Seaman's Hut is one of several old huts scattered across the high country that are ideal refuges for bushwalkers and cross-country skiers in bleak weather. The huts were built by the early graziers.

Even in midsummer there is the chance of heavy snowfalls and freezing conditions occurring.

There is a daily entry fee into Kosciuszko National Park, per vehicle, or you can purchase an annual pass that also provides access to all other parks in New South Wales. The pass is available from the National Park Centre, phone 1 300 361 967 or (02) 9585 6068, or from any national park in the state.

The major camping ground for tents and caravans in the park is at Sawpit Creek. Here you will find toilets, hot showers, fireplaces and even cabins for rent. However, bookings need to be made in advance.

It is possible to camp anywhere in the park provided you are not in sight of a road or near a watercourse. Some of the better camp sites for the car-based camper are found at Tom Groggin beside the Murray River, near Geehi on the Murray Flats, in the old town site of Ravine, or Lobbs Hole below the Yarrangobilly Caves, and at Cooleman Caves on the Long Plain east of Rules Point. In the north there are several short-term camp sites beside Blowering and Talbingo reservoirs.

There are commercial camping grounds in Jindabyne and Cooma and a huge number of ski chalets, motels and hotels in both these towns as well as in Thredbo and Perisher Valley, some providing on-snow accommodation.

For the avid bushwalker there are countless excellent bush camp sites along the many hundreds of kilometres of walking trails.

tourist info

There are many commercial tour operators offering overnight walks, whitewater rafting, horse-riding, mountain-bike rides, abseiling and photography tours

The Kosciuszko express chairlift operates in summer, enabling access to the summit boardwalks

Information on a variety of tours and activities is available from the Snowy Region Visitor Information Centre (02) 6450 5600

Barrington Tops National Park

A major attraction of the Barrington Tops is the clean, fresh air. But visitors are also rewarded with a vast array of walking tracks, magnificent scenery and lookouts, superb wildflowers, spectacular rainforest, snow gums and peat swamps. It is easy to say that Barrington offers everything. The park covers 73 884 hectares that vary from snowplains to impenetrable forests dissected by raging rivers with some wonderful waterfalls.

fact file

WHERE: 320 km north of Sydney and 30 km west of Gloucester
Map: NSW 6 K3

WHEN: September to February; winter is cold and many trails are closed

WHY: Great bushwalks, dramatic scenery, 4WD

SIZE: 73 884 ha

RANGER: National Parks and Wildlife Service, Nelson Bay (02) 4984 8200 or Gloucester (02) 6538 5300

State Forests Newcastle West (02) 4927 0977, or State Forests Information Centre 1300 655 687 or (02) 9871 3377

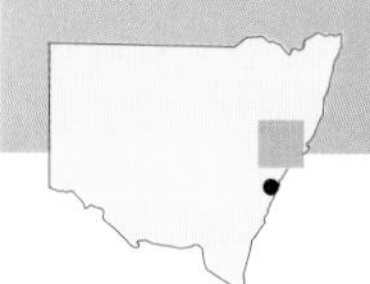

The many different species of flora and fauna are also a feature of the park. As well, the park is surrounded by vast areas of state forest which cater to the traveller with provision of trails, camping and picnic areas.

Activities

The Barrington Tops provide a wide variety of activities, the most popular ones being camping and bushwalking, and there is a very good network of walking trails throughout the park. Some are easy, short walks, while others are demanding and involve overnight camps in high altitude areas.

Anglers will find trout in the mountain streams, but check with local National Parks and Wildlife Service personnel regarding permits and seasons. You will need a New South Wales fishing licence.

The area has always been attractive to drivers with 4WD vehicles but track closures and wilderness declarations in recent years have greatly reduced these opportunities. Check with the National Parks and Wildlife Service and State Forests as to access and track availability.

In the lower reaches of the mountains, rafting and canoeing are favourite pastimes on the Barrington, Cobark and Gloucester Rivers.

Access

Good roads lead to most areas but during winter many of these can be slippery or covered with snow. Vehicle access from the south via Dungog or Gresford leads to the well-known Barrington Guest House and its surrounding superb walking trails. It also provides access to the state forest areas of Chichester Dam and Telegherry Forest Park where excellent picnic and camping facilities are available.

From the east, access is via Gloucester to either the Gloucester Tops or further west into the area's highest peaks along the Scone–Gloucester road.

If approaching from the west, travel via Scone and Moonan Flat before ascending the range

Right: *Barrington Tops National Park provides a protected environment for this mountain brushtail possum or bobuck* (Trichosurus caninus) *and her baby.*

on the Scone–Gloucester road. This is the most direct route to the more remote camp sites around Careys Peak and the Big Hole.

Camping

If you are bushwalking, you can camp almost anywhere, as long as you are more than 300 metres from a trail or official camp site.

If you wish to camp with your vehicle there are well-maintained camping sites in the southern section, in the Chichester State Forest, at Telegherry Forest Park and Allyn River Forest Park. In the Gloucester Tops region is a well-kept but more restricted camping area.

The state forest camping area at Polblue Swamp is excellent. The camping sites at Junction Hole and the Big Hole are favoured by more adventurous bushwalkers.

It would be wise to check with the National Parks and Wildlife Service for availability and access to most of the camping sites.

Left: *Superb World Heritage listed rainforests are a feature of the park, which also contains Antarctic beech forests, snow gum woods, wild rivers and wilderness areas.*

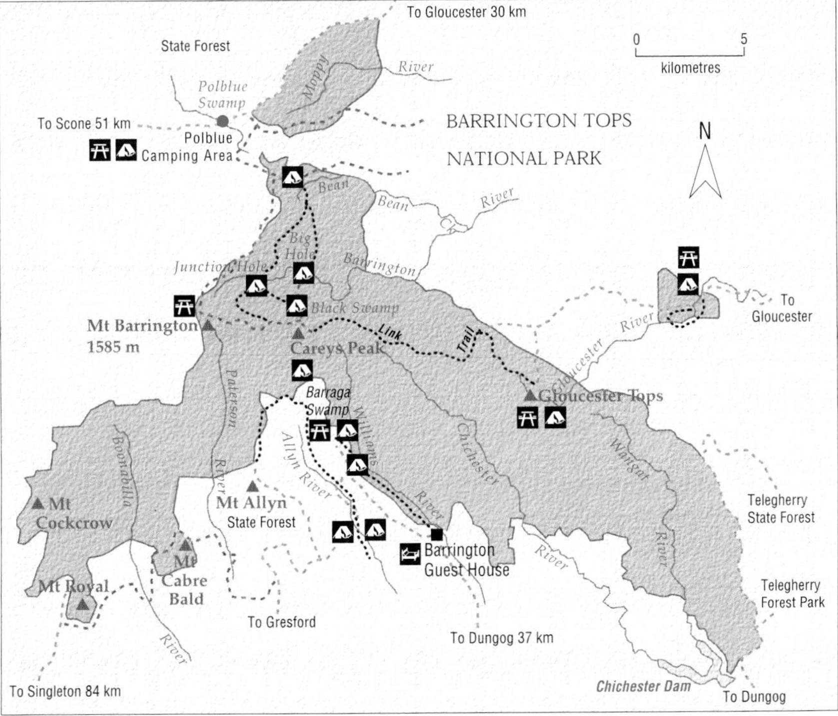

This part of the Great Dividing Range is subject to dramatic weather changes—one of the forces which helped shape this natural rock sculpture.

Deua National Park

The Deua National Park encompasses the mountains inland from the south coast towns of Moruya and Narooma. Although it is primarily a wilderness park, everyone can enjoy the wilderness areas. There are great camping spots beside clear rivers, 4WD trails, fabulous walks, caves, diverse flora and a huge range of wildlife. There have been 80-odd species of birds recorded from the park and a wide range of mammals, of which swamp wallabies are one of the most common.

Vegetation in Deua National Park changes markedly with altitude, providing a rich diversity of habitats for a variety of birds and other animals.

fact file

WHERE: 100 km south-east of Canberra
Map: NSW 7 K5

WHEN: September to May

WHY: Scenery, 4WD, camping, canoeing

SIZE: 82 926 ha

RANGER: National Parks and Wildlife Service, Narooma (02) 4476 2888

Activities

The park includes a number of challenging 4WD tracks from which drivers can enjoy superb views, and one of the best camp sites in New South Wales waiting at the end of the day in the Bendethera Valley. Although the roads are not particularly difficult, all visitors should know how to use their 4WD vehicles in rough terrain. Organised 4WD tag-along tours are conducted by Great Divide Tours, phone (02) 9913 1395.

Speleologists can explore the Bendethera and Wyanbene Caves, while remote country bushwalkers can venture into the rugged southern end of the park. Canoeists can paddle in the upper reaches of the Shoalhaven River, and mountain bike riders will also enjoy the 4WD trails.

Access and Camping

The Araluen–Moruya Road runs along the Deua River and gives access to the Bendethera–Merricumbene Fire Trail that gives the easiest access into the park from the north or from the coast.

The Braidwood–Nimmitabel Road, often referred to as the Krawarree Road, passes along the backbone of the Great Divide and the western boundary of the park. This provides access to the Big Hole, Wyanbene Caves and 4WD access onto the Mount Dampier and Bendethera Trails that lead into the heart of the park.

From the coast there's also 4WD access via a network of forestry trails out of Moruya that eventually lead to the Bendethera Trail.

Once in the park the trails are the domain of the 4WD; the Bendethera, Merricumbene, Mount Dampier and Minuma Trails provide varying degrees of difficulty. 4WD tracks should not be used in wet conditions. The few trails that dissect the park have remained open thanks to appropriate management by the National Parks and Wildlife Service.

There are established camp sites with pit toilets and barbecues on the Araluen Road at the Deua River Camping Area, approximately halfway between Araluen and Moruya, and at Bakers Flat. This road is very narrow as it twists and follows the river, but it is accessible to conventional vehicles.

Right: *The tawny frogmouth owl* (Podargus strigoides) *is resident in Deua National Park. Unlike other owls it does not hide during the day but roosts, motionless and head erect, on branches.*

On the Krawarree Road from Braidwood, the Berlang Camping Area provides picnic and camping opportunities. The Shoalhaven River is nearby and it is a 30 minute walk to the Big Hole. The Big Hole is a result of the hillside collapsing into an underground limestone cavern, creating a hole 30 metres across and 90 metres deep.

The Bendethera Valley deep in the heart of the national park stretches for over 4 km, and it provides the best opportunity for camping for those with 4WD vehicles. There are pit toilets and fire pits provided. The valley can be reached from both east and west.

Entry and camping fees apply.

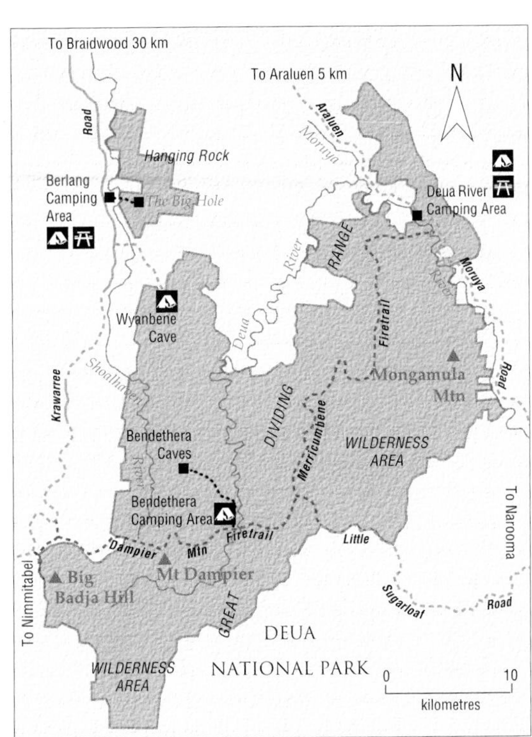

Deua National Park contains a number of rivers which have carved their way down the steep ridges to the valleys. In some places there are sparkling waterfalls, in others tranquil pools.

Kanangra–Boyd National Park

This spectacular park is only three hours' drive from Sydney and has some of the most inspiring scenery in Australia. In the heart of the park are the awesome Kanangra Walls and everyone should see them at least once in their lifetime. The Blue Mountains National Park joins its eastern and southern boundary, while state forests border much of the rest.

fact file

WHERE: 3 hours' drive west of Sydney via Jenolan Caves
Map: NSW 6 F8

WHEN: Spring and summer

WHY: Wilderness areas, lookouts, walks, 4WD

SIZE: 68 661 ha

RANGER: National Parks and Wildlife Service, Oberon (02) 6336 1972, or Blackheath (02) 4787 8877

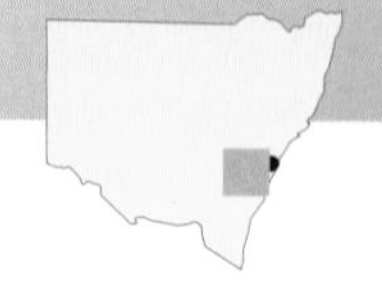

Attractions

The scenery and the isolation of the area are the major interest points of the park. There are sheer cliffs of several hundred metres, magnificent waterfalls and superb walking trails. There are also some great camping spots and an abundance of wildlife. The park is primarily wilderness, covering 68 661 hectares stretching from Jenolan Caves to Colong Caves.

Activities

There are some brilliant walks and views in the park. At the end of the Kanangra Walls Road there are easy, level walking trails leading to several magnificent lookouts over the Walls. There is wheelchair access at this point.

Here you will also find the Waterfall Walk that takes only 30 minutes to the base of the Kalang Falls, while the Plateau Walk gives you some great views over the wilderness areas.

There are many longer walks that entail overnight camps and you need to be experienced and very fit. These walks wind their way into deep gorges, passing mountains with such evocative names as Cloudmaker, Strongleg, Wild Dog, Stormbreaker and High and Mighty.

The walk out to the top of Morong Falls on the Boyd River is also worth the effort. Here you'll find impressive cascades and swimming holes; the walk will take at least one hour.

Cycling is only allowed on the public roads and trails. Bikes are not allowed on walking trails.

Caving is popular, and canyoning and abseiling are growing activities within the park.

There is limited four-wheel driving in the park, however, there is some exciting driving to be had crossing the Kowmung River.

Access

Although this is a wilderness area, access is quite reasonable. The major route from Sydney is via the Jenolan Caves Road from the Great Western Highway to the caves and then onto the Kanangra Walls Road. This road is 30 km of all-weather gravel but caution is needed in wet weather. You can also approach this road from Oberon or, if

This abandoned slab hut in the rugged terrain of Kanangra–Boyd National Park was originally a bushman's home.

NSW

tourist info

CAVING: Permits for Tuglow and Colong Caves required in advance from the National Parks and Wildlife Service

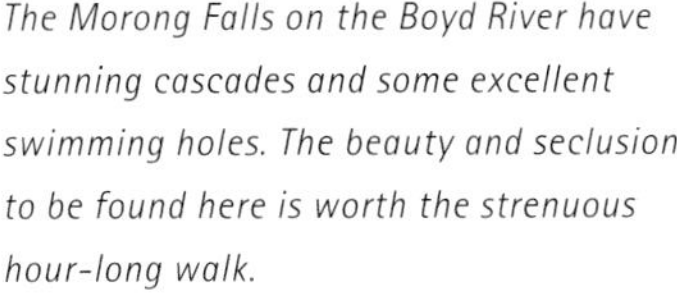

The Morong Falls on the Boyd River have stunning cascades and some excellent swimming holes. The beauty and seclusion to be found here is worth the strenuous hour-long walk.

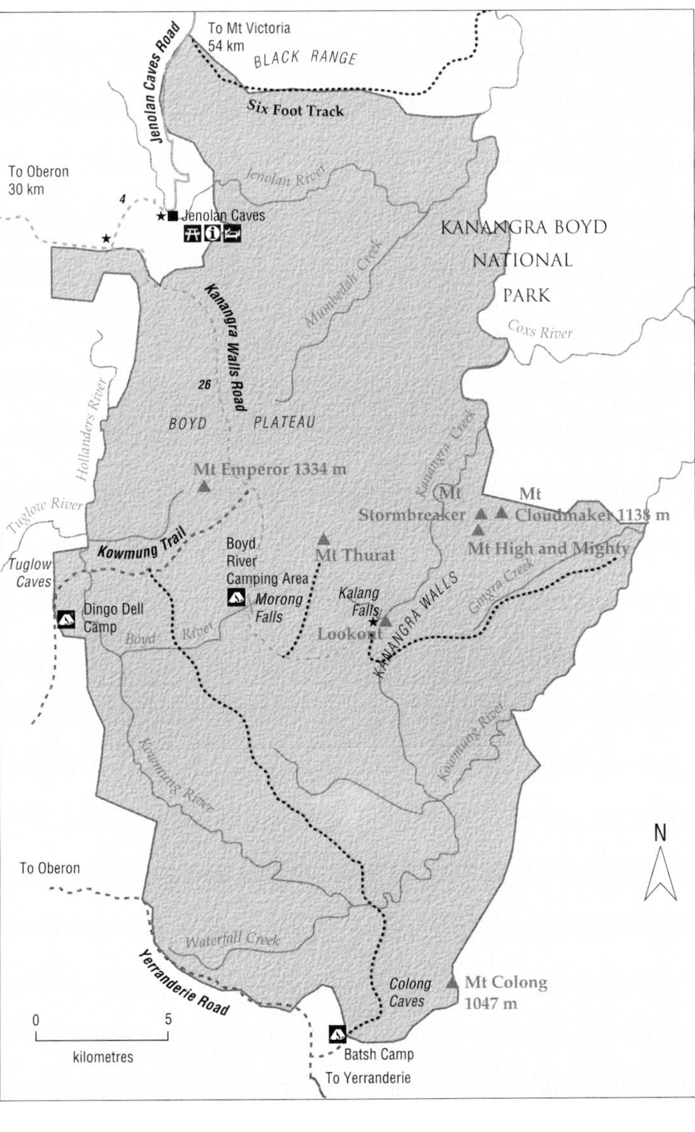

you have a 4WD vehicle, you would find the route through the Dingo Dell Camping Area and across the Kowmung River the most interesting.

All other access into the very heart of the park is by foot.

Camping

There is a vehicle-based camping area on the Kanangra Walls Road at the Boyd River crossing that has toilets and barbecues. Accessible by conventional vehicles, it is subject to extreme weather conditions and snow can fall at any time. The Dingo Dell Camping Area, with pit toilets but plenty of fresh water, is 4WD-accessible only and it is better protected from bad weather.

Sturt National Park

Here red kangaroos, emus and wedge-tail eagles reign supreme, the heat shimmers off the burnt red rock and the mulga bushes whistle in the breeze. This is the outback, and it is here where you'll find the driest and most remote of the New South Wales national parks. Established in 1972 and situated in the far north-west corner of the state, Sturt National Park covers an area of 310 634 hectares.

The pink cockatoo (Cacatua leadbeateri) *is also known as the Major Mitchell cockatoo, after the explorer. It is becoming a rare sight in this park.*

fact file

WHERE: 330 km north of Broken Hill
Map: NSW 1 B1

WHEN: March to November

WHY: Remote semi-desert landscape, wildlife, history, 4WD

SIZE: 310 634 ha

RANGER: National Parks and Wildlife Service, Tibooburra
(08) 8091 3308

In the Past

There is ample evidence of Australian Aboriginal occupation in the form of middens and stone relics throughout the area. Charles Sturt, after whom the park is named, spent a year in and around this region in 1844 on his central Australian expedition. In 1880 gold was discovered and pastoralists soon followed. The longest fence in the world, the Dog Fence, was constructed along the New South Wales borders with Queensland and South Australia.

Attractions

The vastness of the outback is the major attraction of this park, but there is much more of interest. The park has a huge kangaroo and emu population and there is ample opportunity to see these magnificent animals at close range. Of equal appeal is the evidence of human endeavour, in the form of explorers' camps at Depot Glen and Fort Grey, and the sheep stations such as Olive Downs and Mount Wood.

Visitors who drive through the area after rain will be rewarded with brilliant displays of wildflowers.

Activities

There are a number of short walking trails including trails from Dead Horse

don't miss

The world's longest fence goes through Sturt National Park. The Wild Dog Fence, or Great Dingo Fence, is 5614 km long, stretching from Jimbour in Queensland to the Great Australian Bight.

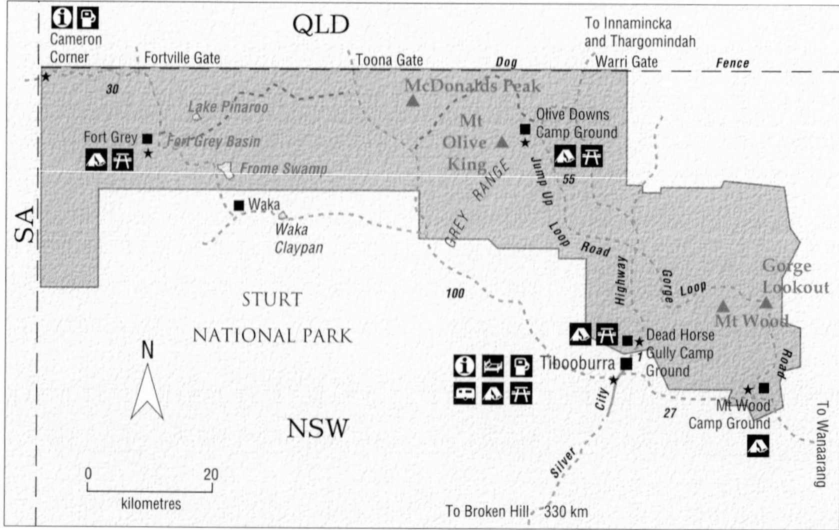

Gully, and at Mount Wood and Olive Downs. At Fort Grey you can walk to the old holding yard constructed by Sturt during his exploration as he searched for the inland sea.

For those interested in history there is also a reconstruction of gold mining techniques at Golden Gully.

The park also has a self-guided and well-mapped drive tour. The drive encompasses 110 km and takes travellers via Mount Wood and Olive Downs through what is the prettiest part of the park.

Access

Sturt National Park stretches from the state's northern and western borders at Cameron Corner east to the Silver City Highway and south to Tibooburra.

The park is very remote and travel in summer is best avoided. Autumn through to spring is a much better time to visit, but you can expect very cold nights in winter.

A mixture of bitumen and graded gravel road stretches for 330 km between Broken Hill and Tibooburra, or there is an unsealed route via Bourke and Wanaaring. Both routes can be impassable after rain so always check the condition of the roads with local police.

The roads within the park and to each of the camping sites and picnic areas are generally gravel with some sandy sections.

Camping

Sturt National Park caters for the tourist with three well-appointed camp sites. Just 1 km out of Tibooburra is the Dead Horse Gully Camp Ground, while further north, just outside the old homestead of Olive Downs, is another camp site which provides a beautiful setting among the mulga trees.

The other recognised camping area is at Fort Grey on the western fringe of the park, just 30 km before Cameron Corner on the state border.

Above: *Remote and semi-arid, the park has a diverse landscape, containing vast stony plains, rolling red sand dunes, remnant gidgee woodland, ancient granite tors and even some wetlands.*

Left: *Sturt's desert pea* (Swainsona formosa), *with its distinctive scarlet and black flowers, grows in the wild only in dry outback conditions.*

tourist info

4WD TOURS: Tri State Safaris (08) 8088 2389

Ku-ring-gai Chase National Park

The Ku-ring-gai Chase National Park lies just north of Sydney and protects some of the most fascinating and beautiful sandstone escarpment country and Australian Aboriginal art sites found in Australia. The rugged landscape discouraged early settlers, and by 1894 its environmental importance was recognised by national park status.

Akuna Bay Marina in Ku-ring-gai Chase National Park is situated in the quiet, sheltered waters of Coal and Candle Creek.

fact file

WHERE: 30 km north of the centre of Sydney
Map: NSW 6 J8

WHEN: All year

WHY: Picnic areas, walking tracks, Australian Aboriginal art sites

SIZE: 14 883 ha

RANGER: (02) 9457 8900

Activities

Numerous walking trails throughout the park cater for all levels of fitness and ability. There are magnificent views over Broken Bay and from West Head Lookout. The Australian Aboriginal rock engravings and stencils are best seen along Resolute Track.

The park is a wonderful place to explore by boat, and in spring and summer wildflowers colour the scene.

Picnic facilities, including tables, fireplaces and toilets, are available at Apple Tree Bay, Bobbin Head, The Basin, West Head, Cottage Point and Akuna Bay, and there are kiosks at Bobbin Head, Apple Tree Bay, Akuna Bay and Cottage Point.

Access

Access to the park is easy, as it's only a 40 minute drive along sealed roads from the centre of Sydney. Each of these access routes passes through fee collection gates and a daily fee per vehicle applies.

If travelling by train you can reach the park from Mount Colah, Mount Ku-ring-gai, Berowra and Cowan stations.

Access by water is also possible to the camping and picnic area at The Basin, with ferries leaving from the Pittwater side of Palm Beach.

Camping

This park is primarily for day visitors. There is only one camping area—at The Basin on Pittwater. It is accessible by ferry from Palm Beach or is a 3 km walk from West Head Road.

The best way to see the wonders of Ku-ring-gai Chase National Park is to walk. There are marked tracks which vary from easy to difficult, taking in a range of environments.

tourist info

Kalkari Visitor Centre
(02) 9472 9300

Palm Beach Ferry Service
(02) 9974 2411

South East Forest National Park

The South East Forest National Park has a continuous but convoluted border. It spreads over the rugged forested mountain country that stretches north from the Victorian border to join with the southern boundary of Wadbilliga National Park. The park, covering 115 372 hectares, straddles the spine of the Great Dividing Range.

Creeks and waterfalls, ferny gullies and superb old-growth forests are home to a diversity of native flora and fauna in this outstanding park.

fact file

WHERE: 450–550 km south of the centre of Sydney
Map: NSW 7 K8

WHEN: All year

WHY: Old-growth forest, scenic drives, 4WD

SIZE: 115 372 ha

RANGER: National Parks and Wildlife Service, Bombala (02) 6458 4080, Narooma (02) 4476 2888 or Merimbula (02) 6495 5000

The park protects outstanding old-growth forest, heathlands, swamps and fern-lined gullies. Over 110 species of birds have been recorded from the region and swamp wallabies are the most common large mammal seen. The old-growth forests are also home to a wide variety of possums and gliders along with bandicoots and potoroos.

Activities

Scenic drives provide access to picnic areas at Six-Mile Creek, Wolumla Peak, White Rock River, Myrtle Mountain, Big Jack and Myanba Creek.

A viewing platform with wheelchair access at Myanba Gorge gives great views over the Towamba Valley. Another viewing platform can be found at Pipers Lookout on the west side of the park, just off the Mountain Highway 60 km west of Bega.

Off the Pambula–Wyndham road you'll find parking and a barbecue area near the interesting and scenic Goodenia Rainforest Walk.

Horseriding, mountain bike touring and bushwalking are also enjoyed in this park.

Access and Camping

The Mountain Highway from Bega cuts through the park, along with a number of other bitumen roads. Good gravel roads are accessible to conventional vehicles, while forestry trails that are suitable for a 4WD open up more of the park to keen travellers.

Car-based camping is available at Six Mile Creek and Postmans Track (accessible only by 4WD), with toilets and drinking water provided.

Around sunset is when you are most likely to see koalas (Phascolarctos cinereus) *here, as this is the time they move around in search of food. Noted for their sleepy demeanour, they sleep 80 per cent of the time.*

Warrumbungle National Park

The Warrumbungle National Park is situated 27 km west of Coonabarabran and it attracts over 80 000 people annually to experience the clear mountain air and enjoy the extensive range of walking trails that crisscross the Warrumbungle Ranges.

Warrumbungle National Park is one of the country's best natural habitat havens for kangaroos and other wildlife.

fact file

WHERE: 27 km west of Coonabarabran in central New South Wales
Map: NSW 4 B10

WHEN: May to March and September to November; very crowded in school holidays

WHY: Bushwalks, rugged mountain scenery, 4WD

SIZE: 21 534 ha

RANGER: Visitor Centre (02) 6825 4364, or National Parks and Wildlife Service, Coonabarabran (02) 6842 1311

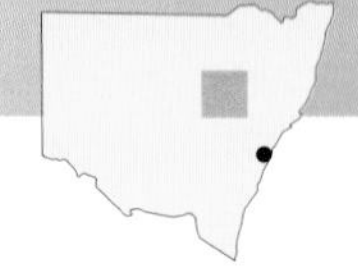

Right: *The Breadknife is a wall of rock with a serrated edge resembling a bread knife. The rock is the remnant of volcanic action, which took place some 13 to 18 million years ago.*

tourist info

Rock climbing permit and access to Burbie Camp (02) 6825 4364

Activities

Bushwalking is the major attraction and there is a huge selection of excellent walking trails. The scenery of the Warrumbungles is a feature of most walks and the well-known Breadknife, a 90 metre wall of solid rock, is one of the renowned features of the park.

There are a number of easy, short walks including Whitegum Lookout and Gurianawa Track that are only 1 km long and wheelchair accessible.

Rock climbers may pursue this activity in selected areas but must obtain a permit from the ranger.

Access

The park is easily accessed by conventional vehicle from either Coonabarabran or Coonamble. The road through the range is gravel. The southern section of the park can be accessed via Gilgandra, again over a gravel road.

There are limited vehicle trails within the park. The track to Camp Burbie is open to 4WD vehicles only.

Camping

There are a number of delightful camp sites, including Camp Blackman, Camp Wambelong and Camp Elongery. Camp Burbie is accessible only by 4WD. In the southern section of the park, accessed from Gilgandra, is Camp Guneemooroo.

For bushwalkers there are designated camp sites along the longer walking trails but you must register with the ranger to camp at these sites.

The lighting of wood fires is not permitted in the park.

More National Parks of Importance

Ben Boyd National Park

SIZE: 10 260 ha
MAP: NSW 7 L9

This park stretches along the southern coast of New South Wales in two sections separated by Twofold Bay and the town of Eden.

The southern section is of major historic interest with the ruins of the bygone whaling era, while the northern section contains interesting coastal flora and a unique formation known as the Pinnacles. Here fragile sand gullies capped with red clay form an unusual eroded gully off Long Beach.

Fishing, diving and surfing are popular pastimes along this coast and there are some great walks in the northern section of the park, including a 1 km nature trail to the Pinnacles. The nearby woodchip mill has an excellent tour each Thursday.

Access to both sections of the park is possible in conventional vehicles.

There are no camping facilities in the northern section. In the south, basic facilities (pit toilets and fireplaces) are provided at Saltwater Creek and Bittangabee Bay. Booking for camp sites in holiday periods is essential.

For more information, contact the National Parks and Wildlife Service, Merimbula, on (02) 6495 5000.

Beautiful beaches with clear waters are hallmarks of Ben Boyd National Park, which edges the Sapphire Coast. The area is excellent for both beach and estuary fishing.

Border Ranges National Park

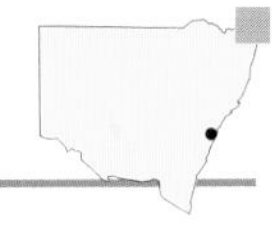

SIZE: 31 683 ha
MAP: NSW 4 M1

This unique area of rainforest and mountain wilderness straddles the Queensland–New South Wales border and shares a common boundary with the better-known Lamington National Park to the north.

This area is home to large numbers of grey kangaroos and red-necked wallabies which can often be seen feeding. The Tweed Range scenic drive winds up through the lush rainforest for about 60 km and can be comfortably driven in about 2 hours.

There are a number of walking trails and picnic areas in the park.

Access is either via Kyogle or Murwillumbah.

Camping in the park is free and permits are not required. There are camping grounds at Sheep Station Creek and at Forest Tops. Bush camping is possible west of the Bar Mountain rest area.

Phone the National Parks and Wildlife Service, Kyogle, (02) 6632 0000 for more information.

The restless flycatcher (Myiagra inquieta) *is a small bird similar to the willie wagtail. In Border Ranges National Park it lives in the eucalypt forests in the southern part of the park.*

Morton National Park

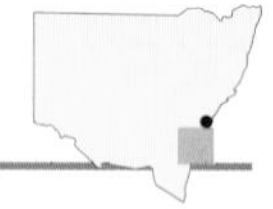

SIZE: 170 635 ha
MAP: NSW 7 M2

did you know?

The Wandandian people who lived on the coastal plains between Jervis Bay and Ulladulla regarded the towering cliffs of the Budawang Range in Morton National Park as a place of mystery, where Dreamtime creatures lived.

Bushwalking and sightseeing are the most popular activities in Morton National Park. Around the spectacular 82 metre high Fitzroy Falls are easy walking trails, some accessible by wheelchair. There are also several great walks around the escarpment behind Bundanoon. The best walks though are around Pigeon House and the Castle.

The easiest and most popular access into the park is via Moss Vale, or from near Nowra or Ulladulla. If you intend to explore further you will need a 4WD vehicle, or be a keen bushwalker.

Car-based camping is available (for a fee) at Gambells Rest at Bundanoon—bookings essential, (02) 4887 7270—with hot showers, toilets and barbecues.

In the southern section there are small camping sites at Blue Gum Flat near Pigeon House, where the road crosses the Yadboro River, and on Long Gully Road. No camp fees apply here.

For more details, contact the National Parks and Wildlife Service, Nowra, (02) 4423 2170, or the Fitzroy Falls Visitor Centre, (02) 4887 7270.

Sawn Rocks, in the northern section of Mount Kaputar National Park, are towering basalt 'organ pipe' formations created by volcanic eruptions eons ago.

Mount Kaputar National Park

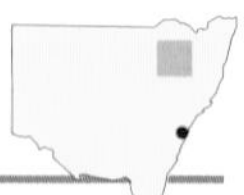

SIZE: 36 817 ha
MAP: NSW 4 E7

This park is dominated by the tall peaks of Mount Kaputar (1520 metres) and Mount Coryah (1400 metres).

Great walking trails (that vary greatly in length and difficulty), lookouts and unusual rock formations are the features that attract visitors.

All visitors must approach the park from Narrabri. It is 30 km of good gravel road to the entrance and another 20 km of steep, winding road (too narrow for caravans) to the main camping grounds.

A small fee, payable on an honour system, applies to the camp sites at Dawsons Spring. There are also two huts that can be hired. At Bark Hut, you must leave your vehicle in the car park and walk into the camp ground with all your gear.

For more information, contact the National Parks and Wildlife Service, Narrabri, (02) 6792 7300.

Mungo National Park

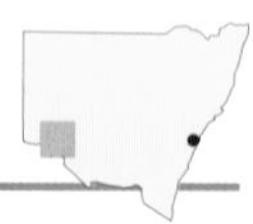

SIZE: 27 847 ha
MAP: NSW 5 F4

The arid Mungo National Park is unique. Set in outback New South Wales, it is part of the Willandra Lakes World Heritage Region. Evidence of Australian Aboriginal occupation dates back more than 60 000 years and the bones of some of the oldest known humans in Australia have been found here.

The major point of interest in the park is the landform known as the Walls of China, while the nearby dry lake bed

is an archaeological goldmine of bones, middens and artefacts.

While road access is unsealed, it is open to conventional vehicles, as are the tracks inside the park.

There are camp sites at the park entrance and at Belah Camp. Bring your own firewood and water. Bunk-style accommodation is available at the shearers' quarters in the park, and just outside the park at Mungo Lodge Motel, phone (03) 5029 7297.

Contact the National Parks and Wildlife Service, Buronga, (03) 5021 8900, for additional information.

The Walls of China, an outstanding 30 km long area containing unusually shaped sand dunes, is a highlight of a visit to Mungo National Park.

Mutawintji National Park

SIZE: 68 912 ha
MAP: NSW 1 D6

There are several outstanding Australian Aboriginal art sites at what is known as the Mutawintji Historic Site, and the surrounding area has been declared a national park.

Mutawintji has a great deal to offer the visitor. There is the colour and grandeur of the real outback, ancient art sites and ceremonial grounds, the incredible Aboriginal Mutawintji Historic Site (486 hectares), and hidden rock pools amid deep red gorges.

The main features of the park are best seen on foot and there is a good network of walking trails, including wheelchair accessible tracks.

The 2 hour drive from Broken Hill is mostly along dry gravel roads that become impassable to all vehicles after rain. There is good camping with basic facilities at Homestead Creek.

Contact the National Parks and Wildlife Service, Broken Hill, (08) 8080 3200, for more details.

An example of the Australian Aboriginal rock art found in Mutawintji National Park. As well as its visual impact, this art has symbolic meaning.

don't miss

At the Mutawintji Cultural Centre, near the entrance of the park, you can sit on the floor in the dark while a Dreamtime story is told. You can also learn more about Mutawintji, which became the first national park in the state to be returned to its traditional owners in 1998.

Myall Lakes National Park

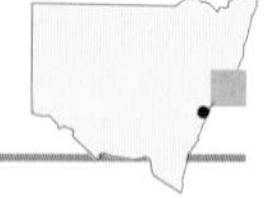

SIZE: 44 172 ha
MAP: NSW 6 L4

Myall Lakes National Park is a great place to enjoy water sports. Sailing, windsurfing and canoeing are very popular. Fishing, and netting fresh prawns late at night are also favourite pastimes.

Bushwalking is well catered for and everyone should experience the unique rainforest trail at Mungo Brush. Houseboats are another great way to experience the peace of the lakes.

Drivers of 4WD vehicles have beach access at designated points along the Mungo Brush Road. Permits for travel along the beach north from Hawks Nest are available from the Great Lakes Tourist Information Centre, Forster, phone (02) 6554 8799, or Tea Gardens, phone (02) 4997 0111.

Broughton Island, off the coast, is also within the national park and the fishing and diving are excellent.

One of New South Wales' most popular parks, Myall Lakes is 230 km north of Sydney and about 1 hour's drive from Newcastle.

The National Parks and Wildlife Service, Nelson Bay, (02) 4984 8200, has provided good camping facilities at a number of places.

did you know?

Myall Lakes is the largest coastal lakes system in New South Wales. The brackish, generally shallow waters here attract a wide variety of birds, including waterfowl, sea eagles and whistling kites.

Oxley Wild Rivers National Park

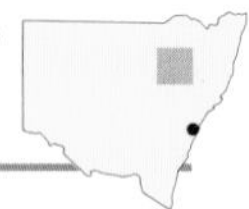

SIZE: 92 926 ha
MAP: NSW 4 K8

The Oxley Wild Rivers National Park preserves an area that includes up to 10 separate river gorges. These gorges are separated by farming and forestry land on the higher plateaus.

The waterfalls tumbling off the escarpment into the wild gorges of the many river beds are spectacular and the lookouts over Wollomombi, Apsley, Dangars and Tia Falls are all easily accessed by vehicle. The adventurous bushwalker will also find the park extremely rewarding. Canoeing is possible on the rivers, especially at Georges Junction where access is easiest.

Travellers can access the park from many different points, including along the Oxley Highway.

Remote camping is permitted anywhere in the park except at designated

Boating is one of the best ways to appreciate the vast and tranquil waterways of Myall Lakes. Anglers can fish for mullet, bream, flathead and luderick.

picnic areas and there are many beautiful spots to choose from.

Contact the National Parks and Wildlife Service, Armidale, (02) 6776 0000, for more details.

Royal National Park

SIZE: 15 000 ha
MAP: NSW 6 J9

Royal National Park, gazetted in 1879, was Australia's first national park. It was severely affected by the Christmas 2001 bushfires.

Bushwalkers will find a huge number of trails to explore in the park and while the coast track is the most spectacular, its total length of 30 km would require an overnight camp.

There are many beaches where swimming is very popular, as are beach and rock fishing.

The park can be accessed by car, train and ferry. Road access is from the Princes Highway. There are walking trails into the park from the railway stations at Engadine, Loftus, Heathcote and Waterfall. A ferry service runs from Cronulla to Bundeena.

There is limited camping in the park at Bonnie Vale. Bookings are essential. There is bush camping or undeveloped sites at various spots including Werrong Beach, Curracurrang, Winifred Falls, Uloola Falls, Deer Pool and Karloo Pool.

For more information contact the National Parks and Wildlife Service, Visitor Centre, on (02) 9542 0648.

Above: *The Royal National Park is the world's second oldest national park. Only 32km from Sydney, it offers a variety of activities, including swimming, cliff-top walks and rainforest cycle tracks.*

Washpool National Park

SIZE: 58 320 ha
MAP: NSW 4 K4

This park is a wilderness area that protects the largest area of old-growth, warm-temperate rainforest in New South Wales. Declared a national park in 1983, it has since been included on the World Heritage List.

Visitors wishing to see a wide variety of wildlife will not be disappointed as the region is one of the richest fauna areas in New South Wales.

A number of interesting walks within the park range from a pleasant one hour stroll along the banks of Coombadjha Creek to difficult 3 day hikes in more remote areas.

Washpool is on the Gwydir Highway between Grafton and Glen Innes in northern New South Wales. The park is accessible to conventional vehicles.

The main camping ground at Bellbird Camping Area has fireplaces, firewood, picnic tables and toilets. There are walk-in camp sites at the Coombadjha Camping Area.

For more details, contact the ranger at Glen Innes on (02) 6732 5133.

The wonga pigeon (Leucosarcia melanoleuca) *is one of the 260 species of birds found in Washpool National Park. It roosts in trees at night, but spends most of the day on the ground.*

Left: *Coast banksias* (Banksia integrifolia) *can be seen in abundance on the Royal's magnificent Coast Track which follows the park's cliffs, escarpments and beaches.*

Willandra National Park

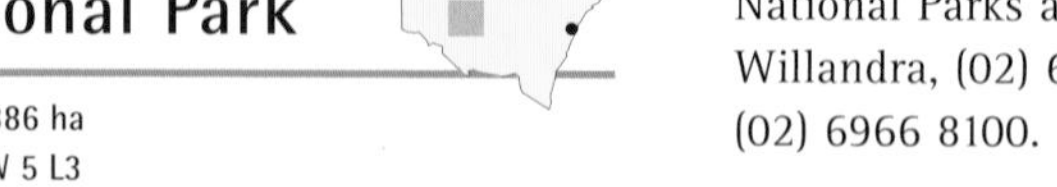

SIZE: 19 386 ha
MAP: NSW 5 L3

Willandra, 64 km northwest of Hillston, was once famous for merino wool. Now the flat country is home to numerous red kangaroos, while the sheep station homestead and other outbuildings have been retained to preserve this part of the state's outback history.

There are a number of walks in the park, with details available from the National Parks and Wildlife Service.

The Merton Motor Trail provides an unsealed road tour of the park. The western section of the park has no vehicle access and is restricted to bushwalkers only.

Access is via unsealed roads that are impassable in wet weather. It is possible to stay in the 'Men's Quarters' where bunks and cooking utensils are provided, but bookings must be made in advance, on (02) 6967 8159. Camping is also available near the homestead. Remote camping within the remainder of the parks possible for backpackers. The area becomes extremely hot in summertime.

The recently discovered Wollemi pine (Wollemia nobilis) *was hidden in a sheltered rainforest gorge in Wollemi National Park. Only three small stands of the trees are known to exist.*

For further information, contact the National Parks and Wildlife Service, Willandra, (02) 6967 8159, or Griffith, (02) 6966 8100.

Wollemi National Park

SIZE: 492 220 ha
MAP: NSW 6 H5

Wollemi is the second largest park in New South Wales and while it is primarily a wilderness park, it is within 2 hours of the busiest city in the country. In 1994, the Wollemi pine was found deep in the park. This is significant because this previously unknown species of tree can trace its descent directly from plants from the Jurassic period.

The park's major feature is its wilderness value and the intrepid bushwalker will find a fascinating range of places to enjoy amid stunning scenery.

For those interested in history the Newnes shale mine site has plenty to offer, while birdwatching, canoeing, li-loing and swimming are popular activities in a number of places in the park.

Vehicle access is restricted to the park's perimeter; after that the park is really only for the fit, experienced and self-sufficient bushwalker.

On the eastern side there is camping at Wheeney Creek, while on the western boundary there is a pleasant large camping area at Newnes. Dunns Swamp is another good camping spot.

For more details contact the National Parks and Wildlife Service, Richmond, (02) 4588 5247; Blackheath, (02) 4787 8877; or Mudgee, (02) 6372 7199.

Quietly floating or canoeing down the Colo River in Wollemi National Park provides an opportunity to observe wildlife that might not otherwise be seen.

Popular Parks at a Glance

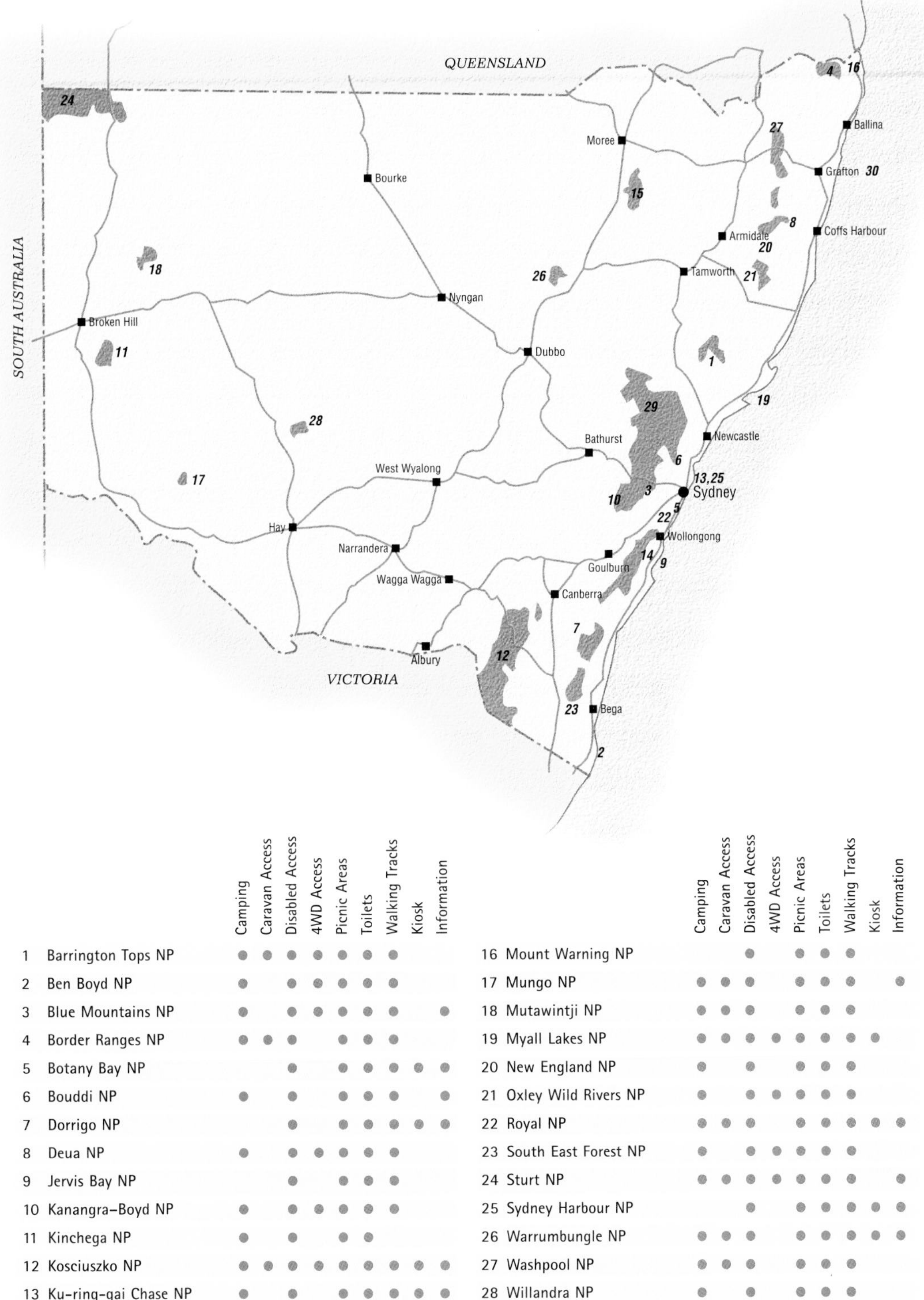

	Park	Camping	Caravan Access	Disabled Access	4WD Access	Picnic Areas	Toilets	Walking Tracks	Kiosk	Information
1	Barrington Tops NP	●	●	●	●	●	●	●		
2	Ben Boyd NP	●		●	●	●	●	●		
3	Blue Mountains NP	●		●	●	●	●	●		●
4	Border Ranges NP	●	●	●		●	●	●		
5	Botany Bay NP			●		●	●	●	●	●
6	Bouddi NP	●		●		●	●	●		●
7	Dorrigo NP			●		●	●	●	●	●
8	Deua NP	●		●	●	●	●	●		
9	Jervis Bay NP			●		●	●	●		
10	Kanangra-Boyd NP	●		●	●	●	●	●		
11	Kinchega NP	●		●		●	●			
12	Kosciuszko NP	●	●	●	●	●	●	●	●	●
13	Ku-ring-gai Chase NP	●		●		●	●	●	●	●
14	Morton NP	●	●	●	●	●	●	●	●	●
15	Mount Kaputar NP	●		●		●	●	●		
16	Mount Warning NP			●		●	●	●		
17	Mungo NP	●	●	●		●	●	●		●
18	Mutawintji NP	●	●	●		●	●	●		
19	Myall Lakes NP	●	●	●	●	●	●	●	●	
20	New England NP	●		●		●	●	●		
21	Oxley Wild Rivers NP	●		●	●	●	●	●		
22	Royal NP	●	●	●		●	●	●	●	●
23	South East Forest NP	●		●	●	●	●	●		
24	Sturt NP	●	●	●	●	●	●	●		●
25	Sydney Harbour NP			●		●	●	●	●	●
26	Warrumbungle NP	●	●	●		●	●	●	●	●
27	Washpool NP	●	●	●		●	●	●		
28	Willandra NP	●		●		●	●	●		
29	Wollemi NP	●	●	●		●	●	●		
30	Yuraygir NP	●	●	●		●	●	●		

Map 1

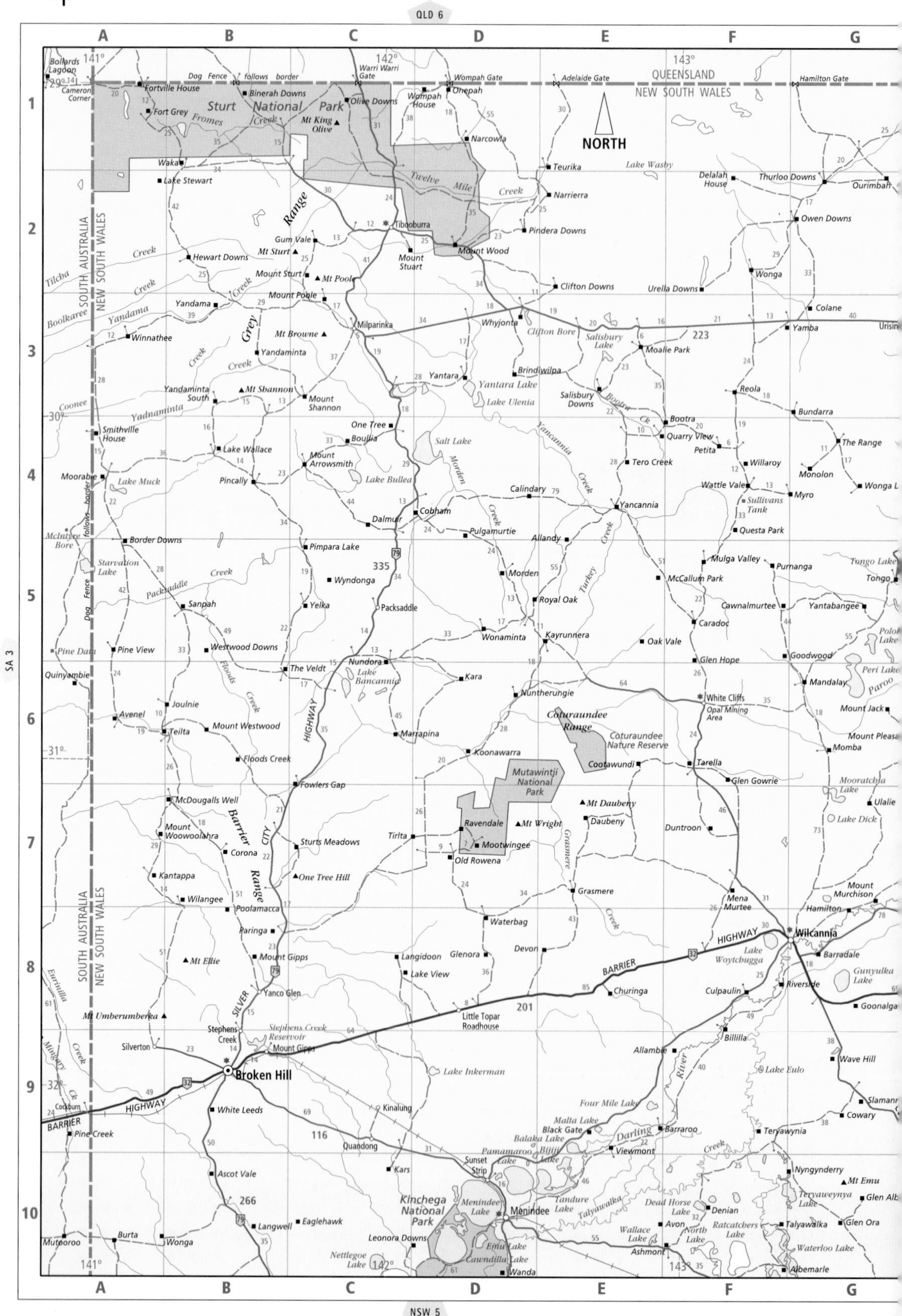
QLD 6
NSW 5
SA 3
NORTH
QUEENSLAND
NEW SOUTH WALES
SOUTH AUSTRALIA
Sturt National Park
Mutawintji National Park
Kinchega National Park
Coturaundee Nature Reserve
Broken Hill
Wilcannia
Menindee
Tibooburra
Milparinka
White Cliffs
Silverton
BARRIER HIGHWAY
SILVER CITY HIGHWAY
Barrier Range
Grey Range
Darling River
Packsaddle
Little Topar Roadhouse

QLD 6

0 10 20 30 40 50
kilometres

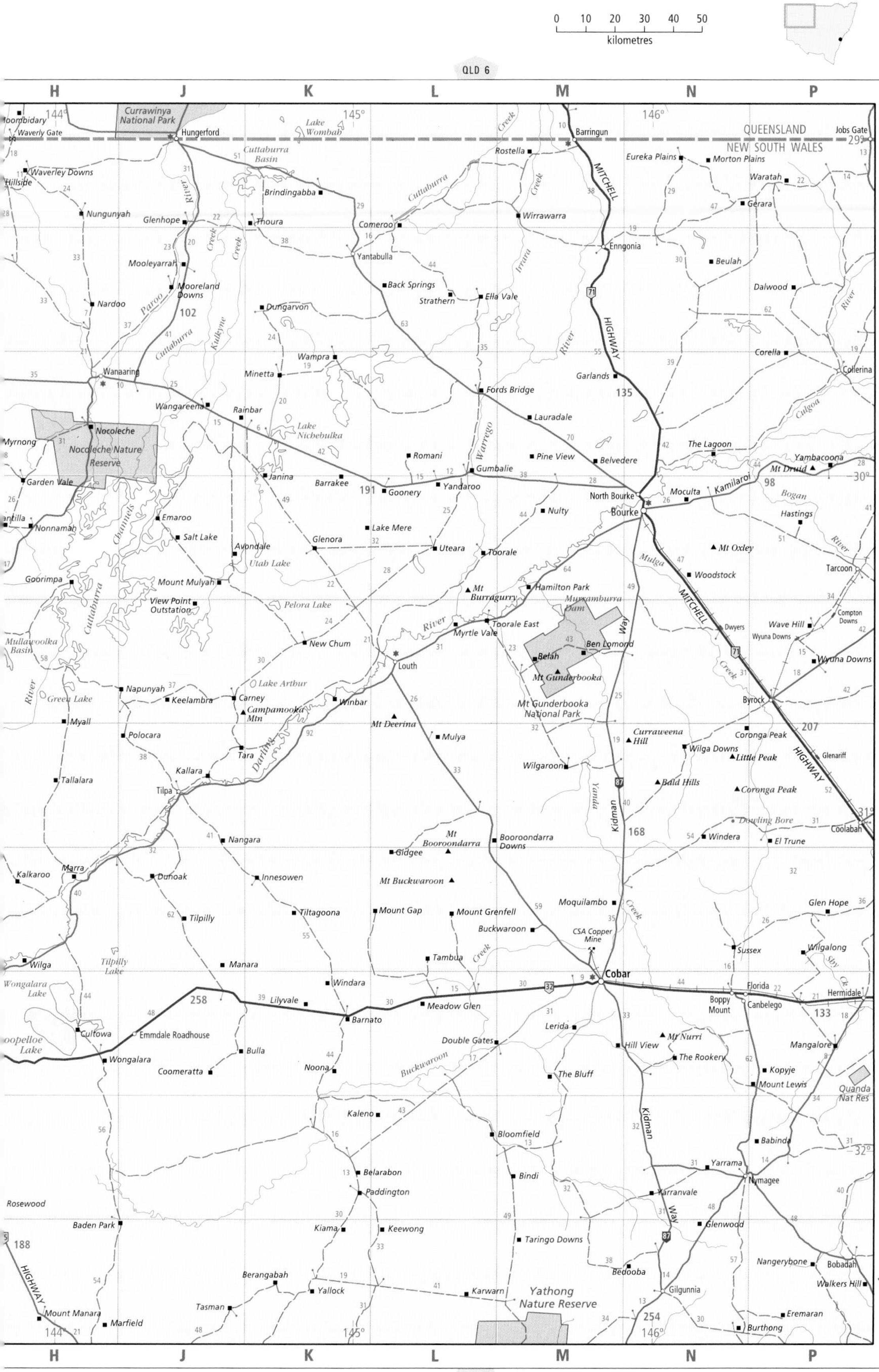

NSW 2

NSW 5

NSW

Map 2

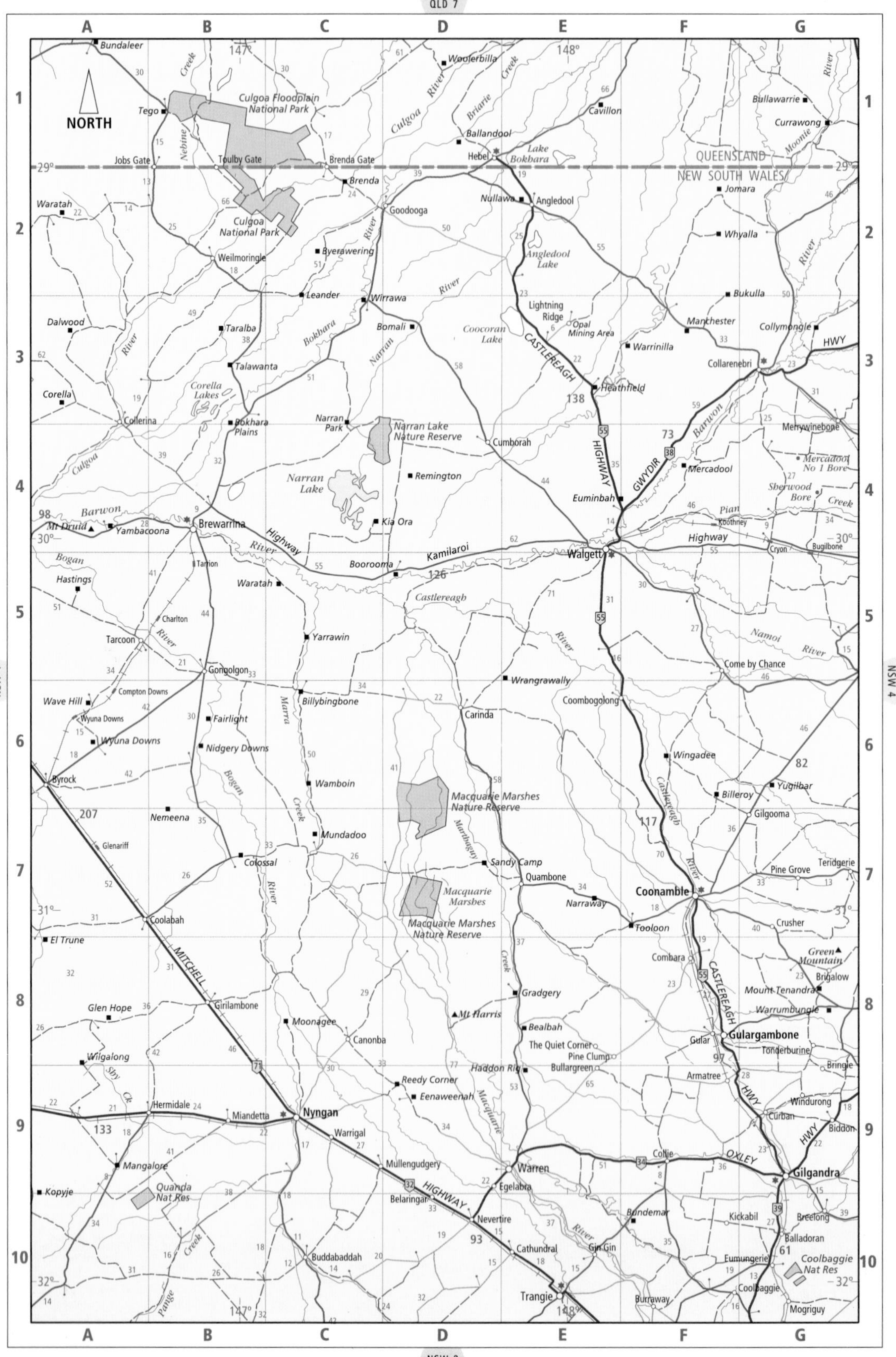
0 10 20 30 40 50
kilometres
QLD 7
NSW 1
NSW 4
NSW 3
NORTH
A B C D E F G
1 2 3 4 5 6 7 8 9 10
147°
148°
29°
30°
31°
32°
QUEENSLAND
NEW SOUTH WALES
Bundaleer
Tego
Culgoa Floodplain National Park
Jobs Gate
Toulby Gate
Brenda Gate
Brenda
Woolerbilla
Cavillon
Ballandool
Hebel
Lake Bokhara
Bullawarrie
Currawong
Waratah
Culgoa National Park
Goodooga
Nullawa
Angledool
Jomara
Whyalla
Weilmoringle
Byerawering
Angledool Lake
Leander
Wirrawa
Bukulla
Dalwood
Taralba
Bomali
Lightning Ridge
Opal Mining Area
Manchester
Collymongle
Coocoran Lake
Warrinilla
Corella
Talawanta
Collarenebri
Corella Lakes
Heathfield
Collerina
Bokhara Plains
Narran Park
Narran Lake Nature Reserve
Cumborah
Merrywinebone
Mercadool
Mercadool No 1 Bore
Narran Lake
Remington
Sherwood Bore
Euminbah
Mt Druid
Yambacoona
Brewarrina
Kia Ora
Koothney
Cryon
Bugilbone
Tarrion
Boorooma
Walgett
Hastings
Waratah
Charlton
Tarcoon
Yarrawin
Come by Chance
Gongolgon
Compton Downs
Wrangrawally
Wave Hill
Billybingbone
Coombogolong
Carinda
Wyuna Downs
Fairlight
Nidgery Downs
Wingadee
Byrock
Wamboin
Yugilbar
Billeroy
Macquarie Marshes Nature Reserve
Nemeena
Gilgooma
Glenariff
Mundadoo
Colossal
Sandy Camp
Teridgerie
Pine Grove
Quambone
Coonamble
Narraway
Macquarie Marshes
Coolabah
Crusher
Macquarie Marshes Nature Reserve
Tooloon
El Trune
Combara
Green Mountain
Brigalow
Mount Tenandra
Gradgery
Warrumbungle
Glen Hope
Girilambone
Mt Harris
Moonagee
Bealbah
Gulargambone
Gular
Canonba
The Quiet Corner
Tonderburine
Pine Clump
Wilgalong
Haddon Rig
Bullargreen
Bringle
Armatree
Reedy Corner
Eenaweenah
Windurong
Hermidale
Miandetta
Nyngan
Curban
Biddon
Warrigal
Mangalore
Mullengudgery
Warren
Collie
Gilgandra
Egelabra
Quanda Nat Res
Kopyje
Belaringar
Bundemar
Kickabil
Breelong
Nevertire
Balladoran
Buddabaddah
Cathundral
Gin Gin
Eumungerie
Coolbaggie Nat Res
Trangie
Burraway
Coolbaggie
Mogriguy
Culgoa River
Briarie Creek
Moonie River
Nebine Creek
Bokhara River
Narran River
Barwon River
Bogan River
Castlereagh River
Namoi River
Pian Creek
Marra Creek
Marthaguy
Macquarie River
Sly Ck
Pange Creek
CASTLEREAGH HIGHWAY
GWYDIR HIGHWAY
Kamilaroi Highway
MITCHELL HIGHWAY
OXLEY HWY
HWY

Map 3

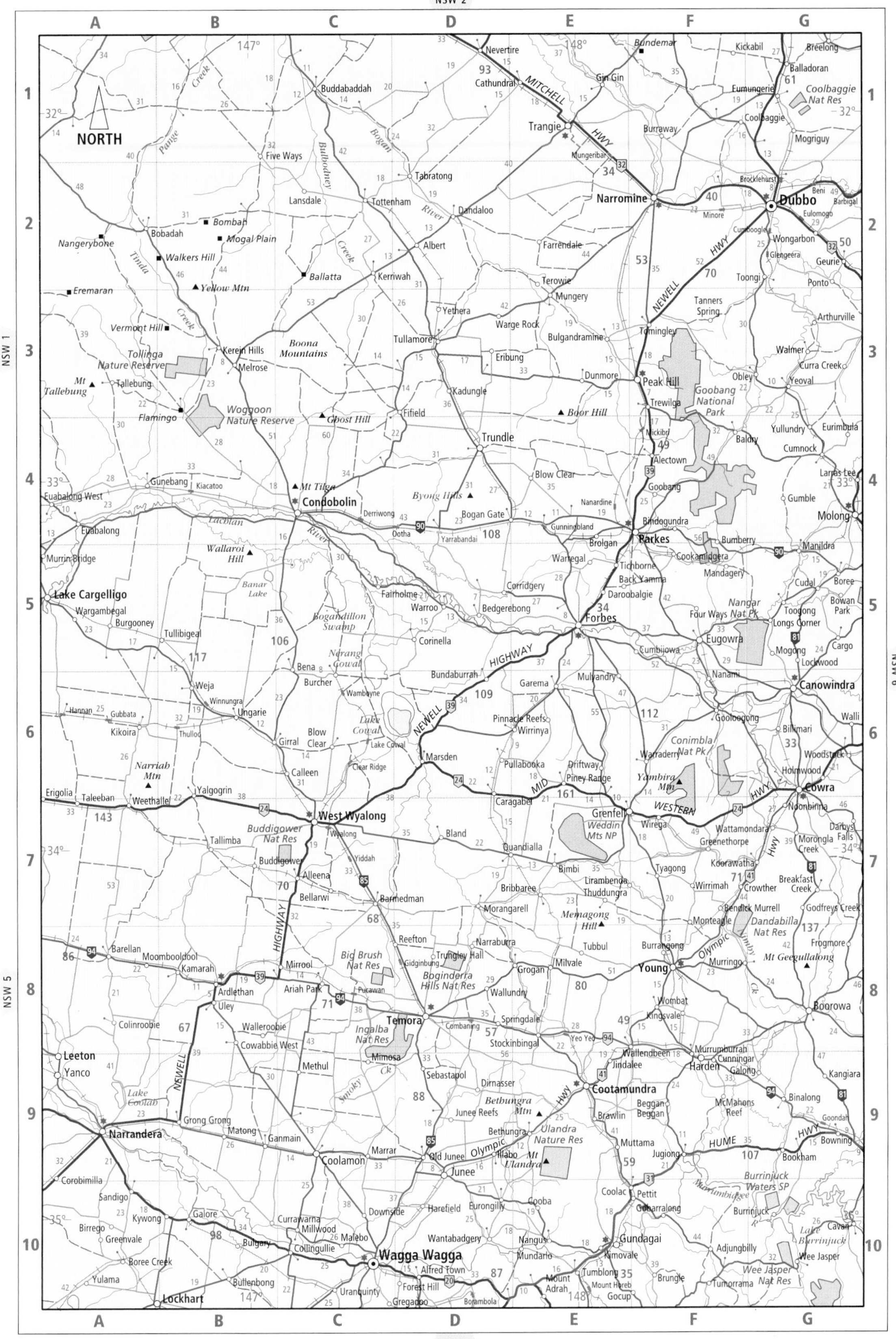
NSW 2
NSW 1
NSW 5
NSW 6
NSW 7
NORTH
kilometres
0 10 20 30 40 50
A B C D E F G
1 2 3 4 5 6 7 8 9 10
147°
148°
32°
33°
34°
35°
MITCHELL HWY
NEWELL HWY
NEWELL HIGHWAY
MID WESTERN HWY
OLYMPIC HWY
HUME HWY
Nevertire
Cathundral
Trangie
Mungeribar
Narromine
Bundemar
Gin Gin
Kickabil
Breelong
Balladoran
Eumungerie
Coolbaggie Nat Res
Coolbaggie
Burraway
Mogriguy
Brocklehurst
Dubbo
Minore
Cumboogle
Wongarbon
Geurie
Ponto
Toongi
Arthurville
Tanners Spring
Buddabaddah
Five Ways
Bulbodney Creek
Bogan River
Tabratong
Tottenham
Lansdale
Dandaloo
Albert
Farrendale
Kerriwah
Ballatta
Bobadah
Nangerybone
Bombah
Mogal Plain
Walkers Hill
Yellow Mtn
Eremaran
Vermont Hill
Pangee Creek
Tinda Creek
Yethera
Tullamore
Mungery
Terowie
Warge Rock
Bulgandramine
Tomingley
Boona Mountains
Kerein Hills
Melrose
Tollingo Nature Reserve
Mt Tallebung
Tallebung
Flamingo
Woggoon Nature Reserve
Ghost Hill
Fifield
Kadungle
Eribung
Dunmore
Peak Hill
Goobang National Park
Trewilga
Boor Hill
Trundle
Nickibri
Alectown
Baldry
Walmer
Obley
Curra Creek
Yeoval
Yullundry
Eurimbula
Cumnock
Larras Lee
Gumble
Molong
Gunebang
Kiacatoo
Mt Tilga
Condobolin
Euabalong West
Euabalong
Derriwong
Byong Hills
Blow Clear
Nanardine
Goobang
Bogan Gate
Bindogundra
Gunningbland
Parkes
Cookamidgera
Bumberry
Manildra
Ootha
Yarrabandai
Lachlan River
Murrin Bridge
Wallaroi Hill
Banar Lake
Lake Cargelligo
Wargambegal
Burgooney
Tullibigeal
Bogandillon Swamp
Fairholme
Warroo
Bedgerebong
Corridgery
Warregal
Brolgan
Tichborne
Back Yamma
Daroobalgie
Forbes
Mandagery
Nangar Nat Pk
Four Ways
Cudal
Boree
Toogong
Bowan Park
Longs Corner
Cargo
Eugowra
Mogong
Lockwood
Cumbijowa
Nanami
Canowindra
Corinella
Nerang Cowal
Bena
Burcher
Bundaburrah
Garema
Mulyandry
Weja
Winnungra
Wamboyne
Hannan
Gubbata
Kikoira
Thulloo
Ungarie
Girral
Blow Clear
Lake Cowal
Marsden
Pinnacle Reefs
Wirrinya
Gooloogong
Walli
Billimari
Woodstock
Holmwood
Cowra
Conimbla Nat Pk
Warraderry
Narriah Mtn
Calleen
Clear Ridge
Pullabooka
Driftway
Piney Range
Yambira Mtn
Erigolia
Taleeban
Weethalle
Yalgogrin
West Wyalong
Wyalong
Caragabal
Grenfell
Wirega
Weddin Mts NP
Noonbinna
Wattamondara
Greenethorpe
Darbys Falls
Moronglla Creek
Tallimba
Buddigower Nat Res
Buddigower
Bland
Quandialla
Yiddah
Alleena
Bimbi
Tyagong
Koorawatha
Bribbaree
Thuddungra
Wirrimah
Crowther
Breakfast Creek
Bellarwi
Barmedman
Morangarell
Memagong Hill
Bendick Murrell
Godfreys Creek
Monteagle
Dandabilla Nat Res
Frogmore
Barellan
Moombooldool
Kamarah
Mirrool
Reefton
Big Brush Nat Res
Trungley Hall
Narraburra
Tubbul
Burrangong
Young
Murringo
Mt Geegullalong
Ardlethan
Ariah Park
Gidginbung
Boginderra Hills Nat Res
Grogan
Milvale
Pucawan
Wallundry
Boorowa
Uley
Colinroobie
Walleroobie
Cowabbie West
Temora
Ingalba Nat Res
Combaning
Springdale
Stockinbingal
Yeo Yeo
Wallendbeen
Wombat
Kingsvale
Murrumburrah
Cunningar
Galong
Harden
Jindalee
Kangiara
Leeton
Yanco
Methul
Mimosa Ck
Sebastopol
Dirnasser
Cootamundra
Binalong
McMahons Reef
Beggan Beggan
Lake Coolah
Narrandera
Grong Grong
Matong
Ganmain
Coolamon
Bethungra Mtn
Junee Reefs
Bethungra
Ulandra Nature Res
Brawlin
Goondah
Bowning
Muttama
Jugiong
Bookham
Marrar
Old Junee
Junee
Illabo
Mt Ulandra
Corobimilla
Sandigo
Kywong
Galore
Currawarna
Millwood
Downside
Harefield
Eurongilly
Cooba
Coolac
Pettit
Gobarralong
Burrinjuck Waters SP
Burrinjuck
Lake Burrinjuck
Cavan
Birrego
Greenvale
Boree Creek
Collingullie
Malebo
Wantabadgery
Nangus
Mundarlo
Gundagai
Kimovale
Adjungbilly
Wee Jasper
Wee Jasper Nat Res
Yulama
Lockhart
Bullenbong
Uranquinty
Wagga Wagga
Alfred Town
Forest Hill
Gregadoo
Borambola
Mount Adrah
Tumblong
Mount Horeb
Gocup
Brungle
Tumorrama

Map 4

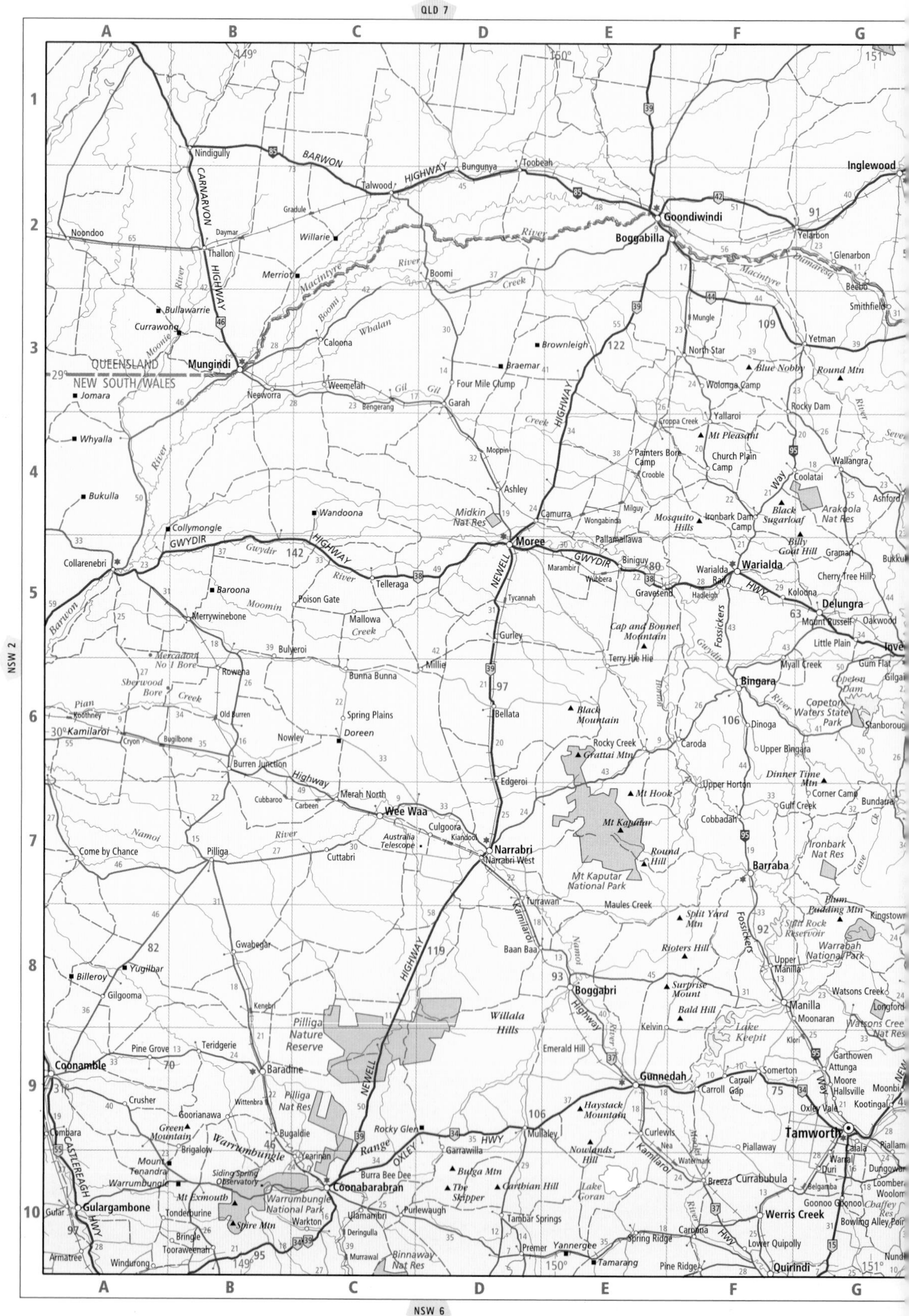
QLD 7
NSW 2
NSW 6
A
B
C
D
E
F
G
1
2
3
4
5
6
7
8
9
10
149°
150°
151°
29°
30°
QUEENSLAND
NEW SOUTH WALES
Nindigully
CARNARVON HIGHWAY
BARWON HIGHWAY
Talwood
Bungunya
Toobeah
Goondiwindi
Boggabilla
Inglewood
Yelarbon
Glenarbon
Beebo
Smithfield
Gradule
Willarie
Noondoo
Daymar
Thallon
Merriot
Boomi
Macintyre River
Dumaresq
Bullawarrie
Currawong
Moonie River
Mungindi
Caloona
Whalan
Boomi
Weemelah
Neeworra
Bengerang
Gil Gil
Four Mile Clump
Garah
Braemar
Brownleigh
HIGHWAY
Mungle
North Star
Yetman
Blue Nobby
Round Mtn
Wolonga Camp
Rocky Dam
Yallaroi
Croppa Creek
Mt Pleasant
Church Plain Camp
Painters Bore Camp
Crooble
Moppin
Jomara
Whyalla
Bukulla
Collymongle
Wandoona
Ashley
Midkin Nat Res
Camurra
Wongabinda
Milguy
Mosquito Hills
Ironbark Dam Camp
Black Sugarloaf
Coolatai
Wallangra
Arakoola Nat Res
Ashford
Billy Goat Hill
Graman
Bukkulla
Collarenebri
GWYDIR
Guwydir River
HIGHWAY
Telleraga
Moree
Pallamallawa
Marambir
GWYDIR
Biniguy
Wubbera
Gravesend
Warialda
Warialda Rail
Hadleigh
HWY
Kolodna
Cherry Tree Hill
Delungra
Mount Russell
Oakwood
Barwon
Baroona
Poison Gate
Mallowa Creek
Moomin
Merrywinebone
NEWELL
Tycannah
Gurley
Cap and Bonnet Mountain
Terry Hie Hie
Fossickers
Little Plain
Myall Creek
Gum Flat
Mercadool No 1 Bore
Rowena
Bulyeroi
Millie
Bunna Bunna
Sherwood Bore
Creek
Bingara
Copeton Dam
Copeton Waters State Park
Pian
Koothney
Old Burren
Spring Plains
Bellata
Black Mountain
Dinoga
Stanborough
Kamilaroi
Cryon
Bugilbone
Nowley
Doreen
Rocky Creek
Grattai Mtn
Caroda
Upper Bingara
Burren Junction
Highway
Edgeroi
Upper Horton
Dinner Time Mtn
Corner Camp
Bundarra
Cubbaroo
Carbeen
Merah North
Wee Waa
Mt Hook
Gulf Creek
Cobbadah
Namoi River
Culgoora
Kiandool
Australia Telescope
Mt Kaputar
Come by Chance
Pilliga
Cuttabri
Narrabri
Narrabri West
Round Hill
Mt Kaputar National Park
Ironbark Nat Res
Barraba
Turrawan
Maules Creek
Split Yard Mtn
Plum Pudding Mtn
Split Rock Reservoir
Kingstown
Warrabah National Park
Gwabegar
HIGHWAY
Kamilaroi
Baan Baa
Rioters Hill
Upper Manilla
Billeroy
Yugilbar
Gilgooma
Kenebri
Boggabri
Surprise Mount
Watsons Creek
Longford
Manilla
Moonaran
Bald Hill
Pilliga Nature Reserve
Willala Hills
Kelvin
Lake Keepit
Watsons Creek Nat Res
Klori
Pine Grove
Teridgerie
Emerald Hill
Garthowen
Attunga
Coonamble
Baradine
NEWELL
Gunnedah
Carroll
Carroll Gap
Somerton
Moore
Hallsville
Moonbi
Crusher
Wittenbra
Pilliga Nat Res
Haystack Mountain
Oxley Vale
Kootingal
Goorianawa
Combara
Green Mountain
Warrumbungle
Bugaldie
Rocky Glen
HWY
Mullaley
Curlewis
Nea
Tamworth
Piallaway
Piallamore
Brigalow
Yearinan
Range
OXLEY
Garrawilla
Nowlands Hill
Watermark
Kamilaroi
Calala
Mount Tenandra
CASTLEREAGH
Siding Spring Observatory
Burra Bee Dee
Bulga Mtn
Warral
Duri
Dungowan
Warrumbungle
Coonabarabran
The Skipper
Carthian Hill
Lake Goran
Breeza
Currabubula
Belgamba
Loomberah
Woolomin
Mt Exmouth
Warrumbungle National Park
Ulamambri
Purlewaugh
Goonoo Goonoo
Chaffey Res
Gular
Gulargambone
Tonderburine
Warkton
Tambar Springs
Werris Creek
Bowling Alley Point
Spire Mtn
Deringulla
Bringle
Tooraweenah
Carroona
Spring Ridge
Lower Quipolly
Murrawal
Binnaway Nat Res
Premer
Yannergee
Tamarang
HWY
Armatree
Windurong
Pine Ridge
Quirindi
Nundle

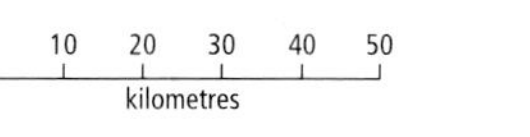

H J K L M N P

NSW

1
Warwick
Karara
Lake Leslie
Main Range National Park
Rockbrae
Emu Vale
Koreelah Nat Pk
Mt Barney Nat Park
Mt Barney
Rathdowney
Laravale
Tamrookum
Limpinwood Nat Res
Numinbah Valley
Springbrook NP
Mt Numinbah Nat Res
Lamington Nat Park
Burleigh Heads
Coolangatta
Tweed Heads
Fingal Head
Banora Point
Chinderah
Kingscliff
Bilambil
Numinbah
Chillingham
Tumbulgum
Condong
Bogangar
Bald Mtn
Tyalgum
Murwillumbah
Pottsville Beach
Killarney
Cougal
Lindesay View
Border Ranges NP
Mt Warning Nat Pk
Uki
Mount Lion
Old Grevillia
Burringbar
Lake Coolmunda
Tank Mtn
Legume
Old Koreelah
Dalman
Woodenbong
MT LINDESAY HWY
GREAT DIVIDING RANGE

2
Dalveen
Maryland Nat Pk
Tooloom Nat Park
Urbenville
Grevillia
Roseberry
Wiangaree
Horseshoe Creek
Mt Jerusalem Nat Park
Kunghur
Wooyung
Ocean Shores
Brunswick Heads
Mullumbimby
Wylie Creek
Captains Ck Nat Res
Toonumbar Nat Pk
Blue Knob
Nightcap NP
Mt Matheson
The Summit
Rivertree Peak
Liston
Tooloom
Yabbro Nat Pk
Eden Creek
Kyogle
Cawongla
Nimbin
Goonengerry
Stanthorpe
Browns Mtn
Pikedale
Amosfield
Old Bonalbo
Ettrick
Cedar Point
The Channon
Dunoon
Rosebank
Byron Bay
Clarence
Dyraaba Central
Modanville
Bangalow
Suffolk Park
Nashua
Paddys Flat
Bonalbo
Doubtful Creek
Rock Valley
Goolmangar
Glen Aplin
Sundown National Park
Boonoo Boonoo Nat Pk
Theresa Creek
Richmond Range NP
Fairy Hill
Bentley
Bexhill
Lennox Head
Mt Gunyah
Ballandean
Mummulgum
Lismore
Wollongbar
Alstonville

3
Glenlyon
Girraween Nat Pk
Bald Rock NP
Boonoo Boonoo
Tabulam
Woodview
Casino
HWY
Ballina
Silver Spur
Lake Glenlyon
Wallangarra
Sandy Hill
BRUXNER
Hogarth Range NP
Greenridge
Empire Vale
Drake
Mallanganee
Leeville
Tuckurimba
Wardell
Mingoola
Tarban
Sunnyside
Basket Swamp NP
Mallanganee Nat Pk
Yorklea
Tatham
Coraki
Dungarubba
Broadwater
Broadwater NP
Mole River
Riverton
Bryans Gap
Leechs Gully
River
Coombell
Ellangowan
Bonshaw
Mt Bowman
Tenterfield
Demon Nat Res
Alice
Busbys Flat
Bungawalbin Nat Pk
Woodburn
Evans Head
Snapper Point
Black Mtn
Wyan
Rappville
Mt Pikapene Nat Park
Torrington SRA
Bluff Rock
Surface Hill
Mt Neville Nat Res
Tabbimoble
Tabbimoble Swamp NP
Maidenhead
Spirabo
Bluff Rock Nat Pk
Billyrimba
Baryulgil
Pacific
Range

4
Round Hill
Kathida
Sandy Flat
Tent Ck
Burnt Down Scrub Nat Res
Camira Creek
Bundjalung National Park
Torrington
Bolivia
Whiporie
Summerland Way
Mororo
Pindari Dam
Stannum
Washpool National Park
Barretts Creek
Banyabba Nat Res
Richmond
Mulloway Point
Coaldale
Chatsworth
Iluka
Tent Hill
Emmaville
Washpool Nat Pk
Timbarra
Gibraltar Range
Gordon Brook
Harwood
Yamba
Deepwater
Butterleaf Nat Pk
Fortis Ck Nat Pk
The Broadwater
Maclean
Angourie
Strathbogie
Cangai
Lawrence
Wooloweyah Estuary
The Bald Knob
Gibraltar Range NP
Jackadgery
Woodford Dale
Tyndale
Dundee Rail
Dundee
Glen Elgin
Copmanhurst
Yuraygir National Park

5
Kings Plains
Wellingrove
Bald Nob
Black Mtn
GWYDIR
Koolkhan
Ulmarra
Brooms Head
Nullamanna
Yarrowford
Barool Nat Pk
Mann
Grafton
Tucabia
Sandon
Sandon Bluffs
Sapphire
Matheson
Nymboida National Park
South Grafton
Range
GWYDIR
Swan Vale
Glen Innes
Red Range
Mann River Nature Res
Ramornie Nat Pk
Pillar Valley
Minnie Water
Elsmore
Stonehenge
Newton Boyd
OBX Creek
Braunstone
Coutts Crossing
Bare Point
Wooli
Stannifer
Carters Mtn
Pinkett
Dalmorton
Buccarumbi
Louis Point
Koukandowie Nat Res
Halfway Creek
Yuraygir National Park

6
Kangaroo Camp
Maybole
Glencoe
Guy Fawkes River Nat Pk
Chaelundi Nat Pk
Nymboida
Kungala
Red Rock
Corindi Beach
Tingha
Mount Mitchell
Warra Nat Pk
Red Herring Hill
Towallum
Single Nat Pk
Ben Lomond
Llangothlin Lake
Glenreagh
Arrawarra
Basin Nat Res
Wandsworth
Backwater
Chaelundi Mtn
Byrnes Scrub Nat Res
Sherwood Nat Res
Coast
Georges Mtn
Llangothlin
Wards Mistake
Mt Hyland Nat Res
Clouds Creek
Nana Glen
Woolgoolga
Tenterden
Marengo Plain
Billys Creek
Nymboi Binderary Nat Pk
Sandy Beach
Emerald Beach
Moonee Beach
Moonee Beach Nat Pk
Ulidarra Nat Pk
Georges Mtn
Dundurrabin
Tyringham
Paddys Plain
Towanna
Coramba
Korora

7
Guyra
Aberfoyle
Monkey Point
Baldersleigh
Booroolong Nat Res
Wongwibinda
Bostobrick
Cascade
Ulong
Brooklana
Coffs Harbour
Abington
Black Mountain
Hernani
Cascade NP
North Dorrigo
Megan
Bindarri Nat Pk
Pine Mtn
Joeys Knob
Cathedral Rock NP
Fernbrook
Dorrigo
Dorrigo Nat Pk
Boambee
Sawtell
Ebor
Majors Point
Thora
Valery
Bonville
Way
Mt Davidson
Round Mtn
Darkwood
Bellinger River NP
Raleigh
Repton
Mylestom
Torryburn
Mitchells Flat
Yarrowyck
Point Lookout
Bellingen
Armidale
Waterfall
Wollomombi
Killiekrankie Mtn
Badwin Nat Res
Missabotti
Brierfield
Urunga
Jaanyigga Nat Res
Hillgrove
Jeogla
Valla Beach
SOUTH

8
Rocky River
Castle Doyle
New England National Park
Bowraville
Nambucca Heads
Uralla
Oxley Wild Rivers National Park
Dunggir Nat Pk
Talarm
Macksville
Gostwyck
Enmore
Georges Creek
Five Day Creek
Burrapine
PACIFIC
ENGLAND
Kentucky
Borah Mtn
Comara
Taylors Arm
Bulingary
Warrell Creek
Scotts Head
Grassy Head
Stuarts Point
Wollun
Oven Mtn
Macleay
Bellbrook
Eungai
TASMAN
Carrai Nat Pk
River
Baynes Mtn
Ngambaa Nat Res
Trial Bay
South West Rocks
Arakoon
Smoky Cape
SEA

9
Walcha Road
Walcha
Moona Plains
Daisy Plains
Boonanghi Nat Res
Toorooka
Willawarrin
Clybucca
Jerseyville
Woolbrook
Turners Flat
Smithtown
Kinchela
Gladstone
Fredericton
Korogoro Point
Hat Head
Kookaburra
Sherwood
Kempsey
South Kempsey
Hat Head NP
OCEAN
Aberbaldie
Kemps Pinnacle
Mt Banda Banda
Glen Morrison
Oxley Wild Rivers NP
Mt Werrikimbe
Kangaroo Flat
Willi Willi Nat Pk
Kumbatine Nat Pk
Crescent Head
Thunderbolts Way
Weabonga
Brackendale
Werrikimbe Nat Pk
Kundabung
Maria River Nat Pk

10
Niangala
Mt Sugarloaf
Mummel Gulf Nat Pk
OXLEY
Yarrowitch
Upper Rollands Plains
Rollands Plains
Limeburners Creek Nat Res
Mt Seaview
Point Plomer
Saltwater Lake
Ogunbil
Doyles River Nat Pk
Forbes River
Bellangry
Telegraph Point
Myrtle Scrub
Pappinbarra
Nowendoc Nat Park
Mount Seaview
Kindee
Pembrooke
Blackmans Point
Riamukka
Yarras
Beechwood
Wauchope
Port Macquarie
Raffles Peak
HWY
Ellenborough
Hanging Rock
Nowendoc
Bagnoo

NORTH

29°
30°
31°
152°
153°

H J K L M N P

Map 5

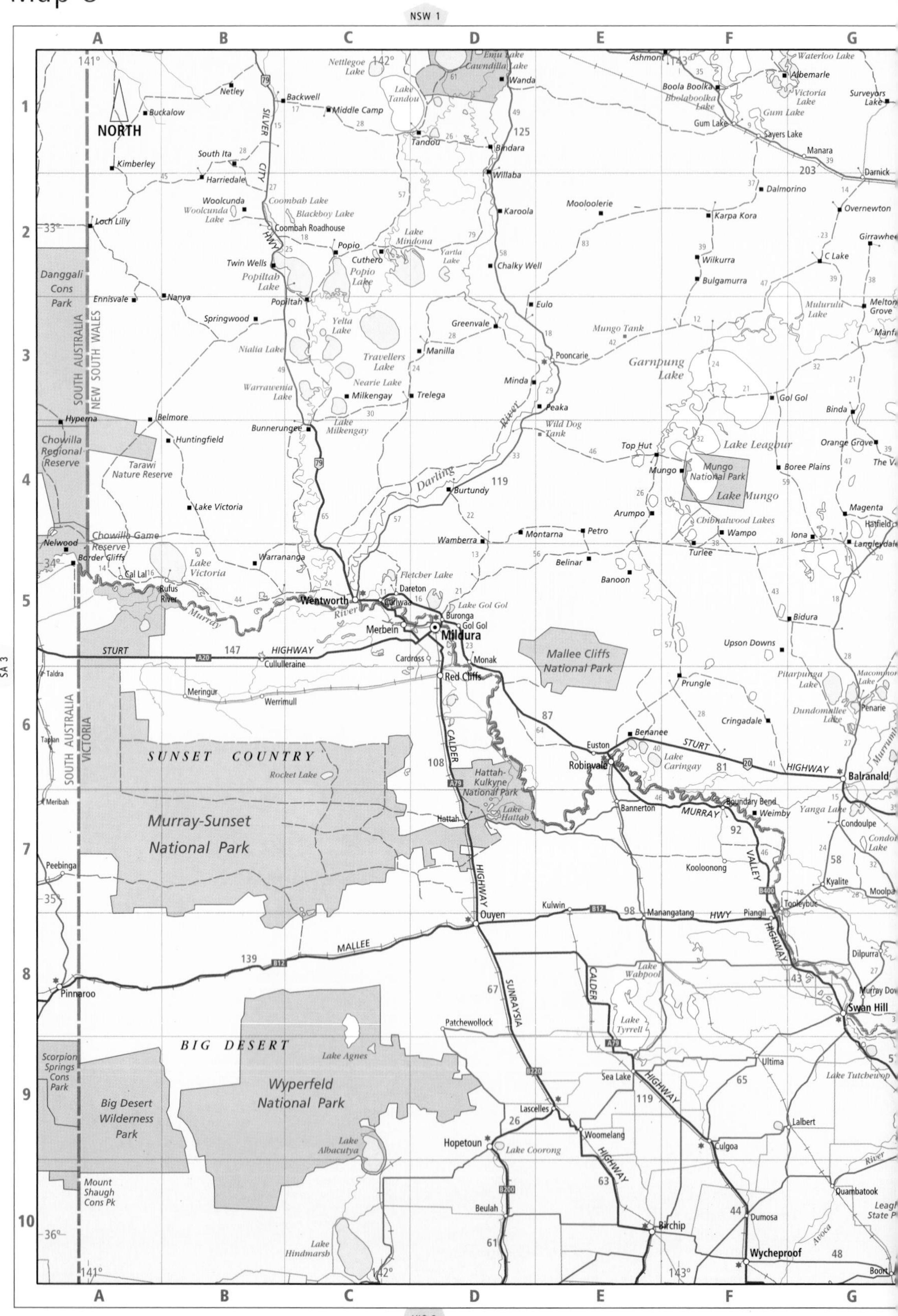
NSW 1
VIC 2
SA 3
NORTH
SOUTH AUSTRALIA
NEW SOUTH WALES
VICTORIA
Netley
Buckalow
Backwell
Middle Camp
Nettlegoe Lake
Emu Lake
Cawndilla Lake
Wanda
Lake Tandou
Tandou
Bindara
Willaba
Ashmont
Boola Boolka
Bbolaboolka Lake
Gum Lake
Sayers Lake
Albemarle
Waterloo Lake
Victoria Lake
Surveyors Lake
Manara
Darnick
Kimberley
South Ita
Harriedale
SILVER CITY HWY
Woolcunda
Woolcunda Lake
Coombah Lake
Blackboy Lake
Coombah Roadhouse
Loch Lilly
Popio
Cuthero
Popio Lake
Lake Mindona
Yartla Lake
Karoola
Mooloolerie
Karpa Kora
Dalmorino
Overnewton
Girrawheen
Twin Wells
Popiltah Lake
Popiltah
Chalky Well
Wilkurra
Bulgamurra
C Lake
Danggali Cons Park
Ennisvale
Nanya
Springwood
Yelta Lake
Eulo
Greenvale
Mungo Tank
Mulurulu Lake
Melton Grove
Nialia Lake
Manilla
Travellers Lake
Pooncarie
Garnpung Lake
Warrawenia Lake
Nearie Lake
Milkengay
Trelega
Minda
Gol Gol
Binda
Hyperna
Belmore
Peaka
Bunnerungee
Lake Milkengay
Wild Dog Tank
Chowilla Regional Reserve
Huntingfield
Top Hut
Lake Leaghur
Orange Grove
Tarawi Nature Reserve
Darling River
Mungo
Mungo National Park
Boree Plains
Burtundy
Lake Mungo
Lake Victoria
Arumpo
Magenta
Chibnalwood Lakes
Hatfield
Chowilla Game Reserve
Wamberra
Montarna
Petro
Wampo
Iona
Langleydale
Nelwood
Border Cliffs
Warrananga
Turlee
Belinar
Cal Lal
Fletcher Lake
Banoon
Rufus River
Murray River
Wentworth
Dareton
Curlwaa
Lake Gol Gol
Bidura
Merbein
Buronga
Mildura
Upson Downs
STURT HIGHWAY
Cullulleraine
Cardross
Monak
Mallee Cliffs National Park
Taldra
Red Cliffs
Prungle
Pitarpunga Lake
Meringur
Werrimull
Macommon Lake
Dundomallee Lake
Penarie
Cringadale
Taplan
Benanee
SUNSET COUNTRY
CALDER
Euston
Robinvale
Lake Caringay
Balranald
Rocket Lake
Hattah-Kulkyne National Park
Meribah
Bannerton
Boundary Bend
Weimby
Yanga Lake
Murray-Sunset National Park
Hattah
Lake Hattah
MURRAY
Condoulpe
Condor Lake
Peebinga
Kooloonong
VALLEY
Kyalite
HIGHWAY
Moolpa
Tooleybuc
Ouyen
Kulwin
Manangatang
HWY
Piangil
MALLEE
Dilpurra
CALDER
Lake Wahpool
Pinnaroo
SUNRAYSIA
Murray Downs
Swan Hill
Patchewollock
Lake Tyrrell
BIG DESERT
Lake Agnes
Scorpion Springs Cons Park
Ultima
Sea Lake
Wyperfeld National Park
Lake Tutchewop
Big Desert Wilderness Park
Lascelles
Lalbert
Lake Albacutya
Hopetoun
Lake Coorong
Woomelang
Culgoa
Mount Shaugh Cons Pk
Quambatook
Beulah
Dumosa
Leaghur State Park
Avoca
Birchip
Lake Hindmarsh
Wycheproof
Boort

0 10 20 30 40 50
kilometres

NSW 1

H J K L M N P

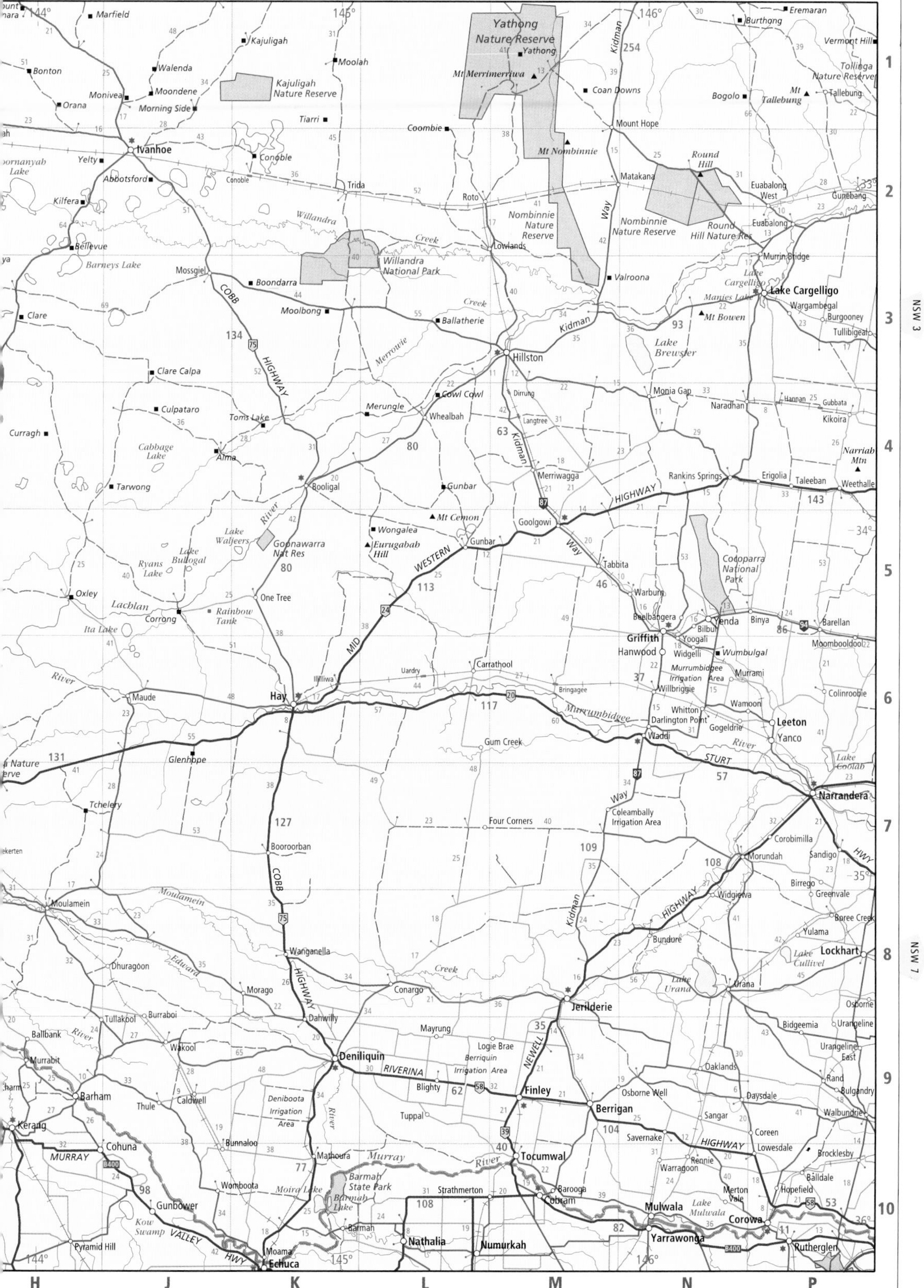

NSW 3
NSW 7

H J K L M N P

VIC 3

Map 6

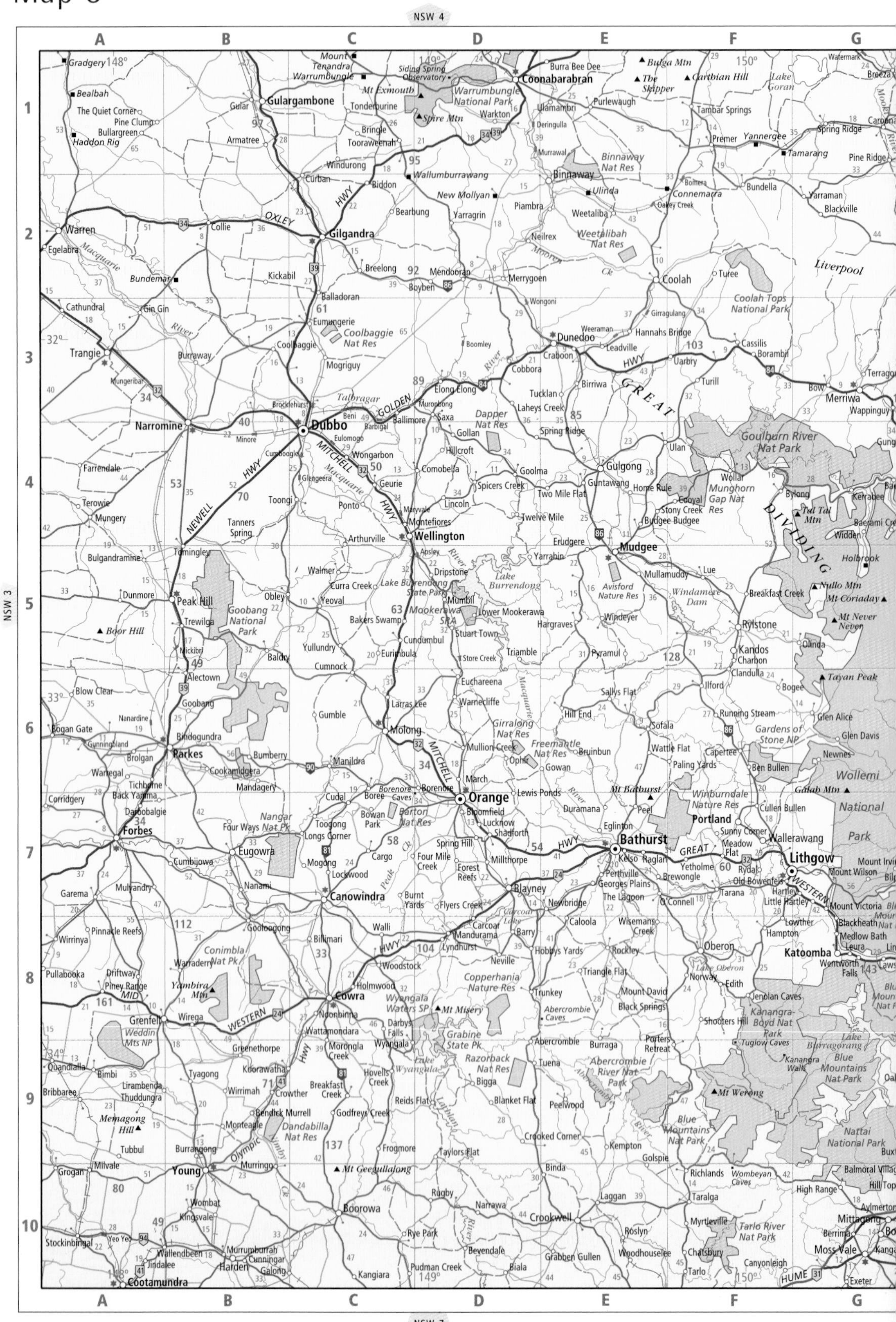
NSW 4
NSW 3
NSW 7
A
B
C
D
E
F
G
1
2
3
4
5
6
7
8
9
10
Gradgery
Bealbah
The Quiet Corner
Pine Clump
Bullargreen
Haddon Rig
Gulargambone
Gular
Armatree
Mount Tenandra
Warrumbungle
Siding Spring Observatory
Mt Exmouth
Warrumbungle National Park
Spire Mtn
Tonderburine
Bringle
Tooraweenah
Coonabarabran
Burra Bee Dee
Bugaldie
Ulamambri
Deringulla
Warkton
Purlewaugh
Bulga Mtn
The Skipper
Carthian Hill
Tambar Springs
Premer
Yannergee
Tamarang
Spring Ridge
Pine Ridge
Breeza
Lake Goran
Windurong
Curban
Biddon
Wallumburrawang
New Mollyan
Binnaway
Binnaway Nat Res
Ulinda
Connemarra
Bundella
Yarraman
Blackville
Warren
Egelabra
Collie
OXLEY
Gilgandra
Bearbung
Yarragrin
Piambra
Weetaliba
Neilrex
Weetalibah Nat Res
Bundemar
Kickabil
Breelong
Mendooran
Boyben
Merrygoen
Coolah
Turee
Liverpool
Cathundral
Gin Gin
Balladoran
Eumungerie
Coolbaggie Nat Res
Wongoni
Girragulang
Coolah Tops National Park
Trangie
Burraway
Coolbaggie
Mogriguy
Boomley
Dunedoo
Weeraman
Craboon
Hannahs Bridge
Leadville
Cassilis
Borambil
Uarbry
Mungeribar
Narromine
Dubbo
Brocklehurst
Talbragar
GOLDEN
Elong Elong
Cobbora
Tucklan
Birriwa
Turill
Merriwa
Terragon
Wappinguy
Minore
Eulomogo
Barbigal
Ballimore
Muronbong
Saxa
Gollan
Dapper Nat Res
Laheys Creek
Spring Ridge
GREAT
Ulan
Goulburn River Nat Park
Farrendale
Cumboogle
MITCHELL
HWY
Wongarbon
Hillcroft
Comobella
Gulgong
Wollar
Goolma
Terowie
Mungery
NEWELL
Toongi
Geurie
Ponto
Spicers Creek
Lincoln
Two Mile Flat
Guntawang
Home Rule
Munghorn Gap Nat Res
Cooyal
Stony Creek
Budgee Budgee
Bylong
Kerrabee
Tanners Spring
Maryvale
Montefiores
Twelve Mile
DIVIDING
Tal Tal Mtn
Baerami Creek
Widden
Bulgandramine
Tomingley
Arthurville
Wellington
Erudgere
Mudgee
Holbrook
Apsley
Dripstone
Yarrabin
Mullamuddy
Lue
Lake Burrendong
Avisford Nature Res
Windamere Dam
Nullo Mtn
Mt Coriaday
Dunmore
Peak Hill
Goobang National Park
Obley
Walmer
Curra Creek
Yeoval
Lake Burrendong State Park
Mumbil
Mookerawa SRA
Lower Mookerawa
Windeyer
Breakfast Creek
Mt Never Never
Trewilga
Boor Hill
Bakers Swamp
Cundumbul
Stuart Town
Hargraves
Rylstone
Olinda
Yullundry
Eurimbula
Triamble
Pyramul
Kandos
Charbon
Clandulla
Nickibri
Alectown
Baldry
Cumnock
Store Creek
Tayan Peak
Euchareena
Bogee
Blow Clear
Goobang
Warnecliffe
Sallys Flat
Ilford
Gumble
Larras Lee
Macquarie
Hill End
Running Stream
Glen Alice
Bogan Gate
Nanardine
Bindogundra
Molong
Girralong Nat Res
Sofala
Gardens of Stone NP
Glen Davis
Gunningbland
Parkes
Bumberry
Mullion Creek
Freemantle Nat Res
Bruinbun
Wattle Flat
Capertee
Newnes
Brolgan
Cookamidgera
Manildra
Ophir
Gowan
Paling Yards
Ben Bullen
Wollemi
Wamegal
Mandagery
March
Mt Bathurst
Winburndale Nature Res
Tichborne
Back Yamma
Corridgery
Cudal
Boree
Borenore Caves
Borenore
Orange
Lewis Ponds
Duramana
Cullen Bullen
Galah Mtn
National
Daroobalgie
Nangar Nat Pk
Bowan Park
Barton Nat Res
Bloomfield
Lucknow
Shadforth
Eglinton
Peel
Portland
Forbes
Four Ways
Toogong
Longs Corner
Spring Hill
Bathurst
Sunny Corner
Wallerawang
Park
Eugowra
Cargo
Four Mile Creek
Millthorpe
Kelso
Raglan
Meadow Flat
Lithgow
Mount Irvine
Cumbijowa
Mogong
Lockwood
Forest Reefs
Perthville
Yetholme
Rydal
Mount Wilson
Garema
Mulyandry
Nanami
Canowindra
Burnt Yards
Flyers Creek
Blayney
Georges Plains
Brewongle
Old Bowenfels
Hartley
Little Hartley
The Lagoon
Newbridge
O'Connell
Tarana
WESTERN
Mount Victoria
Pinnacle Reefs
Gooloogong
Carcoar Lake
Carcoar
Caloola
Wisemans Creek
Lowther
Blackheath
Hampton
Medlow Bath
Wirrinya
Billimari
Walli
Mandurama
Barry
Lyndhurst
Rockley
Oberon
Leura
Katoomba
Conimbla Nat Pk
Neville
Hobbys Yards
Pullabooka
Driftway
Warraderry
Woodstock
Copperhania Nature Res
Triangle Flat
Lake Oberon
Norway
Wentworth Falls
Yambira Mtn
Piney Range
MID
Holmwood
Mount David
Edith
Jenolan Caves
Cowra
Wyangala Waters SP
Mt Misery
Trunkey
Abercrombie Caves
Black Springs
Kanangra-Boyd Nat Park
Grenfell
Wirega
Noonbinna
Wattamondara
Darbys Falls
Shooters Hill
Weddin Mts NP
Greenethorpe
Morongla Creek
Wyangala
Grabine State Pk
Abercrombie
Burraga
Porters Retreat
Tuglow Caves
Lake Burragorang
Quandialla
Bimbi
Koorawatha
Hovells Creek
Razorback Nat Res
Tuena
Abercrombie River Nat Park
Kanangra Walls
Blue Mountains Nat Park
Tyagong
Lake Wyangala
Bribbaree
Thuddungra
Wirrimah
Crowther
Breakfast Creek
Reids Flat
Bigga
Blanket Flat
Peelwood
Mt Werong
Memagong Hill
Bendick Murrell
Godfreys Creek
Lachlan
Blue Mountains Nat Park
Monteagle
Dandabilla Nat Res
Crooked Corner
Nattai National Park
Tubbul
Burrangong
Olympic
Frogmore
Taylors Flat
Kempton
Golspie
Milvale
Young
Murringo
Mt Geegullalong
Binda
Richlands
Wombeyan Caves
Balmoral Village
Hill Top
Grogan
Wombat
Rugby
Laggan
Taralga
High Range
Kingsvale
Boorowa
Narrawa
Crookwell
Mittagong
Stockinbingal
Yeo Yeo
Rye Park
Roslyn
Myrtleville
Tarlo River Nat Park
Berrima
Wallendbeen
Murrumburrah
Cunningar
Harden
Galong
Jindalee
Bevendale
Woodhouselee
Chatsbury
Moss Vale
Cootamundra
Kangiara
Pudman Creek
Biala
Grabben Gullen
Tarlo
Canyonleigh
HUME
Exeter
148°
149°
150°
32°
33°
34°

0 10 20 30 40 50
kilometres

H J K L M N P

1 2 3 4 5 6 7 8 9 10

NSW

SOUTH

TASMAN

PACIFIC

SEA

OCEAN

NORTH

Port Macquarie
Wauchope
Taree
Wingham
Gloucester
Forster
Tuncurry
Bulahdelah
Dungog
Nelson Bay
Raymond Terrace
Maitland
Newcastle
Cessnock
Kurri Kurri
Singleton
Muswellbrook
Scone
Aberdeen
Murrurundi
Quirindi
Werris Creek
Gosford
Wyong
The Entrance
Hornsby
Parramatta
SYDNEY
Bondi Junction
Liverpool
Campbelltown
Richmond
Windsor
Penrith
Wollongong
Port Kembla
Shellharbour

Barrington Tops National Park
Myall Lakes National Park
Royal National Park
Yengo National Park
Wollemi National Park

GREAT DIVIDING RANGE

PACIFIC HWY
NEW ENGLAND HWY
GOLDEN HWY
OXLEY HWY

152°
153°
151°
32°
33°
34°

H J K L M N P

Map 7

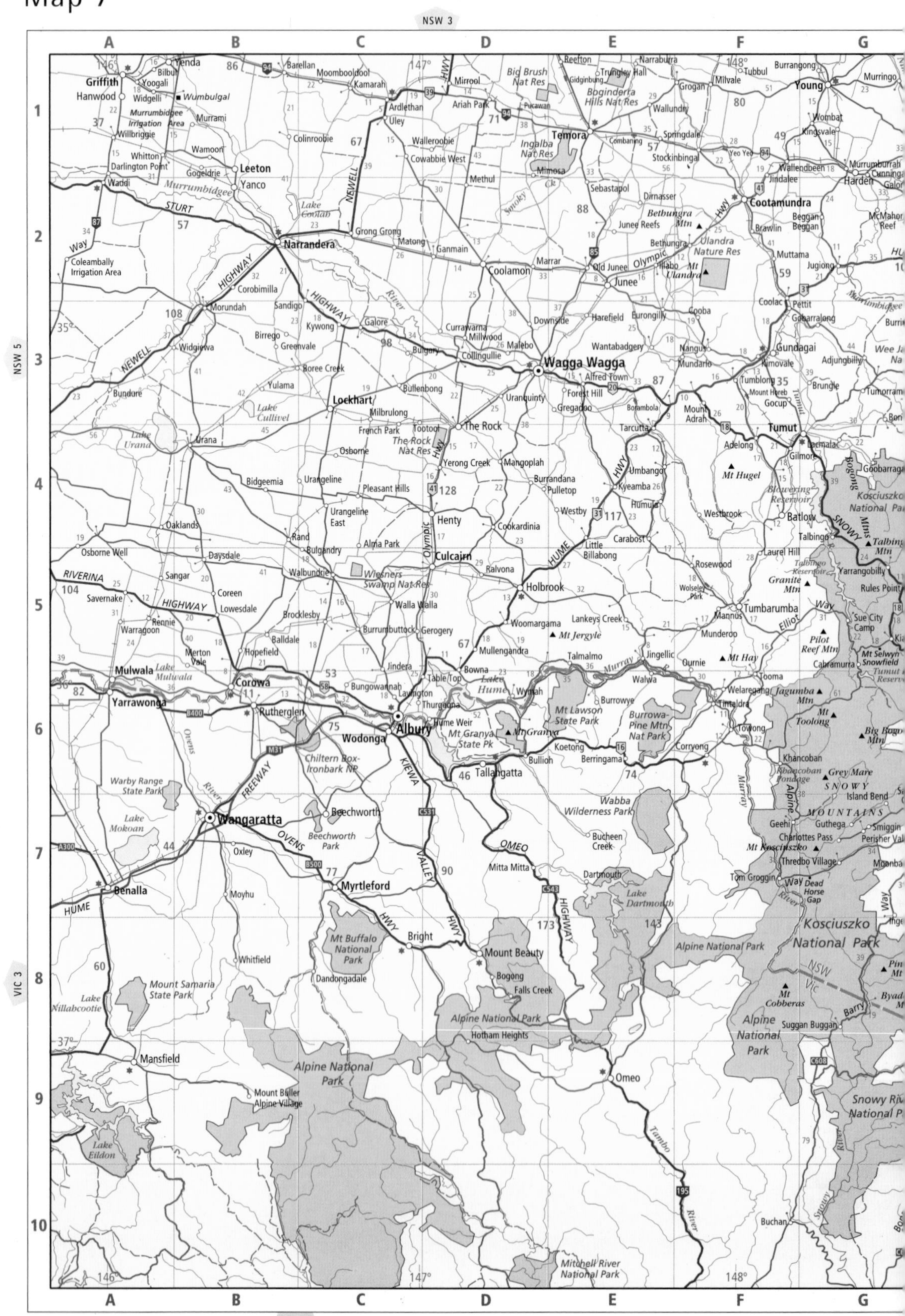
NSW 3
A
B
C
D
E
F
G
1
2
3
4
5
6
7
8
9
10
NSW 5
VIC 3
VIC 3
Griffith
Hanwood
Yenda
Bilbul
Yoogali
Widgelli
Wumbulgal
Murrumbidgee Irrigation Area
Murrami
Willbriggie
Whitton
Darlington Point
Wamoon
Gogeldrie
Leeton
Yanco
Waddi
Murrumbidgee
STURT
Way
Coleambally Irrigation Area
Barellan
Moombooldool
Kamarah
Ardlethan
Uley
Colinroobie
Mirrool
Ariah Park
Big Brush Nat Res
Pucawan
Reefton
Trungley Hall
Narraburra
Gidginbung
Bogindera Hills Nat Res
Temora
Ingalba Nat Res
Combaning
Springdale
Wallundry
Grogan
Milvale
Tubbul
Burrangong
Young
Murringo
Wombat
Kingsvale
Yeo Yeo
Stockinbingal
Wallendbeen
Jindalee
Murrumburrah
Harden
Cunningar
Galong
Cootamundra
Walleroobie
Cowabbie West
Methul
Mimosa Ck
Sebastapol
Dirnasser
Bethungra Mtn
Junee Reefs
Bethungra
Ulandra Nature Res
Mt Ulandra
Illabo
Olympic
Hwy
Brawlin
Beggan Beggan
McMahons Reef
Muttama
Jugiong
Lake Coolah
NEWELL
Grong Grong
Matong
Ganmain
Narrandera
Coolamon
Marrar
Old Junee
Junee
HIGHWAY
Corobimilla
Morundah
Sandigo
Kywong
Galore
River
Currawarna
Millwood
Malebo
Downside
Harefield
Eurongilly
Cooba
Coolac
Pettit
Gobarralong
Murrumbidgee
Burrinjuck
Birrego
Greenvale
Widgiewa
Bulgary
Collingullie
Wagga Wagga
Alfred Town
Wantabadgery
Nangus
Mundarlo
Gundagai
Kimovale
Adjungbilly
Wee Jasper
Bundure
Yulama
Boree Creek
Bullenbong
Uranquinty
Forest Hill
Gregadoo
Bomambola
Tumblong
Mount Horeb
Gocup
Brungle
Tumorrama
Lockhart
Milbrulong
French Park
Tootool
The Rock
The Rock Nat Res
Lake Cullivel
Lake Urana
Urana
Mount Adrah
Tarcutta
Tumut
Lacmalac
Adelong
Gilmore
Osborne
Yerong Creek
Mangoplah
Umbango
Mt Hugel
Goobarragandra
Bidgeemia
Urangeline
Pleasant Hills
Burrandana
Pulletop
Kyeamba
Humula
Blowering Reservoir
Kosciuszko National Park
Bogong
Mtns
Urangeline East
Henty
Westby
Westbrook
Batlow
Oaklands
Rand
Bulgandry
Alma Park
Cookardinia
Carabost
Talbingo
SNOWY
Talbingo Mtn
Osborne Well
Daysdale
Culcairn
Ralvona
Little Billabong
Laurel Hill
Rosewood
Talbingo Reservoir
Yarrangobilly
RIVERINA
Sangar
Walbundrie
Wiesners Swamp Nat Res
Holbrook
HUME
Granite Mtn
Rules Point
Savernake
Coreen
Lowesdale
HIGHWAY
Rennie
Walla Walla
Lankeys Creek
Wolseley Park
Mannus
Tumbarumba
Way
Sue City Camp
Warragoon
Brocklesby
Burrumbuttock
Gerogery
Woomargama
Mt Jergyle
Munderoo
Elliot
Pilot Reef Mtn
Merton Vale
Balldale
Hopefield
Mullengandra
Talmalmo
Jingellic
Ournie
Mt Hay
Cabramurra
Mt Selwyn Snowfield
Tumut Reserve
Mulwala
Lake Mulwala
Corowa
Jindera
Bungowannah
Bowna
Lake Hume
Murray
Walwa
Tooma
Welaregang
Jagumba Mtn
Yarrawonga
Rutherglen
Lavington
Table Top
Thurgoona
Wymah
Burrowye
Tintaldra
Mt Toolong
Big Bogong Mtn
Ovens
Wodonga
Albury
Hume Weir
Mt Granya State Pk
Mt Granya
Mt Lawson State Park
Burrowa-Pine Mtn Nat Park
Towong
Corryong
FREEWAY
Chiltern Box-Ironbark NP
KIEWA
Tallangatta
Bullioh
Koetong
Berringama
Khancoban
Khancoban Pondage
Grey Mare
SNOWY
MOUNTAINS
Island Bend
Warby Range State Park
River
Wangaratta
Beechworth
Wabba Wilderness Park
Alpine
Geehi
Guthega
Smiggin
Perisher Valley
Lake Mokoan
OVENS
Beechworth Park
Bucheen Creek
Charlottes Pass
Mt Kosciuszko
Thredbo Village
Moonbah
Oxley
OMEO
VALLEY
Mitta Mitta
Dartmouth
Lake Dartmouth
Tom Groggin
Dead Horse Gap
Benalla
Moyhu
Myrtleford
HWY
HIGHWAY
HUME
Bright
Mount Beauty
Alpine National Park
Kosciuszko National Park
Mt Buffalo National Park
Whitfield
Bogong
Falls Creek
NSW
Vic
Mt Cobberas
Barry
Mount Samaria State Park
Dandongadale
Lake Nillahcootie
Alpine National Park
Hotham Heights
Alpine National Park
Suggan Buggan
Mansfield
Alpine National Park
Omeo
Mount Buller Alpine Village
Snowy River National Park
Lake Eildon
Tambo
River
Buchan
Snowy
Mitchell River National Park
146°
147°
148°
35°
36°
37°

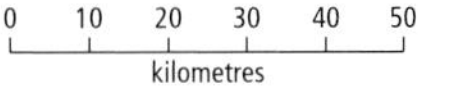

NSW 6

H J K L M N P

NORTH

Frogmore, Taylors Flat, Mt Geegullalong, Kempton, Golspie, Binda, Richlands, Wombeyan Caves, Nattai National Park, Buxton, Balmoral Village, Hill Top, Tahmoor, Wilton, Bargo, Yanderra, Yerrinbool, Coalcliff, Thirroul, Corrimal, Balgownie, Lake Cordeaux, Avon Lake

1

Boorowa, Rugby, Narrawa, Crookwell, Laggan, Taralga, High Range, Mandemar, Aylmerton, Mittagong, Bowral, Wollongong, Unanderra, Dapto, Red Point, Port Kembla, Rye Park, Roslyn, Myrtleville, Tarlo River Nat Park, Berrima, Moss Vale, Kangaloon, Lake Illawarra, Shellharbour, Bass Point, Bevendale, Grabben Gullen, Woodhouselee, Chatsbury, Canyonleigh, Robertson, Albion Park, Kangiara, Pudman Creek, Biala, Tarlo, Exeter, Jamberoo, Minnamurra, Kiama, Blakney Creek, Kingsdale, Towrang, Marulan, HUME, Bundanoon, Lake Yarrunga, Kangaroo Valley, Budderoo NP, Werri Beach, Gerringong, Goondah, Dalton, Kenmore, Tallong, Wingello

2

Bowning, Gunning, Breadalbane, Yarra, Goulburn, Shoalhaven River, Tallowa Dam, Berry, HWY, Gerroa, Jaspers Brush, Yass, HWY, Mt Dixon, Bungonia, Komungla, Morton National Park, Bomaderry, Nowra, Shoalhaven, Shoalhaven Heads, Bight, Culburra, Yass River, BARTON, Bellmount Forest, Collector, Inveralochy, Yalwal, Ettrema Hill, Falls Creek, Crookhaven Bight, Beecroft Head, Currarong, Jervis Bay NP, Point Perpendicular, Murrumbateman, Lake Bathurst, Windellama, Callala Bay, Huskisson, Vincentia, Cavan, Lake Burrinjuck, Gundaroo, Lake George, Sandy Point, Tomerong, Wandandian, Jervis Bay, Jervis Bay Nat Park, Sussex Inlet, St Georges Head, Wee Jasper, FEDERAL, Tarago, Lake Bathurst, Sassafras, Nerriga

3

Brindabella Nat Park, Sutton, Bywong, Boro, Lower Boro, PRINCES, Cudmirrah, Wreck Bay, Ginninderra, Belconnen, Bradon, KINGS, RANGE, Morton National Park, Conjola, Bendalong, Lake Burley Griffin, CANBERRA, Bungendore, Charleyong, Yatteyattah, Lake Conjola, South Canberra, Fyshwick, Burbong, Milton, Mollymook, Ulladulla, Weston Creek, Woden Valley, Queanbeyan, Yadboro Flat, Warden Head, Brindabella, Tuggeranong, Hoskinstown, Braidwood, HWY, Burrill Lake, Bendora Dam, Googong Reservoir, Rossi, Mongarlowe, Budawang Nat Park, Tabourie Lake

4

Tharwa, Royalla, Termeil, Bawley Point, Kioloa, AUSTRALIAN CAPITAL TERRITORY, Williamsdale, Captains Flat, Ballalaba, Majors Creek, East Lynne, Murramarang Nat Park, Durras North, Durras Lake, Durras, Araluen North, Araluen, Nelligen, Tinderry NR, Tantangara Reservoir, Mt Kelly, Scabby Range NR, Namadgi National Park, Michelago, Togganoggera, Deua Nat Park, Batemans Bay, Long Beach, North Head, Batemans Bay, Batehaven, Mogo, Tomakin, Malua Bay, Yaouk, MONARO, Jingera, DIVIDING, Wyanbene Caves Mtn, Wyanbene Caves, Mongamula Mtn, Mossy Point, Broulee

5

Nungar, Colinton, Jerangle, Deua National Park, Garlandtown, Moruya, Moruya Heads, Bugtown, Shannons Flat, Rosedale, Bredbo, Whinstone Hill, Snowball, Big Badja Hill, Congo, MTS, Adaminaby, Old Adaminaby, Peak View, Turlinjah, Tuross Head, Tuross Lake, Potato Point, Lake Eucumbene, Chakola, Bodalla, Nerrigundah, Eurobodalla, Brou Lake

6

Buckenderra, Bunyan, Numeralla, Jillicambra Mtn, Countegany, River, Dalmeny, Kianga, Wagonga Inlet, Narooma, Rocky Plains, HWY, Cooma, Tuross, Montague Island, Central Tilba, Cape Dromadery, Yowrie, PRINCES, Tilba Tilba, Jindabyne, Berridale, Rock Flat, GREAT, Kybeyan, Wadbilliga National Park, Cobargo, Wallaga Lake, Wallaga Lake NP, SOUTH, East Jindabyne, Jindabyne, Hudsons Peak, MONARO, Cooerang, Bermagui, Bermagui South, Dalgety, Snowy, Bobundara, Bald Hill, Dandelong Nature Res, Quaama

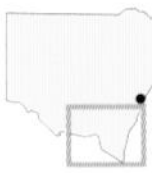

7

Beloka, Nimmitabel, Warrigal Mtn, Biamanga Nat Pk, Goalen Head, Bunga Head, TASMAN, Brogo, Bunga, Paupong, Wapengo, Mimosa Rocks, Bemboka Nat Pk, Tanja, Wapengo Lake National Park, Numbla Vale, Bemboka, Numbugga, Bega, Bungarby, Kameruka, Tathra, SEA, Ando, Tantawangalo National Park, Jellat Jellat, Kalaru, Mt Rix, Candelo, Bemm River, Bukalong, Mount Darrah, Yurammie, Wolumla, Wallagoot Lake, Bournda Nat Pk, PACIFIC

8

Mt Alexander, Bibbenluke, Cathcart, South East Forest NP, Merimbula, Corrowong, Bombala, Wyndham, Pambula, Pambula Beach, Coolangubra National Park, Lochiel, Haycock Point, Yowaka Nat Pk, Ben Boyd NP, Burragate, Genoa Nat Pk, Towamba, Eden, Delegate, Craigie, Mila, Pericoe, Twofold Bay, Bondi Gulf Nat Pk, Mt Wog Wog, East Boyd, Mt Imlay Nat Pk, Kiah, Mowarry Point, OCEAN

9

Bonang, Bendoc, Nungatta Mtn, Mt Poole, Mt Imlay, Wonboyn Lake, Nungatta, Narrabarba, NEW SOUTH WALES, Green Cape, Chandlers Creek, Coopracambra National Park, VICTORIA, HWY, Disaster Bay, Erinundra National Park, Timbillica, Nadgee Nature Reserve, Nadgee Point, CANN VALLEY HWY, Genoa, Gipsy Point, Cape Howe

10

Lind Nat Pk, Cann River, PRINCES, Alfred Nat Pk, Mallacoota, Mallacoota Inlet, Gabo Island

149° 150° 151°

35° 36° 37°

H J K L M N P

VIC 4

NSW

Victoria

The small state of Victoria is truly a wonderland for outdoor enthusiasts, with over a tenth of its area devoted to national or state parks, reserves and protected historical sites. Its natural beauty extends from the mountainous High Country and large tracts of rugged forests to coastlines offering white sandy beaches, remote stretches of seashore and the magical Great Ocean Road. It encompasses the wonderful Gippsland lakes and the Little Desert, the magnificent Grampians and the open plains and low scrub of the mallee. Victoria is indeed fortunate to have such a large number of diverse multi-use parks, where walkers play alongside campers, climbers, horseriders and four-wheel drivers—all joined by their common love of the outdoors and their interest in its conservation.

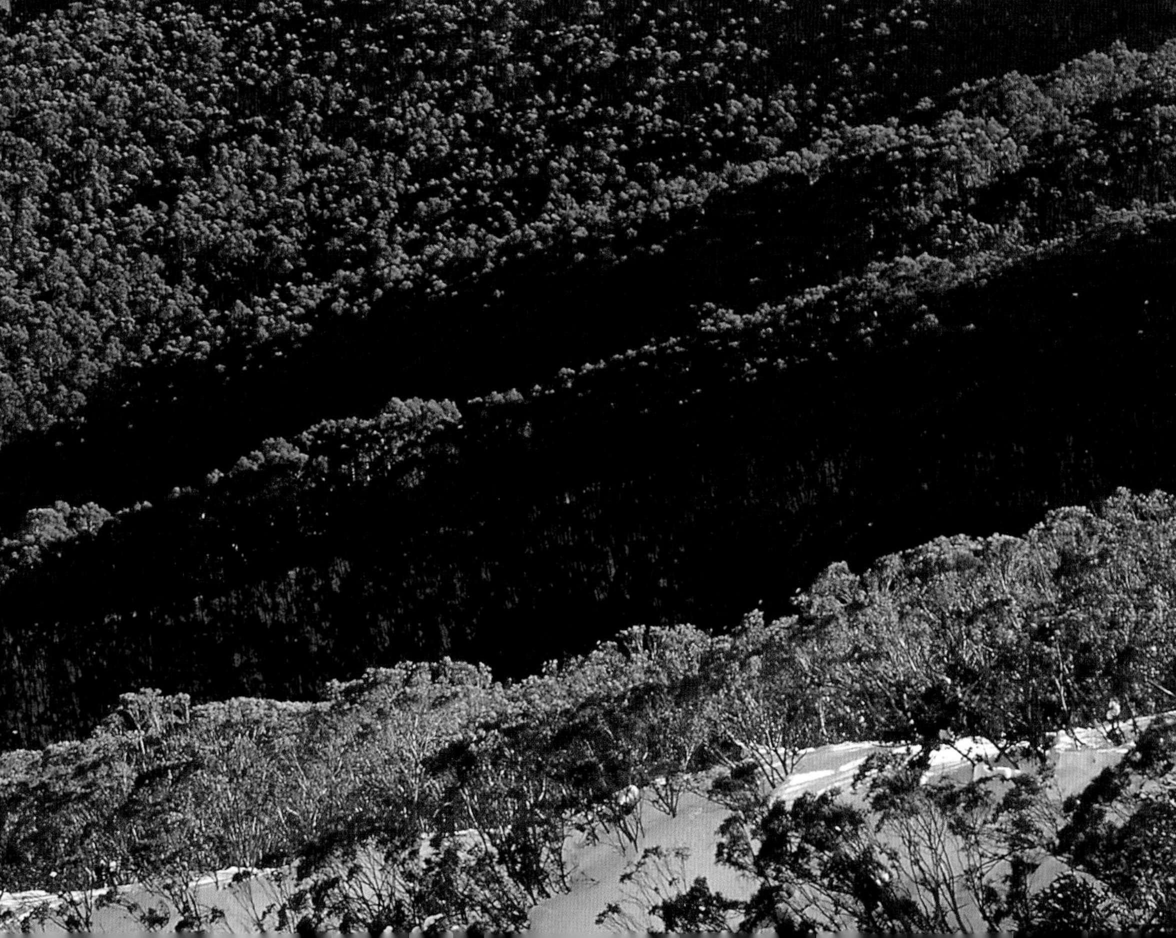

Alpine National Park

Covering a vast area of 646 000 hectares, the Alpine National Park is Victoria's biggest, and one of Australia's finest parks, offering rugged mountains, powerful rivers, remote snowfields, open plains and deep gorges which open out to reveal green valleys. Reaching far across the Dividing Range, this park forms an important natural corridor for its unique flora and fauna and is best treated in six different sections: Mount Hotham–Feathertop; Wombargo–The Cobberas; Tingaringy; Bogong High Plains; Wonnangatta–Moroka; and Mount Buller–Stirling.

fact file

WHERE: Extends across the Great Dividing Range from Mansfield, through to the border with New South Wales, with access 230–500 km from Melbourne
Map: Vic 4 D4

WHEN: All year

WHY: Mountain scenery, skiing in winter, swimming, walking, 4WD tours, cycling, horse-riding, canoeing, nature study, photography, historical interest

SIZE: 646 000 ha

INFORMATION: Parks Victoria 131 963

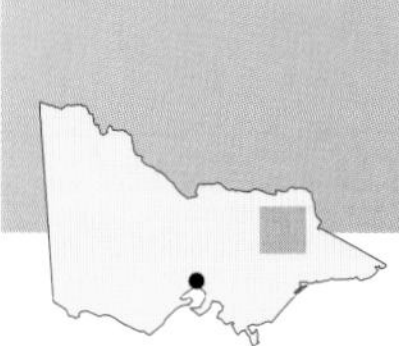

In the Past

Australian Aboriginals resided in this mountain region for thousands of years, but it was in 1824 that Hume and Hovell explored and named the Australian Alps.

Many different types of people were to venture across and inhabit the peaks, including miners during the mining booms, loggers, graziers and workers on hydro-electric schemes.

The push to protect the region as a national park first came from the newly formed Victorian National Parks Association during the 1960s, but it wasn't until December 1989 that the Alpine National Park was proclaimed.

A Diversity of Life

The alpine region is ever-changing; snow covers the upper reaches for most of winter, while summer brings heat to both the lower reaches and the mountain tops. The weather can change from extreme heat to freezing temperatures very quickly, and snow is not uncommon during the warmer months.

Right: *The crimson rosella* (Platycercus elegans) *is found in and around the tall trees in the eucalypt forests and woodlands of the park.*

Perhaps the most enduring image of the High Country is that of tall timbers. The park is dominated by eucalypts such as the mountain gum and stringybark, then further up on the peaks the alpine ash, and above the snow line, the colourful, gnarled, stunted snow gum.

During spring, as the winter snow melts, a carpet of alpine daisies, alpine marsh marigold and the alpine hovea greet walkers who utilise the ski tracks for their forays on foot.

The changing weather and the different types of vegetation lead to diversity in the wildlife. An abundance of bird life will be found on a visit to the park. Species include the noisy gang-gang cockatoo, colourful crimson rosellas and the distinctive long-beaked wattlebird.

Patient visitors will be rewarded by chance meetings with kangaroos, bats and echidnas. Wombats can be found foraging at night.

Many species of animals are endemic to this region, including the brush-tailed rock wallaby and the mountain pygmy possum. At one time the latter was thought to be extinct.

Mount Hotham–Feathertop

Mount Feathertop and Mount Hotham are among Victoria's highest peaks and provide a perfect playground for skiers and snowboarders in winter, and walkers and cyclists during the summer months.

The Hotham Heights village caters for the downhill skier, while the surrounding area boasts a remote mountain range for the ski tourer. Many cross-country skiers base themselves at nearby Dinner Plain, and the adventurous head cross-country along the Razorback trail to Mount Feathertop.

Walking tracks abound after the snow melts, and the Alpine Walking Track cuts through this region towards Falls Creek.

For up-to-date information, contact the Alpine Resorts Commission.

Above: *By far the highest mountain range on this relatively flat continent, the Australian Alps form a distinctive ecological zone, with several plant and animal species only found here.*

Left: *Snow gums* (Eucalyptus niphophila) *dominate the woodlands above the snow line. Its bark sheds in ribbons, leaving a smooth whitish-grey surface.*

Hiking at Falls Creek. When the snow melts, there are many accessible walking tracks. The 650 km Alpine Walking Track passes through the park and can be joined at Falls Creek.

Wombargo–The Cobberas

With only one access road suitable for conventional vehicles, this section in the north of the state abuts the New South Wales Kosciuszko National Park. Visitors with conventional vehicles should use Black Mountain Road to access the popular camping areas of Native Dog Flat, Willis on the Snowy River and the Cobberas Wilderness Area. Four-wheel drivers have a much greater choice of tracks and routes through this region.

The peaks of Mount Cobberas One and Two are popular bases for walks, as is Cowombat Flat with its wreckage of a DC-3 aircraft that crashed in 1954.

Tingaringy

As the highest peak east of the Snowy River, Mount Tingaringy offers commanding views of the New South Wales Kosciuszko Range and the peaks down south towards the Snowy River. Most of this region is classified as a wilderness area and at the border of New South Wales adjoins the Kosciuszko National Park and Byadbo Wilderness Area. Because mechanical means of transport are not permitted, it is mainly bushwalkers who use this remote and inhospitable region. Water can be scarce here in summer, so bushwalkers need to be well prepared and self-sufficient.

Bogong High Plains

The early graziers brought their cattle to the lush, grassy Bogong High Plains during summer and these plains were one of the first places you could ski in Victoria in the early 1900s.

Today the area is popular with visitors in both summer and winter as it still offers snow skiing, and also provides bushwalking, bike and horseriding, and trout fishing in the Rocky Valley Dam and Pretty Valley Pondage.

Wallace's Hut, built by the Wallace Brothers in 1889, is the oldest of the cattlemen's huts still standing in the park and it is classified by the National Trust. This building is not far from the Bogong High Plains Road, near Falls Creek.

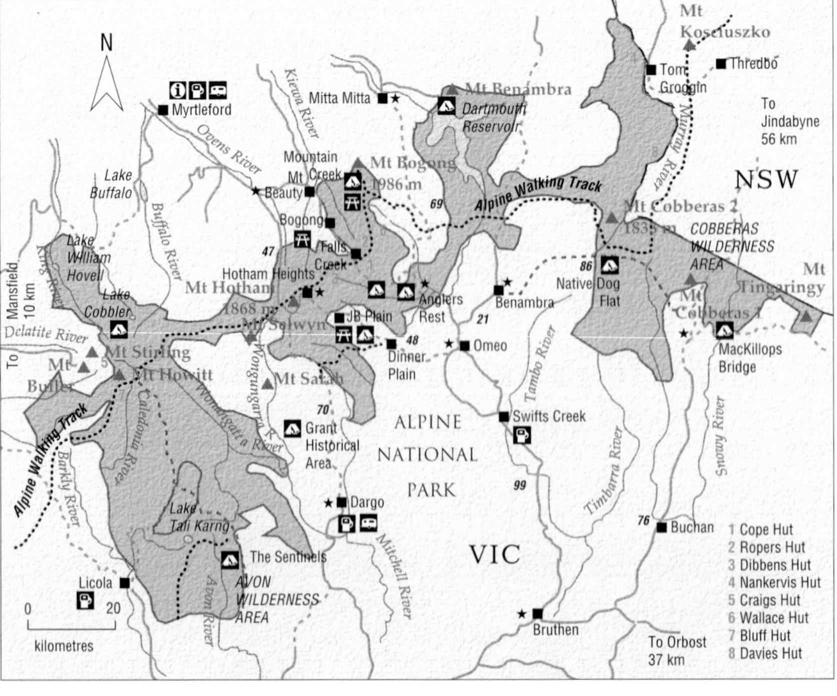

Opposite page: *Visitors to the Alpine National Park can gain access to beautiful Bindaree Falls from Mount Stirling Circuit Road which winds through sub-alpine and alpine forest.*

Right: *The spectacular view of crags and escarpments from The Bluff. This 200 metre high rocky escarpment can be reached either on foot or on horseback.*

Wonnangatta–Moroka

This section of the park is one of the more popular, offering a wide range of walking and 4WD tracks, ski trails in winter for cross-country skiers, and excellent camping areas, many of which have access for conventional vehicles. For many, the main attraction is the Wonnangatta Valley with its majestic green valley floor where many pioneers settled last century.

Hidden deep in the mountains at the head of the Wellington River is the jewel of the High Country, Lake Tali Karng, which is accessible on foot and can only be viewed from the Sentinel and Echo Point on Rigalls Spur. Many walkers enjoy the 28 km hike, spending more than one night camped by the beautiful sapphire blue lake.

did you know?

Victoria's high country is the stuff of legends. The film *The Man from Snowy River*, based on A. B. 'Banjo' Paterson's poem of the same name, was made at Craig's Hut and other locations in the Alpine National Park. The Snowy River runs through the north-east of the park and into New South Wales.

Mount Buller–Stirling and Lake Cobbler

Only 2 hours drive from Melbourne, Mount Buller and Mount Stirling are two of the state capital's favourite playgrounds, with Stirling offering excellent cross-country skiing and popular walking trails, while Buller caters for Melbourne's downhill ski enthusiasts. With many trails surrounding the two mountains and leading up to Lake Cobbler, 4WD touring and cycling are popular pastimes.

Kelly's Hut, in the Victorian Alps. Many such huts were built by the early pioneers. Today the huts are used as temporary and emergency accommodation.

High Country Huts

Scattered throughout the park are a number of huts, most of which once belonged to the pioneers that grazed their cattle on the high plains during summer and which are part of the rich cultural heritage of the alpine region.

The most popular huts to visit include Wallace's Hut on the Bogong High Plains, and Bluff Hut and Craig's Hut in the region near Mansfield. Off the Howitt Road you will find Guy's Hut and the ruins of the Old Wonnangatta Station, while Davies Plain Hut is in the northern part of the park.

Activities

4WD touring is a very popular way to enjoy the park, especially where access is impossible by conventional vehicles.

One of the favourite areas to visit, Wonnangatta Valley, is in the centre of the park, north of Licola. There is camping aplenty in the valley and attractions include the site of a burnt-out station on the banks of Conglomerate Creek and a cemetery perched on the hillside under towering pine trees.

Other interesting tours in the alpine park include Dargo and the Crooked River–Talbotville area, Jacksons Crossing on the Snowy River and the Deddick Trail. The more adventurous and experienced might like to tackle Butcher Country Track or the mountain country around Davies Plain.

This park is very popular with walkers. Popular short walks include the return trek from the Bogong High Plains to Wallace's Hut and another fairly easy walk from Howitt Road to Bryces Gorge.

While there are many walks within the park, by far the most impressive is the Alpine Walking Track which extends 650 km from the old goldmining town of Walhalla, across the rugged mountain range, into New South Wales, finishing in the Australian Capital Territory.

The Alps of Victoria also offer premium fishing, mountain-bike riding, horseriding and canoeing country. In fact, here in this vast park, there is something for everybody.

Camping in the high country. Many bitumen and good quality roads give access to camping sites with facilities, but hikers have the best opportunity to access more remote wilderness areas.

Access and Camping

Many bitumen and good quality roads lead to the major regions within the park.

The Mount Buller–Stirling area can be reached via Mansfield, north of Melbourne, along good quality gravel roads, while the Wonnangatta–Moroka area is accessed via Licola, on a well-maintained gravel road, or from Dargo on 4WD tracks.

Mount Hotham is serviced by a good bitumen road from Harrietville to the north and Dargo from the south. The Snowy River Road provides access for the Tingaringy unit, while Benambra and the Black Mountain Road lead to the Cobberas region in the north-east of the park.

Remote camping is the best way to experience the magnificent Alpine Park in areas where there are no facilities provided. There are, however, some popular camping sites (with pit toilets, fireplaces and picnic facilities) accessible to conventional vehicles. These include MacKillops Bridge on the Snowy River, Sheepyard Flat and Lake Cobbler near Mount Buller, along the Wellington River north of Licola and at Anglers Rest, north of Omeo.

For details of camping locations, contact Parks Victoria, phone 131 963.

Left: *The Victorian Alps are famous for their skiing. Enthusiasts can enjoy cross-country skiing at Mount Stirling and Mount Feathertop, with downhill skiing being popular at Mount Buller and Mount Hotham.*

tourist info

Alpine Resorts Commission, Mount Hotham (03) 5759 3550

Grampians National Park

A series of jagged blue peaks forms a striking outline on the horizon, perched on the western plains of Victoria. A closer inspection reveals the ruggedness and grandeur of massive sandstone sculptures interspersed with a mosaic of colourful wildflowers. The Grampians make up this series of ranges which extend more than 80 km in length and 50 km at their widest point; they signal the end of the Great Dividing Range that starts near Cooktown in far north Queensland.

fact file

WHERE: Central western Victoria, 260 km from Melbourne and 25 km south-west of Stawell
Map: Vic 5 G3

WHEN: September to November for wild-flowers, March to May for mild weather

WHY: Hiking, camping, sightseeing, cycling, scenic driving, rock climbing, and wildflower exhibition (early October)

SIZE: 167 000 ha

INFORMATION: Parks Victoria 131 963

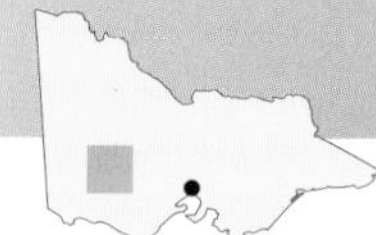

don't miss

Time your visit to the Grampians National Park to coincide with an event hosted by the locals. Choose from the Jazz Festival in February, the Art Exhibition and Shakespeare in the Grampians in April, the Wildflower Spectacular in October, and the Halls Gap Film Festival in November.

These rugged mountains offer outdoor enthusiasts the base for most activities, including walking, rock climbing, cycling and abseiling.

The sculptured structures started to emerge more than 400 million years ago when the land rose to form large areas of mountain. These rock formations have since been weathered by wind and rain and are now the main attraction of the Grampians National Park.

One of the more noticeable features of the range is that the western slopes are modest, while the eastern slopes are very steep. Excellent examples of this can be found on the Wonderland Range, near Halls Gap in the park's centre. This region has not always been protected under national park status, but has long been recognised for its rugged beauty.

In the Past

Early evidence of Australian Aboriginal settlement can be seen in the park's many art sites; it is also believed that these early inhabitants utilised the rock formations and caves for their ceremonies. Many of the line drawings at the art sites such as Wab Manja and Billimina shelters depict animal tracks, human figures and handprints.

Thomas Mitchell was the first European to explore this region in 1836 and it was not long after that graziers occupied the foothills of the mountains. Other settlers included gold miners and loggers, the latter harvesting timber during the area's time as a state forest until the national park was formed in 1984.

Since then, visitor numbers have noticeably increased, and now strict controls are in place to protect the region from the effect of the extra visitors as well as from feral animals, weeds and soil erosion.

Sandstone Formations

The 167 000 hectare national park consists of four main systems of ranges: Victoria and Mount William in the park's lower sections, Mount Difficult in the north, and Serra, which cuts through the centre of the park from Dunkeld to Halls Gap. A smaller range to the south-west of Halls Gap is the Wonderland

Left and below: *Halls Gap is perhaps the most popular area of the Grampians National Park, which is not really surprising as it is the main tourist centre for the region. From Halls Gap you can look at unusual rock formations and towering cliffs, start walking trails, stop in at the Visitor Centre, and go bush camping.*

Range. This range is popular with visitors, and its unusual rock formations and towering cliffs can be appreciated in a variety of walks that begin around Halls Gap.

The rugged sandstone peaks and valleys are home to an extremely diverse plant life, with many rare species of wildflowers. Spring heralds the wildflower season. From August to November the colourful blooms carpet the rocky slopes and valleys, and include species such as the brilliant red flame heath which is widespread on the hillsides and the rare spectral duck orchid.

High up, the plateaus are covered in thick heathlands, while the hillsides and most of the park are covered in woodland forests and eucalypts such as messmate and brown stringybarks. In contrast, the moist valley floors and folds within the rocks provide the nutrients needed for the swamp gums, succulent ferns and silver banksias to flourish.

The diversity of plant life provides a habitat for a large number of birds, with more than 200 different species recorded in the Grampians. Flowering gums attract lorikeets, while yellow-tailed black cockatoos soar above the stringybarks. Walkers will see crimson rosellas and honeyeaters in the heathlands, and campers will often be rewarded with the antics of kookaburras.

Left: *The rainbow bee-eater* (Merops ornatus), *which can be seen in much of mainland Australia, can eat hundreds of bees each day. Over 200 bird species have been recorded in the Grampians.*

Right: *The dramatic sandstone peaks and valleys of the Grampians. As well as providing spectacular scenery, the mountains house some of the premier rock climbing sites in Victoria.*

Below: *The rugged rocky scenery around Halls Gap can be seen up close on this trail that hugs the rock face. The Grampians National Park contains over 200 km of maintained walking tracks.*

Right: *The eastern grey kangaroo* (Macropus giganteus) *is one of the many animals in the park. They are used to humans and come right into the picnic grounds.*

The most common marsupial spotted within the park is the swamp wallaby, but other species such as the grey kangaroo and a number of possums inhabit the park. Zumstein picnic area in the centre of the park is popular for viewing kangaroos, but visitors are asked not to feed these friendly natives. Platypus also reside in many of the creeks, but it takes a keen eye and a great deal of patience to spot one of these reclusive monotremes.

A Bushwalker's Paradise

With more than 200 km of maintained walking tracks throughout the park, it is no wonder that walkers head to this region to sample the many trails and the spectacular scenery. These trails range from short strolls through to overnight treks over rough terrain that are only suitable for the ambitious and fit.

One of the most popular walks for tourists is the Wonderland Long Walk. This walk starts at the Halls Gap camp ground and climbs along the Pinnacle Track

through eucalypt forests to the Pinnacle Lookout, which rewards the energetic walker with spectacular views. Continuing along the Wonderland Track on the return walk to Halls Gap takes in the Grand Canyon, Silent Street and the famous Elephant's Hide. This 10 km walk is of moderate difficulty and should take a day to complete.

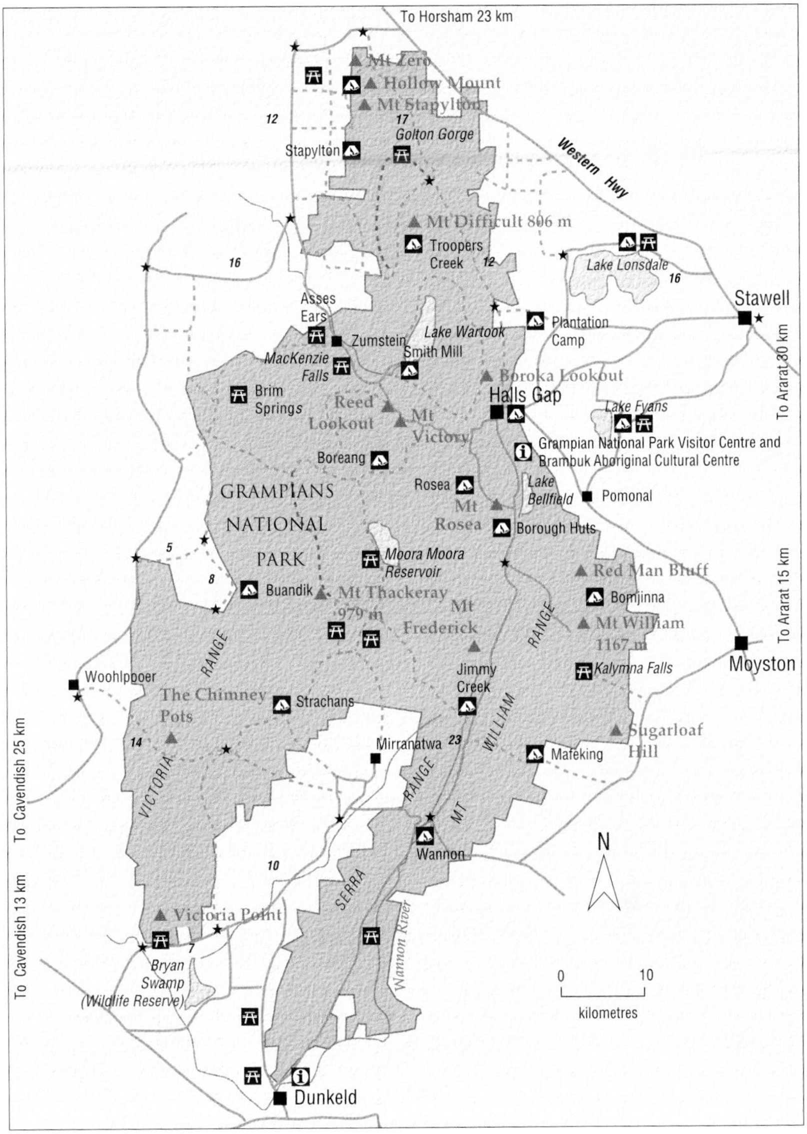

Another walk is Briggs Bluff, which is best undertaken by those without a fear of heights, as it follows the cliff edge. This 10 km walk begins at the car park near Rose Gap and follows the Beehive Falls track and then climbs steeply up onto the plateau for spectacular views of the Wimmera Plains.

The Balconies, which offers scenic views of the Victoria Valley, can be reached via a track from the Reed Lookout car park. This easy walk is less than 2 km long.

Information on all the walks are available from the Grampians National Park Visitor Centre at Halls Gap.

Rock Climbing and Abseiling

Featuring a multitude of large, majestic sandstone formations, the Grampians have a number of popular rock climbs.

don't miss

The Grampians offers some of the most spectacular climbing sites in the whole of Australia. There are many tour operators that can take you climbing, with the climbs ranging from easy to the more difficult, for the experienced climber.

MacKenzie Falls is the most popular of the several waterfalls in the Grampians. After rain, torrents of water rush over 40 metre cliffs into a deep pool.

Hollow Mountain, in the north of the park, is very popular, while Mount Rosea, near Halls Gap, offers one of the best collections of sandstone climbs. For something different, nearby Bundaleer has a range of climbs.

For details on climbing in the Grampians, or nearby Mount Arapiles, contact Parks Victoria 131 963, and the Victorian Climbing Centre. Guided climbing tours can be organised through Base Camp and Beyond at Halls Gap.

Other Activities

There are a number of scenic drives through the ranges. However, most of the vehicular tracks that were used during the logging era have now been closed, so there is little to attract keen four-wheel drivers. Cycling is the next best form of transport and there are a number of pleasant rides in the region.

A popular one-day ride is the Wonderland Trail that leaves from Zumstein picnic area and heads to Wonderland car park before returning to Zumstein. The length of this trek is 53 km and will take a day to complete. The trail takes in MacKenzie Falls and the Pinnacle Lookout.

For the more adventurous, there is a 100 km 3-day ride, leaving also from Zumstein, which heads to the Victoria Range in the south of the park, taking in the Glenelg River, Wallaby Rocks and various Australian Aboriginal sites.

The two lakes in the park—Wartook and Bellfield—offer the visitor canoeing, swimming and fishing. Brown trout, redfin, blackfish and the occasional rainbow trout can be taken; nearby Rocklands Reservoir, Lake Fyans and Lake Toolondo are also popular. Yabbying is also a favourite pastime of the locals in many of the dams and waterholes in and around the park area. Victorian fishing licences must be obtained from Parks Victoria for all waters.

Wartook offers restricted powerboat use, while Rocklands and Lake Fyans are the main bodies of water for powered watercraft and water-skiers.

The park offers a cultural experience through a number of ancient Australian Aboriginal rock art sites, some of which are accessible to visitors.

Brambuk Aboriginal Cultural Centre near Halls Gap gives its visitors an insight into the indigenous culture through displays, bush tucker and performances given by the local Australian Aboriginal people.

The Grampians National Park Visitor Centre and its extensive displays should be your first stop at the beginning of your exploration of the park. Rangers are on hand to answer any questions.

Access

The park is 260 km from Melbourne, and Halls Gap can be reached via Ararat or Stawell. Access to the park's southern section is via Dunkeld, and through Wartook to the west.

Camping

There are bush camping areas throughout the park and a number of excellent camps where fees apply. Most are operated on a self-serve system, where campers fill out forms and deposit them at the camp site.

Camp grounds in the central part of the park include Borough Huts, Mount Rosea and Boreang. To the south-east, covering the Serra and Mount William Ranges, you will find Bomjinna, Jimmy Creek, Mafeking and Wannon Crossing. Victoria Range to the south-west offers camping at Buandik and Strachan Hut. Camping in the northern sector can be found at Troopers Creek, Smith Mill, Hollow Mountain and Mount Stapylton. The most popular camping areas are those at Halls Gap.

tourist info

Brambuk the National Park and Cultural Centre, Halls Gap
(03) 5356 4452

Grampians National Park Visitor Centre
(03) 5356 4381. Open daily 9.00 a.m. to 5.00 p.m.

Stawell Tourist Information Centre
(03) 5358 2314

Victorian Climbing Centre, Seaford
(03) 9782 4222

Right: *Casting for brown trout, redfin or blackfish in the Rocklands Reservoir, a popular fishing spot in the Grampians. Fishing licences must be obtained before you begin.*

Below: *Superb stretches of water in the Grampians include Lake Bellfield, which is the closest to Halls Gap. Water sports, including swimming, canoeing and fishing, are popular.*

Croajingolong National Park

The Croajingolong National Park is a remote wilderness area where cool freshwater streams trickle down from the mountains and from within pockets of temperate rainforest, through the tablelands of the park, before filtering through the sand dunes to finally emerge on the rugged windswept coastline of eastern Victoria.

Above: *The rugged south-eastern coast of Victoria, near Point Hicks. The Thurra River winds through the national park to meet the sea here. A small boat or a canoe will give access to the estuary.*

fact file

WHERE: 500 km from Melbourne, via the Princes Highway, in far eastern Gippsland Map: Vic 4 K9

WHEN: December to February for water sports, September to November for wildflowers

WHY: Walking, camping, coastal scenery, fishing, boating, swimming, nature study, birdwatching

SIZE: 87 500 ha

INFORMATION: Parks Victoria 131 963

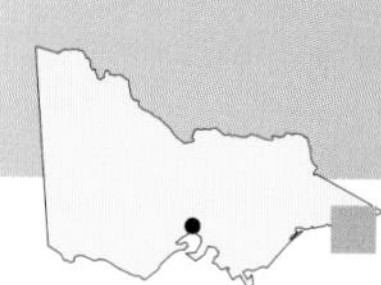

Australian Aboriginals are thought to have lived in the Croajingolong area for over 40 000 years and it's not hard to understand why. With prolific plant life and an abundance of birds, fish and marsupials, this area provided a perfect food source for the local tribal groups.

Croajingolong was established in 1979 from a number of smaller parks. The natural, unspoilt beauty of this park attracts hundreds of visitors each year, especially to the freshwater estuaries of the Thurra, Mueller and Wingan Rivers.

The park features woodlands that lead down into gullies where temperate rainforest plants such as tree ferns, mosses, orchids and vines can be found. As you venture closer towards the coastline, the large trees give way to smaller plants, which offer a riot of colour in spring and, finally, stunted banksias and tea-trees on the windswept cliffs.

Nature study and birdwatching are popular pastimes among park visitors, and over 300 species of birds can be found, including many waterbirds.

Right: *A seagull or silver gull* (Larus novaehollandiae) *on the Croajingolong coast. Over 300 species of birds can be found in the park, including pelicans, lyrebirds, parrots and cockatoos.*

Walking, Canoeing and Fishing

The area is a popular bushwalking destination with the long beaches, relatively good access and availability of fresh water being attractions to those who revel in remote lonely beaches.

Popular shorter walks within the park include the 2 hour Dunes Walk which takes you over the high sand dunes and offers a superb view over Point Hicks. In the same area is the Lighthouse Trek, which is easier and takes 3 hours to explore Point Hicks.

From Wingan River camp site you can take the 5–6 hours return Petrel Point Track which explores the eastern coastline, while for a full day's walk, take the Easby Track from Wingan Point.

To get a different and enjoyable view of the area a small boat or a canoe will give you access to many sections of delightful river and estuary country, its wildlife and fishing.

Keen anglers will be rewarded with a large variety of species, taken from river, beach and headland, with nearby

Below: *Genoa Falls, located in the northern part of the park, form a multi-deck cascade. Water dragons can sometimes be seen sunning themselves on the rocks by the falls.*

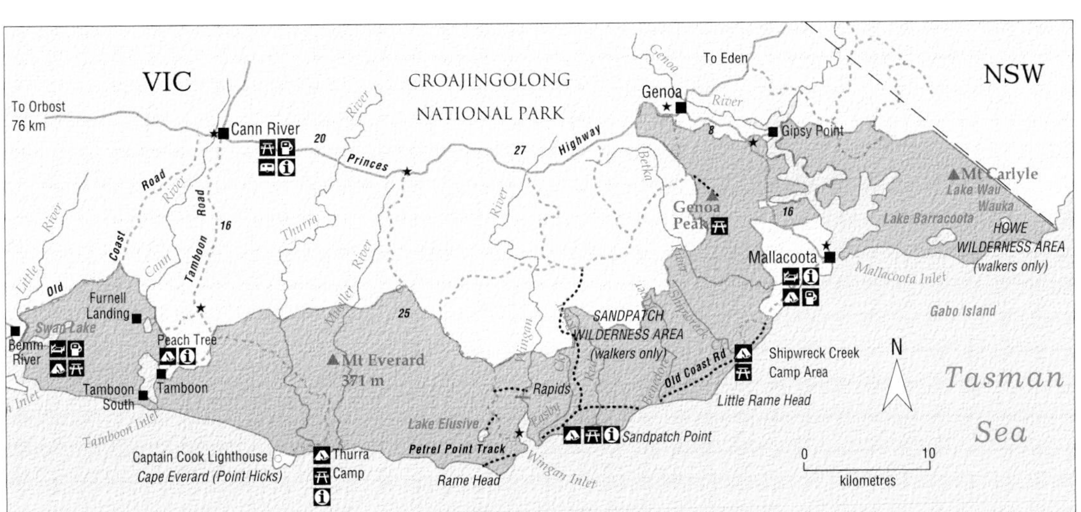

Mallacoota being a popular spot to catch flathead, bream and sand whiting.

Access and Camping

The road to Mallacoota is sealed but the generally good unsealed roads into the park from the Princes Highway may close after rain. Check with the ranger.

Camping is allowed at Peach Tree Camping Area on Tamboon Inlet, Shipwreck Creek, Wingan River, Mueller River and Thurra River. Camping is also allowed outside the park at Cape Conran, Bemm River, Marlo and Mallacoota. Most of the camp sites have basic facilities (pit toilets, fireplaces and tables).

During the peak holiday periods, a ballot system is used for allocation of camping sites. Contact the ranger for camping information.

Dandenong Ranges National Park

Reaching upward from Ferntree Gully on the outskirts of Melbourne, over Mount Dandenong, lies the verdant sanctuary of the Dandenong Ranges National Park. Four large areas of natural bush plus smaller sections in the immediate vicinity have been combined to form the park. Over 130 species of birds and 31 mammal species have been recorded, while there are more than 350 plant species, 16 of which are either rare or restricted in distribution.

Lush tree ferns contrasting with trickling waterfalls and tall eucalypts provide part of the appeal of the Dandenong Ranges National Park.

fact file

WHERE: 40 km east of Melbourne, via the Burwood Highway
Map: Vic 6 E3

WHEN: All year

WHY: Picnics, bushwalking

SIZE: 3215 ha

INFORMATION: Parks Victoria: 131 963

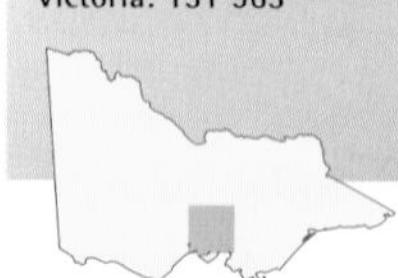

Activities

Apart from lazing underneath the forest canopy on a hot summer's day, the most popular recreation in the park is bushwalking, and a number of excellent trails are on offer.

The Ferntree Gully block offers a variety of interesting walks including the 1000 Steps to the top of the range. There are three picnic areas, including the wheelchair accessible Ferntree Gully and One Tree Hill picnic areas.

The Sherbrooke section boasts natural bushland and the tumbling Sherbrooke Falls. This block also features the Hardy Gully Nature Trail near the Grants Picnic Ground. This walk is about 700 metres and should take visitors only half an hour to complete. Nearby is the Margaret Lester Forest Walk, of similar length, which has a hard surface that is suitable for wheelchairs.

Mount Dandenong itself is in the section known as Doongalla, which means 'place of peace'. It is aptly named, with spectacular views and rugged bush trails leading down the western side of the mountain. Nearby is a kiosk and the Mount Dandenong Observatory. The Doongalla Homestead site is accessible by car, along Doongalla Road, and its lawns and exotic plants make an idyllic picnic area.

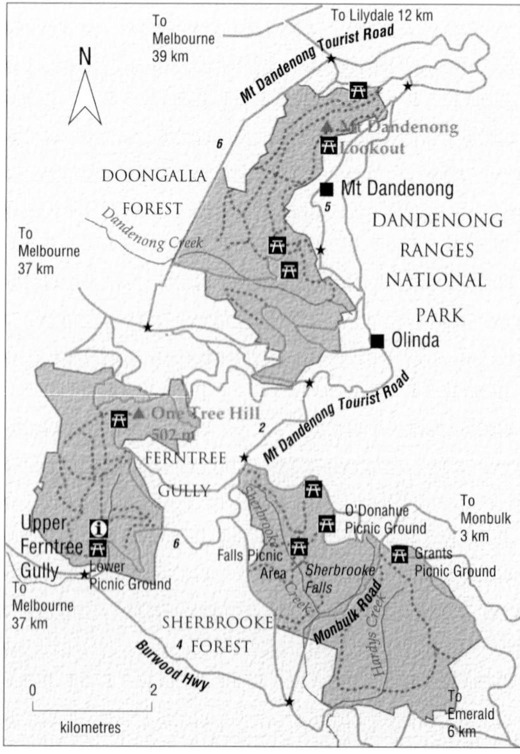

did you know?

The Dandenong Ranges National Park exists because of the efforts of the local residents. In 1882, they persuaded the Victorian Minister for Agriculture to set aside a 168 ha area as a recreational park. In 1927, the area was enlarged and proclaimed as Victoria's second national park.

To the east is the Olinda Forest block that joins with the Silvan Reservoir Water Reserve and the R. J. Hamer Forest Arboretum. While the water reserve is closed to the public there are a large number of trails and a couple of picnic areas through the rest of the area.

There are some long walks in the park, including the 15 km Western Trail and the 18 km Olinda Forest Trail from Mount Dandenong to Kallista.

The Doongalla block can be reached off the Mount Dandenong Tourist Road, or from the Mountain Highway. The Falls Road off the Mount Dandenong Tourist Road gives access to the Olinda Forest section of the national park.

Camping is not permitted within this metropolitan parkland, but there is plenty of accommodation, including charming bed-and-breakfast places, in the hills of the Dandenong Ranges.

Left: *The eastern yellow robin* (Eopsaltria australis) *is one of the many birds that inhabit the park. Visitors will also hear bellbirds, kookaburras and the amazing song of the lyrebird.*

In the surrounding area there are other parks and reserves including the William Ricketts Sanctuary and the National Rhododendron Gardens.

Access

From the city, the Burwood Highway is the best access to the park. The major Melbourne street directories detail access, picnic areas and walking trails in the park.

The first and most accessible section of the park is the Ferntree Gully block, which is just off the Burwood Highway in Upper Ferntree Gully.

Further along the Mount Dandenong Tourist Road, and flanking the Monbulk Road, is the Sherbrooke Forest section.

This park is less than an hour's drive from Melbourne. Access to the park is easy along the Mount Dandenong Tourist Road, but once there, walking is the best way to enjoy the natural bushland.

Wilsons Promontory National Park

One of the most attractive and popular national parks in Victoria, 'The Prom', as it is affectionately known, is one of the country's oldest parks, being established in 1898. The park encompasses 130 km of coastline and has an immense diversity of landscapes, with huge granite headlands protecting secluded white beaches while marshland and sand dunes give sanctuary to a multitude of bird and animal life.

fact file

WHERE: South Gippsland on the Victorian coast, 200 km south-east of Melbourne
Map: Vic 6 J8

WHEN: All year

WHY: Camping, walking, photography, scuba diving, snorkelling, swimming, overnight bushwalking (permit required)

SIZE: 53 000 ha

INFORMATION: Parks Victoria 131 963

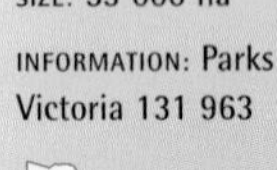

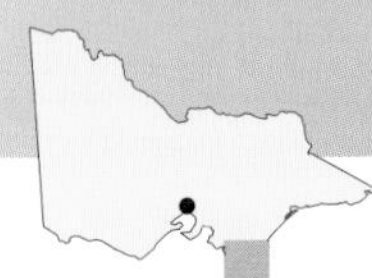

did you know?

The native plants and animals of The Prom have not always been conserved. Sealers Cove was named by George Bass, who sent his men to shoot seals for supplies there in 1798, and in the early 1840s Refuge Cove housed a whaling station. Later, in the 1850s, a timber mill was set up at Sealers Cove.

Further inland, the land reaches up to form rugged forested mountain ranges that play host to fern-filled gullies and temperate pockets of rainforest. The east and west coasts of The Prom have been protected in a Marine Park (some fishing allowed) while a 300 metre wide Marine Reserve (totally protected, no fishing allowed) protects the southern coast and nearby offshore islands.

Water Activities and Walks

Apart from photography, which is a popular pastime in the park, bushwalking is the favoured activity, and the only form of transport, as bicycles are not permitted past vehicle boundaries. There are walks of every degree of difficulty, from short 10 minute strolls to rugged overnight hikes that require overnight permits.

Popular walks include Squeaky Beach to Picnic Bay, while a more difficult 38 km return walk leads to the Lighthouse on the southernmost tip of the Australian mainland.

On the east coast, an energetic and popular 37 km 2–3 day walk, starting at the car park at Mount Oberon, takes in Sealers Cove, Refuge Cove and Waterloo Bay.

Many water activities can be enjoyed in the surrounding ocean and the freshwater streams, including swimming, snorkelling and scuba diving. Fishing is also popular but restrictions apply in the marine parks and reserves. Check with the ranger at Tidal River for details.

Boats can be launched off the beach at Tidal River. A key is available from the ranger.

Access and Camping

The park can be accessed from the South Gippsland Highway via Foster or Meeniyan and Fish Creek.

Tidal River offers the only vehicle access to the park and has camping and caravan sites, along with cabins, flats and group lodges. Demand for the sites and accommodation is extremely heavy, especially during peak holiday times when a ballot is drawn. Facilities for campers include unpowered sites, fireplaces, a kiosk, toilets, showers and picnic tables.

Accommodation is also available in the Lighthouse Cottages, but access is only by walking.

More remote camping areas in the park, which are accessed by walking tracks and have toilets, include Oberon Bay which is close to the Tidal River site, Roaring Meg in the south of the park, and Waterloo Bay. As well there's Refuge Cove and Sealers Cove on the east coast, while in the north of the park is Tin Mine Cove.

There are also some other sites which have no toilet facilities. They include Johnny Souey Cove, Five Mile Beach, Lower Barry Creek and Barry Creek.

Many of the northern camp sites are often closed in summer due to lack of fresh water.

For camp and accommodation bookings or further enquires, contact the Visitor Information Centre at Tidal River on (03) 5680 9555.

Left: *Wilsons Promontory National Park now includes 130 km of unspoilt coastline. The park has been expanded considerably since its establishment in 1898.*

The dramatic granite bluffs and slabs of The Prom are popular with climbers. Whale Rock overlooks the magnificent coastline of the park.

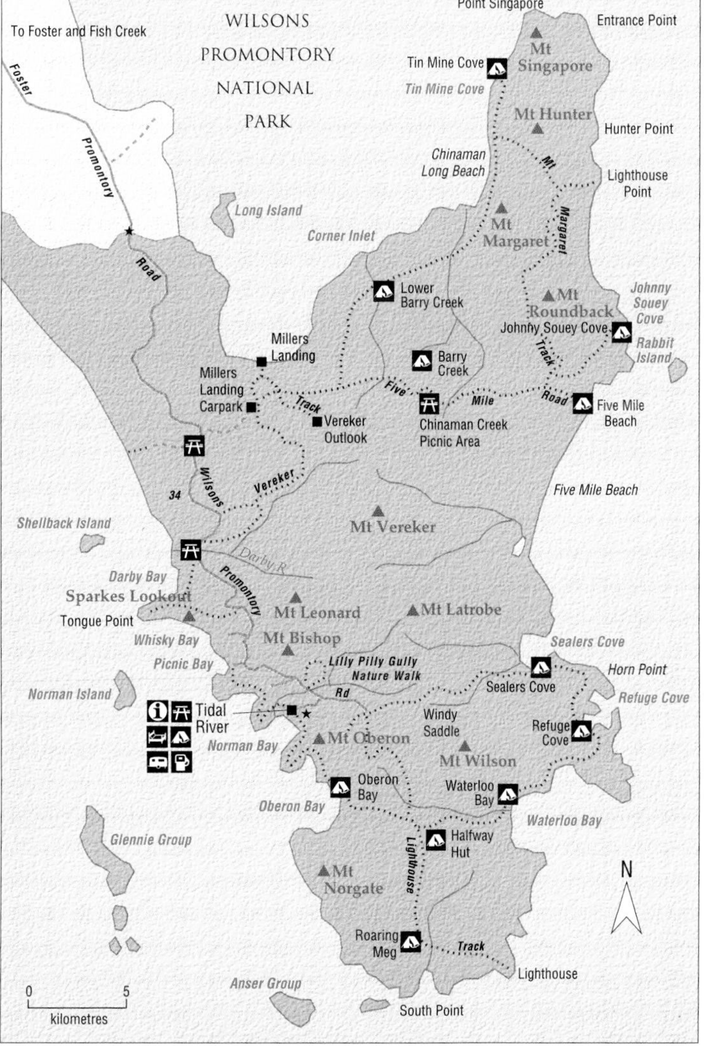

Wyperfeld National Park and Lake Albacutya Regional Park

Wyperfeld National Park was established in the early twentieth century and has now become the third-largest park in Victoria. Lake Albacutya Regional Park adjoins the national park on its southern boundary and boasts a size of 8300 hectares. With much of the north-west of Victoria cleared for grazing and wheat farming, these parks protect one of the last large expanses of mallee country left in the state.

Above: *The raucous sulphur-crested cockatoo* (Cacatua galerita) *can be seen among the red gums and heathlands in the park.*

fact file

WHERE: 450 km north-west of Melbourne, 47 km from Hopetoun
Map: Vic 2 D3

WHEN: March to May; September to November, for wildflowers

WHY: Walking, cycling, scenic drives, 4WD, birdwatching, wildflower study

SIZE: 357 017 ha

INFORMATION: Parks Victoria 131 963

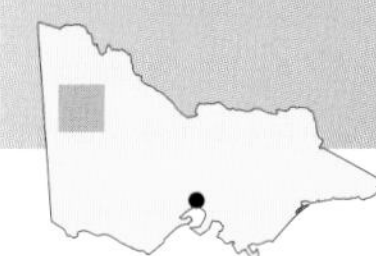

The basis of these parks is the large number of occasionally flooded lakes which are connected by Outlet Creek that runs north through the park from the northern end of Lake Albacutya.

The parks are host to a wide variety of bird and animal life. Emus and kangaroos are common, while the mallee fowl makes its nest amongst the remote mallee-covered dunes.

Activities

There are two self-guided walks within the Wyperfeld Park, both of which are of an easy standard. One trail is located at Lake Brambruk, the other at Black Flat Lake and the return trip takes from 2 to 3 hours.

The Desert Walk is a relatively easy 6 km circuit walk along a sandy track near Nine Mile Square and offers excellent views of the Big Desert and Outlet Creek during the 3 hours it takes.

For more remote walks, use the Casuarina camp ground as your base and seek local information from the park ranger.

Bicycles can be used on the firmer tracks such as the Outlet Creek Track, Lowan Track and Dattuck Track, but other tracks will probably be too sandy.

Drivers of 4WD vehicles will enjoy the drive north from the main Wonga

Right: *Camping facilities are provided at the Wonga Hut site in Wyperfeld. This is near Wonga Lake, which now holds water only rarely, after extremely heavy flooding further north.*

Camping Ground via the Eastern Lookout Road and the Dattuck, North–South and Eagle tracks to Pine Plain and beyond. There's some good remote camping in this northern area.

At Lake Albacutya a 4WD track circles the lake. Duck shooting is also permitted during the season. Dogs are allowed on a leash in the camping areas around the lake only.

West of Lake Albacutya two 4WD tracks cut through this remote region—the Chinaman Well Track and the Milmed Rock Track—and both lead to the main Murrayville-Nhill Road.

Access and Camping

The best access is from the Henty Highway, then west from Hopetoun.

The northern section of the park can be easily accessed via Hopetoun and Patchewollock. The western boundary of the park is along the Murrayville–Nhill Road, a graded dirt road that can be closed after rain.

The main camping area is at Wonga Hut, which has a picnic shelter, limited water, washing block, pit toilets and fireplaces. It is suitable for caravans, although there is no power.

Broken Bucket, on the Murrayville–Nhill Road, has toilets and water. In the north of the park, Casuarina has pit toilets, limited water and fireplaces and is accessible by 4WD vehicles. Remote bush camping for walkers is allowed.

There are also three camping grounds on the shores of Lake Albacutya and these have toilets and picnic tables only.

Water supplies are limited and you may need to bring your own.

Left: *Red kangaroos (Macropus rufus) graze on the grassy plains of the park. Emus and grey kangaroos are also often seen, and there are small desert animals in the mallee areas.*

VIC

don't miss

There are many ways to explore the beauties and wonders of this park. You can try birdwatching, canoeing, 4WD touring, camping and even duck shooting when in season. Bushwalking is popular in the park and there are two self-guided trails.

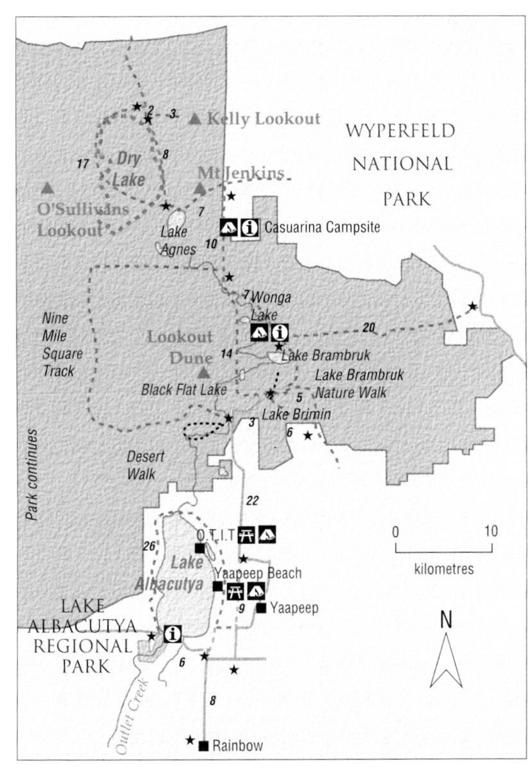

Mornington Peninsula National Park

The Mornington Peninsula National Park covers some 2686 hectares, mainly along the coast from Point Nepean to Cape Schanck in the east, and features craggy headlands, spectacular sandy beaches and an abundance of marine life and history.

The Cape Schanck area was originally protected by the Cape Schanck Coastal Reserve, but is now part of the Mornington National Park.

fact file

WHERE: 95 km south of Melbourne on the eastern side of the entrance to Port Phillip Bay Map: Vic 6 C5

WHEN: September to May

WHY: Military fort, beaches, swimming (not at Point Nepean due to currents), surfing, bush and beach walks, historical significance

SIZE: 2686 ha

INFORMATION: Parks Victoria 131 963

Bookings to visit Point Nepean (03) 5984 4276

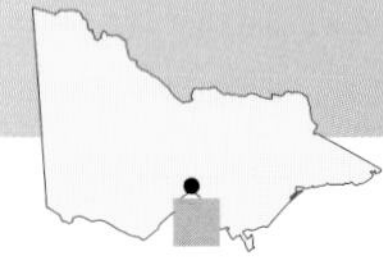

This park includes the old Port Nepean Quarantine Station, which incorporates an historic fort, cemetery and quarantine station that was set up in 1852. The fort was erected in 1882, but only two shots were ever fired in the fort's 63 year history of active duty—at the start of each World War.

Activities

Exploring Point Nepean is possible by boarding the transporter service, or you can cycle any day of the year taking in all the sights. This section of the park is popular and visitor numbers are limited so it is advisable to book ahead.

The back beaches of Sorrento, Portsea and Gunnamatta are well known among surfers, beach lovers and fishermen.

Popular walks include the Farnsworth Track that covers the area between Portsea and London Bridge and offers superb coastal views, while the inland section of the park can be enjoyed along a walking track from Cape Schanck.

Access and Facilities

There's good and easy access to places along the coast including Portsea, the Sorrento Back Beach and Cape Schanck.

The park is for day-use only; toilets and picnic facilities can be found throughout the park.

Cheviot Beach is on the southern side of Point Nepean. It was named after a ship wrecked there in 1887. The surf here can be dangerous, and only experienced scuba divers should explore the wreck.

Murray–Sunset National Park

Located in the far north-west of Victoria, the Murray–Sunset National Park is the second-largest park in the state. It offers salt flats and sand dunes to the north, and thick mallee scrub to the south. Proclaimed in 1991, the park takes in four important wilderness zones.

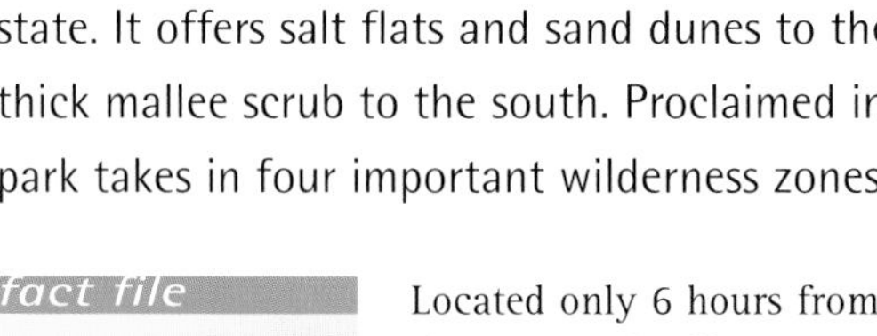

The Pink Lakes derive their hue from carotene, a pigment secreted by algae (Dunaliella salina). *The colour is brightest in spring and summer.*

fact file

WHERE: On the Victorian–South Australian border, 585 km from Melbourne, via Ouyen
Map: Vic 1 C6

WHEN: September to November

WHY: 4WD, walking, nature study, photography, camping, cycling, remote desert

SIZE: 633 000 ha

INFORMATION: Parks Victoria 131 963

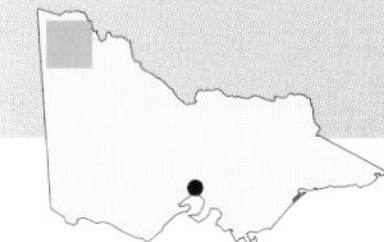

Located only 6 hours from Melbourne, this vast park offers visitors an insight into the arid desert regions of Australia. It is renowned for the magnificent Pink Lakes, and this easily accessible spot is the ideal base for a series of day trips by 4WD, bicycle or on foot.

It is, however, the remoteness of the region that has a lasting impact on visitors, and four-wheel drivers are best equipped to take advantage of this.

Experienced walkers can also take advantage of the wilderness areas, while easier, shorter walks are available near the designated camping areas.

The word 'mallee' is the term used to describe the unusual growth form of the eucalypts in the area. About 20 species of mallee eucalypts grow in this region.

Access and Camping

The Mallee Highway borders the south of the park, while the Calder Highway borders the eastern side.

Camping is very pleasant at Pink Lakes where you will find reasonable facilities. If you have a 4WD vehicle you can reach the camping areas of Mopoke, Pheneeys Track, Mount Crozier and Rocket Lake. These remote camping areas offer basic facilities. Water is not available through most of the park.

Heavy rain can make the tracks inaccessible for conventional vehicles.

Along the northern edge of the park, the Murray and Lindsay Rivers regularly flood the neighbouring plains, creating sizable billabongs.

Snowy River National Park

The powerful Snowy River forces its way through deep, rocky gorges and the rugged Victorian High Country before it finally settles into a large, wide, tranquil waterway and trickles quietly out to the ocean. Covering 98 700 hectares, this remote area is considered to be extremely significant and its remoteness has allowed two wilderness areas to be incorporated within the park.

Canoeing is the best way to enjoy the Snowy River, and to observe the park's river scenery, impressive deep gorges and diverse vegetation.

fact file

WHERE: Far East Gippsland, 390 km from Melbourne via the Princes Highway Map: Vic 4 G6

WHEN: All year, though the Snowy River is best in the warmer months

WHY: Snowy River, MacKillops Bridge, canoeing, camping, bushwalking, scenic drives, mountain bike riding, 4WD, fishing, rafting

SIZE: 98 700 ha

INFORMATION: Parks Victoria 131 963

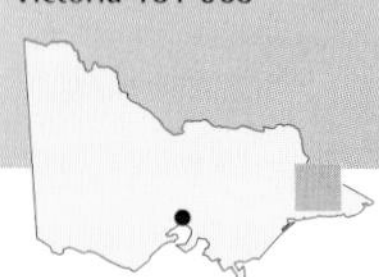

Activities

Although the Snowy Mountains Hydro-Electricity Scheme takes much of the water from the river, there are still rugged gorges and rapids to thrill the most experienced canoeist. The section from MacKillops Bridge to Buchan, which flows through three gorges, is a 3- to 4-day trip.

For walkers there are a number of trails to enjoy. There's the hard 18 km Silver Mine Walking Track and the easier Snowy River Nature Walk from MacKillops Bridge.

Experienced four-wheel drivers will enjoy the Deddick Trail.

Access and Camping

Park access is either from the Buchan–Gelantipy road to the turn-off past Seldom Seen and onto the road to MacKillops Bridge, or via the 4WD Deddick Trail, which is seasonally closed and runs from the south of the park to MacKillops Bridge. There is also access from the north-east via Bonang and the Bonang–Gelantipy road. The road in, however, has very steep drop-offs.

The camping grounds at MacKillops Bridge, Waratah Flat and Balley Hooley have basic facilities; Raymond Falls and Hick's camp sites have none. Camping permits are required.

Near MacKillops Bridge. The walks in this northern part of the park show the harsh grey rock faces and dense vegetation around the Snowy River valley.

tourist info

Canoeing Victoria, (03) 9459 4251

More National Parks of Importance

Baw Baw National Park

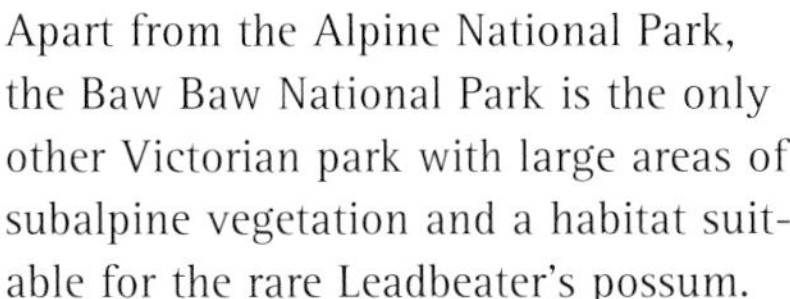

SIZE: 13 300 ha
MAP: Vic 6 J3

Apart from the Alpine National Park, the Baw Baw National Park is the only other Victorian park with large areas of subalpine vegetation and a habitat suitable for the rare Leadbeater's possum.

During winter, skiers enjoy the downhill slopes or the many cross-country trails that lead as far afield as Mount St Gwinear. In the milder months, bushwalkers enjoy the trails scattered over the mountain tops or traversing part of the long-distance Alpine Walking Track. The Silvertop Picnic Ground has excellent views of the Thomson Dam.

The main access to the park is from Drouin through Nerrim South and Tanjil Bren where a narrow, winding bitumen road leads to the village. The Mount Erica car park or Mount St Gwinear are accessible off the Thomson Valley Road.

Dispersed bush camping is allowed on the Baw Baw Plateau, while there are also motels and lodges at the Mount Baw Baw Alpine Village.

For more information contact Parks Victoria, on 131 963.

Errinundra National Park

SIZE: 25 600 ha
MAP: Vic 4 J7

In eastern Victoria, high on the Errinundra Plateau, you will find the largest stand of cool temperate rainforest in the state. Scenic drives and boardwalks help visitors appreciate this priceless beauty. The self-guided nature walk gives a good insight into the park.

Access is restricted in wet conditions, when closures may apply. The main entry is via the Errinundra Road from Club Terrace to the south, or the Bonang Highway from the east, taking the Errinundra Road. The main roads into the park are unsealed and winding, and should be driven with caution. They are unsuitable for caravans.

Camping sites can be found at the Gap Scenic Reserve in the north, on the Bonang River near the intersection of the Bonang Highway and the Gap Road. Goongerah Camping Area is to the west.

Be prepared for wet weather, even in the warmer months.

For further information, contact Parks Victoria, on 131 963.

The snow gum (Eucalyptus pauciflora) *is a cold-climate tree. Baw Baw and Alpine are the only Victorian parks where it can be seen.*

Most of the Errinundra National Park is above 1000 m and is inaccessible during winter due to snow and rain. Springtime also brings heavy rain to the area.

Hattah-Kulkyne National Park

SIZE: 48 000 ha
MAP: Vic 1 F6

The Hattah-Kulkyne National Park takes in a typical mallee environment of native cypress pine woodland and vast mallee scrubland. The park is bordered by the Murray River and the Murray-Kulkyne Regional Park to the east.

In all but the driest years a series of small riverlets feed water from the Murray River along the Chalka Creek, which in turn provides an oasis for the wildlife in the park: birds, kangaroos and other animals can be found in abundance.

The lakes are best explored by canoe, but walking and cycling are also both excellent ways to explore the park.

Access to the park is via the Sunraysia Highway or Robinvale Road east of Hattah. Good gravel roads stretch through the park. Delightful camping areas can be found on the shores of Lake Hattah and Lake Mournpall and along the Murray River.

For more information contact Parks Victoria, on 131 963.

Right: *The sacred kingfisher* (Todiramphus sanctus) *is one of 200 species of birds living in Hattah-Kulkyne National Park. The park has both dry and lake environments, unlike others in this part of the state.*

The trees in the northern part of Kinglake National Park are mainly stringybarks, peppermint gums and other eucalypts.

Kinglake National Park

SIZE: 21 600 ha
MAP: Vic 6 E2

The Kinglake National Park provides Melburnians with a cool respite from the summer heat and offers magnificent views of the city, densely forested mountain tops and fern-filled gullies.

For walkers, the Wombelano Falls on Hirts Creek can be accessed via an easy short walk through the cool, fern-filled gullies; ferns and messmate forests can be seen on the short walk to Mason Falls. The more spectacular journey by foot is the 20 km moderate to hard Everard Circuit Walk. If you want a great view, without the energetic walk, the Frank Thomson Lookout is just out of town.

The park is divided into three sections surrounding Kinglake township and can be accessed via the Melba Highway, or from any of the roads leading to Kinglake.

The region caters more for day-visitors, but there is a camp area at the Gums. The area is small, and sites need to be booked ahead through the ranger. Contact Parks Victoria, on 131 963.

Right: *Mallee vegetation on the shores of Lake Hattah, one in the series of lakes connected by small waterways that are the main feature of the Hattah-Kulkyne National Park.*

Lake Eildon National Park

SIZE: 27 750 ha
MAP: Vic 3 J9

Lake Eildon National Park is a natural playground for campers, walkers and wildlife enthusiasts. It offers steep, rugged mountains and freshwater rivers leading into the vast reservoir of Lake Eildon with its many arms and bays.

Fishing is popular in the lake and the streams that flow into it, while four-wheel drivers can tour the remote parts of the park. Bushwalkers, water-skiers and canoeists will also enjoy the lake, rivers and surrounding forest country.

The park can be accessed via the Eildon–Jamieson road or from Goughs Bay via Mansfield.

Camp sites are located at Fraser Camping area and Jerusalem Creek and should be pre-booked during peak times. Boat-based camp sites are at Taylors Creek, Mountaineer Inlet and Coopers Point. Camping permits are required. For more information, contact Parks Victoria, on 131 963.

There are a number of bushwalks in the southern section of Lake Eildon National Park, varying from energetic five-hour treks, to relaxed one-hour trails.

VIC

Little Desert National Park

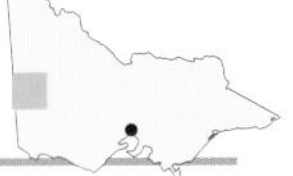

SIZE: 132 000 ha
MAP: Vic 2 C8

The Little Desert National Park conserves an important region of the mallee in far western Victoria. The sandy soils support typical mallee vegetation and heathland areas, and the park has a diverse range of animal and bird life, and vegetation. In spring there is a spectacular display of wildflowers.

As most of the tracks in the sandy region are unsuitable for conventional vehicles, this remote area is perfect for 4WDs. Tracks are often closed due to wet weather and Parks Victoria, phone 131 963, should be contacted for information on track conditions and closures.

Many walks in the area accommodate the day or overnight hiker, while short walks can be taken from the camping areas.

Access to the park is along well-formed gravel roads from Dimboola, Horsham or Edenhope.

Remote bush camping is allowed in the central and western blocks, while at the Horseshoe Bend camping ground on the Wimmera River, you will find sites for caravans and tents. Ackle Bend also has basic camping facilities, with fireplaces, tables and toilets.

don't miss

Try to time your visit to Little Desert National Park to coincide with the spring blooming of wildflowers. Apart from the typical mallee vegetation, you can see smaller plants and shrubs, such as holly grevillea, flame heath and the colourful broom bush.

Lower Glenelg National Park

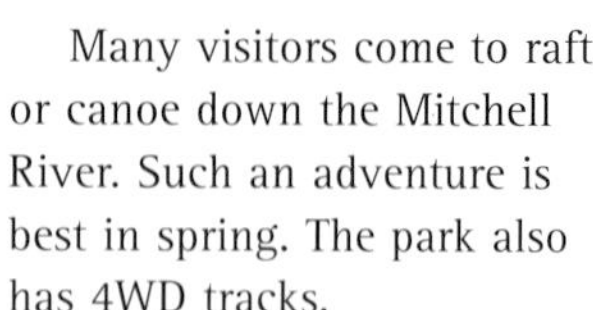

SIZE: 27 300 ha
MAP: Vic 5 C6

Before it meets the Southern Ocean in western Victoria, the Glenelg River carves a magnificent gorge lined with tall limestone cliffs that form the most popular feature of this park. With plenty of overnight camps and easy paddling, the Glenelg River offers newcomers the perfect canoeing adventure.

A limestone column in Princess Margaret Rose Caves in the Lower Glenelg National Park. The caves were discovered in 1936.

The Glenelg River Gorge and the river itself are popular for canoeing, fishing and boating. The Princess Margaret Rose Caves, which are open for guided tours, are another attraction—phone (03) 8738 4171. Limited camping and accommodation are also available at the caves.

Many walking tracks crisscross the park, and bushwalkers can see large number of plants and animals as well as wildflowers in spring.

Dartmoor and Nelson give easy access to all the sections of the park. Camp grounds are scattered along the Glenelg River and also at Dartmoor. Camping is by permit only, from the Nelson Visitor Centre, (08) 8738 4051.

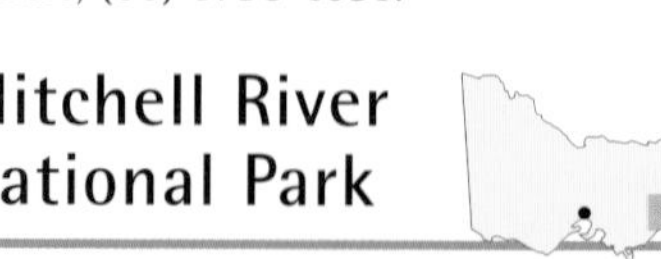

Right: *An Australian king parrot* (Alisterus scapularis) *in Mitchell River National Park. They join about 150 other bird species in the park, which includes excellent forest country.*

Mitchell River National Park

SIZE: 11 900 ha
MAP: Vic 4 C8

The Mitchell River National Park offers a remote mountain wilderness just north of the Princes Highway in East Gippsland, 300 km from Melbourne.

Many visitors come to raft or canoe down the Mitchell River. Such an adventure is best in spring. The park also has 4WD tracks.

Apart from the river, the best known feature of this park is the Den of Nargun, where a steep walking track, about 1 km long, leads from the car park at the south of the park to a limestone cave featuring stalactites. This car park is the most accessible and most favoured entry into the park. Other points of interest are the Bluff Lookout and Billy Goat Bend.

Access is from the Princes Highway before Bairnsdale, taking the Dargo Road.

Numerous bush camping sites can be found throughout the park, particularly along the Mitchell River.

For more information contact Parks Victoria, on 131 963.

Mount Buffalo National Park

SIZE: 31 600 ha
MAP: Vic 3 M7

Encircled by the Ovens, Buffalo and Buckland Rivers, this year-round park offers snow-covered mountain tops for skiing in winter, and clear, warm days for walking in summer.

It is the rugged nature of this park that beckons a wide variety of outdoor enthusiasts. There's excellent bushwalking with more than 90 km of marked trails in the park, and for the more adventurous there are some fantastic long rock climbs.

During the winter months cross-country skiers are well catered for, while downhill skiers have many trails to choose from. Anglers will find brown trout in Lake Catani, and mountain-bike riders have use of the vehicle access roads through the park.

Access to the park from Melbourne is via the Hume Highway on a sealed road through Porepunkah. Tyre chains must be carried during winter. Camping is restricted to the camp ground at Lake Catani. Motel or lodge-style accommodation is available at the Mount Buffalo Chalet, phone (03) 5755 1500.

For more information contact Parks Victoria, on 131 963.

Otway National Park

SIZE: 12 876 ha
MAP: Vic 5 L9

The Otway National Park stretches from just west of Apollo Bay along the coastline to Princetown where it merges with the Port Campbell National Park. This park has impressive mountain ash trees, waterfalls and lush, fern-filled ravines as well as its rugged coastline.

Fishing and surfing are popular along the coast and in the rivers, and there are numerous walks to enjoy. Swimming should be restricted to the lakes and rivers, as there are strong sea currents. Horseriding with a permit is allowed, as is mountain-bike riding.

The park can be accessed from the Princes Highway, then south through Apollo Bay or Lavers Hill, or via the Great Ocean Road.

Campers are catered for at the beachside Blanket Bay camping area at Point Lewis. Further west is the Johanna camping area, while Aire River also has camp sites.

Camp sites can be very popular, especially during summer, and should be booked in advance with the ranger. Contact Parks Victoria, on 131 963.

Above: *The huge granite plateau of Mount Buffalo towers over the surrounding river valleys. It was named by the explorers Hume and Hovell.*

Fog along the Great Ocean Road in the Otway National Park. In summer and autumn the park's forests are a cool haven from the heat.

Above: *The Twelve Apostles in Port Campbell National Park. This landmark was once part of a limestone cave system. Gradually the outer limestone wore away, creating these stacks.*

area, and the famous Glenample Homestead is now open to visitors.

The park is accessed via the Great Ocean Road, between Princetown and Peterborough. Camping is available at all the towns. Bookings are essential over the main holiday periods. For more information contact Parks Victoria on 131 963, or call into the Visitor Centre at the Twelve Apostles.

Port Campbell National Park

SIZE: 1750 ha
MAP: Vic 5 J8

The weather-beaten coastline of the Port Campbell National Park stands as a headstone for the numerous shipwrecks that lie on the nearby ocean floor. But it is the significant landmark of the Twelve Apostles that most people remember from their visit to this spectacular coast. These sea stacks—small, sheer-sided islands just offshore—dominate this coast and the drive along it.

The historic shipwreck-trail drive from Port Fairy all the way to Lavers Hill follows the Great Ocean Road. There are many interesting walks in the

Right: *The Lakes National Park and Gippsland Lakes Coastal Park are ideal family holiday locations, offering seaside fun as well as lakes and forest areas.*

The Lakes National Park and Gippsland Lakes Coastal Park

SIZE: 2390 ha/17 584 ha
MAP: Vic 6 N4

Encompassing the coastal region from Seaspray to Lakes Entrance, the Gippsland Lakes Coastal Park boasts such natural features as Ninety Mile Beach and the vast inland coastal lakes system. The smaller Lakes National Park adjoins it, while other reserves are dotted throughout the immediate area.

Visitors can take one of the many walks along the beach or stroll through banksia woodlands. Birdwatchers can use the bird hides in the park, while a trip to Murphy's Hill will reward the energetic with fantastic views of Bass Strait. Wildflowers flourish and visitors in October can enjoy the fine displays. There's also plenty of water to swim in.

There is boat access from Paynesville, and the eastern end of the park is reached from Bairnsdale. Rotomah Island is accessed by boat.

There are many camping areas within the coastal park, but camping in the national park is only allowed at Emu Bight.

Contact Parks Victoria on 131 963 for more details.

Popular Parks at a Glance

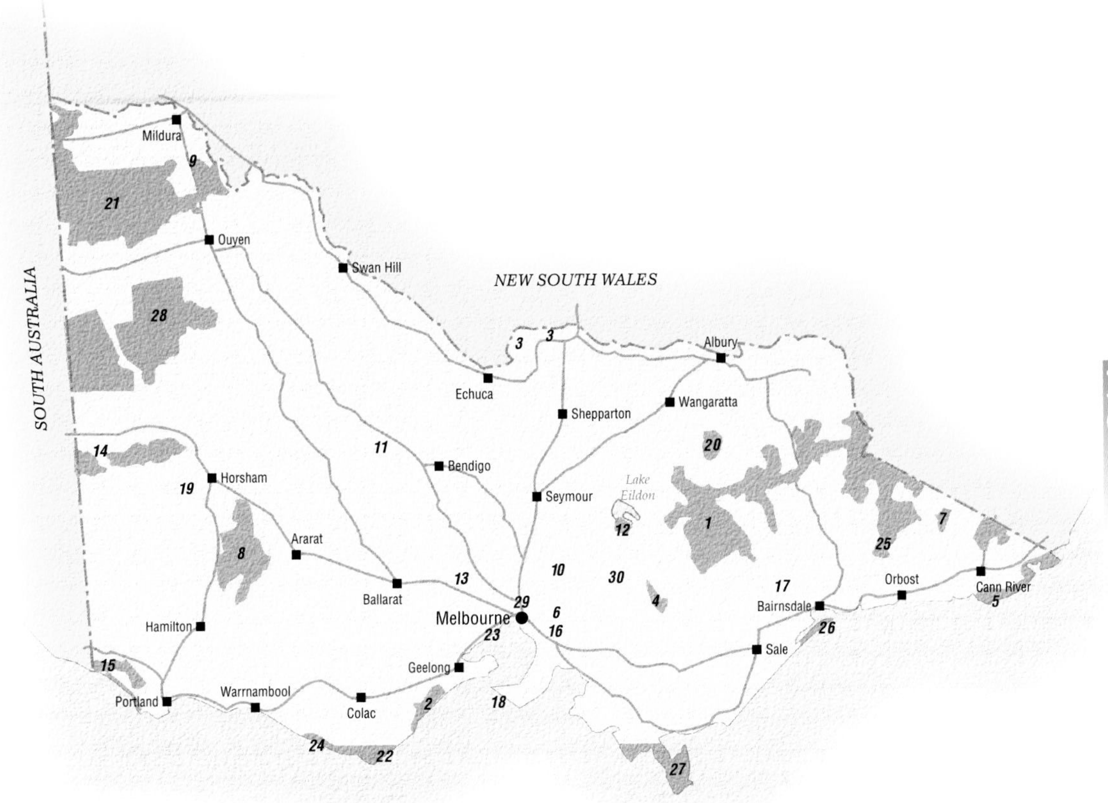

	Park	Camping	Caravan Access	Disabled Access	4WD Access	Picnic Areas	Toilets	Walking Tracks	Kiosk	Information
1	Alpine NP	●			●	●	●	●		●
2	Angahook–Lorne SP	●		●		●	●	●		●
3	Barmah SP	●		●		●	●	●		●
4	Baw Baw NP	●				●	●	●		●
5	Croajingolong NP	●			●	●	●	●		
6	Dandenong Ranges NP			●		●	●	●	●	●
7	Errinundra NP	●			●	●	●	●		●
8	Grampians NP	●		●	●	●	●	●	●	●
9	Hattah–Kulkyne NP	●	●		●	●	●	●		●
10	Kinglake NP	●	●	●	●	●	●	●		●
11	Kooyoora SP	●				●	●	●		
12	Lake Eildon NP	●			●	●	●	●	●	●
13	Lerderderg SP	●			●	●	●	●		●
14	Little Desert NP	●	●		●	●	●	●		●
15	Lower Glenelg NP	●	●			●	●	●		
16	Lysterfield Lake Park			●		●	●	●		●
17	Mitchell River NP	●			●	●	●	●		
18	Mornington Peninsula NP			●		●	●	●		●
19	Mount Arapiles–Tooan SP	●				●	●	●		●
20	Mount Buffalo NP	●				●	●	●		●
21	Murray–Sunset NP	●			●	●	●	●		●
22	Otway NP	●		●	●	●	●	●		●
23	Point Cook CP			●		●	●	●		●
24	Port Campbell NP					●	●	●		●
25	Snowy River NP	●			●	●	●	●		
26	The Lakes NP	●				●	●	●		●
27	Wilsons Promontory NP	●		●		●	●	●		●
28	Wyperfeld NP	●		●	●	●	●	●		●
29	Yarra Ranges NP			●		●	●	●		●
30	Yarra Valley Parklands			●		●	●	●		●

Map 1

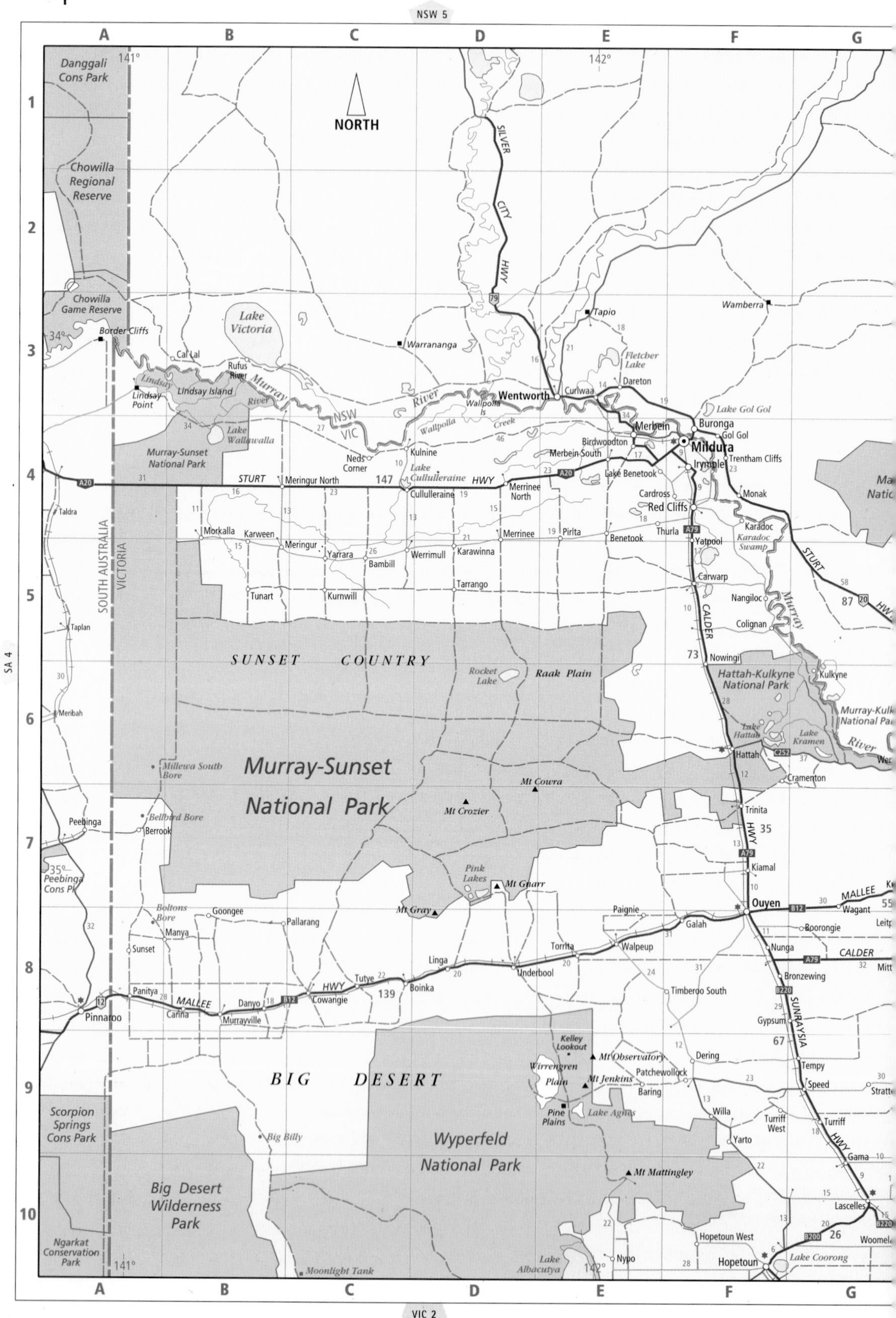
NSW 5
NORTH
Murray-Sunset National Park
SUNSET COUNTRY
BIG DESERT
Wyperfeld National Park
Big Desert Wilderness Park
Hattah-Kulkyne National Park
Mildura
Wentworth
Ouyen
Red Cliffs
Merbein
Hopetoun
Pinnaroo
Lake Victoria
SOUTH AUSTRALIA
VICTORIA
SA 4
VIC 2

Map 2

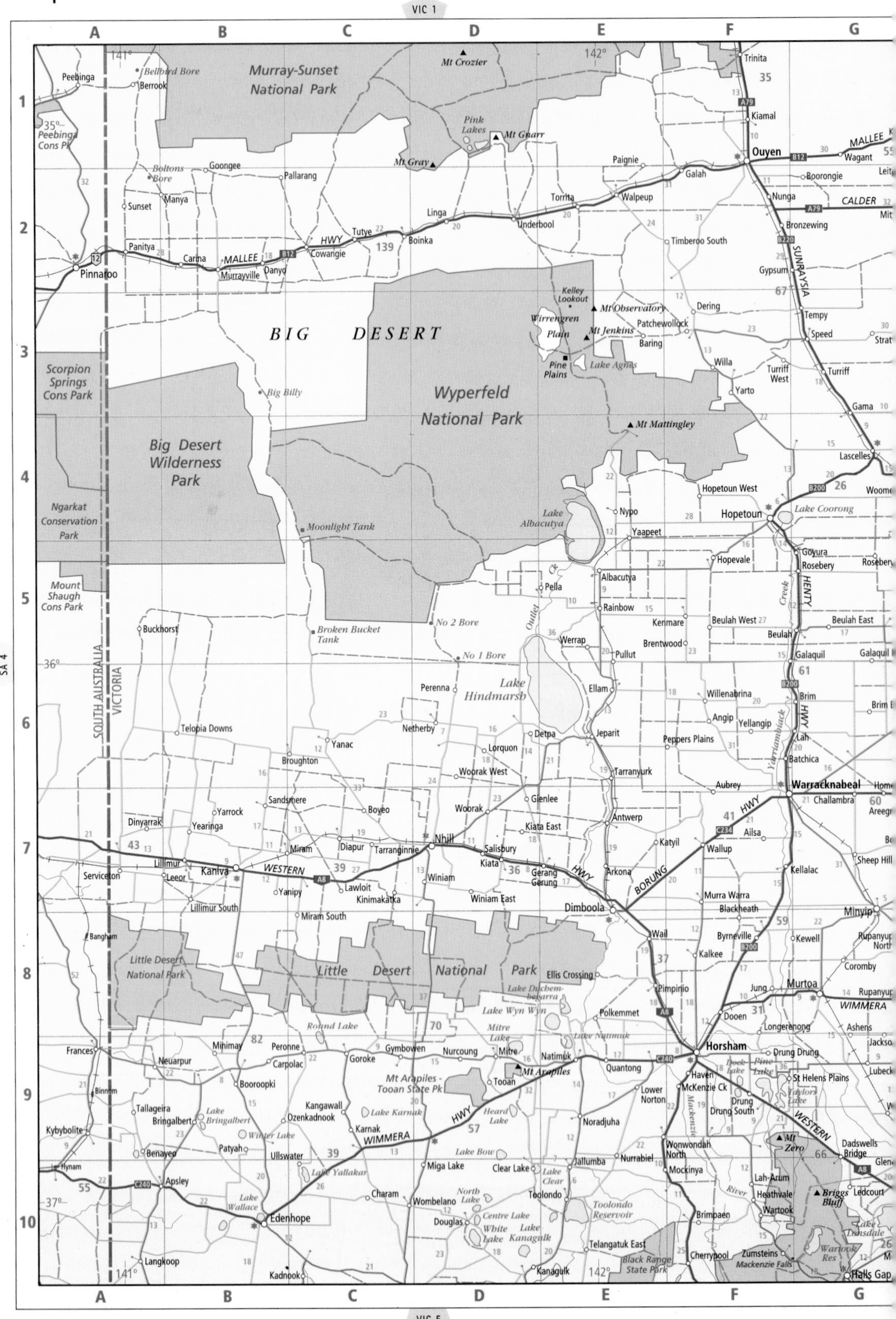

VIC 1
A
B
C
D
E
F
G
1
2
3
4
5
6
7
8
9
10
Murray-Sunset National Park
Mt Crozier
Pink Lakes
Mt Gnarr
Mt Gray
Trinita
Kiamal
Ouyen
Wagant
MALLEE
Boorongie
Nunga
CALDER
Bronzewing
Peebinga
Bellbird Bore
Berrook
Peebinga Cons Pk
Boltons Bore
Goongee
Pallarang
Paignie
Galah
Manya
Sunset
Torrita
Walpeup
Linga
Underbool
Tutye
Boinka
Timberoo South
Panitya
Carina
MALLEE
HWY
Cowangie
Murrayville
Danyo
Pinnaroo
Gypsum
SUNRAYSIA
Kelley Lookout
Mt Observatory
Dering
Wirrengren Plain
Mt Jenkins
Patchewollock
Baring
BIG DESERT
Tempy
Speed
Willa
Turriff West
Turriff
Pine Plains
Lake Agnes
Yarto
Scorpion Springs Cons Park
Big Billy
Wyperfeld National Park
Mt Mattingley
Gama
Lascelles
Big Desert Wilderness Park
Hopetoun West
Ngarkat Conservation Park
Lake Albacutya
Nypo
Hopetoun
Lake Coorong
Moonlight Tank
Yaapeet
Goyura
Rosebery
Hopevale
Albacutya
Pella
Mount Shaugh Cons Park
Rainbow
Kenmare
Beulah West
Beulah East
Beulah
HENTY
Brentwood
Galaquil
Buckhorst
Broken Bucket Tank
No 2 Bore
Outlet Ck
Werrap
Pullut
No 1 Bore
SOUTH AUSTRALIA
VICTORIA
Perenna
Lake Hindmarsh
Ellam
Willenabrina
Brim
Netherby
Angip
Yellangip
Telopia Downs
Yanac
Detpa
Jeparit
Peppers Plains
Lah
Lorquon
Broughton
Batchica
Woorak West
Tarranyurk
Aubrey
Warracknabeal
Sandsmere
Boyeo
Glenlee
Challambra
Yarrock
Woorak
Antwerp
Dinyarrak
Yearinga
Kiata East
Ailsa
Nhill
Diapur
Tarranginnie
Salisbury
Katyil
Wallup
Miram
Lillimur
Kiata
Serviceton
Leeor
Kaniva
WESTERN
Winiam
Gerang Gerung
Arkona
BORUNG
Kellalac
Lawloit
Yanipy
Kinimakatka
Winiam East
Murra Warra
Lillimur South
Miram South
Dimboola
Blackheath
Minyip
Wail
Byrneville
Kewell
Bangham
Kalkee
Little Desert National Park
Little Desert National Park
Ellis Crossing
Corombry
Lake Duchembegarra
Pimpinio
Jung
Murtoa
Lake Wyn Wyn
Polkemmet
Dooen
WIMMERA
Round Lake
Mitre Lake
Lake Natimuk
Longerenong
Ashens
Frances
Minimay
Peronne
Gymbowen
Nurcoung
Mitre
Natimuk
Horsham
Drung Drung
Neuarpur
Carpolac
Goroke
Quantong
Haven
Dock Lake
Pine Lake
Booroopki
Mt Arapiles-Tooan State Pk
Mt Arapiles
Tooan
McKenzie Ck
St Helens Plains
Binnum
Tallageira
Kangawall
Lower Norton
Drung
Taylors Lake
Bringalbert
Lake Bringalbert
Ozenkadnook
Lake Karnak
Heard Lake
Drung South
Karnak
Noradjuha
Kybybolite
Winter Lake
WIMMERA
HWY
Mackenzie
WESTERN
Benayeo
Patyah
Lake Bow
Nurrabiel
Wonwondah North
Mt Zero
Dadswells Bridge
Ullswater
Jallumba
Hynam
Miga Lake
Clear Lake
Lake Clear
Mockinya
Lake Yallakar
Lah-Arum
Apsley
Briggs Bluff
Charam
North Lake
Toolondo
River
Heathvale
Ledcourt
Lake Wallace
Toolondo Reservoir
Wartook
Edenhope
Wombelano
Centre Lake
Brimpaen
Douglas
White Lake
Lake Kanagulk
Lake Lonsdale
Telangatuk East
Wartook Res
Langkoop
Black Range State Park
Cherrypool
Zumsteins
Mackenzie Falls
Kadnook
Kanagulk
Halls Gap
SA 4
VIC 5

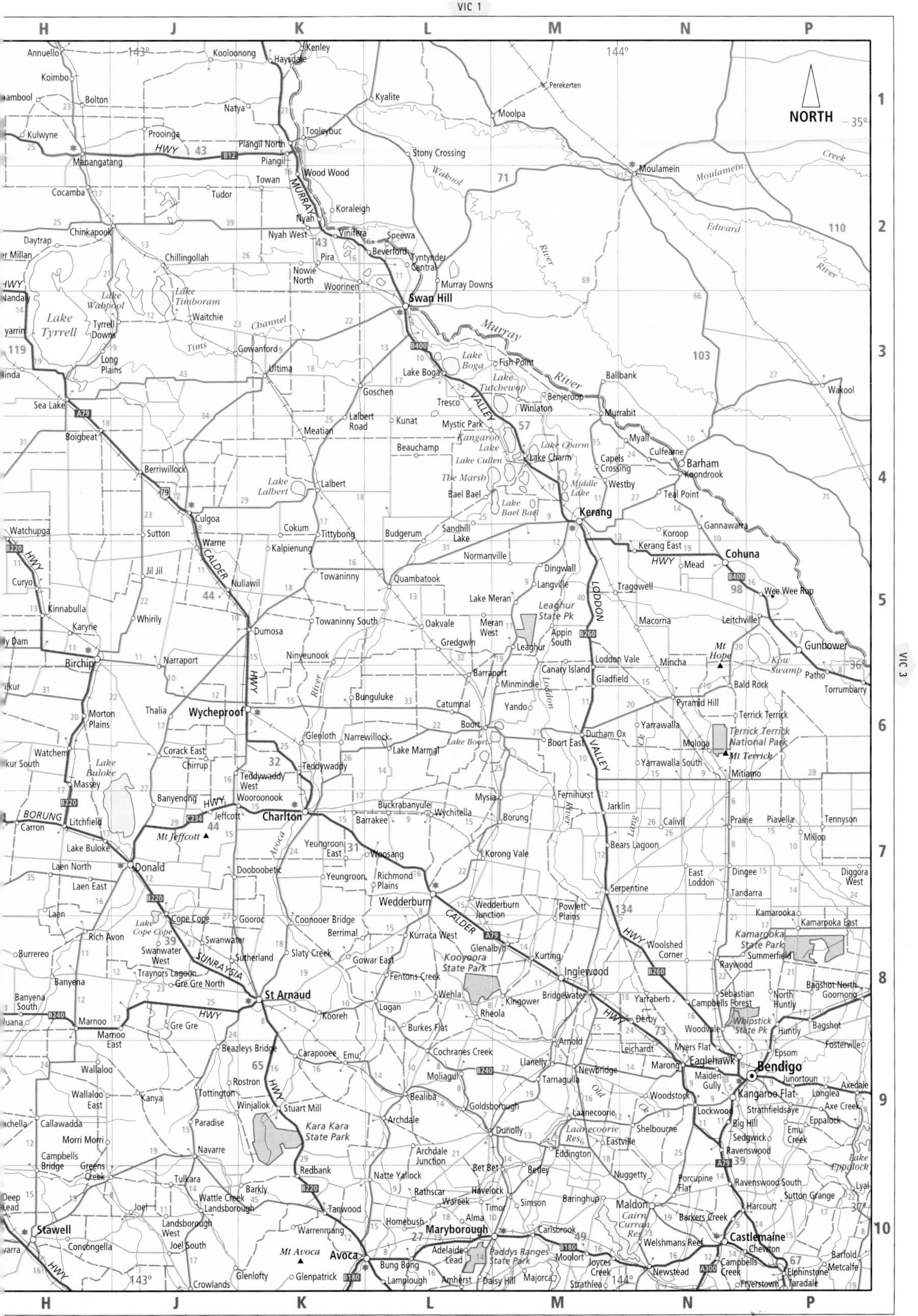

0 10 20 30 40
kilometres
VIC 1
NORTH
Swan Hill
Kerang
Cohuna
Barham
Moulamein
Wycheproof
Charlton
Donald
St Arnaud
Wedderburn
Inglewood
Bendigo
Eaglehawk
Castlemaine
Maryborough
Avoca
Stawell
Birchip
Sea Lake
Boort
Dunolly
Maldon
Kara Kara State Park
Kooyoora State Park
Leaghur State Pk
Terrick Terrick National Park
Kamarooka State Park
Whipstick State Pk
Paddys Ranges State Park
Lake Tyrrell
Lake Buloke
Murray River
Loddon River
Avoca River
CALDER HWY
LODDON VALLEY HWY
SUNRAYSIA HWY
MURRAY VALLEY
BORUNG HWY
VIC 3
VIC 5

Map 3

NSW 5

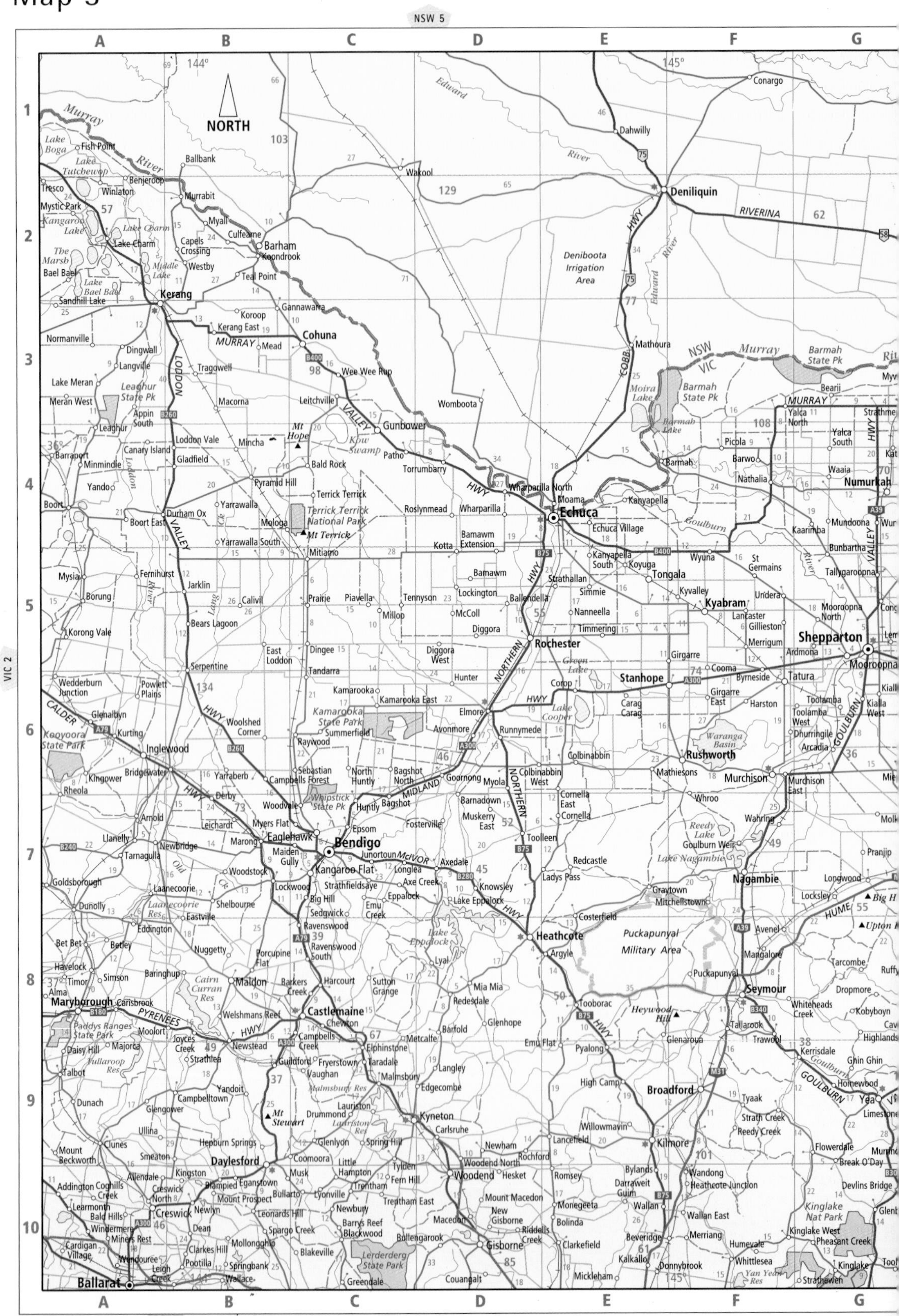

VIC 2

VIC 5

0 10 20 30 40
kilometres

NSW 7

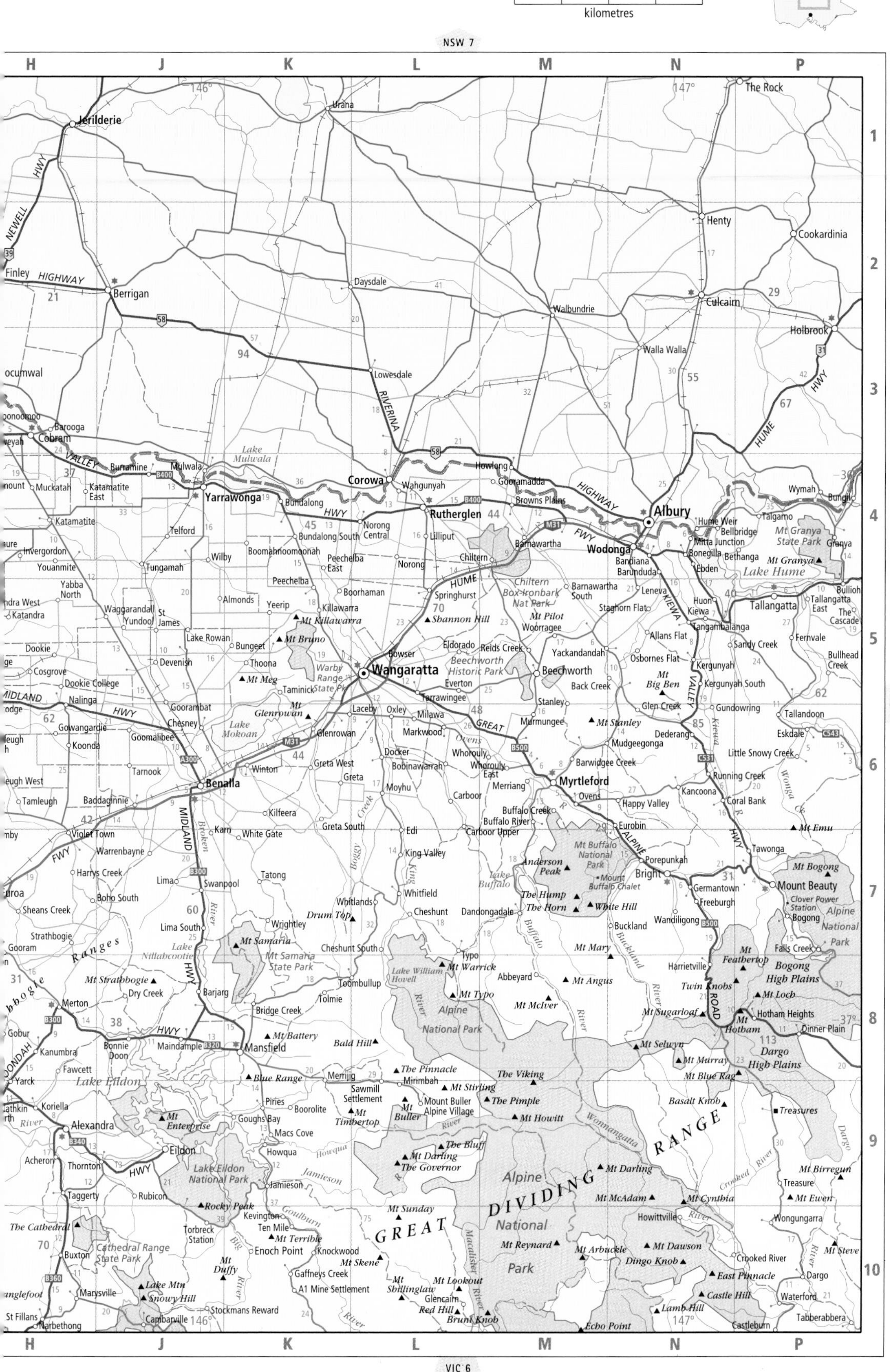

VIC 4

VIC 6

Map 4

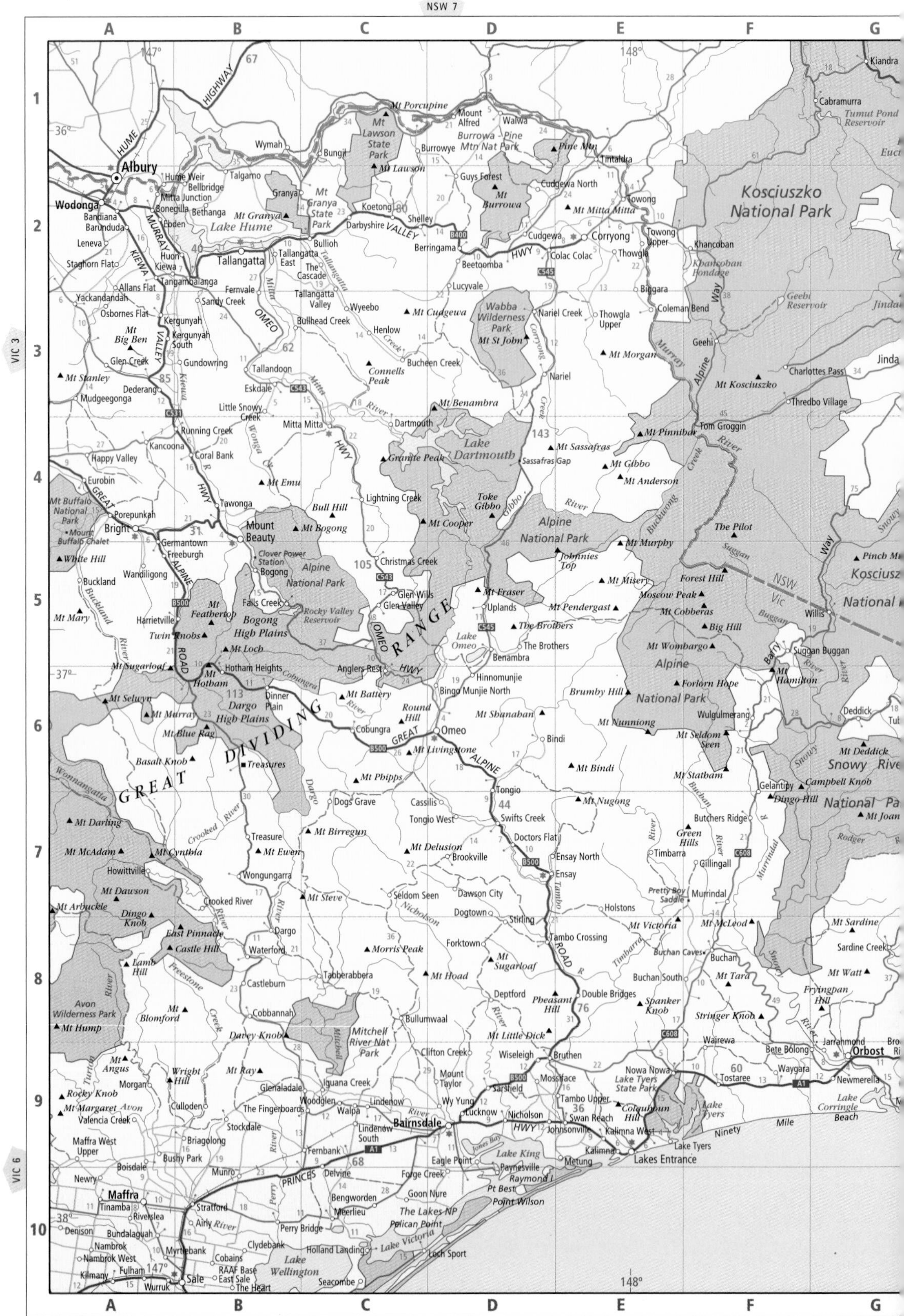
NSW 7
VIC 3
VIC 6
A
B
C
D
E
F
G
1
2
3
4
5
6
7
8
9
10
147°
148°
36°
37°
38°
HUME
HIGHWAY
Albury
Wodonga
Hume Weir
Bellbridge
Mitta Junction
Bonegilla
Bethanga
Ebden
Talgarno
Wymah
Bungil
Mt Porcupine
Mount Alfred
Walwa
Burrowa - Pine Mtn Nat Park
Pine Mtn
Tintaldra
Mt Lawson State Park
Mt Lawson
Burrowye
Guys Forest
Mt Burrowa
Cudgewa North
Towong
Mt Mitta Mitta
Kiandra
Cabramurra
Tumut Pond Reservoir
Kosciuszko National Park
Granya
Mt Granya State Park
Mt Granya
Lake Hume
Koetong
Shelley
Darbyshire
VALLEY
Berringama
Cudgewa
Corryong
Towong Upper
Khancoban
Khancoban Pondage
Bandiana
Barunduda
Leneva
Staghorn Flat
MURRAY
KIEWA
Huon
Kiewa
Tangambalanga
Tallangatta
Bullioh
Tallangatta East
The Cascade
Beetoomba
HWY
Colac Colac
Thowgla
Allans Flat
Yackandandah
Osbornes Flat
Fernvale
Sandy Creek
Tallangatta Valley
Lucyvale
Biggara
Coleman Bend
Geebi Reservoir
Wyeebo
Mt Cudgewa
Wabba Wilderness Park
Mt St John
Nariel Creek
Thowgla Upper
Mt Big Ben
Kergunyah
Kergunyah South
Bullhead Creek
OMEO
Henlow
Geehi
Glen Creek
Gundowring
Connells Peak
Bucheen Creek
Mt Morgan
Murray
Alpine
Way
Jinda
Mt Stanley
Tallandoon
Nariel
Charlottes Pass
Mt Kosciuszko
Dederang
Eskdale
Mudgeegonga
Little Snowy Creek
Mt Benambra
Thredbo Village
Mitta Mitta
Dartmouth
Mt Pinnibar
Tom Groggin
Running Creek
Kancoona
Coral Bank
Lake Dartmouth
Mt Sassafras
Sassafras Gap
Happy Valley
Granite Peak
Mt Gibbo
Mt Anderson
Eurobin
Mt Emu
Mt Buffalo National Park
Porepunkah
Tawonga
Lightning Creek
Toke Gibbo
Bull Hill
Bright
Mount Beauty
Mt Bogong
Mt Cooper
Alpine National Park
Mt Murphy
The Pilot
Mount Buffalo Chalet
Germantown
Freeburgh
Clover Power Station
Christmas Creek
Johnnies Top
White Hill
Bogong
Pinch Mt
Buckland
Wandiligong
Mt Misery
Forest Hill
Kosciusz
Glen Wills
Glen Valley
Mt Fraser
Uplands
Moscow Peak
Mt Mary
Harrietville
Mt Feathertop
Falls Creek
Bogong High Plains
Rocky Valley Reservoir
RANGE
Mt Pendergast
Mt Cobberas
Willis
NSW
Vic
Twin Knobs
Lake Omeo
The Brothers
Big Hill
Mt Loch
Benambra
Mt Wombargo
Suggan Buggan
Mt Sugarloaf
Mt Hotham
Hotham Heights
Anglers Rest
Hinnomunjie
Mt Hamilton
Mt Selwyn
Dinner Plain
Mt Battery
Bingo Munjie North
Brumby Hill
Forlorn Hope
Deddick
Dargo High Plains
Mt Murray
Round Hill
Mt Shanahan
National Park
Wulgulmerang
Mt Blue Rag
GREAT
DIVIDING
Cobungra
Omeo
Bindi
Mt Nunniong
Mt Seldom Seen
Mt Deddick
Snowy River
Basalt Knob
Treasures
Mt Livingstone
ALPINE
Mt Bindi
Mt Statham
Mt Phipps
Gelantipy
Campbell Knob
Dingo Hill
National Park
Dogs Grave
Cassilis
Tongio
Mt Nugong
Tongio West
Swifts Creek
Butchers Ridge
Mt Joan
Mt Darling
Treasure
Mt Birregun
Doctors Flat
Green Hills
Timbarra
Mt McAdam
Mt Cynthia
Mt Ewen
Mt Delusion
Brookville
Ensay North
Gillingall
Howittville
Wongungarra
Ensay
Mt Dawson
Seldom Seen
Dawson City
Pretty Boy Saddle
Murrindal
Mt Arbuckle
Crooked River
Mt Steve
Dogtown
Holstons
Dingo Knob
Stirling
Mt Victoria
Mt McLeod
Mt Sardine
East Pinnacle
Dargo
Tambo Crossing
Sardine Creek
Castle Hill
Waterford
Morris Peak
Forktown
Mt Sugarloaf
Buchan Caves
Buchan
Lamb Hill
Mt Hoad
ROAD
Buchan South
Mt Tara
Mt Watt
Castleburn
Tabberabbera
Deptford
Pheasant Hill
Double Bridges
Spanker Knob
Fryingpan Hill
Avon Wilderness Park
Mt Blomford
Cobbannah
Bullumwaal
Stringer Knob
Mt Hump
Davey Knob
Mitchell River Nat Park
Mt Little Dick
Wairewa
Jarrahmond
Mt Angus
Wright Hill
Mt Ray
Clifton Creek
Wiseleigh
Bruthen
Bete Bolong
Orbost
Morgan
Glenaladale
Iguana Creek
Mount Taylor
Mossiface
Nowa Nowa
Waygara
Tostaree
Newmerella
Rocky Knob
Culloden
Woodglen
Lindenow
Wy Yung
Sarsfield
Lake Tyers State Park
Tambo Upper
Mt Margaret
Valencia Creek
The Fingerboards
Walpa
Lucknow
Nicholson
Swan Reach
Colquhoun Hill
Lake Tyers
Lake Corringle Beach
Stockdale
Lindenow South
Bairnsdale
Johnsonville
Kalimna West
Ninety
Mile
Maffra West Upper
Briagolong
Fernbank
Jones Bay
Lake King
Kalimna
Lakes Entrance
Lake Tyers
Bushy Park
Eagle Point
Paynesville
Metung
Boisdale
Munro
PRINCES
Delvine
Forge Creek
Raymond I
Newry
Maffra
Tinamba
Stratford
Bengworden
Goon Nure
Pt Best
Point Wilson
Riverslea
Meerlieu
The Lakes NP
Pelican Point
Denison
Airly
Perry Bridge
Bundalaguah
Nambrok
Clydebank
Holland Landing
Lake Victoria
Nambrok West
Myrtlebank
Cobains
Loch Sport
Lake Wellington
Kilmany
Fulham
RAAF Base East Sale
Wurruk
Sale
Seacombe
The Heart

0 10 20 30 40
kilometres

NSW 7

H J K L M N P

NORTH

VIC

Deua National Park
Moruya
Turlinjah
Tuross Lake
Bodalla
Narooma
Tilba Tilba
Cobargo
Bermagui
Adaminaby
Old Adaminaby
Numeralla
Cooma
Yowrie
Berridale
Wadbilliga National Park
Biamanga Nat Park
Dalgety
Nimmitabel
Brogo
Bemboka Nat Park
Numbugga
Bega
Mimosa Rocks National Park
Tathra
Ando
Mt Rix
Tantawangalo National Park
Candelo
Wallagoot Lake
Bournda Nat Park
South East Forest National Park
Cathcart
Merimbula
Bombala
Wyndham
Coolangubra National Park
Yowaka National Park
Ben Boyd National Park
Delegate
Eden
Craigie
Delegate River
Bendoc North
Towamba
Haydens Bog
Mt Delegate
Bondi Gulf Nat Pk
Genoa National Park
Pericoe
East Boyd
Bonang
Bendoc
Mt Imlay National Park
Ben Boyd National Park
Mt Tennyson
Mt Poole
Mt Canterbury
Granite Mtn
Narrabarba
Brown Mtn
Buldah
Coopracambra National Park
NEW SOUTH WALES
VICTORIA
Green Cape
Disaster Bay
Goongerah
Cobb Hill
Errinundra National Park
Chandlers Creek
Mealing Hill
Wroxham
Combienbar
Weeragua
Wangarabell
Errinundra
Mt Ellery
Mt Kaye
Maramingo Hill
Nadgee Nature Reserve
Nadgee Point
Waldron Mtn
Noorinbee North
Mt Carlyle
Bee Tree Hill
Genoa
Gipsy Point
Fairhaven
Pike Hill
Cape Howe
Lake Barracoota
Pyramid Hill
Noorinbee
Tonghi Creek
Genoa Peak
Gabo Island
Club Terrace
Alfred Nat Park
Mallacoota
Mallacoota Inlet
Lind Nat Park
Cann River
Murrungowar
Croajingolong National Park
Mt Cann
Bellbird Creek
Little Rame Head
Wingan Bay
Furnell
Mt Everard
Croajingolong National Park
Sandpatch Point
Cape Conran Coastal Park
Lake Furnell
Swan Lake
Tamboon
Bemm River
Wingan Point
Rame Head
East Cape
Pearl Point
Sydenham Inlet
Tamboon Inlet
Petrel Point
Cape Everard
Cape Conran

GREAT DIVIDING RANGE
MONARO HIGHWAY
SNOWY MOUNTAINS HWY
PRINCES HWY
CANN VALLEY HWY

149° 150° 36° 37° 38°

1 2 3 4 5 6 7 8 9 10

H J K L M N P

Map 5

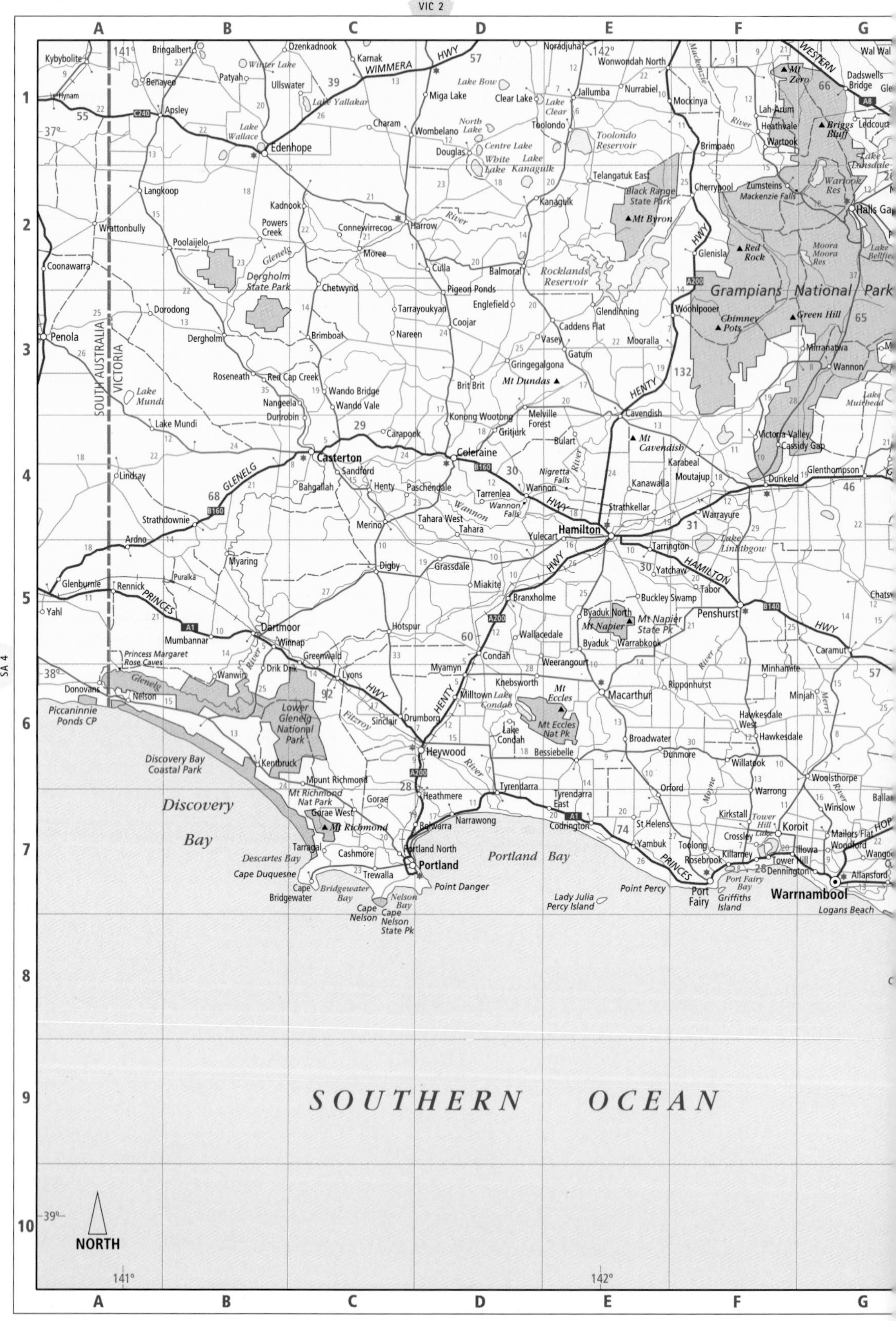
VIC 2
SA 4
A
B
C
D
E
F
G
1
2
3
4
5
6
7
8
9
10
141°
142°
37°
38°
39°
SOUTH AUSTRALIA
VICTORIA
Kybybolite
Hynam
Bringalbert
Benayeo
Patyah
Winter Lake
Ozenkadnook
Ullswater
Karnak
WIMMERA HWY
Apsley
Lake Wallace
Lake Yallakar
Edenhope
Charam
Miga Lake
Wombelano
North Lake
Douglas
Centre Lake
White Lake
Lake Kanagulk
Lake Bow
Clear Lake
Lake Clear
Noradjuha
Wonwondah North
Jallumba
Nurrabiel
Mockinya
Mackenzie River
Toolondo
Toolondo Reservoir
Telangatuk East
Black Range State Park
Mt Byron
Kanagulk
Brimpaen
Cherrypool
Lah-Arum
Heathvale
Wartook
Mt Zero
Briggs Bluff
WESTERN
Dadswells Bridge
Wal Wal
Ledcourt
Lake Lonsdale
Wartook Res
Zumsteins
Mackenzie Falls
Halls Gap
Moora Moora Res
Lake Bellfield
Grampians National Park
Red Rock
Green Hill
Chimney Pots
Glenisla
Woohlpooer
Langkoop
Kadnook
Powers Creek
Connewirrecoo
Harrow
Glenelg River
Moree
Culla
Balmoral
Rocklands Reservoir
Wrattonbully
Poolaijelo
Coonawarra
Dergholm State Park
Chetwynd
Pigeon Ponds
Englefield
Tarrayoukyan
Coojar
Nareen
Glendinning
Caddens Flat
Vasey
Mooralla
Gatum
Dorodong
Penola
Dergholm
Brimboal
Gringegalgona
Mt Dundas
Mirranatwa
Wannon
Roseneath
Red Cap Creek
Wando Bridge
Wando Vale
Brit Brit
Lake Mundi
Nangeela
Dunrobin
Konong Wootong
Melville Forest
Cavendish
Mt Cavendish
HENTY
Lake Muirhead
Victoria Valley
Cassidy Gap
Carapook
Gritjurk
Bulart
Casterton
Coleraine
Karabeal
Moutajup
Dunkeld
Glenthompson
Sandford
Lindsay
GLENELG
Bahgallah
Henty
Paschendale
Tarrenlea
Nigretta Falls
Wannon Falls
Wannon River
Kanawalla
Strathkellar
Warrayure
Strathdownie
Merino
Tahara West
Tahara
Hamilton
Yulecart
Tarrington
Lake Linlithgow
Ardno
Myaring
Digby
Grassdale
Yatchaw
HAMILTON
Tabor
Glenburnie
Rennick
Puralka
PRINCES
Miakite
Branxholme
Buckley Swamp
Yahl
Byaduk North
Mt Napier
Mt Napier State Pk
Penshurst
Chatsworth
Dartmoor
Hotspur
Wallacedale
Byaduk
Warrabkook
Caramut
Mumbannar
Winnap
Princess Margaret Rose Caves
Greenwald
Condah
Weerangourt
Minhamite
Drik Drik
Myamyn
Knebsworth
Mt Eccles
Ripponhurst
Donovans
Wanwin
Lyons
Milltown
Lake Condah
Macarthur
Minjah
Nelson
Piccaninnie Ponds CP
Lower Glenelg National Park
Fitzroy
Sinclair
Drumborg
Mt Eccles Nat Pk
Hawkesdale West
Hawkesdale
Lake Condah
Broadwater
Heywood
Bessiebelle
Dunmore
Discovery Bay Coastal Park
Kentbruck
Willatook
Woolsthorpe
Mount Richmond
Tyrendarra
Orford
Moyne
Warrong
Winslow
Mt Richmond Nat Park
Gorae
Heathmere
Tyrendarra East
Ballangeich
Discovery Bay
Gorae West
Mt Richmond
Narrawong
Codrington
St Helens
Kirkstall
Tower Hill Lake
Koroit
Mailors Flat
Woodford
Tarragal
Bolwarra
Yambuk
Toolong
Crossley
Descartes Bay
Cashmore
Portland North
Portland Bay
Rosebrook
Killarney
Illowa
Tower Hill
Wangoom
Cape Duquesne
Trewalla
Portland
Dennington
Allansford
Cape Bridgewater
Bridgewater Bay
Point Danger
Lady Julia Percy Island
Point Percy
Port Fairy
Port Fairy Bay
Griffiths Island
Warrnambool
Logans Beach
Nelson Bay
Cape Nelson
Cape Nelson State Pk
SOUTHERN OCEAN
NORTH

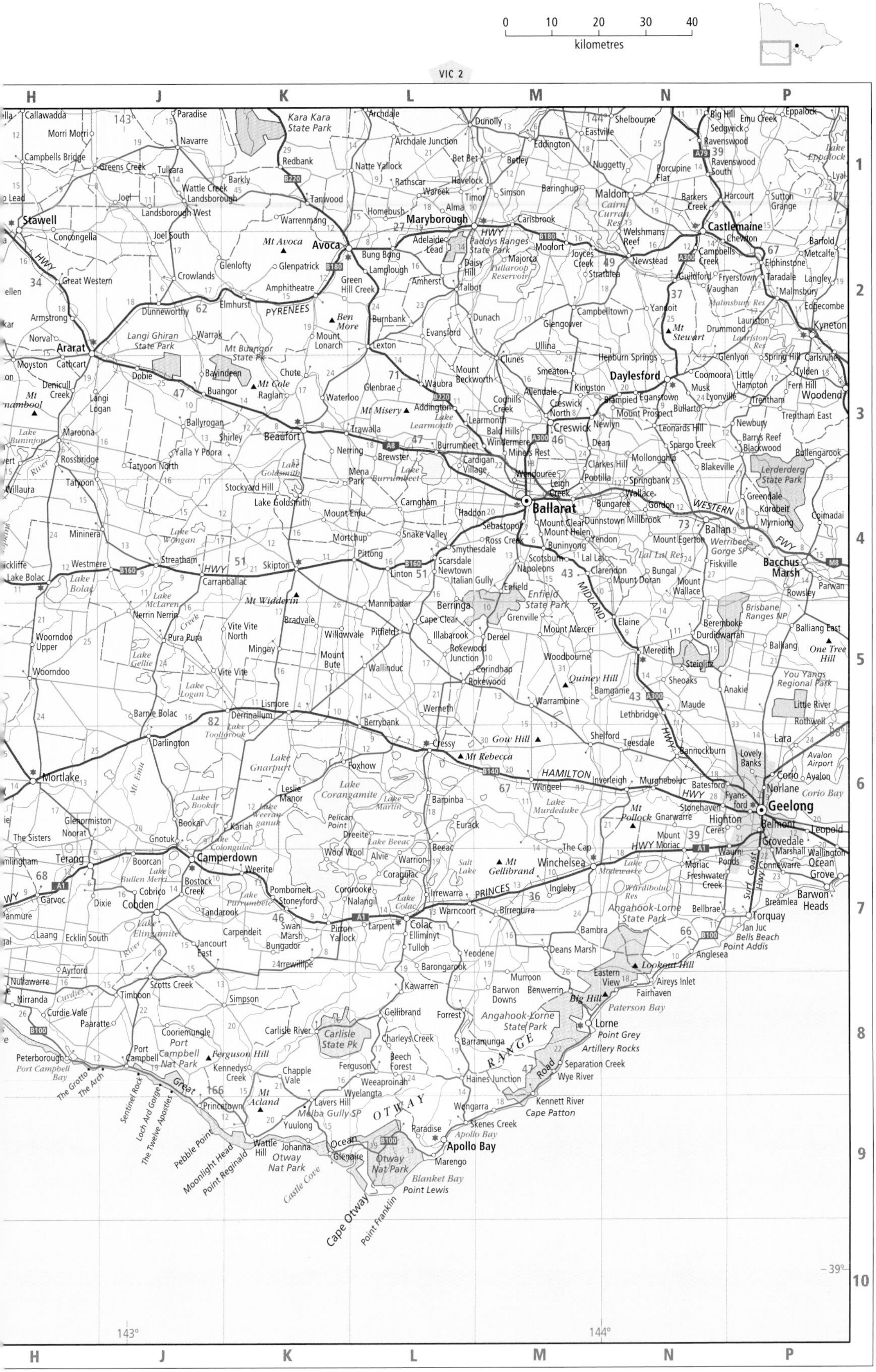

0 10 20 30 40
kilometres

VIC 2

H J K L M N P

1 2 3 4 5 6 7 8 9 10

VIC 6

143° 144° 39°

H J K L M N P

Map 6

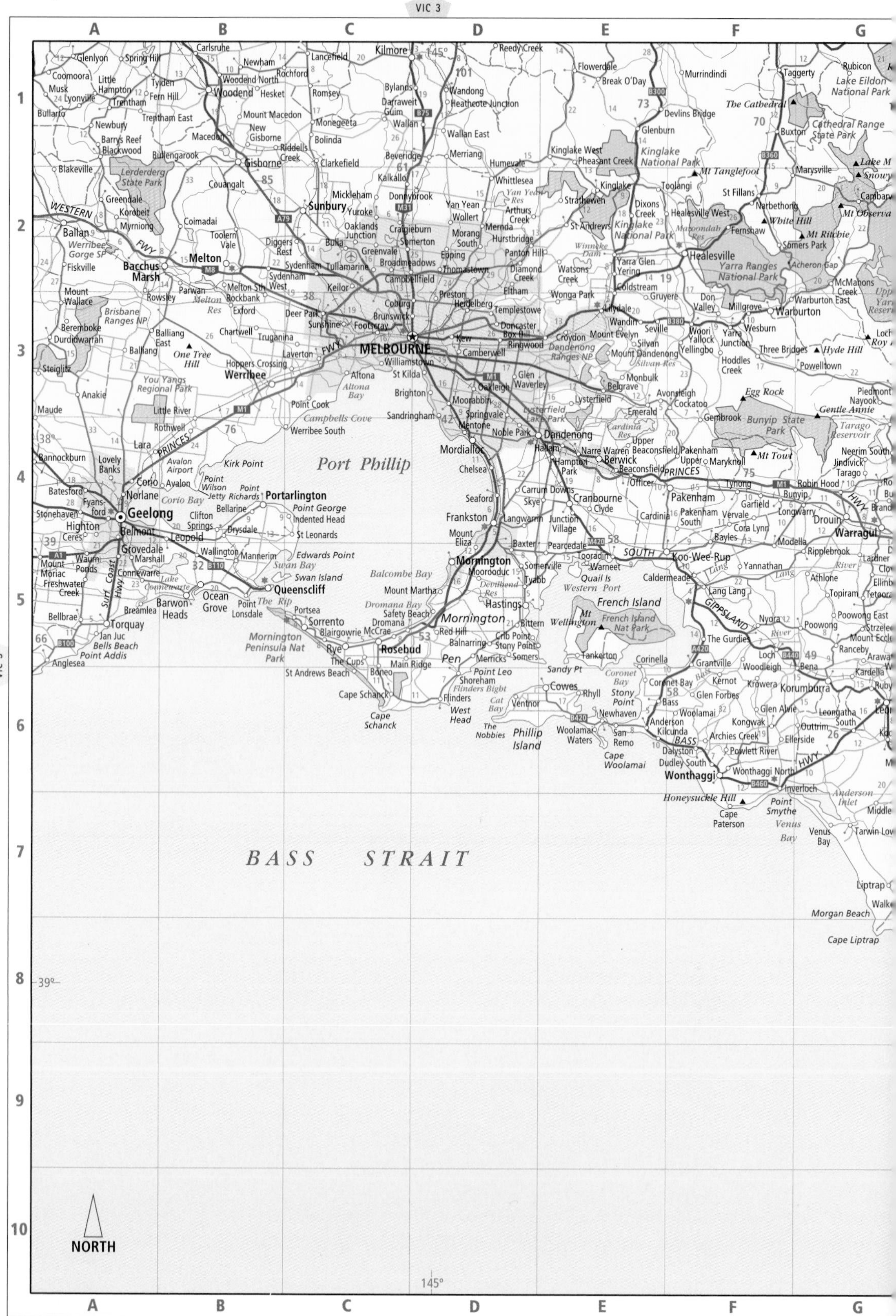
VIC 3
VIC 5
A
B
C
D
E
F
G
1
2
3
4
5
6
7
8
9
10
145°
38°
39°
NORTH
MELBOURNE
Geelong
Port Phillip
BASS STRAIT
Western Port
French Island
Phillip Island
Kilmore
Woodend
Gisborne
Sunbury
Melton
Bacchus Marsh
Werribee
Lara
Torquay
Ocean Grove
Queenscliff
Portarlington
Sorrento
Rosebud
Mornington
Frankston
Dandenong
Cranbourne
Pakenham
Berwick
Healesville
Warburton
Warragul
Drouin
Koo-Wee-Rup
Wonthaggi
Cowes
Hastings
Korumburra
Whittlesea
Lilydale
Ringwood
Box Hill
Kinglake National Park
Yarra Ranges National Park
Bunyip State Park
Dandenong Ranges NP
Lerderderg State Park
Brisbane Ranges NP
You Yangs Regional Park
Mornington Peninsula Nat Park
Cathedral Range State Park
Lake Eildon National Park
Cape Schanck
Cape Woolamai
Cape Paterson
Cape Liptrap
Point Lonsdale
Anglesea
Marysville
WESTERN FWY
PRINCES
SOUTH GIPPSLAND HWY
BASS HWY

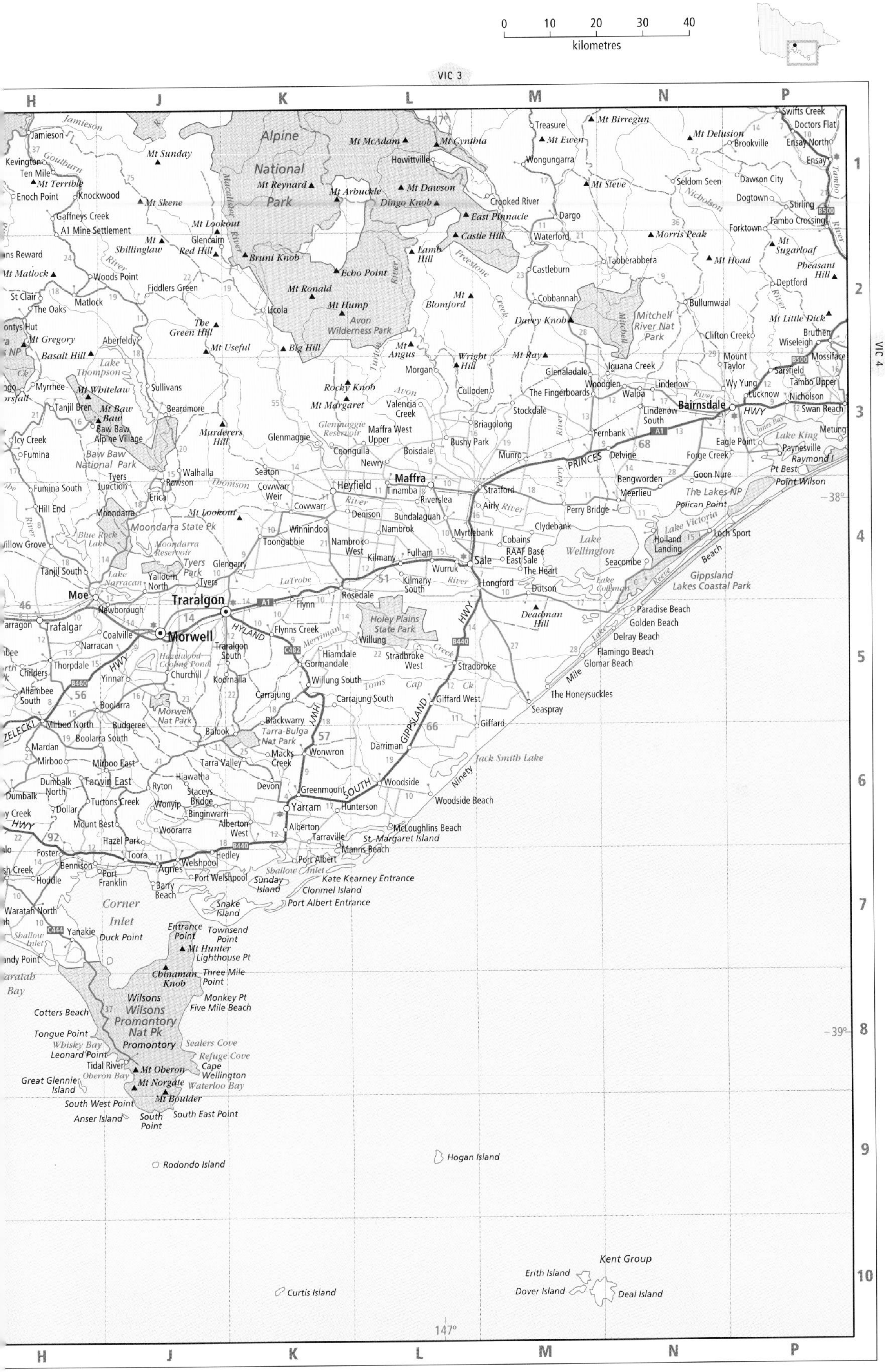

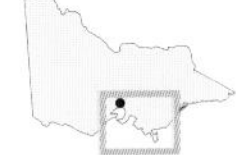

0 10 20 30 40
kilometres

VIC 3

H J K L M N P

Jamieson
Kevington
Ten Mile
Mt Terrible
Enoch Point
Knockwood
Gaffneys Creek
A1 Mine Settlement
Mt Sunday
Mt Skene
Alpine National Park
Mt McAdam
Mt Cynthia
Howittville
Mt Reynard
Mt Arbuckle
Mt Dawson
Dingo Knob
Crooked River
East Pinnacle
Castle Hill
Lamb Hill
Mt Lookout
Glencairn
Red Hill
Mt Shillinglaw
Bruni Knob
Echo Point
Mt Ronald
Mt Hump
Avon Wilderness Park
Licola
Big Hill
Treasure
Mt Birregun
Mt Ewen
Wongungarra
Mt Steve
Dargo
Waterford
Castleburn
Mt Delusion
Brookville
Seldom Seen
Dawson City
Dogtown
Stirling
Tambo Crossing
Forktown
Morris Peak
Mt Sugarloaf
Mt Hoad
Tabberabbera
Pheasant Hill
Deptford
Swifts Creek
Doctors Flat
Ensay North
Ensay
Mt Matlock
Woods Point
Matlock
St Clair
The Oaks
Fiddlers Green
The Green Hill
Mt Useful
Mt Gregory
Aberfeldy
Basalt Hill
Lake Thompson
Mt Whitelaw
Tanjil Bren
Mt Baw Baw
Baw Baw Alpine Village
Baw Baw National Park
Sullivans
Beardmore
Murderers Hill
Mt Blomford
Cobbannah
Davey Knob
Mitchell River Nat Park
Bullumwaal
Clifton Creek
Mt Little Dick
Bruthen
Wiseleigh
Mt Angus
Wright Hill
Mt Ray
Morgan
Rocky Knob
Mt Margaret
Culloden
Glenaladale
Iguana Creek
Woodglen
Lindenow
Walpa
The Fingerboards
Stockdale
Lindenow South
Bairnsdale
Mount Taylor
Wy Yung
Lucknow
Sarsfield
Mossiface
Tambo Upper
Nicholson
Swan Reach
Metung
Lake King
Eagle Point
Paynesville
Raymond I
Forge Creek
Pt Best
Goon Nure
Point Wilson
The Lakes NP
Pelican Point
Icy Creek
Fumina
Fumina South
Hill End
Willow Grove
Tyers Junction
Walhalla
Rawson
Erica
Moondarra
Moondarra State Pk
Mt Lookout
Blue Rock Lake
Moondarra Reservoir
Tyers Park
Glenmaggie
Glenmaggie Reservoir
Valencia Creek
Maffra West Upper
Coongulla
Boisdale
Briagolong
Bushy Park
Newry
Seaton
Heyfield
Maffra
Tinamba
Riverslea
Cowwarr Weir
Cowwarr
Denison
Bundalaguah
Munro
Stratford
Airly
Fernbank
Delvine
Bengworden
Meerlieu
Perry Bridge
Winnindoo
Toongabbie
Nambrok
Nambrok West
Myrtlebank
Cobains
Clydebank
Lake Wellington
Holland Landing
Lake Victoria
Loch Sport
Tanjil South
Yallourn North
Lake Narracan
Glengarry
Tyers
Kilmany
Fulham
Wurruk
Sale
RAAF Base East Sale
The Heart
Seacombe
Kilmany South
Longford
Dulson
Gippsland Lakes Coastal Park
Moe
Newborough
Traralgon
Flynn
Rosedale
Holey Plains State Park
Deadman Hill
Paradise Beach
Golden Beach
Delray Beach
Flamingo Beach
Glomar Beach
Trafalgar
Coalville
Morwell
Narracan
Flynns Creek
Willung
Traralgon South
Hiamdale
Gormandale
Stradbroke West
Stradbroke
Thorpdale
Hazelwood Cooling Pond
Churchill
Childers
Yinnar
Koornalla
Willung South
Carrajung
Carrajung South
Giffard West
The Honeysuckles
Seaspray
Allambee South
Boolarra
Morwell Nat Park
Blackwarry
Giffard
Mirboo North
Budgeree
Balook
Tarra-Bulga Nat Park
Boolarra South
Mardan
Mirboo
Mirboo East
Tarra Valley
Macks Creek
Wonwron
Darriman
Jack Smith Lake
Ninety Mile Beach
Dumbalk North
Dumbalk
Tarwin East
Ryton
Hiawatha
Staceys Bridge
Devon
Greenmount
Woodside
Woodside Beach
Dollar
Turtons Creek
Wonyip
Binginwarri
Yarram
Hunterson
Mount Best
Woorarra
Alberton West
Alberton
Tarraville
McLoughlins Beach
St Margaret Island
Manns Beach
Hazel Park
Foster
Toora
Hedley
Port Albert
Bennison
Port Franklin
Agnes
Welshpool
Port Welshpool
Hoddle
Sunday Island
Shallow Inlet
Kate Kearney Entrance
Clonmel Island
Port Albert Entrance
Barry Beach
Snake Island
Waratah North
Corner Inlet
Yanakie
Duck Point
Entrance Point
Townsend Point
Mt Hunter
Lighthouse Pt
Chinaman Knob
Three Mile Point
Sandy Point
Waratah Bay
Wilsons Promontory Nat Pk
Monkey Pt
Five Mile Beach
Cotters Beach
Tongue Point
Whisky Bay
Leonard Point
Sealers Cove
Refuge Cove
Tidal River
Mt Oberon
Oberon Bay
Cape Wellington
Great Glennie Island
Mt Norgate
Waterloo Bay
Mt Boulder
South West Point
Anser Island
South Point
South East Point
Rodondo Island
Hogan Island
Kent Group
Erith Island
Dover Island
Deal Island
Curtis Island

147°
38°
39°

VIC 4

1 2 3 4 5 6 7 8 9 10

H J K L M N P

VIC

Tasmania

With over one-quarter of the state set aside as national parks, state reserves, historic sites and similar, Tasmania offers a wonderfully rich diversity of protected wilderness, startling natural beauty and amazing history. A National Parks Holiday Pass, valid for two months, gives you entry into all 33 national parks and is available for a small fee. The parks offer a variety of activities, from gentle strolls to week-long bushwalks, from river and lake cruises to scenic flights. You can ski; fish; canoe; sail; dive; abseil; ride a horse, a jet boat or camel; four-wheel drive along vast ocean beaches and giant sand dunes; or raft down wild rivers. Tasmania's parks are blessed with a wealth of attractions and facilities; lacking only deserts and coral reefs, there really is something here for everyone.

Cradle Mountain–Lake St Clair National Park

Cradle Mountain–Lake St Clair National Park is one of the most famous and spectacular national parks in Australia. Part of the Tasmanian Wilderness World Heritage Area, it is listed by the World Heritage Commission as one of the most precious places on earth. This stunningly beautiful area contains rugged mountain peaks, steep forested gorges, moorlands, rainforest, glacial lakes and tarns.

fact file

WHERE: Cradle Valley is 85 km (about 1 hour's drive) from Devonport via Sheffield or Wilmot, or from Burnie airport; Lake St Clair is 175 km from Hobart, via the Lyell Highway and Derwent Bridge. Roads may be closed in winter
Map: Tas 1 J9

WHEN: November to April

WHY: Bushwalking, rock climbing, fishing, canoeing, windsurfing, trail rides, boat cruising, wildlife, 4WD

SIZE: 161 204 ha

RANGER: Cradle Mountain (03) 6492 1133; Lake St Clair (03) 6289 1172

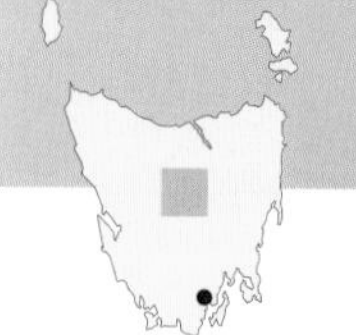

Erosion by glaciers and water, which took place more than 500 000 years ago, carved out the valleys and lakes. Plants in the area reflect their ancient heritage, bearing a closer relationship to species found in New Zealand and South America than to those seen on the mainland of Australia. With snow gums and giant grass trees, or moss- and lichen-clad pencil pine forests, the varied terrain contains a wide range of flora including buttongrass sedges, daisies and herbs.

The Twisted Lakes were created over 500 000 years ago, during a glacial period. Their calm surface mirrors the beauty of their surrounds.

Left: *Plants in Cradle Mountain–Lake St Clair National Park add to its incredible beauty. The deciduous beech* (Nothofagus gunnii) *creates a splash of golden colour during autumn.*

Below: *Pencil pines* (Athrotaxis cupressoides) *are found throughout Cradle Mountain–Lake St Clair National Park. This hardy species survives in an extremely harsh environment.*

With rain falling on an average of 275 days per year and snowfalls occurring on around 54 days a year, you can expect clear and sunny weather only on about 32 days! But even in winter the park has a unique splendour and beauty; under a mantle of snow it takes on a fantasy land appearance.

Cradle Mountain

Father of Cradle Mountain

Gustav Weindorfer, an Austrian naturalist, is considered the 'father' of this 161 204-hectare national park. He built his forest home, Waldheim Chalet, in the wilderness at Cradle Valley in 1911 when everything, including the bathtub, had to be carried in on foot.

After Weindorfer's death in 1932, Waldheim was purchased by his friends and continued to be run as a guesthouse until 1975 when it was closed because of its dilapidated state. Faithfully restored by the Parks and Wildlife Service, with woodwork fashioned from native King Billy pine trees, it is now a monument to this far-sighted pioneer.

Wildlife

The national park is a veritable magnet for all lovers of nature. Prolific wildlife found in the region incorporates many migratory species of birds, such as wrens, honeyeaters and robins, which depart the high country in winter and head towards coastal areas, leaving the park to the resident birdlife, which includes eagles, currawongs and parrots.

A largely nocturnal marsupial population includes wombats, possums, spotted-tailed quolls (tiger cats), and Tasmanian devils. During the day the many Bennett's wallabies and pademelons will approach people, looking for handouts.

don't miss

While you're in Cradle Mountain–Lake St Clair National Park, take the opportunity to test your angling skills against the famous Tasmanian rainbow and brown trout that are found in the lakes and streams.

A lone bushwalker enjoys the view from the top of Barn Bluff overlooking Cradle Mountain–Lake St Clair National Park. There are many walking tracks crisscrossing the park.

Walking

There are numerous signposted walks within Cradle Valley, starting with a reasonably gentle half-hour return stroll along the Enchanted Walk. The King Billy Track (one hour return) takes you through beautiful moss-clad forests of myrtle beech, sassafras, celery-top pine and ancient—1500 to 1700 years old—King Billy pines.

The Pencil Pine Falls near Cradle Mountain Lodge flow downstream through Cradle Valley from Lake Dove, one of the many glacial lakes scattered throughout the park.

There's also the very easy, 500-metre Rainforest Walk starting from behind the visitor centre, which takes you right around roaring Pencil Pines Falls, while a very popular 3-hour return walk goes to the Ballroom Forest. This superb walk follows the western shore of Lake Dove, which reflects the craggy peaks of Cradle Mountain, to a primeval wonderland full of myrtle, sassafras and deciduous beech.

Mountain guides from the Cradle Mountain Lodge lead regular daily walks, but if you are trekking independently, it's important to register at the Ranger's Office in the visitor centre for any walk over an hour. Weather in these regions is notoriously fickle and you'll need to be well prepared for sudden changes. Japara coats, waterproof pants and even gumboots can be hired from the store if necessary.

The Overland Track

For the dedicated trekker, the 60-km Overland Track from Cradle Valley to Lake St Clair offers one of the world's great walks. Evocative names, such as Cathedral Mountain, the Acropolis and Mount Olympus, indicate the reverence which trekkers, from the earliest times, have accorded this stunning area.

The track winds around Lake Dove and Cradle Mountain to Barn Bluff, past many glacial lakes, around Mounts Pelion (both East and West) and Mount Ossa—Tasmania's highest peak at 1617 metres—and down to Lake St Clair, headwater of the Derwent River.

The Overland Track requires a minimum of 5 days and is not for the unfit

or ill-prepared. Although there are some public huts found along the trail, tents should always be carried.

Guided treks are available from Craclair Tours. Those seeking a little luxury can indulge themselves in a fabulous 'walk on the wild side' with Cradle Huts, a Launceston-based company which has four well-appointed lodges along the Overland Track—it is the only private accommodation allowed in this wilderness area.

Cradle Huts run 6-day walks, averaging a daily walking time of 5 hours, including a full day at Pelion (midway) to rest—or, if you are feeling energetic, you can climb Mount Ossa. A 17-km boat trip down Lake St Clair completes the trek which begins and ends in Launceston. You can contact Cradle Huts in Launceston on (03) 6391 9339.

Other Activities

Tasmania's lakes and streams are renowned as some of the best in the world for chasing the elusive trout. All the major waterways are open to the public for fishing from July until April (an annual Inland Fisheries licence is necessary).

Other activities within Cradle Valley include canoeing, whitewater rafting,

Left: *Fly-fishing is one of the big drawcards of the Cradle Mountain–Lake St Clair National Park. The deep, crystal-clear lakes are brimming with trout.*

Below left: *A 6-km track winds around the shores of Lake Dove and past the imposing spires of Cradle Mountain. Many believe it to be one of Tasmania's premier walking trails.*

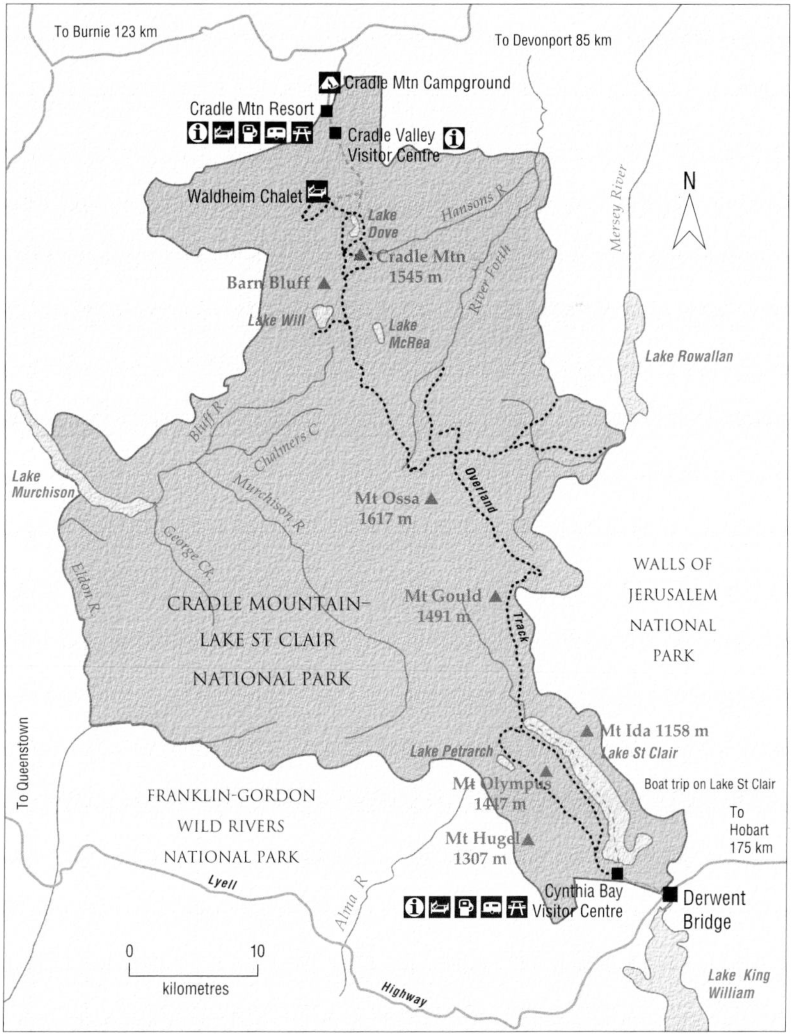

panning for gold, 4WD tours, trail rides on mountain ponies, and even abseiling for the more adventurous.

The Cradle Mountain Visitor Centre, at Cradle Valley (open from 8 a.m. to 5 p.m. daily), has a wealth of information on this World Heritage Area, while the store in Cradle Valley has a wide range of souvenirs plus enough provisions so you can handle your own catering. Petrol (unleaded only) is also available. Scenic flights are on offer from a small runway nearby.

Weather-beaten and covered in moss, some of the King Billy pines (Athrotaxis selaginoides) *found in the park are up to 1500 years old.*

Within the national park itself there are no roads, apart from the road to Lake Dove. There are numerous 4WD tracks around Cradle Valley, to places such as Lake Lea and over the Middlesex Plains, but most tracks are on private property and permission must be granted before use. Cradle Mountain Lodge runs regular 4WD tours of the area.

Wilderness Retreat

Cradle Mountain Lodge is also a wonderfully relaxing wilderness retreat, offering a wide range of accommodation options from camping—in one of the prettiest and best-equipped camp grounds in the country—through to dormitories and the self-contained Waldheim Cabins to the upmarket Cradle Mountain huts.

The highlight of an evening at Cradle Mountain Lodge is the 9.30 p.m. animal feeding on the 'Critter Stand' outside the Tavern Bar. Fresh fruit and vegetables are offered to the rufous wallabies, quolls, brush-tail possums, tiger cats, Tasmanian devils and wombats. The very fat possums are so tame they climb onto the verandah railing to be hand fed and are not even fazed by blinding camera flashes! You can contact Cradle Mountain Lodge on 1300 134 044.

Cradle Mountain Lodge offers the weary traveller a warm haven against the fickle and often inclement weather of the Tasmanian highlands.

Lake St Clair

This beautiful lake in the south of the national park is an easy half-day drive from Hobart. Surrounded by magical mountains, Lake St Clair is Australia's deepest lake (up to 200 metres in places) and is very cold. Its beauty and serenity, where its shallow fringes lap large boulders and sandy beaches, backed by gnarled cypress pines and eucalypts, create a very contemplative mood. Lake St Clair is one of the prettiest spots in Tasmania and one of the most popular with day visitors, particularly people passing through to the west coast, but it is not hard to escape the tourist hordes to find peace and quiet.

Facilities

Cynthia Bay on the south-west corner of the lake is a popular picnic area, with barbecues, toilets, picnic shelter, kiosk, and frequently, hordes of tourist buses and mobs of wallabies.

The visitor centre has interpretation displays of the geology of the region, a video on glaciers and a giant hologram of a family of thylacines (the Tasmanian tiger). The centre also houses the offices of the Parks and Wildlife Service, a shop and a restaurant. It is a fantastic place for children to learn about animals and places in Tasmania. Information on trout fishing is also available here.

Spikes of vibrant scarlet flowers from the Tasmanian native kerosene bush (Richea scoparia) *cover the lower slopes of Cradle Mountain–Lake St Clair National Park during summer.*

TAS

Walking

A beautiful, 3- to 4-hour (return) walk following the roaring Hugel River leads to the lovely Shadow and Forgotten Lakes. Two short, new walks at Cynthia Bay are the Platypus Bay Loop (1 hour return) and the Woodland Nature Walk (1 hour return).

Another easy track, suitable for families, (45 minutes return) is the Watersmeet Nature Trail which leads to the start (or the end) of the Overland Track, passing through eucalypts, rainforest and across buttongrass plains to the Hugel and Cuvier Rivers. Abundant native wildlife, particularly birds and wallabies, can be seen along all these tracks.

Other Activities

A ferry runs regular cruises to the mouth of the Narcissus River at the northern end of the lake and is frequently utilised by walkers finishing the Overland Track. Lake St Clair is a great spot for canoeing, windsurfing, trout fishing and swimming (if you're feeling brave!).

Camping

Phone the ranger's office or the National Parks and Wildlife Service Information Centre on (03) 6492 1133 for details of camp sites. On the Overland Track it is preferable to camp near the huts to prevent degradation of the country. There is no camping in the Cradle Mountain day-walk areas.

Shadow Lake has camp sites where you can enjoy superb lake and mountain views, and Lake St Clair Wilderness Holidays, 5 km north of the Derwent Bridge, has camp sites, backpackers' accommodation and luxury cabins for four to eight people. Contact them for more information on (03) 6289 1137.

tourist info

Craclair Walking Tours (03) 6339 4488

Cradle Mountain Visitor Centre (03) 6492 1133

Franklin–Gordon Wild Rivers National Park

Born out of the greatest environmental battle fought in this country, the Franklin–Gordon Wild Rivers National Park now protects the Franklin River and much of the lower reaches of the Gordon River. One of the greatest wilderness adventure trips in Australia is to raft down the often tranquil, sometimes rapid-churned Franklin River to its junction with the mighty Gordon River in south-west Tasmania.

Above: *Whitewater rafting is definitely not for the faint-hearted, especially on the wild rapids of the Franklin River. A safety helmet and a life jacket are essential items for those tackling the rapids.*

fact file

WHERE: 180 km west of Hobart, along the Lyell Highway via the Derwent Bridge. There is no vehicular access to the park, apart from 4WD access to Mount McCall Map: Tas 3 D3

WHEN: November to February

WHY: Beautiful rivers, magnificent scenery, rafting, walks, 4WD

SIZE: 446 342 ha

RANGER: Queenstown (03) 6471 2511; Strahan (03) 6471 7122

A Wild River

The Franklin River is the largest river in Tasmania to run free for its entire length, from its source in the Cheyne Range to its meeting with the Gordon River 45 km from the sea at Macquarie Harbour.

For many adventurers, a rafting trip on the Franklin begins on one of the Franklin's tributaries, the Collingwood. Once on the Franklin, the river begins its great arc around the sheer bluff of Frenchmans Cap before entering a series of gorges separated by rapids of varying intensity. These are known by such descriptive names as the Churn, Thunder Rush and the Cauldron. Once out of the Great Ravine the river is more placid, and below Big Fall the river slows and spreads out, waiting to join the Gordon.

A Mighty River

The Gordon is regarded by many as the monarch of all rivers. The lower reaches are magnificent, known for their fantastic reflections that, like the very best mirror, reflect the images of the dense forests crowding the pristine river bank.

Apart from the placid stretches of the lower Gordon (accessible from Strahan), much of the river is out of bounds as it is too dangerous to raft or paddle.

Right: *In the 1980s, the Franklin River was at the centre of a heated debate between conservationists and the state government, who wanted to dam the river. It was a debate that bitterly divided the state.*

Access and Camping

Most people experience the wonders of the region on one of the many cruise boats which operate daily out of Strahan,

taking sightseers to the lower reaches of the Gordon. However, powered craft are only allowed up the river as far as Horseshoe Bend. Contact the Tourist Visitor Information Centre in Strahan for a list of the cruises.

There is very limited vehicular access to the Franklin and Gordon areas. Only the Mount McCall 4WD track gives access to the Franklin. This track goes through spectacular country and ends, 22 km later, near Mount McCall and well above the river! You need a permit and a key for the gate from the Queenstown office of the Parks and Wildlife Service.

A few walking trails delve into this wilderness, including short ones off the Lyell Highway and others that are only suitable for well-equipped, experienced bushwalkers. A number of companies with float planes, such as Wilderness Air, operate out of Strahan taking tourists over the rivers and peaks. This is a great way to see this rugged area.

Camping is limited in the park but there are a few bush camps scattered through the area suitable for bushwalkers. The bridge over the Collingwood is one such spot, Irenabyss Camp on the Franklin is another, along with Warners Landing on the Gordon. Otherwise you pitch a tent where you find room in amongst the dense forest or on a flattish slope on the edge of a cliff!

The town of Strahan has all facilities and is really quite a delightful place to spend a few days.

tourist info

Tasmanian Wild River Adventures
0409 977 506

Visitor Information Centre, Strahan
(03) 6471 7622

Wilderness Air
(03) 6471 7280

TAS

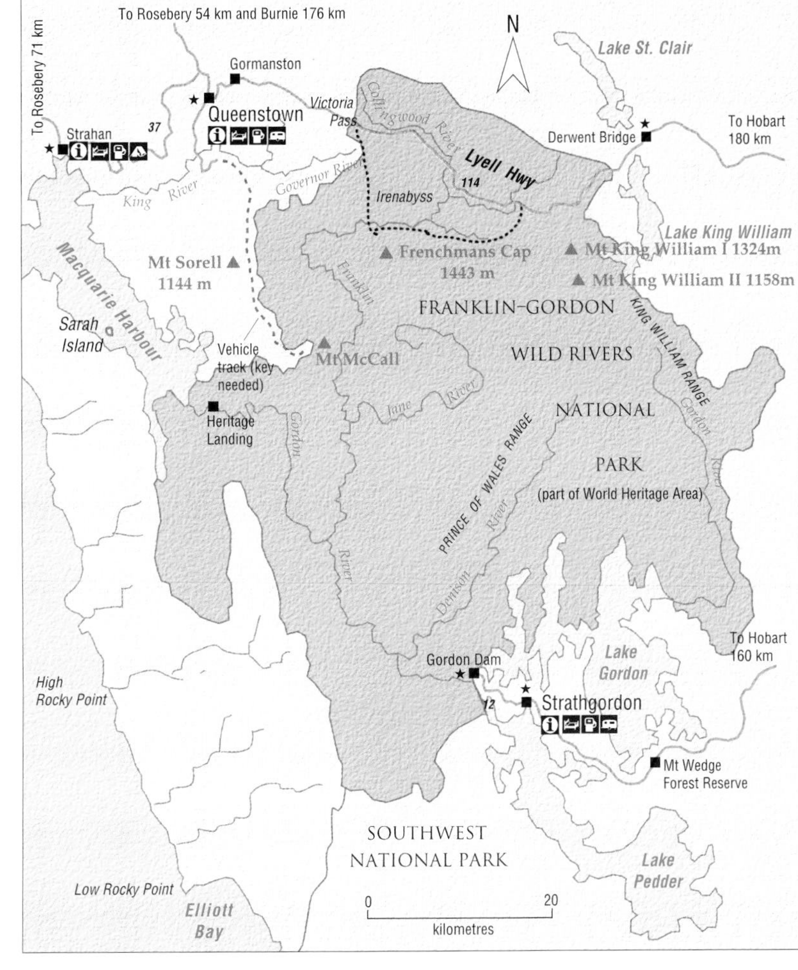

Freycinet National Park

Spectacular coastal scenery is everywhere you look on the Freycinet Peninsula, where dramatic red granite peaks are reflected in clear blue waters lapping sands of dazzling white. The three peaks of the Hazards dominate the skyline, and long before you reach the peninsula they beckon across the expanse of Great Oyster Bay. Such breathtaking panoramas, abundant wildlife and a wealth of outdoor activities make this national park a great holiday area.

fact file

WHERE: 39 km south of Bicheno, via the Tasman Highway; limited vehicular access
Map: Tas 3 P1

WHEN: November to May

WHY: Walking, wildlife, fishing, water sports, sightseeing cruises, 4WD

SIZE: 16 803 ha

RANGER: (03) 6256 7000

The lookout at Cape Tourville affords visitors a magnificent view of the rugged granite coastline along the eastern side of Freycinet National Park.

Freycinet National Park consists mainly of coastal heathland, which becomes a veritable artist's palette of vibrant colours in spring, dominated by awe-inspiring peaks and cliffs. Magnificent pure white, sandy beaches, such as Wineglass Bay (mostly accessible only by boat or on foot), alternate with towering cliffs above the rocky coastline.

The abundant wildlife is as rich as it is varied. Black cockatoos, green rosellas, yellow wattle-birds, butcherbirds and wedge-tail eagles are all seen, while gannets, fairy penguins and white-breasted sea-eagles are some of the many seabirds. There are also wallabies, possums, echidnas and potoroos.

The Freycinet Peninsula was named in 1802 by the French explorer Nicholas Baudin to honour his cartographer Henri Freycinet, and became a national park in 1916. Together with Mount Field, it is Tasmania's oldest national park.

Activities

Freycinet National Park is largely a wilderness area with very little vehicular access. This is a bushwalker's paradise with a variety of walks ranging from 1 to 10 hours, and there are several camp sites for overnight hikers on the 27-km circuit track of the park.

Another popular walk with visitors—particularly at sunrise—is to the summit of Mount Amos for stunning views south across Wineglass Bay and the peninsula, or north across Coles Bay and beyond (2 hours return).

One of the few areas with vehicular access and one of the most spectacular is Cape Tourville, while Bluestone Bay is reached by a 4WD track.

The Hazards, about 485 metres high, present a real challenge to climbers. The fishing in the park is good, with fishing charters being available from the nearby Coles Bay township. Fuel, supplies, boat and sporting equipment hire are also found in the town. Water sports include swimming, water skiing, diving, sailing and canoeing.

To the north (about 10 km from the highway) are the delightfully named

With the cobalt blue waters of Wineglass Bay crowned by a sublime curve of white sand, it comes as no surprise that this beach is recognised as one of the most beautiful in the world.

don't miss

If you're feeling fit, climb the Hazards that form a formidable backdrop to the Freycinet Lodge. They are over 485 metres high and reward the adventurous climber with beautiful views over the entire national park.

TAS

Friendly Beaches, which are a great area for anglers and four wheel drivers. From here, Freycinet Experience runs 4-day walks in the national park starting with a boat ride to Schouten Island.

Access and Accommodation

The park is approximately a 3-hour drive from Hobart, and about the same from Devonport on the state's northern coast.

Accommodation ranges from the fantastic waterfront camp through youth hostels to B&Bs. The environmentally friendly Freycinet Lodge offers many nature-based and educational activities.

There is also a variety of accommodation available through the Freycinet Experience. They offer simple cabin accommodation for overnight walkers as well as more luxurious lodges—for longer stays—tucked away out of sight at the Friendly Beaches. Call (03) 6223 7565 for more information.

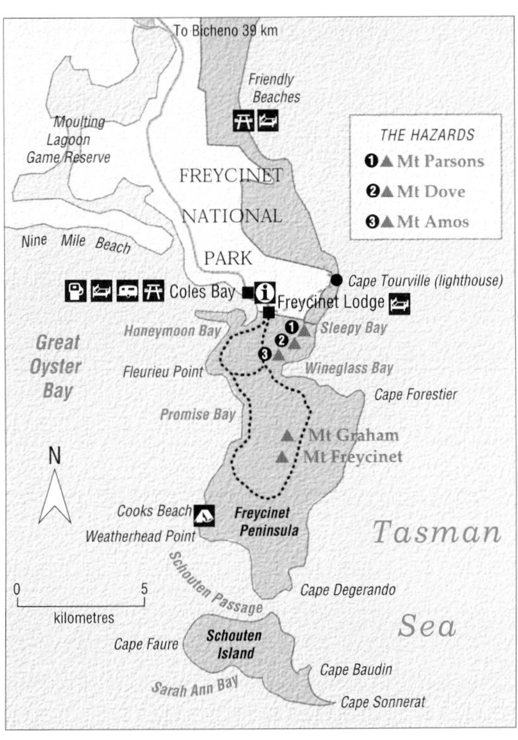

Mount Field National Park

This is Tasmania's oldest national park (along with Freycinet National Park) and is one of the state's prettiest, with a great variety of scenery from low-level rainforest to high-altitude moorlands, brooding mountain ranges, waterfalls and many beautiful lakes. Mount Field has something for everyone, from gentle walks to winter skiing. Lake Dobson, a beautiful mountain lake, is also accessible by car. There's abundant wildlife including Tasmanian devils, spotted-tail quolls and even platypus. Birdlife is also prolific.

The picturesque Russell Falls are the most recognisable and photographed feature of the Mount Field National Park.

WHERE: 75 km north-west of Hobart via New Norfolk Map: Tas 3 G4

WHEN: September to May; June to August

WHY: Wildlife, bush-walking, fishing, picnics, camping, scenic drives, cross-country skiing

SIZE: 16 977 ha

RANGER: (03) 6288 1149

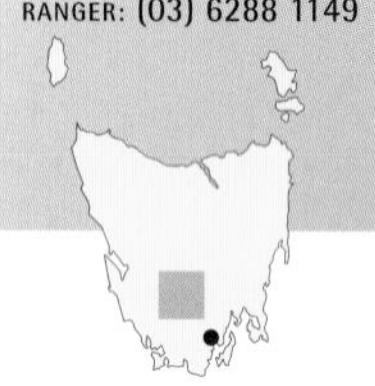

Walking and Skiing

The whole of Mount Field National Park is a walkers' paradise with walks ranging from 10-minute strolls to overnight hikes. A large picnic area at the park entrance is the starting point for a 1-km Nature Walk which winds through giant tree ferns, swamp gums and a great variety of small ferns to the magnificent Russell Falls. Numerous other marked tracks lead to the many lakes and peaks in the national park. Some of these are overnight hikes but there are a number of hikers huts in the park.

Snow-covered in winter, the park offers good cross-country ski tours across the higher plateaus. There is no downhill skiing.

Access and Camping

The park is situated 75 km north-west of Hobart with the entrance 35 km from New Norfolk. There is 4WD access only in late autumn to early spring. Check road conditions before setting out.

At the entrance there is a visitor centre with information about the park. A pretty camping area nearby has full facilities.

The view of Mount Field National Park overlooking Lake Seal is breathtaking. In winter the park can become snow-covered, which adds a new dimension to the already harsh landscape.

More National Parks of Importance

Ben Lomond National Park

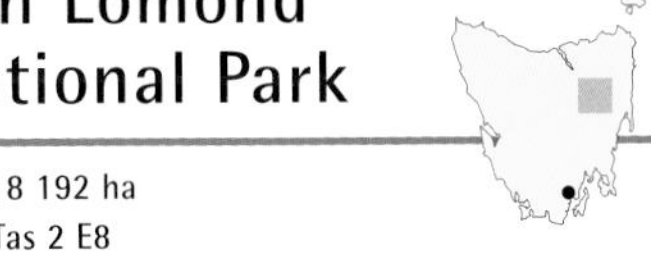

SIZE: 18 192 ha
MAP: Tas 2 E8

Ben Lomond National Park encompasses a 1300-metre high plateau, just 60 km from Launceston, and in winter it becomes the state's major ski resort offering cross-country and downhill skiing from beginners to advanced.

In spring Ben Lomond is a popular spot for day visitors and is a pleasant, unspoilt area for walkers, while the dramatic vertical dolerite columns here attract rock climbers. However, the road up to Ben Lomond is not for the faint-hearted: the final ascent is steep, winding and narrow.

Apart from private clubs, the only accommodation is at Creek Inn which has log-cabin style units. There are no formal camp sites but bush camping is allowed in the national park.

For more information contact the National Parks and Wildlife Service office in Launceston on (03) 6336 5312.

Maria Island National Park

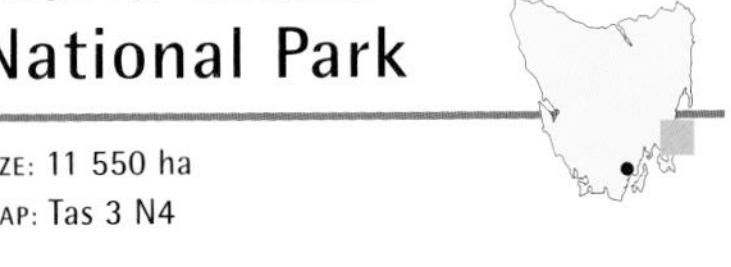

SIZE: 11 550 ha
MAP: Tas 3 N4

This tranquil, beautiful and quite historic island, just 15 km off Tasmania's east coast, boasts magnificent coastal cliffs, dazzling white beaches, open forests and a mountain range that supports a delicate rainforest habitat.

Maria Island was named by explorer Abel Tasman in 1642. In 1825 a penal settlement was established on the island, but it was abandoned in 1832. It was declared a national park in 1972 and the restoration of many of the old buildings, a highlight of a visit here, began. For walkers there are a number of tracks to enjoy, and there is an abundance of tame wildlife to experience.

Ferries operate from Triabunna and Louisville Point, taking less than an hour to reach the island. Triabunna is 84 km from Hobart via the Tasman Highway.

Camp sites are available at the township of Darlington, plus basic dormitory accommodation. You can also camp at French's Farm and Encampment Cove. There is no transport or other facilities on Maria Island.

For more information or to book accommodation, phone (03) 6257 1420.

Ben Lomond National Park, only an hour's drive from Launceston, is Tasmania's only downhill skiing area. It is popular with both visitors and the local population.

The fossil cliffs on Maria Island are only one of the many natural features of this beautiful national park off the east coast. The island also has convict ruins dating back to the early nineteenth century.

Mount William National Park

SIZE: 18 439 ha
MAP: Tas 2 H4

Mount William National Park is an important area for the conservation of Tasmania's coastal flora, including the grass tree (Xanthorrhoea australis).

One of Tasmania's lesser known national parks, Mount William National Park combines natural beauty and abundant wildlife in a coastal setting. Originally set aside to protect the then-rare forester kangaroo, this park covers the north-east tip of Tasmania and encloses coastal heathland, dry sclerophyll forest and a bounty of beautiful beaches.

Swimming, surfing, fishing and diving are popular pastimes; long, white beaches and a network of fire trails allow for a variety of bushwalking. An easy 30-minute walk to the top of Mount William gives sweeping views of the park.

Camp sites are dotted among the sand dunes near Picnic Rocks and on a grassy area beside Deep Creek. In the north there are numerous camp sites around Stumpys Bay and north of Cape Naturaliste.

For more information, phone the ranger on (03) 6376 1550.

Walls of Jerusalem National Park

SIZE: 51 800 ha
MAP: Tas 1 L9

A subalpine wilderness, this national park forms part of the World Heritage Area, and is a gorgeous but fragile place. This park is also strictly for the very fit. Bushwalking, some rock climbing and cross-country skiing are the only activities.

From the car park a strenuous 3-hour walk entails a steep climb up to Trappers Hut and on to Solomons Jewels, a chain of beautiful little lakes. Another steep ridge brings you to Herods Gate and Lake Salome. The West Wall towers 300 metres above this lake, as does the Temple. Mount Jerusalem, the highest mountain in the park at 1458 metres, is to the north. At this altitude weather can be unpredictable at any time of year, so it is important to be well prepared.

There is no vehicular access into the park. There are no facilities in the park, but bush camping is allowed. Only fuel stoves are allowed. For more information, phone the National Parks and Wildlife Service at Molle Creek (03) 6363 5133 or Launceston (03) 6336 5312.

Visitors to the Walls of Jerusalem National Park who make the trip in winter need to be appropriately dressed to combat exposure and frostbite.

Popular Parks at a Glance

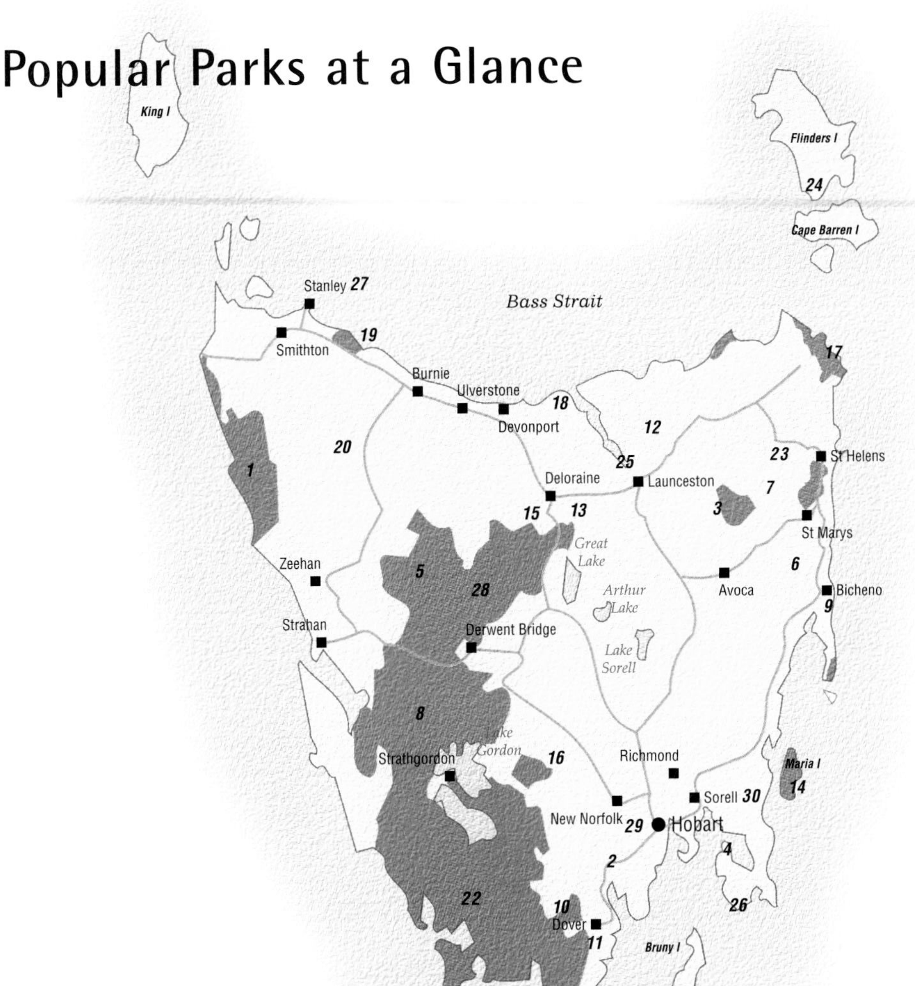

TAS

	Camping	Caravan Access	Disabled Access	4WD Access	Picnic Areas	Toilets	Walking Tracks	Kiosk	Information
1 Arthur Pieman PA	●	●	●	●	●	●	●		
2 Arve River Road/Skywalk	●	●	●	●	●	●	●		
3 Ben Lomond NP	●				●	●	●	●	
4 Coal Mines HS and Lime Bay	●	●	●		●	●	●		
5 Cradle Mtn-Lake St Clair NP	●		●		●	●	●	●	●
6 Douglas Apsley NP	●				●	●	●		●
7 Evercreech FR			●		●	●	●		
8 Franklin-Gordon Wild Rivers NP	●				●	●	●		
9 Freycinet NP	●				●	●	●	●	●
10 Hartz Mountains NP	●				●	●	●		
11 Hastings Caves & Thermal Springs			●		●	●	●	●	●
12 Hollybank FR	●				●	●	●		
13 Liffey Falls			●		●	●	●		
14 Maria Island NP	●				●	●	●		●
15 Mole Creek Karst NP					●	●	●		●
16 Mount Field NP	●	●	●		●	●	●	●	●
17 Mount William NP	●	●		●	●	●	●		
18 Narawntapu NP	●	●			●	●	●		●
19 Rocky Cape NP					●	●	●		
20 Savage River NP									
21 South Bruny NP	●	●			●	●	●		
22 Southwest NP	●				●	●	●		●
23 St Columba Falls							●		
24 Strzelecki NP	●	●			●	●	●		●
25 Tamar Island Wetlands			●		●	●	●		●
26 Tasman NP	●	●			●	●	●		
27 The Nut					●	●	●	●	
28 Walls of Jerusalem NP	●						●		
29 Wellington Park			●	●	●	●	●		
30 Wielangta Forest Drive				●	●	●	●		

Map 1

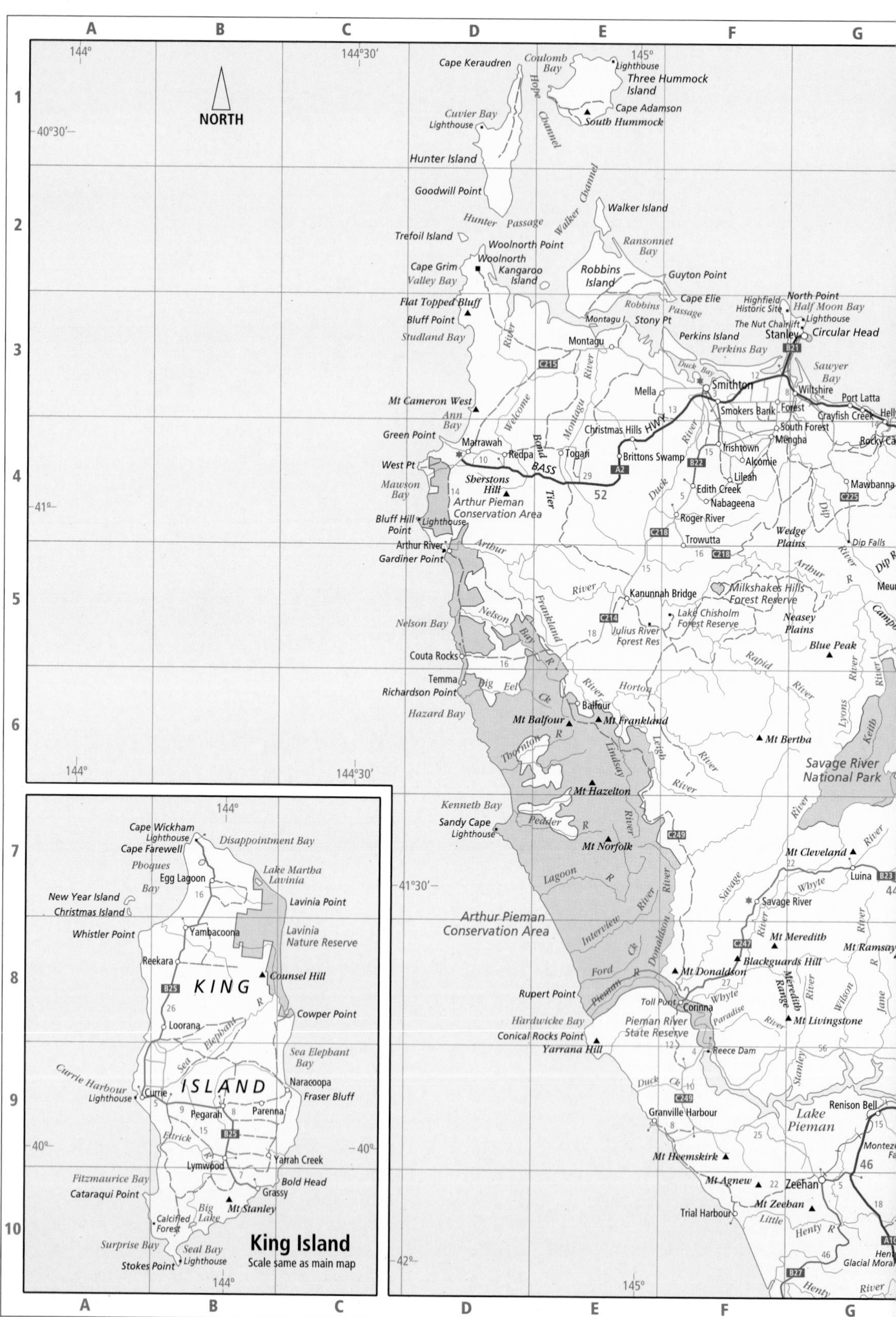
NORTH
Cape Keraudren
Coulomb Bay
Three Hummock Island
Cape Adamson
South Hummock
Hope Channel
Cuvier Bay
Hunter Island
Goodwill Point
Walker Island
Walker Channel
Hunter Passage
Trefoil Island
Woolnorth Point
Woolnorth
Cape Grim
Valley Bay
Kangaroo Island
Robbins Island
Ransonnet Bay
Guyton Point
Cape Elie
Robbins Passage
Flat Topped Bluff
Bluff Point
Studland Bay
Montagu
Stony Pt
Perkins Island
Perkins Bay
Highfield Historic Site
North Point
Half Moon Bay
The Nut Chairlift
Stanley
Circular Head
Sawyer Bay
Smithton
Mella
Wiltshire
Port Latta
Smokers Bank
Forest
Crayfish Creek
Mt Cameron West
Ann Bay
Green Point
Marrawah
Redpa
Togari
Christmas Hills
Brittons Swamp
Irishtown
Mengha
South Forest
Alcomie
Lileah
Edith Creek
Nabageena
Roger River
Trowutta
Mawbanna
West Pt
Mawson Bay
Sherstons Hill
Bond Tier
BASS HWY
Arthur Pieman Conservation Area
Bluff Hill Point
Lighthouse
Arthur River
Gardiner Point
Wedge Plains
Dip Falls
Kanunnah Bridge
Milkshakes Hills Forest Reserve
Lake Chisholm Forest Reserve
Julius River Forest Res
Neasey Plains
Blue Peak
Nelson Bay
Couta Rocks
Temma
Richardson Point
Hazard Bay
Balfour
Mt Balfour
Mt Frankland
Mt Bertha
Savage River National Park
Mt Hazelton
Kenneth Bay
Sandy Cape Lighthouse
Mt Norfolk
Mt Cleveland
Luina
Savage River
Mt Meredith
Mt Ramsay
Blackguards Hill
Mt Donaldson
Meredith Range
Rupert Point
Toll Pnt
Corinna
Hardwicke Bay
Pieman River State Reserve
Mt Livingstone
Conical Rocks Point
Yarrana Hill
Reece Dam
Granville Harbour
Lake Pieman
Renison Bell
Mt Heemskirk
Mt Agnew
Zeehan
Mt Zeehan
Trial Harbour
Glacial Moraine
Cape Wickham Lighthouse
Disappointment Bay
Cape Farewell
Pboques Bay
Egg Lagoon
Lake Martha Lavinia
New Year Island
Christmas Island
Lavinia Point
Whistler Point
Yambacoona
Lavinia Nature Reserve
Reekara
Counsel Hill
KING ISLAND
Cowper Point
Loorana
Sea Elephant Bay
Currie Harbour Lighthouse
Currie
Naracoopa
Fraser Bluff
Pegarah
Parenna
Yarrah Creek
Lymwood
Bold Head
Fitzmaurice Bay
Grassy
Cataraqui Point
Mt Stanley
Calcified Forest
Surprise Bay
Seal Bay Lighthouse
Stokes Point
King Island
Scale same as main map

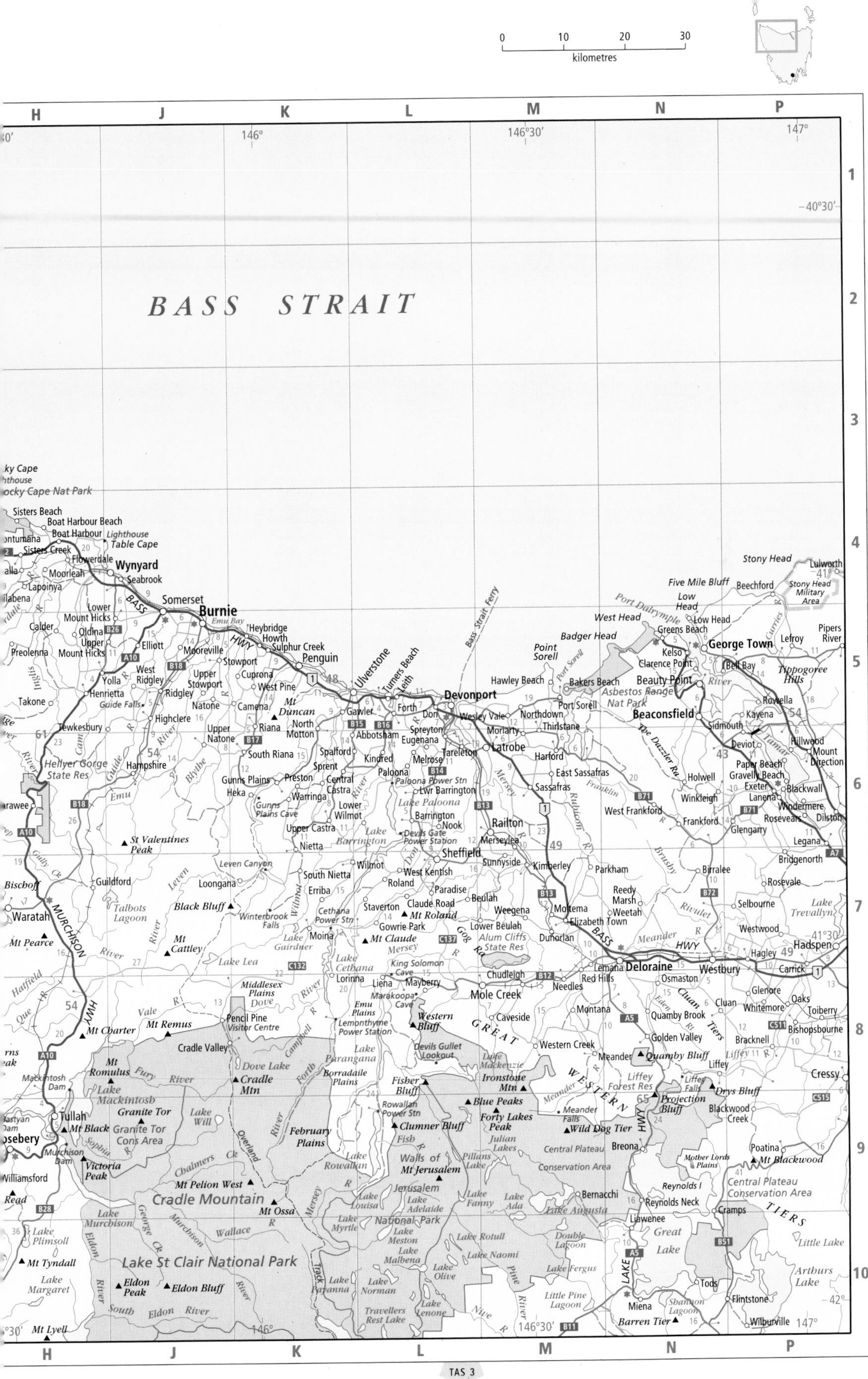

0 10 20 30
kilometres

H J K L M N P

146° 146°30′ 147°

1 2 3 4 5 6 7 8 9 10

–40°30′ –41° –41°30 –42°

BASS STRAIT

ky Cape
thouse
ocky Cape Nat Park
Sisters Beach
Boat Harbour Beach
Boat Harbour
Lighthouse
Table Cape
ontumana
Sisters Creek
Flowerdale
Wynyard
Seabrook
alla
Moorleah
Lapoinya
ilabena
Somerset
Burnie
Emu Bay
Lower Mount Hicks
Calder
Oldina
Upper Mount Hicks
Elliott
Mooreville
Heybridge
Howth
Sulphur Creek
Penguin
Preolenna
Stowport
Cuprona
West Pine
Ulverstone
Turners Beach
Leith
Bass Strait Ferry
West Ridgley
Yolla
Ridgley
Upper Stowport
Henrietta
Guide Falls
Takone
Natone
Camena
Mt Duncan
Gawler
Forth
Devonport
Highclere
Tewkesbury
Upper Natone
Riana
North Motton
Abbotsham
Don
Spreyton
Eugenana
Wesley Vale
Northdown
Moriarty
Thirlstane
Latrobe
Tarleton
Harford
Hellyer Gorge State Res
Hampshire
South Riana
Spalford
Kindred
Melrose
Sprent
Paloona
Central Castra
Gunns Plains
Preston
Heka
Warringa
Gunns Plains Cave
Lower Wilmot
Paloona Power Stn
Lwr Barrington
Lake Paloona
Barrington
Nook
East Sassafras
Sassafras
Railton
Merseylea
Upper Castra
Nietta
Lake Barrington
Devils Gate Power Station
Sheffield
Sunnyside
Kimberley
Parkham
Leven Canyon
Loongana
South Nietta
Wilmot
West Kentish
Roland
Paradise
Beulah
Guildford
Bischoff
Waratah
Erriba
Staverton
Claude Road
Mt Roland
Weegena
Mole Creek
Talbots Lagoon
Black Bluff
Winterbrook Falls
Cethana Power Stn
Gowrie Park
Lower Beulah
Alum Cliffs State Res
Mt Pearce
Mt Cattley
Lake Gairdner
Moina
Mt Claude
Lake Cethana
King Solomon Cave
Lake Lea
Lorinna
Liena
Mayberry
Chudleigh
Middlesex Plains
Dove
Marakoopa Cave
Emu Plains
Lemonthyme Power Station
Western Bluff
Caveside
Great Western Tiers
Mt Charter
Mt Remus
Pencil Pine Visitor Centre
Cradle Valley
Devils Gullet Lookout
Lake Mackenzie
Mt Romulus
Dove Lake
Cradle Mtn
Lake Parangana
Borradaile Plains
Fisher Bluff
Ironstone Mtn
Mackintosh Dam
Lake Mackintosh
Granite Tor
Lake Will
Blue Peaks
Forty Lakes Peak
Tullah
Mt Black
Granite Tor Cons Area
Rowallan Power Stn
Clumner Bluff
Julian Lakes
osebery
February Plains
Fish
Murchison Dam
Victoria Peak
Lake Rowallan
Walls of Mt Jerusalem
Pillans Lake
Williamsford
Mt Pelion West
Jerusalem
Cradle Mountain
Mt Ossa
Lake Louisa
Lake Adelaide
Lake Fanny
Lake Ada
Lake Murchison
Lake Plimsoll
Wallace
Lake Myrtle
National Park
Lake Meston
Lake Malbena
Lake Rotull
Lake Naomi
Double Lagoon
Mt Tyndall
Lake St Clair National Park
Lake Margaret
Eldon Peak
Eldon Bluff
Lake Paranna
Lake Norman
Lake Olive
Lake Fergus
Little Pine Lagoon
Travellers Rest Lake
Lake Lenone
South Eldon River
Nive R
Mt Lyell
Stony Head
Lulworth
Five Mile Bluff
Beechford
Stony Head Military Area
Low Head
Port Dalrymple
West Head
Greens Beach
Badger Head
Kelso
George Town
Lefroy
Pipers River
Point Sorell
Clarence Point
Bell Bay
Tippogoree Hills
Hawley Beach
Port Sorell
Bakers Beach
Beauty Point
Asbestos Range Nat Park
Rowella
Beaconsfield
Kayena
Sidmouth
The Dazzler Ra
Deviot
Hillwood
Mount Direction
Paper Beach
Gravelly Beach
Holwell
Exeter
Blackwall
Winkleigh
Lanena
Windermere
Rubicon R
Franklin
West Frankford
Frankford
Glengarry
Rosevears
Dilston
Legana
Bridgenorth
Brushy
Birralee
Rosevale
Reedy Marsh
Weetah
Selbourne
Lake Trevallyn
Moltema
Elizabeth Town
Rivulet
Westwood
Dunorlan
Meander
Hadspen
Hagley
Deloraine
Westbury
Carrick
Elizabeth Town
Lemana
Red Hills
Needles
Osmaston
Glenore
Whitemore
Oaks
Toiberry
Cluan
Cluan Tiers
Montana
Quamby Brook
Bishopsbourne
Golden Valley
Bracknell
Western Creek
Meander
Quamby Bluff
Liffey
Cressy
Liffey Forest Res
Liffey Falls
Drys Bluff
Projection Bluff
Meander Falls
Blackwood Creek
Wild Dog Tier
Breona
Central Plateau Conservation Area
Poatina
Mt Blackwood
Mother Lords Plains
Reynolds I
Central Plateau Conservation Area
Bernacchi
Reynolds Neck
Lake Augusta
Cramps
Liawenee
Great Lake
Little Lake
Arthurs Lake
Tods
Flintstone
Miena
Shannon Lagoon
Barren Tier
Wilburville
BASS HWY
MURCHISON HWY
LAKE HWY
TIERS

TAS

TAS 2

Map 2

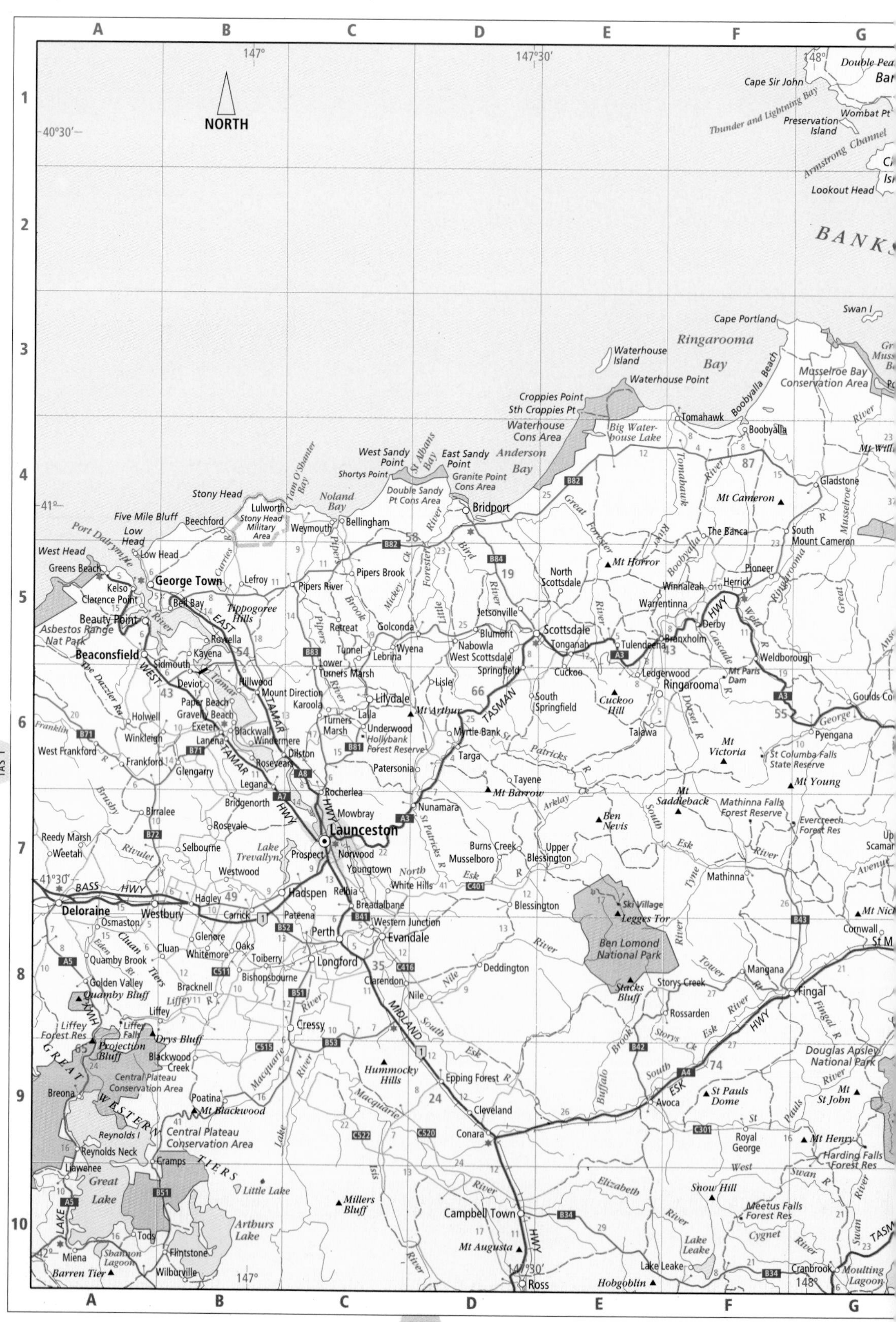

TAS 1

TAS 3

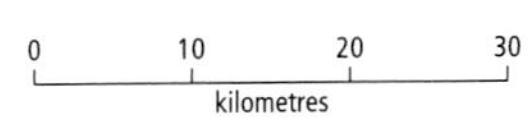

H J K L M N P

Flinders Island

Scale same as main map

FURNEAUX GROUP
FLINDERS ISLAND
148°
148°30′
Outer Sister Island
Inner Sister Island
Lighthouse
Stanley Point
Blyth Point
Palana
Killiecrankie Bay
Mt Killiecrankie
Killiecrankie
Cape Frankland
Mt Tanner
B85
30
Leeka
Roydon Island
Tanners Bay
Marshall Bay
C802
Babel Island
Lighthouse
Cat Island
Sellars Point
40°
Emita
Memana
Wybalenna Historic Site
Furneaux Lookout
The Patriarchs
Sellars Lagoon
Prime Seal Island
Arthur Bay
Blue Rocks
19
Pats R
Walkers Lookout
Mt Leventhorpe
Cameron Inlet
Long Point
Chalky Island
Whitemark
C803
Parrys Bay
B85
Logan Lagoon
Big Green Island
East Kangaroo Island
Ranga
24
Fotheringate Bay
Strzelecki Peaks
Lady Barron
Pot Boil Point
Trousers Point
Little Green Island
Great Dog Island
Mt Chappell Island
Strzelecki NP
Little Dog I
Vansittart Island
Franklin Sound
Pigs Head Point
Puncheon Pt
Goose Island
Lighthouse
Anderson Island
Tin Kettle Island
Apple Orchard Point
Deep Bay
Badger Island
Cape Barren Island
Long Island
Mt Munro
Harleys Point
Cape Barren Island
Double Peak
Cape Sir John
Mt Kerford
Cape Barren
Thunder and Lightning Bay
Kent Bay
Wombat Pt
Preservation Island
Sloping Pt
40°30′
Armstrong Channel
Cone Pt
Forsyth Island
Passage Island
Clarke Island
Black Point
Lookout Head
Moriarty Bay
Moriarty Point
148°
148°30′

1 2 3 4 5 6 7 8 9 10

148°30′
Mt Kerford
Cape Barren
Kent Bay
ng Pt
Cone Pt
Forsyth Island
Passage Island
lack Point
iarty Bay
arty Point
40°30′
TRAIT
pe Naturaliste
umpys Bay
Cod Bay
Purdon Bay
Eddystone Point Lighthouse
Eddystone Point
41°
Ansons Bay
Sharon Point
Bay of Fires Cons Area
Bay Of Fires
The Gardens
Sloop Lagoon
Binalong Bay
Humbug Point Cons Area
11
St Helens Pt
St Helens
St Helens Point Cons Area
Stieglitz
Parnella
Parkside
St Helens Island
20
Dianas Basin
A3
Beaumaris
Scamander Forest Res
Scamander
Henderson Lagoon
Falmouth
Four Mile Creek
Ironhouse Point
22
HWY
Elephant Pass
Chain of Lagoons
9
A3
Picaninny Point
Templestow Lagoon
Seymour
Long Point
Maclean Bay
19
Birdlife and Animal Park
Bicheno
11
95
Cape Lodi
Courland Bay
Freycinet National Park
Friendly Beaches
Mt Peter

149°
149°30′
41°30′
42°
148°30′
149°
149°30′

H J K L M N P

TAS

Map 3

TAS 1
Cradle Mountain Lake St Clair NP
Franklin-Gordon Wild Rivers National Park
Southwest Conservation Area
Southwest National Park
Mount Field Nat Park
Queenstown
Strahan
Derwent Bridge
Strathgordon
Lake Gordon
Lake Pedder
Lake Burbury
Macquarie Harbour
Port Davey
Bathurst Harbour
Maatsuyker Group
De Witt Island
South West Cape
SOUTHERN
OCEAN
NORTH

0 10 20 30
kilometres

H J K L M N P

147° 147°30′ 148° –42°–

1
Flintstone, Great Lake, Wilburville, Mt Franklin, Ross, Hobgoblin, Lake Leake, Lake Leake, Wyefield Rt, Lost Falls Forest Res, Moulting Lagoon, Cranbrook, Freycinet Nat Park, Friendly Beaches, Mt Peter, Mt Paul, A5, LAKE, Woods Lake, Lake Sorell, Steppes, Lagoon of Islands, River, O'Connor Rt, Wye R, River, Nine Mile Beach, Swansea, Hepburn Point, Coles Bay, Coles Bay, Lighthouse, Cape Tourville, Sleepy Bay, Alma Pass, Interlaken, Tunbridge, C305, Macquarie River, Meredith, A3, Great, Mt Dove, Fleurieu Pt, Wineglass Bay, Cape Forestier

2
Woodbury, Antill Ponds, Kittys Rt, Buxton River, Spiky Bridge, Promise Bay, Oyster, Mt Graham, Mt Freycinet, Lake Crescent, Old Mans Head, Blackman River, 86, Vincent Hill, Faddens Tier, Tooms Lake, Mayfield Bay Cons Area, Weatherhead Point, Freycinet Pen, 81, HWY, Table Mtn, Exe Rt, York Plains, Mayfield Bay, Buxton Pt, Bay, Bryans Beach, Baldy Bluff, Cape Degerando, Clyde River, Woods Quoin, Oatlands, Callington Mill Historic Site, Pawtella, Lemont, Little Swanport, Schouten Passage, Schouten Island, Lake Dulverton, Andover, Little Swanport, Seaford Point, Cape Faure, Rooster Point, Cape Sonnerat, Nicholas Sugarloaf, Northumbria Hill, Parattah, Pt Bailly, Freycinet National Park

3
Thorpe Water Mill, Bothwell, Jericho, Pike Hill, Little Swanport R, Little Swanport Hill, Ravensdale Rt, 58, Boltons Beach Cons Area, A5, Green Hill, Spring Hill, Mount Seymour, Whitefoord, Buckland Military Training Area, Grindstone Point, Clyde, Stonor, Baden, Tunnack, Mt Reid, Jordan, Lake Tiberias, HWY, Mt Murray, B110, Black Tier, Melton Mowbray, B31, Rhyndaston, Woodsdale, Bluestone Tier, Eldon, Coal River, Mt Hobbs, Triabunna, –42°30′–, Cape Bougainville

4
Hollow Tree, Levendale, Stony Rt, Sand R, Back R, Louisville, Okehampton Bay, Hamilton, Kempton, MIDLAND, Colebrook, Craigbourne Dam, Prosser, Orford, Lighthouse, Mt Spode, Pelham, Quoin Mtn, Prosser River, Prosser Bay, Passage, Cape Boullanger, Dysart, Spring Beach, Darlington, Maria Island National Park, Derwent, Elderslie, 36, Native Hut Rt, Brown Mtn, 52, Buckland, Tea Tree Rt, Thumbs Picnic Area, Johnsons Pt, Mercury Passage, Mangalore Tier, Jordan, Bagdad, Lowdina, TASMAN, Return Pt, Maria Island, Mt Maria, A10, 48, Mangalore, Runnymede, Rheban, Booming Bay, Mistaken Cape, Broadmarsh, R, C321, Mt Morrison, Curryjong Rt, Prossers Sugarloaf, Pt Lesueur, Gretna, Campania, A3, Shoal Bay, Riedle Bay, Glenora, Rosegarland, HWY, Pontville, Sandspit River Forest Res, Oyster Bay, Mt Dromedary, Tea Tree, Brighton, Sandspit, Nugent, Cape Maurouard, Bushy Park, Macquarie Plains, Plenty, Black Hills, Dromedary, Bridgewater, Richmond, Pawleena, Cape Bernier, Cape Peron

5
Hayes, Magra, B10, Salmon Ponds, Moogara, Granton, Grasstree Hill, Orielton, Wattle Hill, Kellevie, Marion, Feilton, New Norfolk, Boyer, Old Beach, Claremont, B31, Sorell, Midway Point, Bream Creek, Glenfern, Malbina, Molesworth, Otago, B32, Risdon Vale, Pitt Water, Forcett, ARTHUR, Carlton River, Bay, Lachlan, Glenlusk, Cambridge, Lewisham, Copping, Mount Lloyd, Collinsvale, Glenorchy, A3, 27, Seven Mile Beach Protected Area, Dodges Ferry, A9, Cape Paul Lamanon, North Bay, Collins Cap, Mt Rumney, Lookout, Seven Mile Beach, Carlton, Dunalley, Cape Frederick Hendrick, Trestle Mtn, Lookout, Mt Wellington, HOBART, Rokeby, Frederick Henry, Primrose Sands, Dunalley Bay, Blue Hill, Fern Tree, Ridgeway, River, Lauderdale, Green Head, Mt Forestier, HWY, Forestier, High Yellow Bluff

6
Lonnavale, Mt Misery, Crabtree, Mountain River, B64, Neika, Leslie Vale, A6, Taroona, Shot Tower, Ralphs Bay, Sandford, Sloping I, Lime Bay Nat Res, Smooth I, Murdunna, Cape Surville, Judbury, Lucaston, Grove, HWY, Longley, Kingston, Cremorne, Bay, Chronicle Pt, Coal Mines Historic Site, Peninsula, Ranelagh, Lower Longley, 42, Sandfly, Blackmans Bay, Derwent, Opossum Bay, B33, Cape Deslacs, Clifton Beach, Norfolk Bay, 75, Eaglehawk Neck, Tessellated Pavement, Pirates Bay, –43°–, Glen Huon, Huonville, Kaoota, Howden, South Arm, Saltwater River, Tasmanian Blowhole, Tasman Arch, Devils Kitchen, Waterfall Bay, Scotts Divide, HUON, Pelverata, Electrona, Margate, North West Bay, Tinderbox, Iron Pot Lighthouse, Betsey Island, Premaydena, Tasmanian Devil Park, Taranna, Pelverata Falls, Snug Falls, Snug, Dennes Point, Outer North Head, Koonya, B37, A9, O'Hara Bluff

7
Franklin, Woodstock, Coningham, Killora, One Tree Point, Tasman, Peninsula, Tasman Trail, Cradoc, Oyster Cove, Kettering, Barnes Bay, Wedge Bay, Nubeena, Fortescue Bay, South Franklin, Ferry, The Yellow Bluff, White Beach, Castle Forbes Bay, Glaziers Bay, Nicholls Rt, Nicholls Rivulet, Trumpeter Bay, Two Island Bay, Port Arthur, Cape Huay, Port Huon, Wattle Grove, Cygnet, Woodbridge, STORM, Highcroft, Palmers Lookout, Convict Ruins, Munro Bight, Geeveston, Petcheys Bay, Birchs Bay, Variety Bay, Curio Bay, Remarkable Cave, Tasman National Park, Cairns Bay, Lymington, Gardners Bay, B68, Great Bay, North Bruny Island, BAY, Tasman National Park, Maingon Bay, Cape Pillar, Waterloo, Surges Bay, Huon River, Port Cygnet, Middleton, B66, Raoul Bay, Tasman I Lighthouse, Glendevie, Garden Island Creek, Channel, Simpsons Pt, Cape Queen Elizabeth, Police Point, Hideaway Bay, Esperance River, Verona Sands, Gordon, Isthmus Bay, Cape Raoul

8
Surveyors Bay, Huon I, Simpsons Bay, Adventure Bay, 64, Dover, Maggot Pt, D'Entrecasteaux, Raminea, Port Esperance, Esperance Pt, Alonnah, Fluted Cape, Strathblane, Ventenat Point, South, Adventure Bay, Capt Cook's Landing Place, Bligh Museum, A6, Hastings Caves, Lunawanna, Partridge Island, Bruny Island, Cape Connella, Thermal Pool, Great Taylors Bay, Bay of Islands, Lune River, Hopwood Point, Southport, Mangana Bluff

9
Ida Bay, South Bruny Nat Park, South Bruny National Park, Southport Lagoon, Historic Lighthouse, Cloudy Bay, Mt Bruny, Boreel Head, TASMAN SEA, –43°30′–, Cape Bruny, West Cloudy Head, East Cloudy Head, Tasman Head, The Friars, Eliza Point, Recherche Bay, Catamaran, Whale Sculpture, Cockle Creek, Bare Hill, Whale Head

10

147° 147°30′ 148°

H J K L M N P

TAS

South Australia

When they think of South Australia, lovers of the outdoors will immediately call to mind such places as the Flinders Ranges, the Simpson Desert, or the cliffs lining the Great Australian Bight where the flat plains of the Nullarbor Plain plunge into the rolling swells of the Southern Ocean. There are many other natural wonders, and they have one thing in common—some form of park or reserve protects them all. With more than 17 per cent of South Australia protected in some form of conservation area, the state can boast one of the most dynamic and forward-thinking reserve systems in the country. From the parks in the remote north, to the Flinders Ranges, to the south-east and to the mighty Murray, there are many rare jewels hidden away in the vastness of South Australia.

Flinders Ranges National Park

This semi-arid mountain country is among the most spectacular regions of the Australian outback. The changing moods of these mountains enchant all who gaze upon them. The ranges stretch 300 km from near Gladstone in the relatively well-watered parts of the state, north to the low hill of Mount Hopeless on the edge of the Strzelecki Desert. But it is in the central Flinders, around the unique geological structure of Wilpena Pound, that the ranges take on their grandest and most distinctive character.

fact file

WHERE: 460 km north of Adelaide
Map: SA 3 K4

WHEN: April to October; September is best for wildflowers

WHY: Great camping, remote mountain scenery, wildflowers

SIZE: 92 746 ha

INFORMATION: Wilpena Pound Visitor Centre (08) 8648 0048

While Wilpena Pound is the linchpin of the surrounding Flinders Ranges National Park, it really does vie with other natural wonders nearby to provide a seemingly never-ending extravaganza of scenery.

In the Past

The Adnyamathanha people, or 'Hill People', were the original inhabitants of this area and they have left a rich legacy of rock art sites in the region.

Although the mountains were named after Matthew Flinders, who was the first European to view the ranges on his circumnavigation of Australia in 1802, it was Edward John Eyre in 1839 and 1840 who settled the area. Other explorers and surveyors followed, and two doctors, the Browne brothers, opened up the area around Wilpena Pound and the Aroona Valley just to the north.

Since the early 1950s, the Pound has had a tourist resort located at the Wilpena Creek entrance. In 1970 a national park was founded to the north-east of Wilpena Pound, and two years later the new national park was amalgamated with the Pound. Since then the park has grown to its present size of 92 746 hectares.

The little eagle (Hieraaetus morphnoides) *feeds mostly on live prey such as reptiles, small animals and small birds.*

Wilpena Pound

The centrepiece of the park is Wilpena Pound, which attracts most of the visitors and the acclaim. The name Wilpena is said to mean in the local Aboriginal dialect, 'a cupped hand', which is a perfect description of this huge natural amphitheatre, while a 'pound' was the early settlers' name for a stock enclosure. Nearly 5 km wide and 11 km long, the undulating grassland inside the Pound sweeps up on its edges to the lofty craggy peaks of the all-encircling Wilpena Pound Range, that on the edges plummet to the surrounding plains.

There are only two exits from the Pound. One, in the north-west, through Edeowie Gorge, is narrow, rocky and

Grassland sweeps up to the edges of the ranges which encircle Wilpena Pound in the Flinders Ranges. St Mary Peak, part of the range which forms the north-eastern wall of Wilpena Pound, is the highest point in South Australia.

Below: *Wilpena Pound, the centrepiece of this national park, covers over 83 sq km. This crater-like area with its more permanent waterholes, rich vegetation and bountiful wildlife provides a contrast to the stark, dry surrounding plains.*

cliff-strewn, while the other follows the gum-lined Wilpena Creek through a steep-sided valley on the eastern side of the Pound. The park's tourist resort and all the amenities are located close to this entrance.

Few people would come to this area and not take at least a short stroll through the gap carved by Wilpena Creek. Ancient, giant red gums tower over the track and crowd the rocky, often reed-shrouded creek bed, making the walk a shady delight, especially welcome after a long walk across rocky ridges or sun-scorched open plains.

The shorter walks take you to the old homestead and then up the ridge on a short but steep climb to Wangarra

The unusual bearded dragon (Pogona vitticeps). *When threatened, this lizard intimidates predators by standing with its mouth open and puffing out the spiny pouch under its jaw.*

Lookout. The return walk of 2 to 3 km takes 1 to 2 hours. From the entrance to the Pound there is also an hour-long walk along a nature trail and a more strenuous walk of about 2 hours to the lookout on top of Mount Ohlssen Bagge.

Longer walks of a day or more can take you south to Bridle Gap, on the edge of the park, or north to Edeowie Gorge, while a circuit route via the heart of the Pound and Cooinda Camp can take you north to Tanderra Saddle and the top of St Mary Peak. From there it turns south along the battlements of the range to bring you back to the starting point at Wilpena Creek.

Part of the long-distance Heysen Walking Trail cuts through the park, entering at the southern end of the Pound via Bridle Gap. It then heads north from Wilpena Creek along the ABC Range to the Aroona Valley and out of the park to Parachilna Gorge. You can enjoy this trail for a day, a week or even longer, but you need to be experienced and well equipped for extended forays.

Sacred Canyon

Sacred Canyon is one of the best Australian Aboriginal art sites in the Flinders Ranges and is only accessible via a good dirt road that heads off the main Blinman road, just north of the Wilpena Pound Resort turn-off.

A brief walk from the car park along a tree-lined creek brings you to the short narrow canyon. There are rock engravings, or petroglyphs, which can be seen on the sheer rock faces on both sides of the canyon. This ancient form of indigenous art includes animal tracks, circles and other symbols.

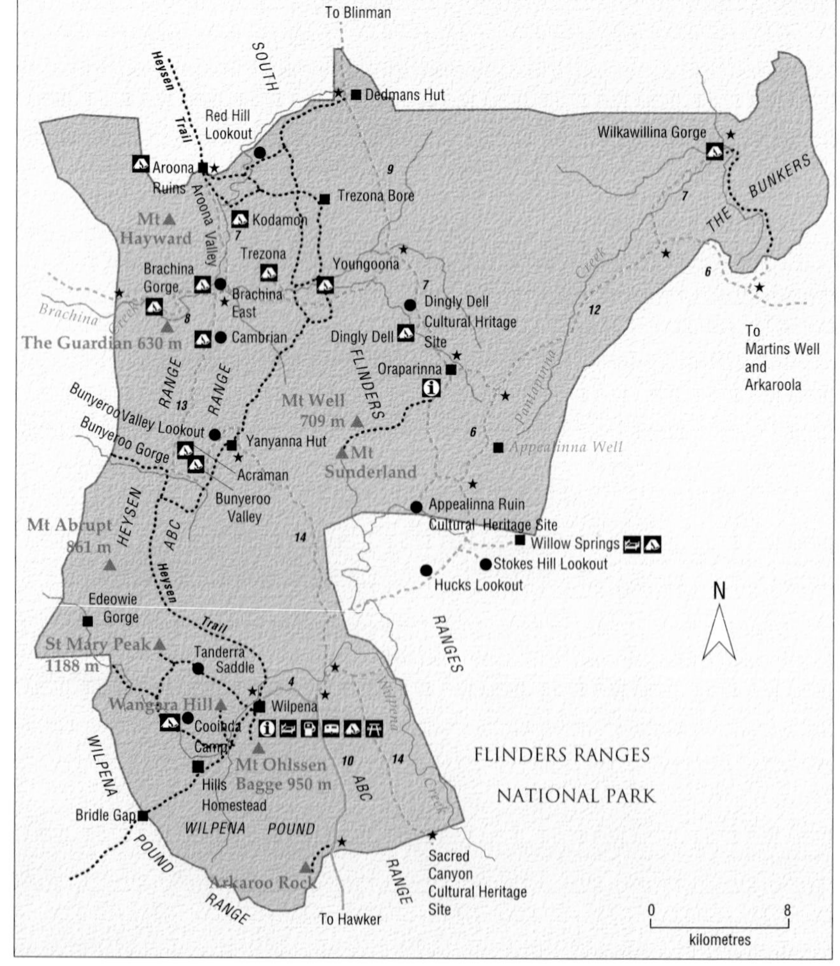

Aroona Valley

The scenic Aroona Valley tucks in beside the northern peaks of the ABC Range, but it is the Heysen Range immediately to the west that dominates the view. The partially restored mud brick and pine Aroona

Opposite page: *White cypress pine* (Callitris glaucophylla) *growing in the local rugged sandstone; its roots penetrate the rock crevices in their search for water.*

Grass trees (Xanthorrhoea australis) *grow on the rocky hillsides. In spring, their white flower spikes blend wih the pinks and reds of Sturt's desert pea, bottlebrush and Sturt's desert rose.*

homestead is perfectly situated to make the most of the view and it also shows how hard life was here back in the boom days of the late 1800s.

You can enjoy a short or long stroll along the Heysen Walking Trail or along the nearby creek. Another walking trail leads out to Red Hill Lookout, a 9 km, 3 to 4 hour, return trip, while other walks will take you out to the Trezona Range or along the Yuluna loop and through the ABC Range.

Brachina Gorge

Where the Brachina Creek meanders through the Heysen Range it forms one of the most delightful features in the area. Gums line the creek, which often has a slow trickle of water running along it. In places, fairly large pools, protected by a rugged bluff or group of shady trees, provide a permanent water source for the area's wildlife.

There are no designated walks, but a stroll along the creek is very pleasant and informative, as it is part of the Brachina Gorge Geological Trail which takes you right through the range. For those who feel energetic, a climb of one of the nearby peaks will give a grand view of the gorge and the surrounding mountains. This really is a special place.

Wilkawillina Gorge

Located in the very north-east of the park is Wilkawillina Gorge, where the Mount Billy Creek has cut its way through the Bunkers Range.

There is a camping ground close to the vehicle track end and a walk of about a kilometre will take you into the gorge proper. This part of the Flinders is much drier than the Wilpena side.

Spectacular Brachina Gorge was formed by Brachina Creek cutting through the ABC and Heysen Ranges. The white gums of the area were immortalised by artist Hans Heysen (1877–1968).

Recommended Drive

One of the best drives in the park is to take the Yanyanna Hut–Bunyeroo Valley road in the early morning. It is especially colourful after rain when the wildflowers bloom. Once you are off the main Blinman road, red kangaroos are very common, and as you get closer to the main range and the hills begin to crowd in, euros and western grey kangaroos may be seen.

The views are superb, with the pine-clad hills rolling away to the sheer bluffs of the Heysen Range. If you want to make a day of it, head up to the Prairie Hotel in Parachilna for lunch and then in the evening head back taking the Moralana Scenic Drive to Wilpena. Although this 36 km drive is actually out of the park, it gives wonderful views of the western walls of Wilpena—in the dying light of day, they are just fabulous.

Access

You can travel on bitumen all the way from Adelaide to the resort at the entrance to Wilpena Pound via Wilmington and Quorn (400 km), while the slightly shorter way (370 km) through Orroroo and Jamestown has a 40 km section of good dirt road south of Hawker.

Elsewhere, good dirt roads suitable for conventional vehicles lead through the park to all the points of interest. Only after occasional heavy rains or floods are any of the roads closed, and then generally only for a short time.

Camping

At Wilpena Pound there is a well-established motel and caravan park, including a general store, fuel outlet, ranger base and visitor information centre.

There is some very good camping in the Aroona Valley, as well as along the headwaters of Brachina Creek, at Dingley Dell on the Blinman road 30 km north of Wilpena Pound, along the main road through Bunyeroo Gorge and at Wilkawillina Gorge in the far north-east of the park. A favourite camping area is along Brachina Gorge where you'll find a number of pleasant spots to stop a while.

No matter where you camp a fee is payable, and no firewood is allowed to be collected in the park. Gas fires are preferred.

Above: *Climbing the Great Wall, a sheer sandstone cliff face 50 m high. The Great Wall is one of the highlights of Moonarie, South Australia's most significant climbing site, on the outer wall of Wilpena Pound.*

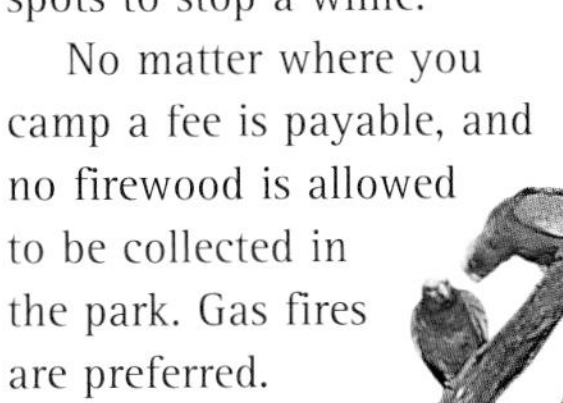

Galahs (Cacatua roseicapilla) *range over grasslands and savannah throughout much of Australia, including the Flinders. These seed-eating parrots will travel as much as 15 km in a day to search for food.*

SA

tourist info

Visitor Centre Wilpena
(08) 8648 0048

Coffin Bay National Park

This park takes up the whole of the Coffin Bay Peninsula, with its 30 380 hectares of sand and limestone country covered mainly with mallee, tea-tree and she-oak woodlands, and low swampy areas covered in samphire. In places, sterile white drifting sand dunes engulf all living things. On one side of the great T-shaped peninsula are the placid protected waters of Coffin Bay, an ideal place to swim, sail a boat or to fish for whiting.

fact file

WHERE: 625 km west of Adelaide, via Port Lincoln Map: SA 4 B2

WHEN: October to April

WHY: Spectacular coastal scenery, good fishing, safe swimming, surfing, 4WD

SIZE: 30 380 ha

RANGER: National Parks and Wildlife, Eyre District Office (08) 8688 3111

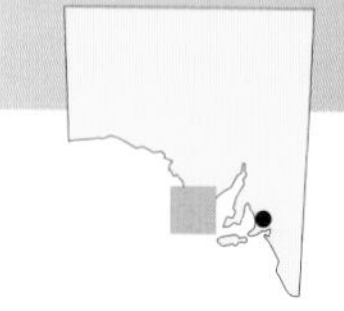

On the opposite side of Coffin Bay Peninsula, along its south-western coast, the surf generated from the great Southern Ocean pounds the coast continuously.

Of course, such an untamed area has other attractions as well. The beaches, headlands, rich shallow coastal waters and scrub-covered sand ridges provide a rich and bountiful habitat for birds. Ospreys are common, rock parrots nest in the scrub above the cliff-lined beaches, and shearwaters skim the nearby waters; occasionally, the rare and elusive western whipbird can be seen.

In the Past

The Nauo people once inhabited the area around Coffin Bay, and shell middens along the coast are a reminder of their early way of life.

Matthew Flinders was the first European to see this coast in 1802 and the area was colonised in the 1840s. Early graziers shipped their hard-earned bales of wool from Morgans Landing, on the north-western coast of Coffin Bay.

Coffin Bay offers superb fishing, both from the protected bayside beaches and on the wilder sea coast. Fishing boat charters are also available.

Activities

There are a number of walking trails in the park, most of which follow old vehicle tracks. It is also very enjoyable to walk along the beaches.

At Yangie Bay there is a very short walk of just 300 metres to the Yangie Lookout, or a longer 1.5 km Kallara Nature Trail walk. Other walks from here include the 5 km walk to Yangie Island or to Long Beach.

In the Whidbey Wilderness area there are a number of short walks, while overnight walks include the 26 km walk south along the Whidbey Trail.

The fishing is superb everywhere. The protected bay beaches are a mecca for King George whiting, garfish, trevally,

The township is only 50 km from Port Lincoln.

The entrance to the park is just through the township. Buying an annual Eyre Park Pass will help you save a few dollars if you are visiting a few parks on Eyre Peninsula.

Conventional vehicles can get as far as Yangie Bay. From this point a series of soft, sandy 4WD tracks head west to the furthermost points of the peninsula. The Whidbey Wilderness area has no vehicle access.

There is a fair range of camping and accommodation in the nearby Coffin Bay township. The local general store can supply food and fuel, while Beachcomber Agencies, phone (08) 8685 4057, has tourist information.

In the national park you are only allowed to camp at Yangie Bay, Black Springs, Morgans Landing, The Pool, and near Sensation Beach.

Left: *Sand dunes at Coffin Bay National Park. The coastal landscape of barren drifting dunes contrasts sharply with protected bays backed by black tea trees.*

did you know?

There are wild ponies in this park! Managed by the Coffin Bay Pony Preservation Society and National Parks and Wildlife, SA, the ponies are believed to be descended from animals brought to the area by the early settlers in the 1840s.

Many conservationists believe that allowing the ponies to live in the park sends the wrong message about feral animals in national parks.

SA

flathead and salmon, while along the wilder coast you can try your luck for salmon, snapper, whiting and a wide variety of reef fish.

Of course, swimming, surfing, diving and sailing are popular pastimes.

Access and Camping

Access to Coffin Bay is easy and on good roads from the main Flinders Highway.

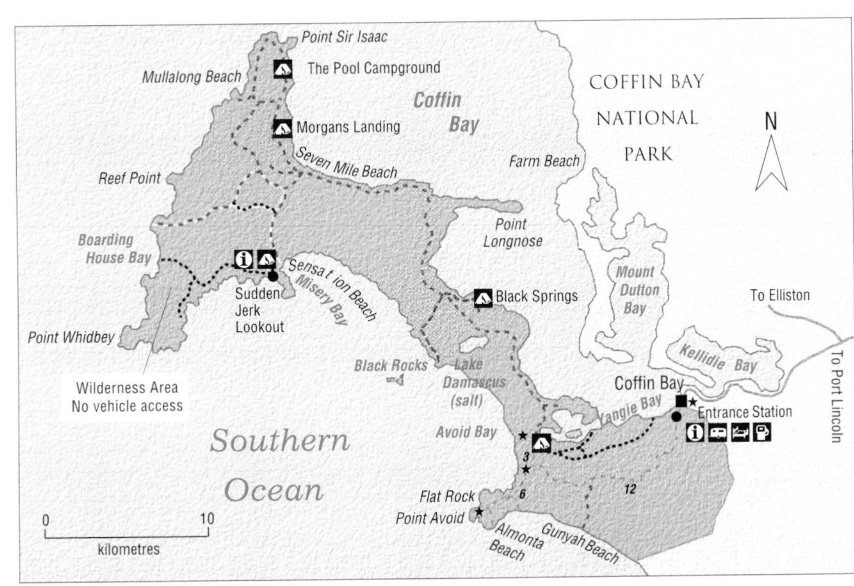

Flinders Chase National Park

The Flinders Chase National Park is renowned for its wildlife, as well as for the amazing view, through Admirals Arch, of a wild, turbulent Southern Ocean pounding a rocky inlet on the far western coast of Kangaroo Island. The park consists of 73 920 hectares of wild virgin scrub and bush country and takes up the whole of the western end of the island. Because of its undisturbed nature and its wide variety of habitats and fauna, it is one of South Australia's most important parks.

Amazing shapes of seemingly delicately balanced boulders sit on top of a remnant granite outcrop at the Remarkable Rocks area.

fact file

WHERE: On Kangaroo Island, 270 km south-west of Adelaide
Map: SA 4 E5

WHEN: November, December, March to May

WHY: Coastal scenery, wildlife, fishing

SIZE: 73 920 ha

RANGER: Rocky River (08) 8559 7235

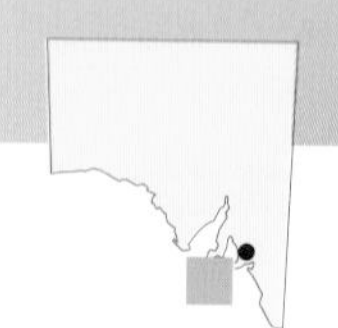

Wildlife

Kangaroos, koalas, ringtail possums and even platypus are commonly seen. Over a dozen species of mammals are native to the park including tammar wallabies, the southern brown bandicoot, the Australian sea lion and the Australian and New Zealand fur seals.

A number of reptiles also live in the park including Gould's sand goanna, a handsome monitor lizard that reaches 1.6 metres in length. Black tiger snakes and copperhead snakes can also be seen but these should be left alone.

There are nearly 200 species of birds found in the park with yellow-tailed black cockatoos and Cape Barren geese being the most common. The rare western whipbird and the glossy black cockatoo may also be sighted on occasion.

The strikingly marked harlequin fish (Othos dentex). *These are a reasonably common catch on the deeper reefs around Kangaroo Island.*

Activities

A number of pleasant, relatively easy walking trails can be found throughout the park including those at Cape du Couedic, Remarkable Rocks, Rocky River (where platypus waterholes may allow a viewing of this elusive monotreme) and Sandy Creek. The Ravine des Casoars trail to the wild and scenic west coast in the northern section of the park is a moderate-to-hard walk of 7 km. Well-equipped and experienced walkers could attempt a much longer trek along the entire west coast.

Kangaroo Island is known for its great fishing. West Bay and Harveys Return are also popular and produce good catches of snapper, sweep, rock cod, whiting and salmon.

A number of wrecks have occurred along this coast including that of the *Loch Vennachar,* a 250-foot clipper which disappeared in 1905 and was finally discovered in 1976 a kilometre north of West Bay. A grave of an unknown sailor can be seen just up from the beach at West Bay.

Access

Access to Kangaroo Island is via the SeaLink ferry from Cape Jervis, 105 km south of Adelaide. The ferry takes you to the small island town of Penneshaw. Flinders Chase National Park is down the other end of the island from Penneshaw, 150 km away, either on bitumen or excellent dirt roads.

The park headquarters is located at Rocky River on the South Coast Road. Within the park most roads are good dirt, and the many points of interest are accessible in a conventional vehicle.

Camping and Accommodation

At Rocky River there is a good camping area with showers, toilets and limited supplies. West Bay, Snake Lagoon and Harveys Return all have small camping areas. Only gas fires are allowed in the Island parks. Accommodation is available at the old Rocky River homestead, in the lighthouse keeper's quarters at Cape Borda and Cape du Couedic, or at Flinders Chase Farmstay and Hostel, phone (08) 8559 7223.

Entry fees and camping fees apply. If you are staying and touring the island an 'Island Pass' will work out more convenient and economical.

tourist info

FERRY: SeaLink 13 13 01 or (08) 8202 8688; www.sealink.com.au

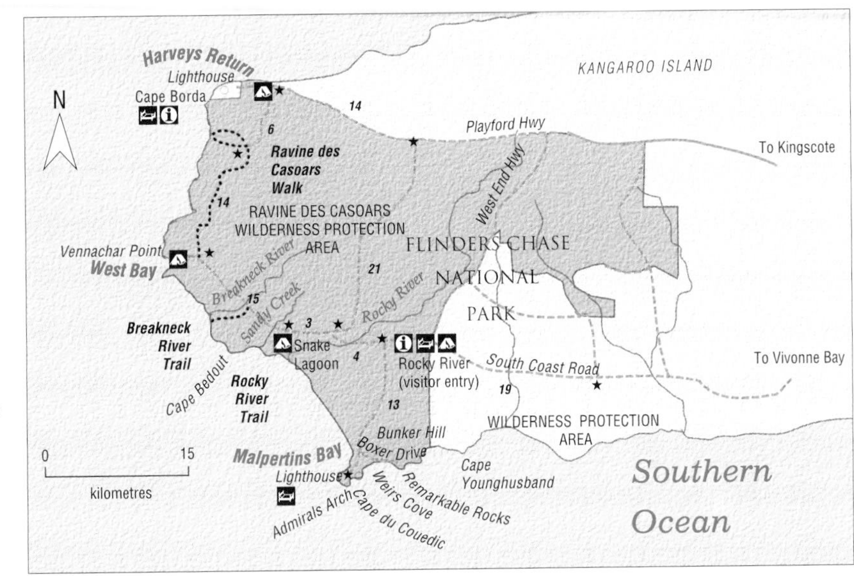

Below: *The land bridge of Admiral's Arch at Cape du Couedic is one of the scenic highlights of Kangaroo Island. Many of the filaments hanging from the roof of the arch are actually fossilised tree roots.*

SA

Witjira National Park, Simpson Desert Regional Reserve & Park

Many people believe that there is no finer desert oasis in Australia than the warm waters of Dalhousie Springs located in the far north of South Australia, in the very west of Witjira National Park. Located on the western edge of the Simpson Desert, the group of 70 or so springs that make up the Dalhousie group of mound springs comprises the most significant natural outflowings of the vast artesian basin that underlies much of outback Australia.

fact file

WHERE: 1360 km north of Adelaide, on the border with Queensland and the Northern Territory
Map: SA 2 C1

WHEN: May to September

WHY: Desert landscape, 4WD, remote camping, warm springs

SIZE: 776 900 ha

RANGER: Desert Parks Hotline 1800 816 078

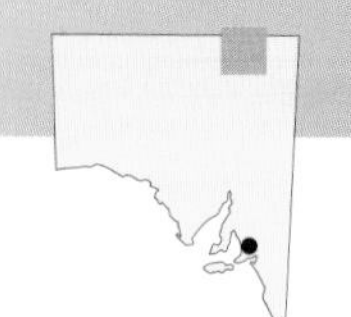

did you know?

The 70 thermal springs in the Dalhousie complex were one of the main reasons for establishing this national park. Dalhousie Springs are home to several species of fish which are found nowhere else in the world.

In the Past

Several groups of Australian Aboriginals included different areas of the Simpson Desert in their tribal lands. Dalhousie Springs and the permanent water points on the western edge of the desert were of spiritual significance as well as an important water source to the Lower Southern Aranda people and the Wangkangurru people.

Charles Sturt was the first European to see the desert in 1845, but the Dalhousie Springs were not discovered until the early 1870s.

Interest in the desert was revived in the 1950s when oil exploration began and this continued through to the 1970s. All the tracks across the desert from Dalhousie east are the result of that exploration work.

In 1967 the Simpson Desert Conservation Park of 6927 sq km was proclaimed. In 1988 the Simpson Desert Regional Reserve of 29 642 sq km was declared linking all the parks, while the Witjira National Park of 7770 sq km, was also established at that time.

Places to Experience

It is the desert ambience, the peace and the solitude, that makes the great memories of a trip to the Simpson Desert parks. The springs around Dalhousie, once you can tear yourself away from the warm water, are worth exploring and the variety of birds is remarkable. Likewise, Purni Bore, deeper into the desert, is a gem and the wetlands created by this bore attract much wildlife.

The ruins of the old Dalhousie homestead should also be visited.

Access

No matter what direction you come from, only dirt roads lead to these parks. The area is really the realm of a 4WD, but in good conditions the main track from Oodnadatta is passable to a conventional vehicle, driven with care.

From Dalhousie the route across the desert strikes the first of the sand ridges

just over 50 km east. The French Line is the roughest but shortest track east (430 km to Birdsville), the WAA Line a good alternative, while the Rig Road is the longest. However, all are definitely 4WD routes and you need to be well prepared and equipped for a crossing of the desert to Birdsville.

All of these routes may be closed after rain. Check with the rangers before setting off.

Left: *Sand dunes in the Simpson Desert. Witjira National Park, one of the gateways to the Simpson Desert, is jointly managed by the Irrwanyere Aboriginal Corporation and National Parks and Wildlife, South Australia.*

Camping

In the very north of the park, 70 km from Dalhousie Springs, the old homestead of Mount Dare offers accommodation, camping, meals, fuel, tyres and minor repairs, as well as a breakdown service and a cold beer.

The only other designated camping grounds are at Dalhousie Springs and Purni Bore where you can find toilets and water. Elsewhere you can camp close to the track on any one of the designated routes across the desert.

The shingleback or stumpy-tailed lizard (Trachydosaurus rugosus) is found throughout arid parts of Australia. Unlike many reptiles, these lizards give birth to very large, live young which weigh about 35 per cent of the mother's weight.

Desert Parks Pass

To enter or travel this reserved land in the state's north, you need a Desert Parks Pass. For an economical fee, the pass includes a good range of maps and booklets and is valid for a year.

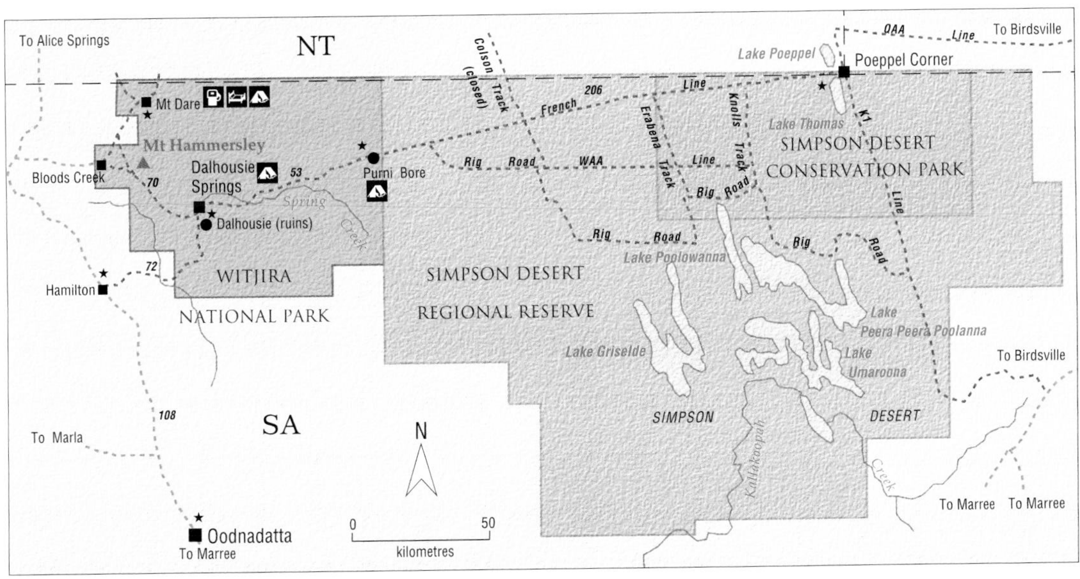

Canunda National Park

The south-eastern coast of South Australia has one of the wildest, most untouched coastlines on the continent. Canunda National Park takes up 9358 hectares of coast that is dominated by large sand dunes and, in the north of the park, rugged limestone cliffs.

Southern right whale (Eubalaena australis) *and calf. These whales and the minke whale pass along this coast on their annual migrations.*

fact file

WHERE: 390 km south-east of Adelaide, via the Princes Highway
Map: SA 4 M9

WHEN: December to February

WHY: Wild, spectacular coast, fishing, beach driving, wildlife, 4WD

SIZE: 9358 ha

INFORMATION: DEH Mt Gambier (08) 8735 1177

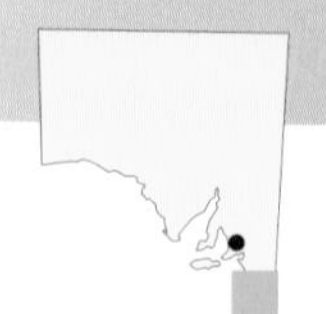

Walking, Fishing and Wildlife

There are a number of walking trails, giving travellers an opportunity to experience this park first-hand. Some trails lead along the edge of the cliffs while others take you to good vantage points or historic places of interest.

For the keen angler this part of South Australia's coast can provide good catches of salmon, mulloway, flathead and the occasional shark.

Nature watchers may sight some of the world's rarest birds, including the orange-bellied parrot and the hooded plover, as well as having the chance to see penguins and seals which are regular visitors along this coast.

don't miss

Walking trails that shouldn't be missed include the Khyber Pass Walk (a short stroll from the car park to a spectacular area of sand dunes) and the Seaspray Walk (a 1.5 km walk along the cliff edge).

Access and Camping

Access by conventional vehicles is limited to Cape Buffon and Boozy Gully in the north of the park, and to Oil Rig Square in the central section of the park.

For those with a 4WD, the complete park is accessible by following the orange marker posts that lead through the park from Southend to Carpenter Rocks. Excellent sand driving techniques are required and you must stick to the marked track. This route can be challenging.

You can camp near Southend, Oil Rig Square and Number Two Rocks. A permit from the ranger is required to camp in the park. There are caravan parks in Millicent and Carpenter Rocks.

Right: *Huge sand dunes dominate the southern part of Canunda National Park. Much of the park is accessible only by 4WD.*

Coorong National Park

The Coorong is a series of shallow lagoons that provide a rich habitat for hundreds of thousands of waterbirds. It is protected from the rolling surf of the Southern Ocean by a narrow strip of sand dunes known as the Younghusband Peninsula.

A surf angler on the Younghusband Peninsula. Ninety Mile Beach on the ocean side of the peninsula is quite remote and relatively lightly fished.

fact file

WHERE: 140 km south-east of Adelaide
Map: SA 4 K5

WHEN: November to February

WHY: Fishing, wildlife, coastal scenery, 4WD

SIZE: 46 745 ha

RANGER: Meningie (08) 8575 1200

Fishing and Birdwatching

There is excellent surf fishing for mulloway, whiting, flathead, salmon and shark. In the lagoon, mullet, bream and flounder abound.

The whole area is one of Australia's most important wetlands and it is a birdwatcher's paradise, with over 200 species of birds being recorded. The lakes regularly support over 120 000 waders, a large number of black swans, and an abundant population of Cape Barren geese, as well as being the largest pelican breeding area in Australia.

Access, Camping and Accommodation

The mainland side of the park is accessible to conventional vehicles while the ocean beaches are strictly 4WD territory. All vehicles must stay on the marked routes. Access tracks across the dunes to the beach are well marked.

The route north along the beach from Tea Tree Crossing is closed from late October to late December each year to protect the endangered hooded plover during its breeding season.

There are plenty of places to camp that can be accessed by car, 4WD or boat. These include Mark Point, Long Point, and Tea Tree Crossing. A camping permit is needed.

Noonameena House, in the heart of the park, offers accommodation for up to eight people.

tourist info

Salt Creek Visitor Centre
(08) 8575 7014

Murray River National Park

The Murray River National Park is made up of three distinct sections of floodplain spread along the Murray River from above Renmark to just north of Loxton in the heart of the Riverland of eastern South Australia. The park protects not only the natural wonders and rich wildlife, but also preserves ancient Australian Aboriginal middens, canoe trees, ceremonial rings of stone, and burial sites found throughout the park.

Fishing on the Murray River. Golden perch and Murray cod remain popular target species, but catfish and silver perch are now quite rare.

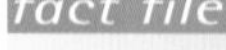

fact file

WHERE: 180 to 240 km east of Adelaide, via the Sturt Highway
Map: SA 4 N2

WHEN: September to April

WHY: Camping, fishing, magnificent river scenery, birdwatching

SIZE: 13 250 ha

RANGER: Murraylands Regional Office (08) 8595 2111

Activities

Fishing, camping, birdwatching, canoeing and cruising on a houseboat are popular pastimes, while bushwalks can be enjoyed throughout the park.

Canoeing here is very pleasant and trips of up to 4 days can be done in the Bulyong Island area, incorporating Ral Ral Creek and the Murray, while 1 or 2 day trips can be planned in the Katarapko section of the park. Both the Bulyong Island and the Katarapko sections are very popular with canoeists.

There are boat launching facilities in a number of places, except in the Lyrup Flats section.

Access and Camping

Access to the Katarapko section is off the Sturt Highway, west of the township of Berri. Dirt roads lead to numerous camping sites along Katarapko Creek and the Murray River.

Lyrup Flats is located upstream from Berri with the Sturt Highway giving good access to an all-weather dirt road that leads to a number of large camping areas and to tracks that head to smaller individual camps along the river.

Bulyong Island, not far upstream from Renmark, is a popular spot and while it doesn't have any designated camping areas, it is possible to camp at many points along the river.

Camping permits, available from the ranger, are required for camping anywhere in the park.

The Murray River National Park offers pleasant places for houseboats to pull up and enjoy a bit of fishing. All three sections of the national park are popular for houseboat cruising.

More National Parks of Importance

Belair National Park

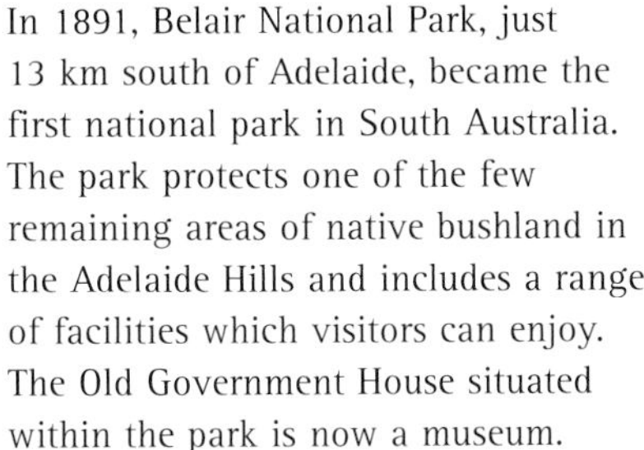

SIZE: 840 ha
MAP: SA 4 J3

In 1891, Belair National Park, just 13 km south of Adelaide, became the first national park in South Australia. The park protects one of the few remaining areas of native bushland in the Adelaide Hills and includes a range of facilities which visitors can enjoy. The Old Government House situated within the park is now a museum.

A number of sealed roads head off through the park giving good access to much of it and the park's facilities. Barbecue facilities abound and walks radiate to all corners of the park.

Playford Lake, close to the developed area, supports good numbers of waterbirds and a 1 km walk around the lake is a pleasant way to view the birdlife.

The park is open to day visitors only and an entrance fee is charged. For further information, phone the ranger on (08) 8278 5477.

Vulkathunha-Gammon Ranges National Park

SIZE: 128 228 ha
MAP: SA 3 K2

The Gammon Ranges, a maze of twisted landforms, steep-sided gorges and rugged bluffs, make up the most northern extension of the Flinders Ranges.

A couple of 4WD tracks cut through the park but the heart of the area, around the Plateau and Mainwater Pound, is really the realm of the adventurous and experienced bushwalker. For the not so adventurous there are a couple of shorter walks available.

Access is via reasonable dirt roads for the last 115 km from Copley, which is 570 km from Adelaide.

There are a number of designated bush camps such as Italowie Gorge, Weetootla Gorge and Grindells Hut (the homestead near the hut can be rented).

For details contact the Department for Environment and Heritage, Port Augusta (08) 8648 5300.

Contrary to its name, the Port Lincoln parrot (Barnardius zonarius) *has a wider distribution and is seen across much of southern Western Australia, into South Australia, and can be seen in Belair National Park.*

The white cypress pine (Callitris glaucophylla) *grows clinging to a cliff face in the Vulkathunha-Gammon Ranges National Park. Under better conditions these trees can grow to 30 metres high.*

Cooper Creek, Innamincka Regional Reserve. In drought years, the creek dries up and only some waterholes, such as Cullyamurra Waterhole which is the largest in Central Australia, remain.

did you know?

The Innamincka Regional Reserve headquarters and Information Centre is located in the restored, stone-walled Elizabeth Symon Nursing Home. It was built in 1928 as part of the Australian Inland Hospital Mission network that provided medical services for people in remote areas.

Innamincka Regional Reserve

SIZE: 13 800 sq km
MAP: SA 2 N4

The Cooper Creek and the Coongie Lakes complex of northern South Australia make up one of the great wetland areas of outback Australia. Surrounded by harsh gibber plain and the sand ridges of the Strzelecki Desert, Cooper Creek brings life to this arid region. In good years water fills the Congie Lakes creating an oasis that teems with life.

All the roads leading to Innamincka are dirt for some distance. They can be closed after heavy rain.

All tracks in the reserve require a South Australian Desert Parks Pass (this can be purchased for an economical fee), which is also necessary for camping. Along Cooper Creek or out at Coongie Lakes you will find some of the best camping spots in Central Australia.

Accommodation is available at the Innamincka pub, phone (08) 8675 9901, or at the Innamincka Trading Post, phone (08) 8675 9900, where all fuels and supplies are also available.

For more information contact the Desert Parks Hotline on 1800 816 078.

Innes National Park

SIZE: 9141 ha
MAP: SA 4 F4

The outstanding coastal scenery, the top surfing, the magical diving and the great fishing bring people back time and again to the southern toe of Yorke Peninsula and Innes National Park.

This wild coast is protected in most places by sheer high cliffs and probably the best spot to experience such a dramatic scene is at the Gap, near Reef Heads. Further north is the protected waters of delightful Pondalowie Bay.

There are a number of small camping spots dotted around the coast, including Gym Beach and Shell Beach, but the most popular is Pondalowie Bay itself.

Entrance and camping fees are payable. Accommodation is also available—contact the ranger on (08) 8854 3200, for details.

The Stenhouse Bay Trading Post, phone (08) 8854 4078, offers basic supplies and fuel.

Lake Eyre National Park

SIZE: 1 225 000 ha
MAP: SA 2 F6

At over 8000 sq km, Lake Eyre is the largest salt lake in Australia, the largest saltpan in the world, and also the lowest point in Australia. In the last 100 years the lake has only had a significant amount of water in it six times, the most spectacular being in 1974, when it filled to capacity with about 34 cubic km of water.

Lake Eyre South, just off the Oodnadatta Track, 90 km west of Marree, is the easiest access. A 4WD track via Muloorina homestead and another south of William Creek lead to the lake's shore.

A South Australian Desert Parks Pass (available for an economical fee) is required for access and camping. For more information contact the Department for Environment and Heritage, Port Augusta (08) 8648 5300 or the Desert Parks Hotline on 1800 816 078.

Lincoln National Park

SIZE: 29 000 ha
MAP: SA 4 D3

Great camping, good fishing, diving, surfing and four wheel driving plus a variety of coastal scenery and wildlife make this region an ideal summer destination although dangerous freak waves can occur in rough weather.

A 4WD track from Sleaford Mere heads west behind the dunes to Wanna and leads to many popular surf fishing spots. Another 4WD track leads east to West Point and Memory Cove. A permit and key are required to drive this route.

A sealed road leads south from Port Lincoln. Entry and camping permits are available at the park entrance. A good dirt road heads into the park.

Camping is allowed at a number of spots in the park. At Taylors Landing you can also launch small boats. Donington Cottage is available to rent, while an Eyre Park Pass will save you money. Contact National Parks and Wildlife Service in Port Lincoln on (08) 8688 3111.

The Australian sea lion (Neophoca cinerea) *is one the most endangered of the world's seals and sea lions. They can be seen off the coast of Lincoln National Park.*

don't miss

In the north of Lincoln National Park take the 1.1 km walk uphill to the Flinders Monument which commemorates Matthew Flinders' visit in 1802. There are stunning views of Port Lincoln and the nearby islands.

SA

Gym Beach in the north of Innes National Park. There are some great walks in the park, including the 3-hour walk from Browns Beach to Gym Beach.

Giant gum tree in Mount Remarkable National Park. The area has a relatively high rainfall of up to 600 mm per year, allowing large areas of quite dense woodland to develop.

Mount Remarkable National Park

SIZE: 15 632 ha
MAP: SA 3 H7

This park in the southern Flinders Ranges takes in the area around Alligator Gorge, Mambray Creek and the high peak of Mount Remarkable. The area is rich in wildflowers and birds, as well as red kangaroos, euros and the delightful, but rarer, yellow-footed rock wallaby.

There are plenty of great walks in the park such as the walk through Alligator Gorge and from Alligator Gorge to Mambray Creek. Longer walks are also possible.

Access to Alligator Gorge is via a good dirt road from Wilmington, while Mount Remarkable itself is accessible from Melrose.

The Mambray Creek camping area is reached off Highway 1. You'll need to book in advance and obtain a camping permit. There are a number of back-packing camp sites, some with water.

Campfires are banned in the park from 1 November to 30 April.

For more information contact the ranger at Mambray Creek, on (08) 8634 7068.

Naracoorte Caves National Park

SIZE: 70 ha
MAP: SA 4 N8

This small park, 370 km south-east of Adelaide, is on the World Heritage List because of the discovery of rich fossil beds in Victoria Cave, which include the remains of marsupials and other extinct animals. Provision has been made for visitors to view the 'dig'.

A number of other caves are open to tourists, including Blanche Cave, Wet Cave and Alexandra Cave. There are tours conducted daily.

Between November and February, thousands of common bentwing bats make a spectacular sight at dusk as they leave the caves in search of food.

The camping ground in the park is well set up and a permit is required before you can camp.

For further information, contact the ranger at Naracoorte, on (08) 8762 2340, or Mount Gambier, on (08) 8735 1177.

The little red flying fox (Pteropus scapulatus) *is common in much of southern Australia, and can be seen with bentwing bats near Naracoorte.*

Popular Parks at a Glance

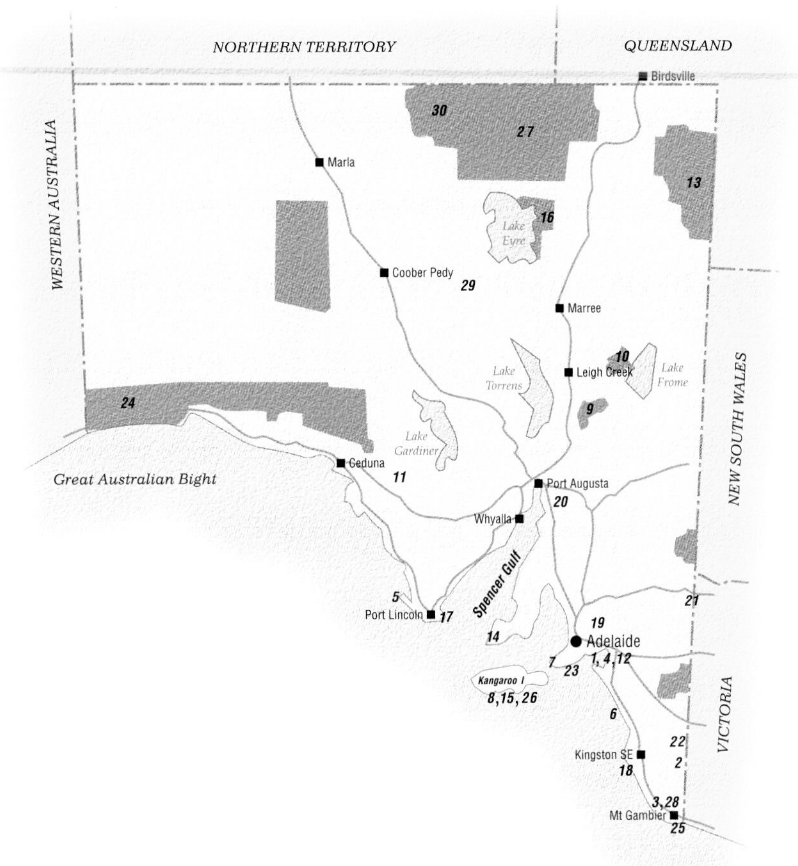

	Park	Camping	Caravan Access	Disabled Access	4WD Access	Picnic Areas	Toilets	Walking Tracks	Kiosk	Information
1	Belair NP	●		●		●	●	●	●	●
2	Bool Lagoon NP	●				●	●	●		
3	Canunda NP	●			●	●	●	●		
4	Cleland WP & CP			●		●	●	●	●	●
5	Coffin Bay NP	●	●		●	●	●	●		●
6	Coorong NP	●	●		●	●	●	●		
7	Deep Creek CP	●	●			●	●	●		●
8	Flinders Chase NP	●	●	●		●	●	●	●	●
9	Flinders Ranges NP	●	●			●	●	●	●	●
10	Vulkathunha-Gammon Ranges NP	●			●			●		●
11	Gawler Ranges NP	●	●		●			●		
12	Granite Island RP						●	●	●	●
13	Innamincka RR	●			●		●			
14	Innes NP	●	●			●	●	●	●	●
15	Kelly Hill CP			●		●	●	●	●	●
16	Lake Eyre NP	●			●					
17	Lincoln NP	●			●	●	●	●		
18	Little Dip NP	●	●		●	●	●	●		
19	Morialta CP			●		●	●	●	●	●
20	Mount Remarkable NP	●		●		●	●	●		●
21	Murray River NP	●					●	●		
22	Naracoorte Caves NP	●	●	●		●	●	●	●	●
23	Newland Head CR	●				●	●	●		
24	Nullarbor NP	●	●		●					
25	Piccaninnie Ponds CP	●					●	●		
26	Seal Bay CP	●		●			●	●	●	●
27	Simpson Desert CP & RR	●			●					
28	Tantanoola Caves CP			●		●	●	●	●	●
29	Wabma Kadarbu Mound Springs CP							●		
30	Witjira NP	●			●		●	●		

SA

Map 1

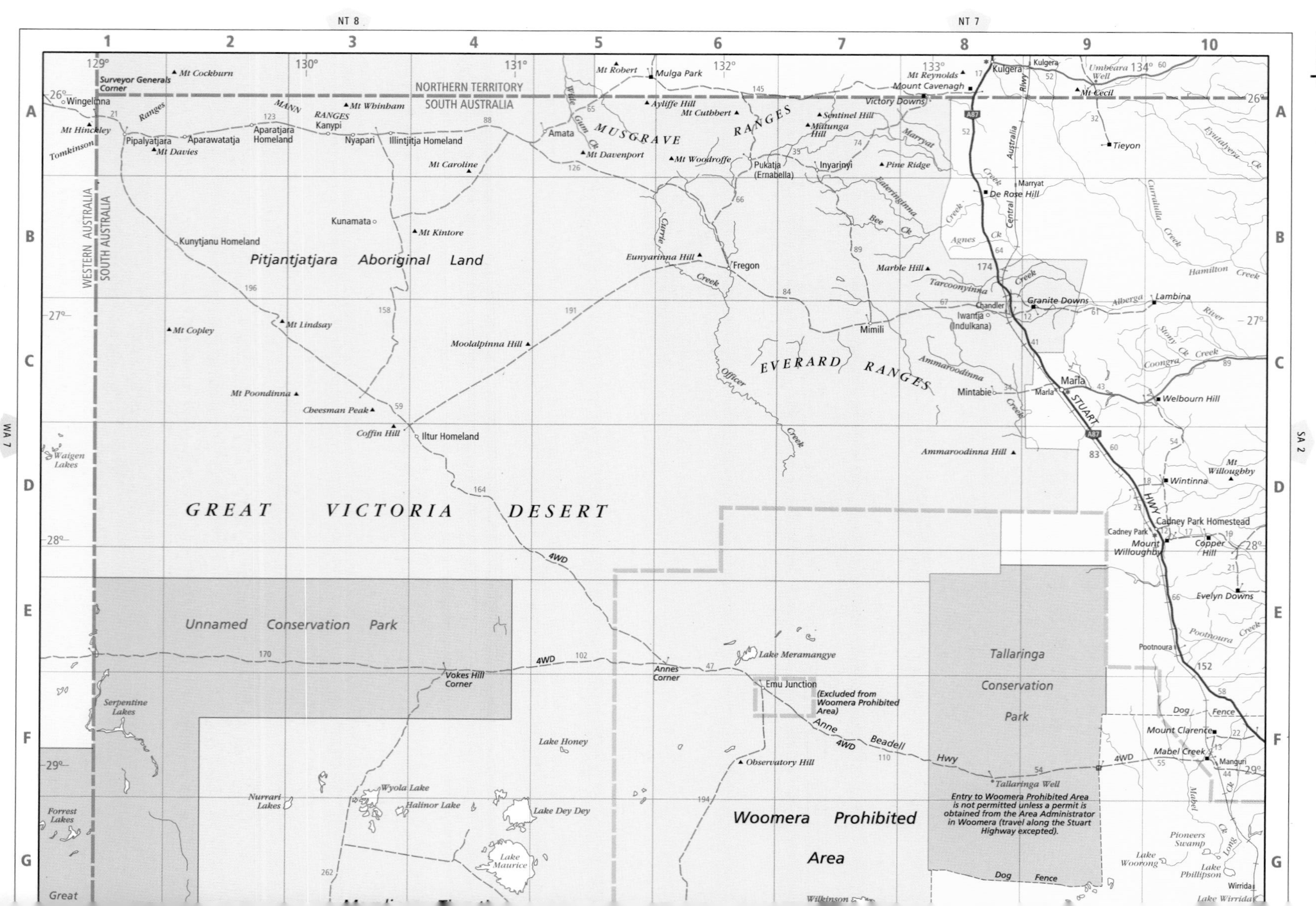

SA 2
NT 7
NT 8
WA 7
NORTHERN TERRITORY
SOUTH AUSTRALIA
WESTERN AUSTRALIA
GREAT VICTORIA DESERT
Pitjantjatjara Aboriginal Land
EVERARD RANGES
MUSGRAVE RANGES
MANN RANGES
Unnamed Conservation Park
Tallaringa Conservation Park
Woomera Prohibited Area
Entry to Woomera Prohibited Area is not permitted unless a permit is obtained from the Area Administrator in Woomera (travel along the Stuart Highway excepted).
(Excluded from Woomera Prohibited Area)
STUART HWY
Anne Beadell Hwy
Dog Fence
4WD
Surveyor Generals Corner
Wingellina
Pipalyatjara
Aparawatatja
Aparatjara Homeland
Kanypi
Nyapari
Illintjitja Homeland
Amata
Pukatja (Ernabella)
Inyarinyi
Mimili
Fregon
Iwantja (Indulkana)
Kunamata
Kunytjanu Homeland
Iltur Homeland
Mulga Park
Victory Downs
Mount Cavenagh
Kulgera
Marryat
De Rose Hill
Granite Downs
Chandler
Marla
Mintabie
Lambina
Welbourn Hill
Wintinna
Cadney Park Homestead
Copper Hill
Mount Willoughby
Evelyn Downs
Pootnoura
Mount Clarence
Mabel Creek
Manguri
Emu Junction
Annes Corner
Vokes Hill Corner
Tallaringa Well
Lake Meramangye
Lake Honey
Lake Dey Dey
Lake Maurice
Halinor Lake
Wyola Lake
Nurrari Lakes
Serpentine Lakes
Forrest Lakes
Waigen Lakes
Mt Cockburn
Mt Davies
Mt Hinckley
Mt Whinbam
Mt Caroline
Mt Kintore
Mt Davenport
Mt Woodroffe
Mt Cuthbert
Ayliffe Hill
Mt Robert
Mt Reynolds
Mt Cecil
Umbeara Well
Tieyon
Sentinel Hill
Matunga Hill
Pine Ridge
Marble Hill
Eunyarinna Hill
Moolalpinna Hill
Mt Lindsay
Mt Copley
Mt Poondinna
Cheesman Peak
Coffin Hill
Ammaroodinna Hill
Observatory Hill
Mt Willoughby
Officer Creek
Currie Creek
Wide Gum Ck
Currallulla Creek
Hamilton Creek
Alberga River
Agnes Creek
Eateringinna
Bee Ck
Tarcoonyinna Creek
Ammaroodinna Creek
Lake Phillipson
Pioneers Swamp
Lake Woorong

WA 9

SA 3

Aboriginal Land

Nature Reserve

Maralinga Restricted Area

Maralinga

Ooldea

Yarle Lakes

Range

NULLARBOR PLAIN

Trans Australian Railway

Deakin

Hughes

Denman

Cook

Fisher

O'Malley

Watson

Ooldea

Bates

Barton

Mungala

Mount Christie

Wynbring

Dog Fence

Lyons

Malbooma

Tarcoola

Central Aust Railway

Mobella

Jumbuck Outstation

Lake Anthony

Half Moon Lake

Commonwealth Hill

Gina

Carne Outstation

Mulgathing

Mt Christie

Lake Bring

Partridge Lakes

WESTERN AUSTRALIA

SOUTH AUSTRALIA

Nullarbor Regional Reserve

Ifould Lake

Lake Tallacootra

Yellabinna Regional Reserve

Mt Finke

Googs Track 4WD

Nullarbor National Park

Koonalda

Nullarbor Roadhouse

EYRE HIGHWAY

Border Village

Eucla

Wilson Bluff

Eucla National Park

Great Australian Bight Marine Park

Yalata Swamp

Yalata Aboriginal Land

Head of Bight

Great Australian Bight Whale Sanctuary

Yalata Roadhouse

Yalata

Black Hill

Yumbarra Cons Res

Euria Well

Yumbarra Conservation Park

Dog Fence

Charoba Tank

Radio Astronomy Station

Kalanbi

Koonibba Community

Pureba Cons Res

Pureba Cons Park

Wahgunyah Cons Res

Great Australian Bight Marine Park

Nundroo

Bookabie

Bookabie Hill

Coorabie

Fowlers Bay Cons Res

Fowlers Bay

Chadinga Cons Res

Penong

Woolshed Hill

Cape Adieu

Nyuts Reef

Nuyts Reef Conservation Park

Cactus Beach

Point Sinclair

Lake MacDonnell

Point Bell

Denial Bay

Denial Bay

Wandana

Ceduna

Maltee

Thevenard

Mudamuckla

Nunnyah CR

Puntabie

Chinbingina

Nunjikompita

Laura Bay

Smoky Bay

Smoky Bay

Carawa

Wirrulla

St Peter I

Goat I

Evans I

Lacy Islands

Eyre I

Franklin Is

St Francis Island

Nuyts Archipelago Cons Park

Point Dillon

Pt Brown

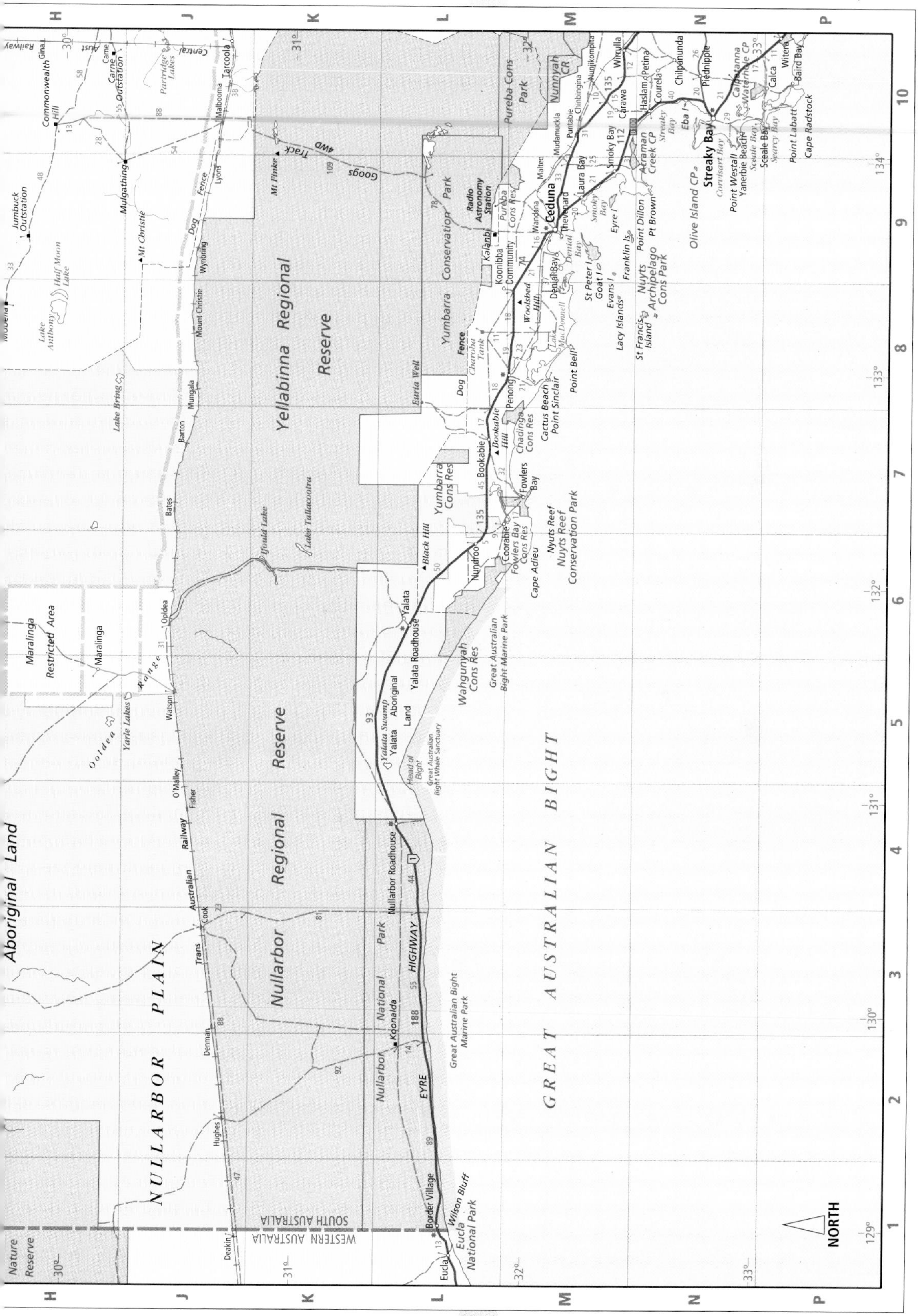

Acraman Creek CP

Streaky Bay

Haslam

Petina

Courela

Chilpanunda

Eba I

Olive Island CP

Streaky Bay

Piednippie

Corvisart Bay

Point Westall

Yanerbie Beach

Calpatanna Waterhole CP

Sceale Bay

Sceale Bay

Searcy Bay

Calca

Witera

Point Labatt

Baird Bay

Cape Radstock

GREAT AUSTRALIAN BIGHT

NORTH

0 20 40 60 80 100
kilometres

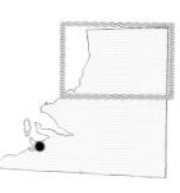

SA

Map 2

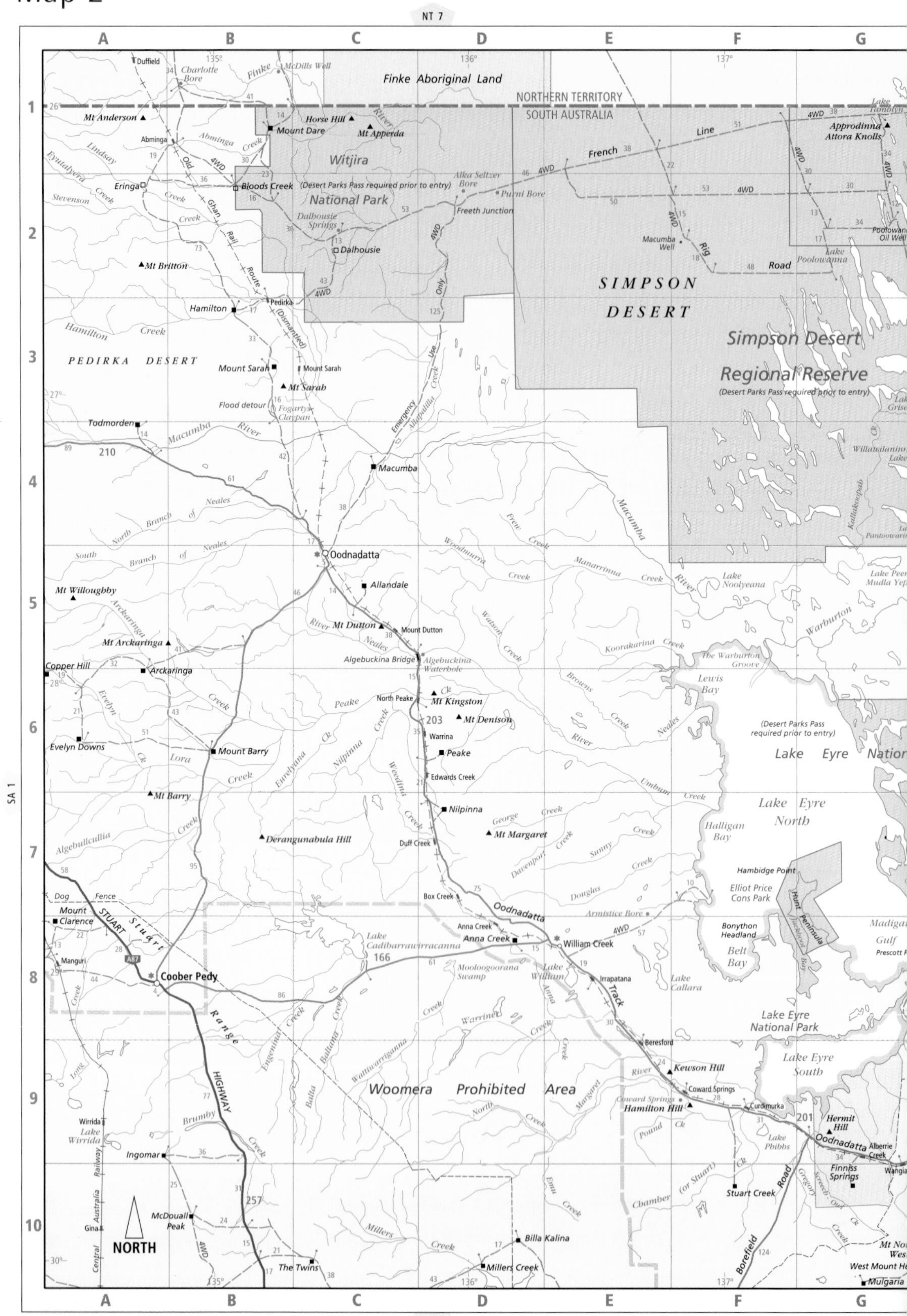
NT 7
SA 3
SA 1
A
B
C
D
E
F
G
1
2
3
4
5
6
7
8
9
10
135°
136°
137°
26°
27°
28°
30°
Finke Aboriginal Land
NORTHERN TERRITORY
SOUTH AUSTRALIA
Duffield
Charlotte Bore
McDills Well
Finke
Mt Anderson
Horse Hill
Mount Dare
Mt Apperda
Abminga
Witjira
National Park
(Desert Parks Pass required prior to entry)
Eringa
Bloods Creek
Alka Seltzer Bore
Purni Bore
Freeth Junction
Dalhousie Springs
Dalhousie
French Line
4WD
Approdinna Attora Knolls
Macumba Well
Rig Road
Lake Poolowanna
Poolowanna Oil Well
SIMPSON
DESERT
Simpson Desert
Regional Reserve
(Desert Parks Pass required prior to entry)
Mt Britton
Old Ghan Rail Route (Dismantled)
Pedirka
Hamilton
4WD Only
Emergency Use
PEDIRKA DESERT
Mount Sarah
Mt Sarah
Flood detour
Fogartys Claypan
Todmorden
Macumba River
Macumba
Algebuckina Bridge
Algebuckina Waterhole
Oodnadatta
Allandale
Mt Willoughby
Mt Dutton
Mount Dutton
Mt Arckaringa
Arckaringa
Copper Hill
Evelyn Downs
Mount Barry
Mt Barry
North Peake
Mt Kingston
Mt Denison
Warrina
Peake
Edwards Creek
Nilpinna
Mt Margaret
Derangunabula Hill
Duff Creek
Box Creek
Anna Creek
William Creek
Lake Cadibarrawirracanna
Mooloogoorana Swamp
Lake William
Irrapatana
Lake Callara
Oodnadatta Track
Dog Fence
Stuart Range
Mount Clarence
Manguri
Coober Pedy
STUART HIGHWAY
A87
Woomera Prohibited Area
Beresford
Kewson Hill
Coward Springs
Hamilton Hill
Curdimurka
Hermit Hill
Alberrie Creek
Finniss Springs
Wangianna
Stuart Creek
Borefield Road
Lake Phibbs
Wirrida
Lake Wirrida
Ingomar
Central Australia Railway
McDouall Peak
Gina
The Twins
Millers Creek
Billa Kalina
West Mount Hope
Mulgaria
Lake Eyre National Park
Lake Eyre North
Lake Eyre South
Halligan Bay
Hambidge Point
Elliot Price Cons Park
Bonython Headland
Belt Bay
Hunt Peninsula
Lewis Bay
The Warburton Groove
Lake Noolyeana
Warburton
Madigan Gulf
Prescott Point
Lake Eyre
(Desert Parks Pass required prior to entry)
Armistice Bore
Chamber (or Stuart) Ck
NORTH
210
166
203
201
257

0
20
40
60
80
100
kilometres

H
J
K
L
M
N
P
1
2
3
4
5
6
7
8
9
10
138°
139°
140°
141°
26°
27°
28°
29°
30°
QUEENSLAND
SOUTH AUSTRALIA
NEW SOUTH WALES
Simpson Desert National Park
Poeppel Corner
Lake Thomas
Simpson Desert Conservation Park
(Desert Parks Pass required prior to entry)
K1 Line
Rig Road
4WD
SIMPSON DESERT
Big Red
Birdsville
Lake Nappanerica
Eyre Creek
Dickeree Waterhole
Pandie Pandie
Karrathunka Waterhole
Diamantina
Inside Track
New Alton Downs
Andrewilla Waterhole
Goyder Lagoon
Koonchera Waterhole
Outside Track
Geake Hill
STRZELECKI DESERT
Shallow Lake
Moonda Lake
Frew Hill
Lake Cooninnie
Cadelga Outstation
Lake Short
Lake Etamunbanie
Lake Uloowaranie
The Sisters
Haddon Corner
Haddon Creek
Nullah Outstation
Providence Creek
Cordillo Downs
Arrabury
Montkeleary Creek
Lake Goyder
Lake Apanburra
Coongie
Lake Marroocutchanie
Coongie Lake
Innamincka Regional Reserve
(Desert Parks Pass required prior to entry)
Kudriemitchie Outstation
Mulga Bore
Leap Year Bore
Patchawarra Bore
Cooper Creek
Walkers Crossing
Scrubby Camp Waterhole
Tirrawarra Oil and Gas Field
Gidgealpa
Nappa Merrie
Burke and Wills Dig Tree
Innamincka
Cullyamurra Waterhole
Lake Andree
Gidgealpa Gas Field
Moomba
Moomba Gas Field
Della Gas Field
Burke-Dullingari Oil and Gas Field
Epsilon
Big Lake Gas Field
Big Lake Moomba
Lake Moomba
Strzelecki Creek
Toolache Gas Field
Lake Murteree
Merty Merty
Omicron
Bollards Lagoon
Cameron Corner
Fort Grey
Lindon
Lake Stewart
Clifton Hills
Warburton Crossing
Warburton Creek
Tippipilla Creek
Birdsville Track
Mt Gason Bore
Mt Gason
Sturt Stony Desert
Lake John
Lake Koodnanie
Lake Umaroona
Kallakoopah Creek
Lake Howitt
Cowarie
Kalamurina
Mirra Mitta Bore
Lake Perigundi
Mt Hogarth
Mungeranie Gap
Uwinya Hill
Mungeranie
Mungeranie Roadhouse
Kalamurra Lake
Lake Kittakittaooloo
Lake Warrakalanna
Lake Ngapakaldi
Lake Hope or Panda
Mulka
Lake Mulapula
Lake Puntawolona
Lake Killalpaninna
Lake Killamperpunna
Etadunna
Cannuwaukaninna Bore
Lake Kopperamanna
Strzelecki Regional Reserve
Pipeline Track
Gas
Strzelecki Track
Lake Gregory
Lake Florence
Dulkaninna
Conical Hill
Strzelecki Crossing
Yaningurie Waterhole
Coonyanna
Clayton
Muloorina
Lake Blanche
Montecollina Bore
Dog Fence
Lake Harry
Clayton River
Tooncatchyn Creek
Duck Ponds Creek
Lake Arthur
Blanchewater
Mount Hopeless
Lake Callabonna
Attraction Hill
Marree
Callanna
Track
Murnpeowie
George Creek
Petermorra Creek
Yerila
Mt Hopeless
Lake Delusion
Frome
Mundowdna
Old Ghan Rail
Route
Witchelina
Hayes
Kingsmill
Wilpoorinna
Mt Freeling
Mount Freeling
Mt Babbage
Moolawatana
Mt Fitton Talc Mine
Mount Fitton
Hamilton Ck
Mt Neill
Farina
Strzelecki
Lake Yannerpi
Tilcha Creek
Bookaree
Yandama
Smithville House
308
351
106
174
203
195

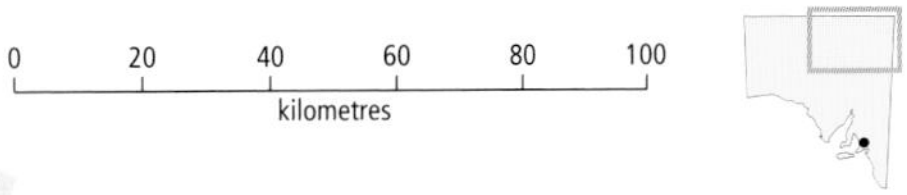

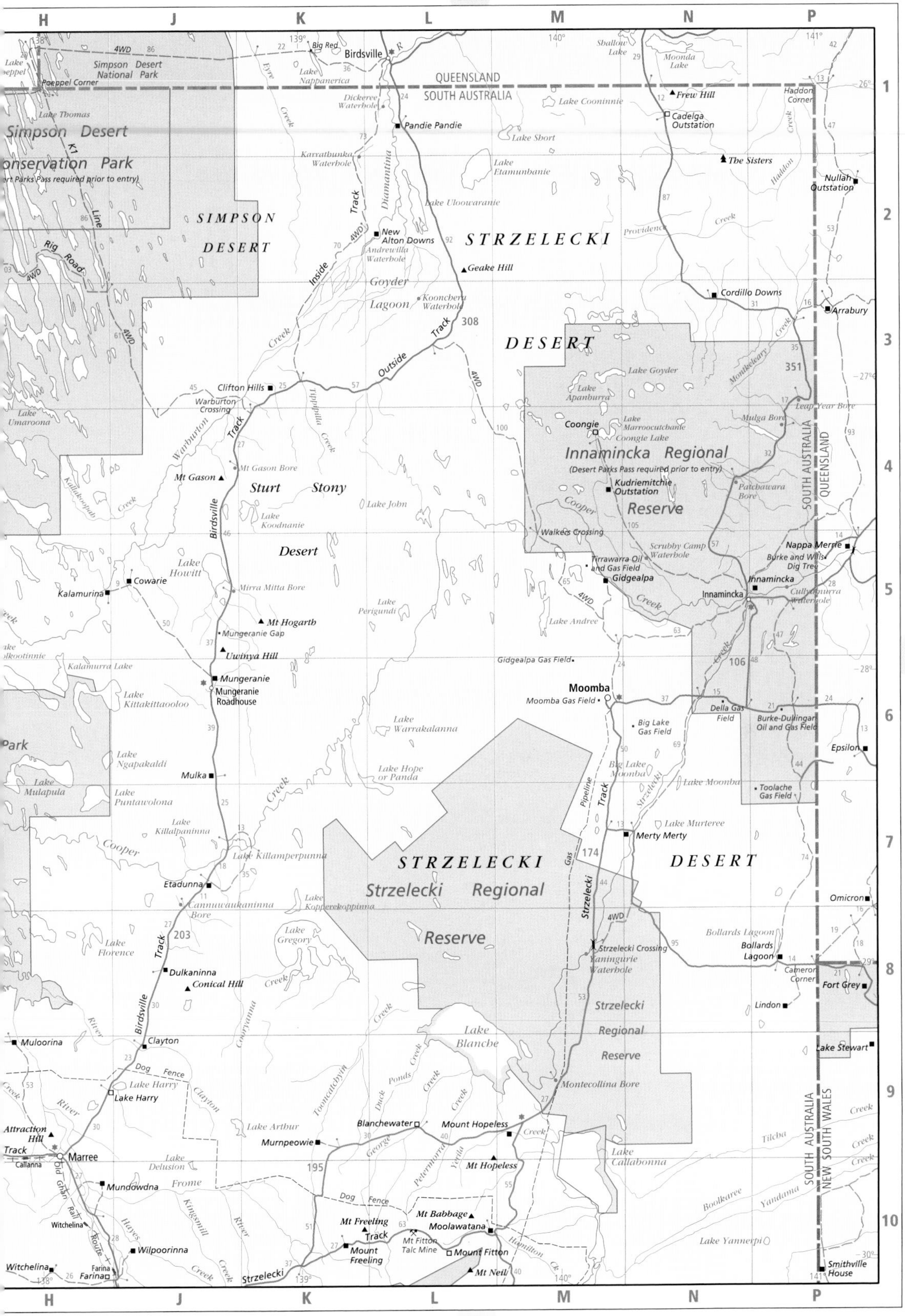

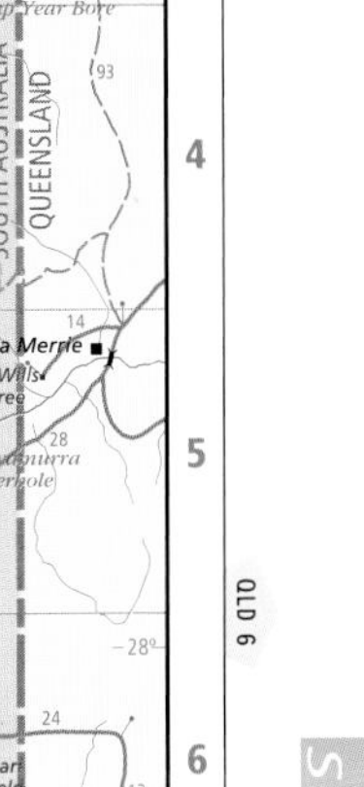

Map 3

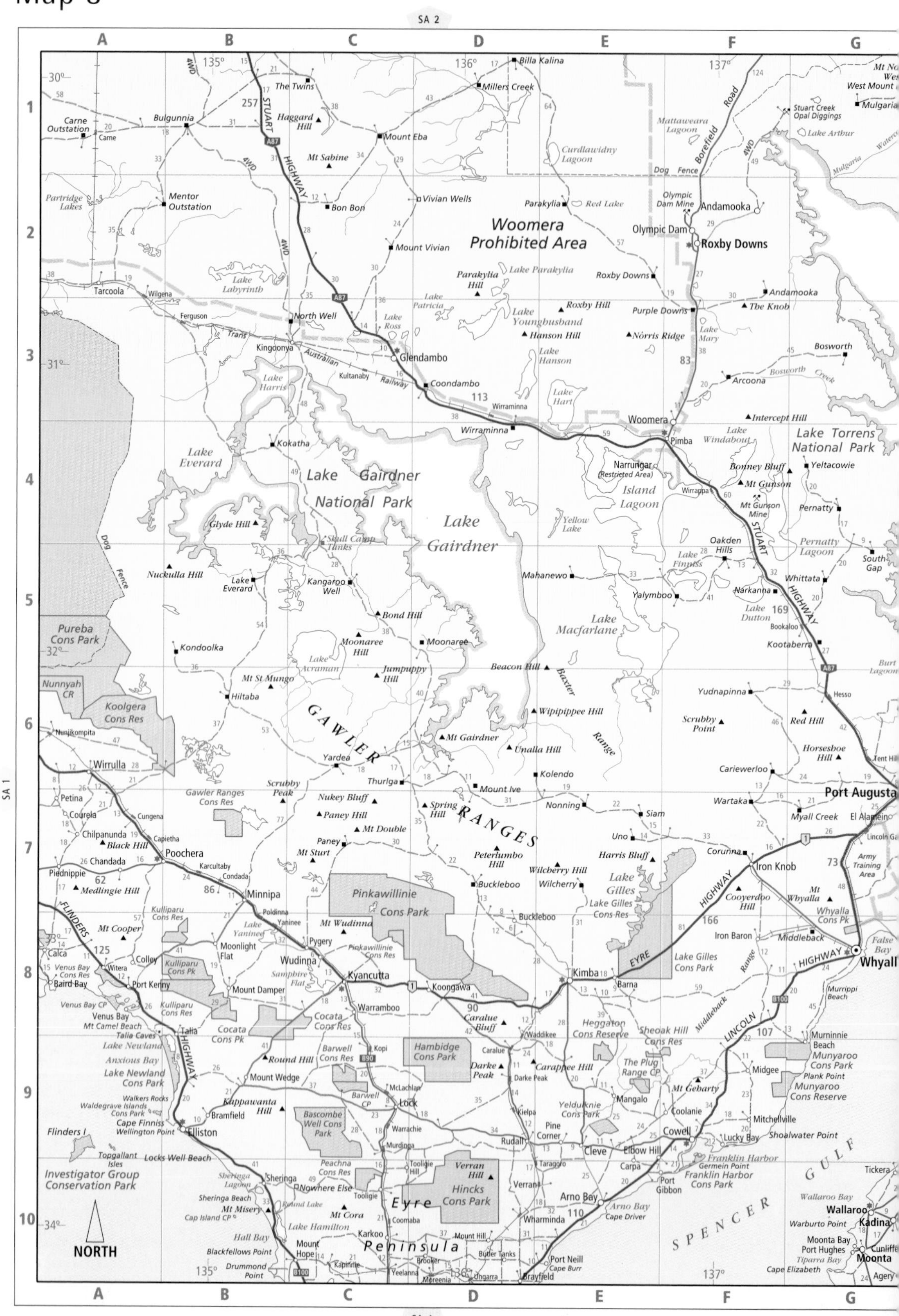
SA 2
SA 4
SA 1
NORTH
Woomera Prohibited Area
Lake Gairdner National Park
Lake Gairdner
Lake Torrens National Park
GAWLER RANGES
Eyre Peninsula
SPENCER GULF
STUART HIGHWAY
EYRE HIGHWAY
LINCOLN HIGHWAY
FLINDERS HIGHWAY
Trans Australian Railway
Dog Fence
Borefield Road
Baxter Range
Middleback Range
Billa Kalina
Millers Creek
The Twins
Haggard Hill
Mount Eba
Mt Sabine
Bulgunnia
Carne Outstation
Mentor Outstation
Partridge Lakes
Bon Bon
Vivian Wells
Mount Vivian
Curdlawidny Lagoon
Parakylia
Red Lake
Mattaweara Lagoon
Olympic Dam Mine
Andamooka
Olympic Dam
Roxby Downs
Stuart Creek Opal Diggings
Lake Arthur
Mulgaria
West Mount
Lake Labyrinth
Tarcoola
Wilgena
Ferguson
North Well
Kingoonya
Glendambo
Kultanaby
Coondambo
Wirraminna
Lake Parakylia
Parakylia Hill
Lake Patricia
Lake Ross
Lake Youngbusband
Hanson Hill
Roxby Hill
Norris Ridge
Purple Downs
The Knob
Lake Mary
Lake Hanson
Lake Hart
Bosworth
Bosworth Creek
Arcoona
Lake Harris
Woomera
Pimba
Intercept Hill
Lake Windabout
Narrungar (Restricted Area)
Island Lagoon
Wirrappa
Bonney Bluff
Yeltacowie
Mt Gunson
Mt Gunson Mine
Pernatty
Pernatty Lagoon
Kokatha
Lake Everard
Glyde Hill
Skull Camp Tanks
Yellow Lake
Oakden Hills
Lake Finniss
South Gap
Nuckulla Hill
Kangaroo Well
Mahanewo
Yalymboo
Narkanna
Whittata
Lake Dutton
Bookaloo
Bond Hill
Lake Macfarlane
Pureba Cons Park
Kondoolka
Moonaree Hill
Moonaree
Kootaberra
Burt Lagoon
Lake Acraman
Jumpuppy Hill
Mt St Mungo
Beacon Hill
Nunnyah CR
Hiltaba
Yudnapinna
Hesso
Koolgera Cons Res
Wipipippee Hill
Scrubby Point
Red Hill
Nunjikompita
Mt Gairdner
Unalla Hill
Horsesboe Hill
Tent Hill
Wirrulla
Yardea
Thurlga
Kolendo
Cariewerloo
Mount Ive
Port Augusta
Petina
Gawler Ranges Cons Res
Scrubby Peak
Nukey Bluff
Spring Hill
Nonning
Siam
Wartaka
Myall Creek
El Alamein
Courela
Cungena
Paney Hill
Mt Double
Chilpanunda
Black Hill
Capietha
Poochera
Paney
Mt Sturt
Peterlumbo Hill
Uno
Harris Bluff
Corunna
Iron Knob
Lincoln Gap
Army Training Area
Chandada
Karcultaby
Condada
Wilcherry Hill
Wilcherry
Lake Gilles
Piednippie
Medlingie Hill
Minnipa
Pinkawillinie Cons Park
Buckleboo
Cooyerdoo Hill
Mt Whyalla
Poldinna
Kulliparu Cons Res
Lake Yaninee
Yaninee
Mt Wudinna
Lake Gilles Cons Res
Whyalla Cons Pk
Mt Cooper
Pygery
Pinkawillinie Cons Res
Iron Baron
Middleback
False Bay
Calca
Moonlight Flat
Wudinna
Lake Gilles Cons Park
Whyalla
Venus Bay Cons Res
Witera
Colley
Kulliparu Cons Pk
Sampbire Flat
Kyancutta
Koongawa
Kimba
Barna
Baird Bay
Port Kenny
Mount Damper
Murripi Beach
Venus Bay CP
Kulliparu Cons Res
Warramboo
Caralue Bluff
Venus Bay
Mt Camel Beach
Talia Caves
Talia
Cocata Cons Pk
Cocata Cons Res
Heggaton Cons Reserve
Sheoak Hill Cons Res
Murninnie Beach
Lake Newland
Waddikee
Anxious Bay
Kopi
Barwell Cons Res
Hambidge Cons Park
Caralue
Lake Newland Cons Park
Round Hill
Darke Peak
Carappee Hill
The Plug Range CP
Munyaroo Cons Park
Mount Wedge
McLachlan
Midgee
Plank Point
Walkers Rocks
Mt Gebarty
Munyaroo Cons Reserve
Waldegrave Islands Cons Park
Kappawanta Hill
Barwell CP
Lock
Mangalo
Yeldulknie Cons Park
Cape Finniss
Bramfield
Kielpa
Coolanie
Mitchellville
Wellington Point
Elliston
Bascombe Well Cons Park
Warrachie
Pine Corner
Flinders I
Cowell
Shoalwater Point
Murdinga
Rudall
Cleve
Elbow Hill
Lucky Bay
Topgallant Isles
Locks Well Beach
Franklin Harbor
Tooligie Hill
Verran Hill
Hincks Cons Park
Taragoro
Carpa
Germein Point
Franklin Harbor Cons Park
Tickera
Investigator Group Conservation Park
Sheringa Lagoon
Sheringa
Peachna Cons Res
Nowhere Else
Verran
Port Gibbon
Sheringa Beach
Round Lake
Tooligie
Arno Bay
Wallaroo Bay
Mt Misery
Mt Cora
Coomaba
Wharminda
Arno Bay
Cape Driver
Wallaroo
Cap Island CP
Lake Hamilton
Warburto Point
Kadina
Hall Bay
Karkoo
Mount Hill
Moonta Bay
Port Hughes
Blackfellows Point
Mount Hope
Butler Tanks
Port Neill
Tiparra Bay
Cunliffe
Drummond Point
Kapinnie
Brooker
Cape Burr
Moonta
Yeelanna
Moreenia
Ungarra
Brayfield
Cape Elizabeth
Agery

0 20 40 60 80 100
kilometres

SA 2

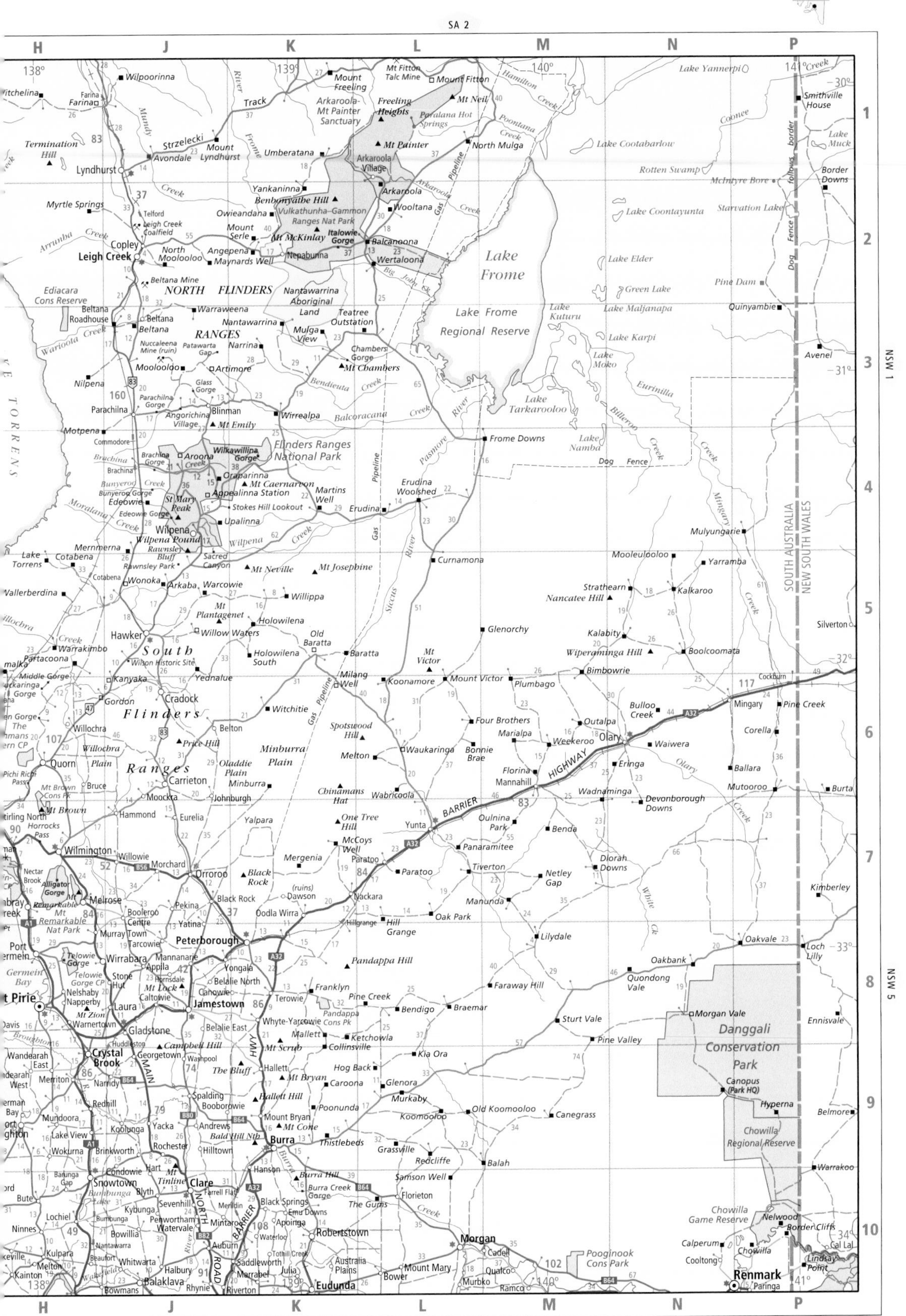

SA 4

Map 4

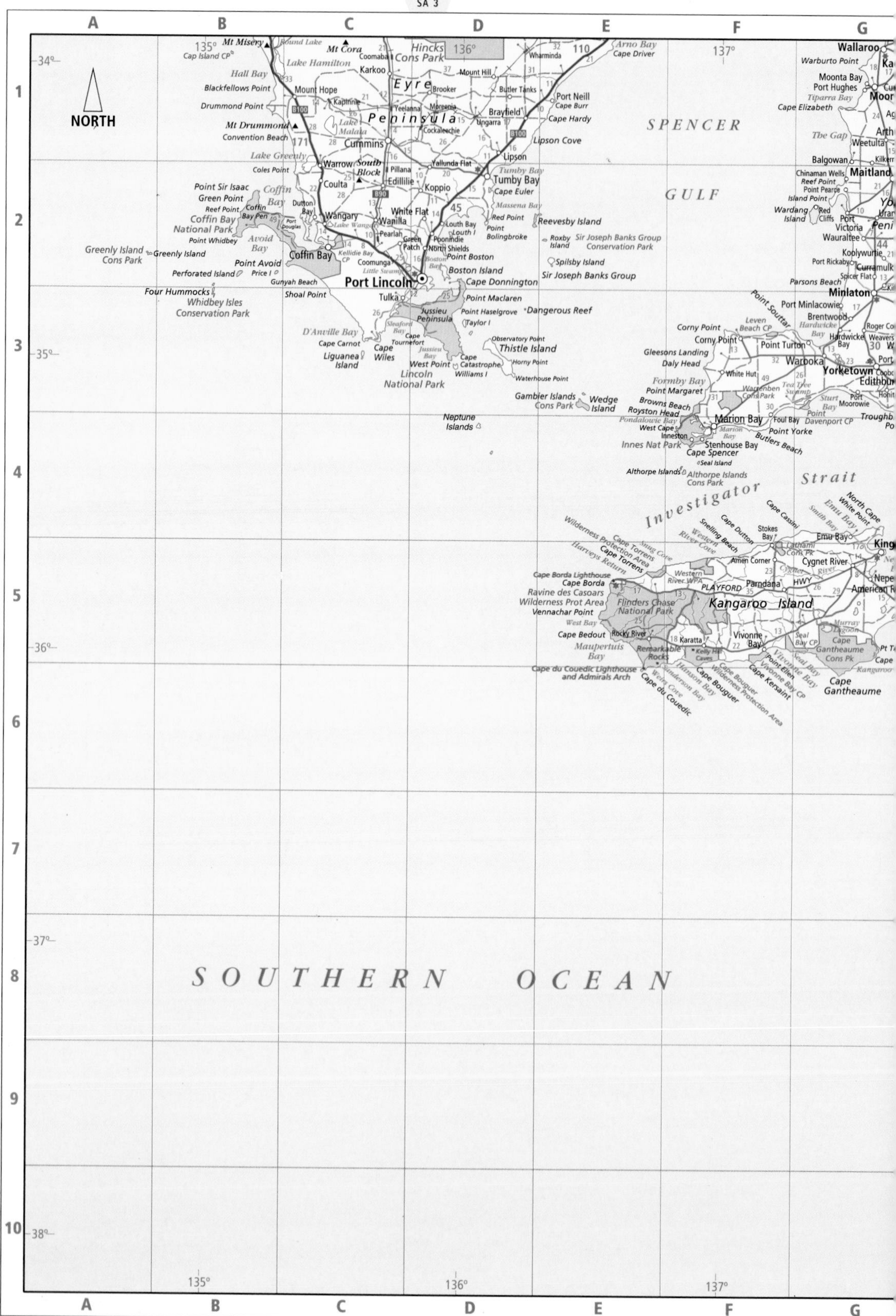
SA 3
A
B
C
D
E
F
G
1
2
3
4
5
6
7
8
9
10
34°
35°
36°
37°
38°
135°
136°
137°
NORTH
Mt Misery
Round Lake
Mt Cora
Cap Island CP
Lake Hamilton
Coomaba
Hincks Cons Park
Karkoo
Mount Hill
Wharminda
110
Arno Bay
Cape Driver
Hall Bay
Blackfellows Point
Mount Hope
Eyre
Brooker
Butler Tanks
Port Neill
Cape Burr
Drummond Point
Kapinnie
Yeelanna
Mercenia
Peninsula
Brayfield
Ungarra
Cape Hardy
Mt Drummond
Convention Beach
Lake Malata
Cockaleechie
Cummins
B100
Lipson Cove
SPENCER
Lake Greenly
Lipson
Coles Point
Warrow
South Block
Pillana
Yallunda Flat
Tumby Bay
Point Sir Isaac
Green Point
Reef Point
Coffin Bay
Coulta
Edillilie
Koppio
Cape Euler
GULF
Coffin Bay National Park
Dutton Bay
Massena Bay
White Flat
Wangary
Wanilla
Red Point
Reevesby Island
Point Whidbey
Avoid Bay
Pearlah
Louth Bay
Louth I
Point Bolingbroke
Roxby Island
Sir Joseph Banks Group Conservation Park
Greenly Island Cons Park
Greenly Island
Coffin Bay
Green Patch
Poonindie
North Shields
Point Boston
Spilsby Island
Point Avoid
Kellidie Bay CP
Coomunga
Boston Island
Sir Joseph Banks Group
Perforated Island
Price I
Little Swamp
Gunyah Beach
Port Lincoln
Cape Donnington
Four Hummocks
Whidbey Isles Conservation Park
Shoal Point
Tulka
Point Maclaren
Jussieu Peninsula
Point Haselgrove
Dangerous Reef
D'Anville Bay
Sleaford Bay
Taylor I
Cape Carnot
Cape Tournefort
Observatory Point
Thistle Island
Liguanea Island
Cape Wiles
Jussieu Bay
West Point
Cape Catastrophe
Williams I
Horny Point
Lincoln National Park
Waterhouse Point
Gambier Islands Cons Park
Wedge Island
Neptune Islands
Wallaroo
Warburto Point
Moonta Bay
Port Hughes
Tiparra Bay
Cape Elizabeth
The Gap
Weetulta
Balgowan
Chinaman Wells
Reef Point
Point Pearce
Island Point
Maitland
Wardang Island
Red Cliffs
Port Victoria
Wauraltee
Koolywurtie
Port Rickaby
Curramulka
Spicer Flat
Parsons Beach
Minlaton
Point Souttar
Port Minlacowie
Brentwood
Hardwicke Bay
Corny Point
Leven Beach CP
Corny Point
Point Turton
Gleesons Landing
Daly Head
Warooka
Yorketown
White Hut
Formby Bay
Point Margaret
Warrenben Cons Park
Tea Tree Swamp
Browns Beach
Royston Head
Pondalowie Bay
West Cape
Inneston
Marion Bay
Foul Bay
Davenport CP
Innes Nat Park
Stenhouse Bay
Point Yorke
Butlers Beach
Cape Spencer
Seal Island
Althorpe Islands
Althorpe Islands Cons Park
Strait
Investigator
North Cape
White Point
Emu Bay
Cape Cassini
Cape Dutton
Stokes Bay
Snelling Beach
Western River Cove
Snug Cove
Cape Torrens
Wilderness Protection Area
Harveys Return
Lathami Cons Pk
Amen Corner
Cygnet River
Cape Borda Lighthouse
Cape Borda
Western River WPA
PLAYFORD
Parndana
HWY
Ravine des Casoars Wilderness Prot Area
Vennachar Point
Flinders Chase National Park
Kangaroo Island
West Bay
Cape Bedout
Rocky River
Karatta
Vivonne Bay
Seal Bay CP
Cape Gantheaume Cons Pk
Maupertuis Bay
Remarkable Rocks
Kelly Hill Caves
Cape du Couedic Lighthouse and Admirals Arch
Cape du Couedic
Weirs Cove
Sanderson Bay
Hanson Bay
Cape Bouguer
Cape Bouguer Wilderness Protection Area
Point Ellen
Vivonne Bay CP
Cape Kersaint
Cape Gantheaume
SOUTHERN OCEAN

0 20 40 60 80 100
kilometres

H J K L M N P

Lochiel, Bumbunga, Penwortham, Watervale, Mintaro, Apoinga, Waterloo, Robertstown, Bowillia, Nantawarra, Kulpara, Beaufort, Whitwarta, Halbury, Auburn, Tothill Creek, Saddleworth, Marrabel, Julia, Tarnma, Australia Plains, Sutherlands, Bower, Mount Mary, Morgan, Cadell, Qualco, Murbko, Ramco, Waikerie, Pooginook Cons Park, Lake Bonney, Kingston-on-Murray, Cobdogla, Moorook, Yinkanie, Winkie, Barmera, Glossop, Berri, Lyrup, Renmark, Paringa, Chowilla Game Reserve, Calperum, Cooltong, Nelwood, Border Cliffs, Chowilla, Cal Lal, Lindsay Point

Port Wakefield, Melton, Kainton, Balaklava, Bowmans, Rhynie, Riverton, Eudunda, Hamilton, Hansborough, Brownlow, Brookfield Cons Park, Frankton, Tarlee, Owen, Alma, Inkerman, Avon, Pinery, Stockport, Kapunda, Bagot Well, Stonefield, Blanchetown, Sandy Point, Price, Lorne, Wild Horse Plains, Long Plains, Hamley Bridge, Calomba, Windsor, Dublin, Mallala, Light, Freeling, Greenock, Dutton, Truro, STURT, Ardrossan, Tiddy Widdy Beach, Parham, Wasleys, Port Prime, Roseworthy, Nuriootpa, Angaston, Tanunda, Keyneton, Sedan, Swan Reach, Lower Light, Two Wells, Gawler, Lyndoch, Swan Reach Cons Park, Notts Well, Maggea, Wunkar, Loxton, Loxton Nth, Gerard, Murray River National Park, Taldra, Morkalla, Pata, Taplan, Bakara CP, Mantung, Mercunda, Bakara, Nildottie, Veitch, Pines Wells, James Well, Black Point, Middle Beach, Port Julia, Port Gawler, Virginia, Smithfield, Elizabeth, Williamstown, Eden Valley, Springton, Mount Pleasant, Cambrai, Black Hill, Angas Valley, Walker Flat, Galga, Cobera, Alawoona, Paruna, Meribah, Murray-Sunset Nat Park, Oak Flat, St Kilda, Salisbury, Kersbrook, Barossa Ranges, Punthari, Caurnamont, Purnong, Copeville, Wanbi, Mindarie, Halidon

Gulf St Vincent, Surveyor Point, Port Vincent, Outer Harbor, Largs Bay, Port Adelaide, ADELAIDE, Gumeracha, Birdwood, Mount Torrens, Palmer, Apamurra, Bowhill, Coolcha, Lobethal, Woodside, Tungkillo, Harrogate, Mannum, Sandalwood, Billiatt Conservation Park, Peebinga, Berrook, Glenelg, Holdfast Bay, Brighton, Stirling, Balhannah, Hahndorf, Mylor, Belair, Nairne, Rockleigh, Tepko, Pompoota, Kalyan, Perponda, Borrika, Peebinga Cons Pk, Sunset, Reynella, Clarendon, Mount Barker, Mount Lofty, Pallamana, Callington, Mypolonga, Karoonda, Karte, Karte CP, Noarlunga, Kangarilla, Echunga, Macclesfield, Murray Bridge, Wynarka, Kulde, Mulpata, Kulkami, Wirha, Sturt Island Cons Park, McLaren Vale, Meadows, Aldinga, Hartley, Woodchester, Brinkley, Naturi, Tailem Bend, Jervois, Strathalbyn, Smithville, Pinnaroo, Panitya, Murrayville, Aldinga Bay, Aldinga Beach, Willunga, Langhorne Creek, Moorlands, Sherlock, Buccleuch, Lameroo, Parilla, Sellicks Beach, Fleurieu, Ashbourne, Belvidere, Sandergrove, Tolderol Point, Wellington, Peake, MALLEE HWY, Bews, Parrakie, Wilkawatt, Jabuk, Geranium, Myponga Beach, Mount Compass, Myponga, Milang, Lake Alexandrina, Cooke Plains, Carrickalinga, Normanville, Yankalilla, Finniss, Currency Creek, Clayton, Narrung, Raukkan, Poltalloch, Ashville, Coomandook, Netherton, One Tree Hill, Baan Hill, Scorpion Springs Cons Pk, Second Valley, Rapid Bay, Torrens Vale, Inman Valley, Pen, Goolwa, Middleton, Hindmarsh Island, Port Elliot, Malinong, Yumali, Carcuma Cons Park, Mount Timothy, Big Desert Wilderness Park, Delamere, Cape Jervis, Parawa, Waitpinga, Victor Harbor, Murray Mouth, Barrages, Lake Albert, Ki Ki, Ngarkat Conservation Park, Backstairs Passage, Deep Creek Cons Park, Tunk Head, Newland Head, Newland Head CP, Waitpinga Beach, Encounter Bay, Younghusband Peninsula, Coorong National Park, Coonalpyn, Mt Little Doughboy, Penneshaw, Cape Coutts, Cape St Albans, Antechamber Bay, Dudley Peninsula, Cape Willoughby, Cape Willoughby Lighthouse, Cape Hart CP, Cape Hart, Black Point, Meningie, Mount Boothby CP, DUKES, Culburra, Mt Shaugh, Mt Rescue, Mount Rescue Cons Park, Mount Shaugh Cons Park, Magrath Flat, Mt Boothby, Tintinara, Woods Well, Messent Cons Park, Baneralla, Policemans Point, Salt Creek, Keith, Telopia Downs, Martin Washpool Cons Pk, HIGHWAY, Lowan Vale, Mt Monster, Cannawigara, Gum Lagoon Cons Park, PRINCES, Bordertown, Yearinga, Buckingham, Mundulla, Wolseley, Serviceton, Lillimur, Willalooka, Mt Willalooka, RIDDOCH, Lillimur South, Western Flat, Padthaway Cons Park, Bangham, Little Desert NP, Padthaway, Bangham Cons Park, Mt Taratap, Lacepede Bay, Long Beach, Lake Nadzab, Keppoch, Frances, Minimay, Mount Scott Cons Park, Fairview Cons Park, Binnum, Kingston SE, Kybybolite, Bringalbert, Reedy Creek, Avenue, Hynam, Margaret Brock Reef Lighthouse, Cape Jaffa, Lucindale, Naracoorte, Apsley, Mount Benson, Lake Hawdon North, Moyhall Swamp, Naracoorte Caves, Cape Thomas, Guichen Bay, Big Heath Cons Park, Bool Lagoon, Langkoop, Robe, Lake Hawdon South, Conmurra, Bool Lagoon Game Reserve, Wrattonbully, Lake Eliza, Greenways, Dergholm State Park, Little Dip CP, Coonawarra, Nora Creina, Clay Wells, Penola Cons Park, Dorodong, Lake St Clair, Lake George, Furner, Penola, Dergholm, Beachport CP, Beachport, Hatherleigh, Rivoli Bay, Mount Burr, Nangwarry, Lake Mundi, Cape Buffon Lighthouse, Rendelsham, Millicent, Kalangadoo, Southend, Tarpeena, Lindsay, Canunda National Park, Tantanoola, Glencoe, Tantanoola Caves, Wandilo, Strathdownie, GLENELG HWY, Lake Bonney, Mil Lel, Mount Gambier, Glenburnie, Yahl, Lighthouse, Cape Banks, Kongorong, OB Flat, Carpenter Rocks, Blackfellows Caves, Mt Schank, Princess Margaret Rose Caves, Nene Valley CP, Allendale East, Nene Valley, Donovans, Nelson, Douglas Point, Cape Northumberland, Port MacDonnell, Piccaninnie Ponds CP

SOUTH AUSTRALIA, VICTORIA

138°, 139°, 140°, 141°, 34°, 35°, 36°, 37°, 38°

1 2 3 4 5 6 7 8 9 10

VIC 1, VIC 2, VIC 5

SA

H J K L M N P

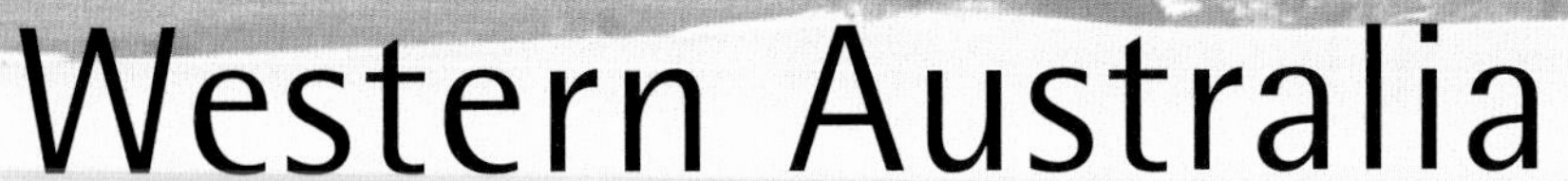

Western Australia

One of the first things visitors to Western Australia notice is space—and with a total area of over 2.5 million sq km taking up about one third of the Australian continent, it's really not surprising. The scenery in the west is full of amazing variety and contrasts, with many of its landscapes like no other place in the country. The state's national parks and reserves, which are all managed by the Conservation and Land Management (CALM) department, are found throughout the whole length and breadth of the state. From the temperate south-west regions and for over 3000 km to the tropical north—even out into the desert heartland of the state—the parks cover a wide range of climates, terrain, wildlife and, importantly for visitors, a vast choice of things to see, do and experience.

Leeuwin–Naturaliste National Park

Here at Cape Leeuwin, which is located on the south-westernmost tip of Western Australia, the balmy waters of the Indian Ocean meet the cooler waters of the wild Southern Ocean. Stretching north from this low cape and its historic lighthouse is a series of rocky headlands, cliff-lined beaches and sweeping bays dotted with reefs and islands, topped at the northern end by Cape Naturaliste and another historic lighthouse.

fact file

WHERE: Cape Naturaliste is 261 km south of Perth; Cape Leeuwin is 324 km south of Perth
Map: WA 8 A8

WHEN: October to May

WHY: Coastal and forest scenery, fishing, swimming, limestone caves, bushwalking, diving, 4WD

SIZE: 19 700 ha

RANGER: CALM Busselton (08) 9752 5555, or Margaret River (08) 9780 5501

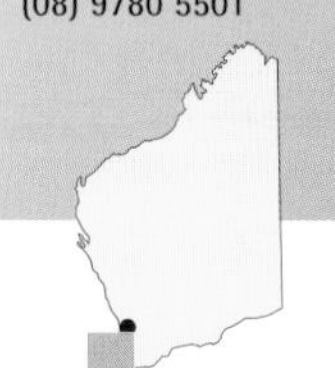

On land a disjointed, convoluted but near continuous strip of land is reserved as national park between these two great capes, with the park taking its name from these two rugged bluffs.

In the Past

Australian Aboriginal occupation of the area dates back to around 40 000 years ago, while the earliest European account of the area was recorded in the log of the Dutch East India Company ship, the *Leeuwin*, in 1622.

Many explorers followed, including England's Matthew Flinders, who named Cape Leeuwin in 1801, and the French navigator, Nicolas Baudin, from whom Hamelin Bay, Cape Naturaliste and Geographe Bay got their names.

Over the past 150 years, the region has been known at different times for its sealing and whaling, grazing and pastoral leases, fishing and timber industry and, more recently, for its world-class vineyards.

Today the park is a popular holiday destination for West Australians, who are attracted by the sheltered bays and beaches, good fishing, dramatic windswept coastal scenery, limestone caves, jarrah and karri forests, excellent surfing and wineries.

Right: *The collared sparrowhawk* (Accipiter cirrhocephalus) *hunts from the cover of open forests and woodlands; the male will return to the nest with food for the female and chicks.*

Cape Naturaliste

Sealed roads lead to the lighthouse built in 1903 and to Bunker Bay, a picturesque spot which is good for a picnic, swim, or for snorkelling and fishing. The West Coast road takes you to Naturaliste Lookout and to Gull Rock, while another sealed road, 3 km south of the lighthouse, takes you to Sugarloaf Rock.

A number of good walking trails, ranging from easy to moderate and taking from 30 minutes to 2 hours to complete, connect these access points.

Canal Rocks to Prevelly Park

At Canal Rocks, a series of rocks extends into the ocean making a natural canal. This is a good fishing spot, but dangerous for swimming. Both the walkway and bridge give good views of the canal and the power of the surging ocean. There is also a protected boat ramp here.

Gracetown is situated on the lovely and scenic Cowaramup Bay, which has a good lookout on the right before you reach the town. Fishing is a popular pastime and when the swells are right, there's some surfing. There are picnic facilities, toilets and a caravan park at the Caves Road turn-off.

Located at the mouth of the Margaret River and just outside the national park, Prevelly Park is famous for its magnificent surfing with the annual 'Margaret River Classic' attracting top surfers from around the world. Canoeing on the pristine waters of the Margaret River, with its myriad birdlife, is also popular.

Left: *Towering jarrah trees* (Eucalyptus marginata) *form almost pure forests, with few other tree species. The column-like trunks are widely spaced, allowing light to reach smaller shrubs.*

Quininup Falls flows freely after winter rains but dries up between mid-spring and late autumn. It can be reached by 4WD track from Quininup Road or on foot from the Moses Road car park.

The Cape to Cape Track starts at the Naturaliste lighthouse and ends 120 km south at the Leeuwin lighthouse; it takes about five to seven days. Cape Naturaliste Lighthouse tours are available Thursday to Tuesday, 9.30 a.m. to 4.00 p.m.

Yallingup and Smiths Beach

These holiday destinations are just a few kilometres apart and both are popular with surfers keen to tackle the huge rolling swells. Fishing from the rocks and along the beach at Smiths Beach is also a favourite sport. There is a choice of caravan parks and other accommodation at both places.

Right: *The tranquil Lefroy Brook flows through a lush tangle of regrowth karri. Ferns and mosses grow among the thick leaf litter and birds are prolific in the dense understorey.*

It is worth visiting the old Ellensbrook Homestead, situated near the mouth of the Margaret River. Alfred Bussell built Ellensbrook in 1857 for himself and his young wife, Ellen. The building has now been restored by the National Trust and is open to the public.

Hamelin Bay and Cosy Corner

Set in a protected bay behind Hamelin Island, this pretty bay is especially popular with families, anglers and divers. A boat ramp is available for launching small craft, while the long beach is ideal for walking and swimming. There is a caravan park beside the beach.

Cosy Corner, which is situated just a few kilometres south, is a reef- and island-studded bay that stretches south to Cape Hamelin. It's a magical dive spot and offers great fishing.

don't miss

A walking track from the Ellensbrook Homestead leads to the appealing Meekadarabee Falls. The name comes from the language of the local Aboriginal people, and means 'the bathing place of the moon'.

Cape Leeuwin

The impressive Leeuwin Lighthouse dominates the Cape and offers startling views of the surrounding coast. Tours of the lighthouse are conducted by the Augusta–Margaret River Tourist Bureau and the lighthouse is generally open between 9.00 a.m. and 4.00 p.m. each day.

Whale Watching

The annual whale migration to and from Antarctica can be seen close up along the Leeuwin–Naturaliste coastline. Humpback and southern right whales swim past on their way to northern breeding grounds during early winter and return south in late spring.

Once the haunt of busy whalers, the coastline is now popular with avid whalewatchers. There are regular sightings from July to November.

The best vantage points to see the whales are Cape Leeuwin, Cape Naturaliste, Gracetown Lookout at Cowaramup Bay, and Sugarloaf Rock. It is estimated that 3000 to 4000 humpbacks make their way along this coast each year.

Fishing, Diving and Sailing

The fishing along this stretch of coastline is excellent all year round, with good catches of skippy, dhufish, snapper, whiting and flathead on offer to keen anglers. During late summer and early autumn Australian salmon make their migratory run up the coast to around Perth and back again, and the fishing can be electric!

Abalone and crayfish are also found in the area. Don't forget that you need a Recreational Fishing Licence to take abalone, rock lobster, marron, and for net fishing or freshwater angling. Contact the Fisheries Department, Perth on (08) 9482 7333 or check out the web at www.fish.wa.gov.au.

There is a multitude of great diving spots in the many protected bays around the islands and reefs. Fourteen ships are known to have sunk during storms and

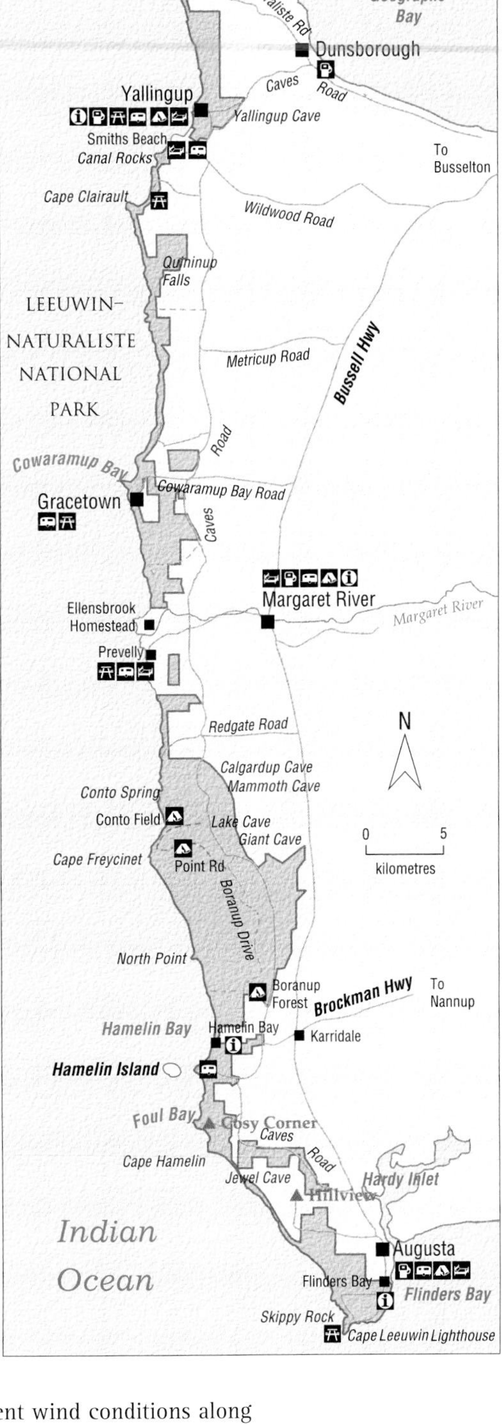

WA

Below: *On the most southwestern tip of Australia, where the Indian and Southern oceans meet, stands the Cape Leeuwin Lighthouse.*

after hitting reefs around Hamelin Bay. A great dive trail has been established which takes in four of those wrecks that are still visible.

The excellent wind conditions along this part of the coastline make both sailing and windsurfing popular summertime attractions here too.

Boranup Forest

Boranup Forest is the largest known karri forest growing in limestone sands and covers 3200 hectares. By 1913, most timber from the area had been cleared and the last mill closed. Remnants of the old mills destroyed by fire some years ago can still be seen at Karridale.

The karri forest has since regenerated, with most trees (some up to 60 metres in height) now less than 100 years old. Grass-trees (balgas) also grow quite prolifically in this region.

There is a pleasant, tall-timber drive through the forest, and the Boranup camping area, set in the bush, is quite basic with barbecues, tables and toilet facilities, but no water.

The karri (Eucalyptus diversicolor) *has adapted to regular fires. Seeds ripen in the heat and fall into the ash beds, to germinate in winter rains.*

Caves

Beneath the sweeping landscape of the park an extraordinary 360 caves have been discovered. Fossils of long-extinct marsupial lions, Tasmanian tigers, a shark, koalas, and even the remains of a gigantic wombat-like creature that was the size of a modern-day horse (dated around 37 000 years ago) have been found here. This cave system is among the oldest and most valuable archaeological sites in Australia.

While most caves are accessible only to experienced speleologists, four of the most spectacular—featuring some shawl and helictite formations—are open to the public with regular guided tours. These are Yallingup Cave, to the north of the park, Mammoth and Lake Caves in Boranup Forest, and Jewel Cave in the south near Augusta.

In addition, there are two adventure caves in Boranup Forest: Giants and Calgardup Caves. Take a torch and wear strong footwear and old protective clothing—the caves are a lot of fun, but care must be taken.

Experienced cavers should contact the ranger for access to other caves in the area.

The Western Australian Christmas tree (Nuytsia floribunda), *named for its December blooms, is actually a member of the parasitic mistletoe family.*

Wildlife and Wildflowers

Native animals that inhabit the national park include western grey kangaroos, brush-tail possums, honey possums and fat-tail dunnarts. There is also a wide range of seabirds, as well as wedge-tailed eagles, kites and the red-tailed tropic bird. In all, around 200 species of birds have been recorded.

The colourful wildflowers are particularly plentiful around headlands and in low heath areas in spring and early summer. Acacias, tiny orchids, coastal daisy bushes, wattles, banksias, cocky's tongue and one-sided bottlebrushes are all found throughout the park.

Right: *Cattle egrets* (Ardea ibis) *forage for insects in wet pastures. In the breeding season their white plumage is tinged with orange.*

Left: *The slow-moving, mostly herbivorous shingleback, or stumpy-tailed, lizard* (Trachydosaurus rugosus) *favours grassland and scrubland.*

Other Attractions

While travelling between various sections of the park, you will encounter other notable features: numerous wineries, cheese factories, craft shops, galleries and studios making anything from gumnut ornaments to jewellery, pottery and furniture.

Most wineries open their cellar doors for both tasting and bottle sales. The art galleries, craft studios and factories often have demonstrations of their craft and samples for sale.

Below right: *The array of flowering shrubs on the coastal plain includes the beautiful chenille honey myrtle* (Melaleuca huegelii) *shown here.*

Access and Camping

Roads to all of the main areas in the park are either sealed or good gravel. In addition, there are several 4WD tracks to remote coastal areas, where the fishing, diving and surfing can be excellent.

You can contact the Boranup camping area and Conto camping area (located off Caves Road, south of Prevelly Park), by phoning CALM at Margaret River, (08) 9780 5501.

There are caravan parks at Yallingup (08) 9755 2164, Augusta (08) 9758 1593, and Hamelin Bay (08) 9758 5540. For Canal Rocks Beach Resort phone (08) 9755 2116.

There are also a number of caravan parks in the surrounding area, including Dunsborough and Margaret River township—all of these make good bases from which to explore nearby sections of the park.

Fuel, water and general supplies are available at Dunsborough, Margaret River township and Augusta.

Cape Range National Park and Ningaloo Marine Park

The Cape Range is the backbone of Cape Range National Park, and its many spectacular gorges are the park's greatest attraction. There are also long stretches of sandy beaches linking the park to Ningaloo Marine Park, which protects the beautiful coral of Ningaloo Reef.

Sheer walls of limestone edge the blue waters of Yardie Creek; black-footed rock wallabies are sometimes spied on the ledges of the southern cliffs.

fact file

WHERE: 400 km north of Carnarvon, off the Great Northern Highway Map: WA 5 C4

WHEN: March to October

WHY: Superb coral reef, great fishing, diving, 4WD

SIZE: 50 581 ha

RANGER: CALM Exmouth (08) 9949 1676

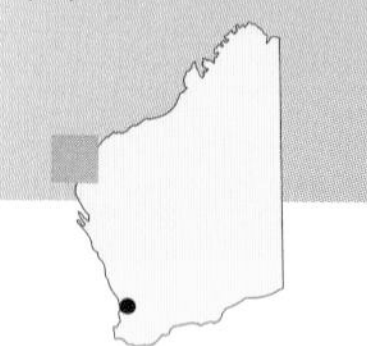

Right: *Long sandy beaches and warm shallow waters sheltered by the offshore reef offer safe swimming. Snorkelling here is also easy for novices.*

Cape Range National Park

Established in 1969, Cape Range National Park takes up much of the west coast and the spine of land known as North West Cape. The most famous gorge here is Yardie Creek Gorge, at the southern end of the park. This rugged country is home to the rare, black-footed rock wallaby.

Exploring the Park

There are some excellent walks in the park, along long stretches of beaches and across rugged range country.

Over on the eastern side of the range from the Thomas Carter Lookout there are a couple of walks up to 8 km in length, while at the Shothole Canyon car park a steep walk will take you to the top of the canyon rim.

On the western side of Cape Range there's the Mandu Mandu Creek walk, while at Yardie Creek, you have a choice of a walk along the creek, another along the northern side of the gorge, or the bird hide and the fauna hide walk.

If you have a canoe you can enjoy a pleasant paddle on Yardie Creek. It's a great way to experience the gorge and see the wildlife. Yardie Creek Tours have boat tours on the creek and operate most days of the tourist season.

Ningaloo Reef and Marine Park

The Ningaloo Marine Park adjoining Cape Range National Park takes in the water from the eastern tip of North West Cape south to Amherst Point. Ningaloo Reef, just offshore, is a truly magnificent coral reef—the fishing is great and the diving superb. The waters provide a home for a great variety of fish, as well as dugongs, turtles, manta rays and whale sharks.

The marine park protecting this coral reef has been divided up into a number of zones and you need to be aware of

did you know?

Whale sharks, the largest sharks in the world, swim in the waters off North West Cape and have put the Ningaloo Marine Park and the adjoining Cape Range National Park on the world stage. You too can swim with them and it is an unforgettable experience!

the regulations, bag limits and what you are allowed to do and not do in each area of the park. Even with such intensive management though, the choices are endless and you won't be disappointed.

Access and Camping

The national park is easily accessible via a bitumen road off the Great Northern Highway. This leads to the small town of Exmouth, or to the holiday hamlet of Coral Bay. Both have a range of accommodation, camping, supplies, tours and other necessities.

From Exmouth the bitumen road heads north, hugging the coast, and then south all the way to Yardie Creek. Inside the park is the Milyering Information Centre, and obtaining a camping permit here opens up the possibility of a number of excellent camp sites dotted along the coast, including the most popular one at Yardie Creek.

South of Yardie Creek and north of Coral Bay is real 4WD territory. Camping is allowed on the Ningaloo Homestead property for a small fee. Phone the owners on (08) 9942 5936.

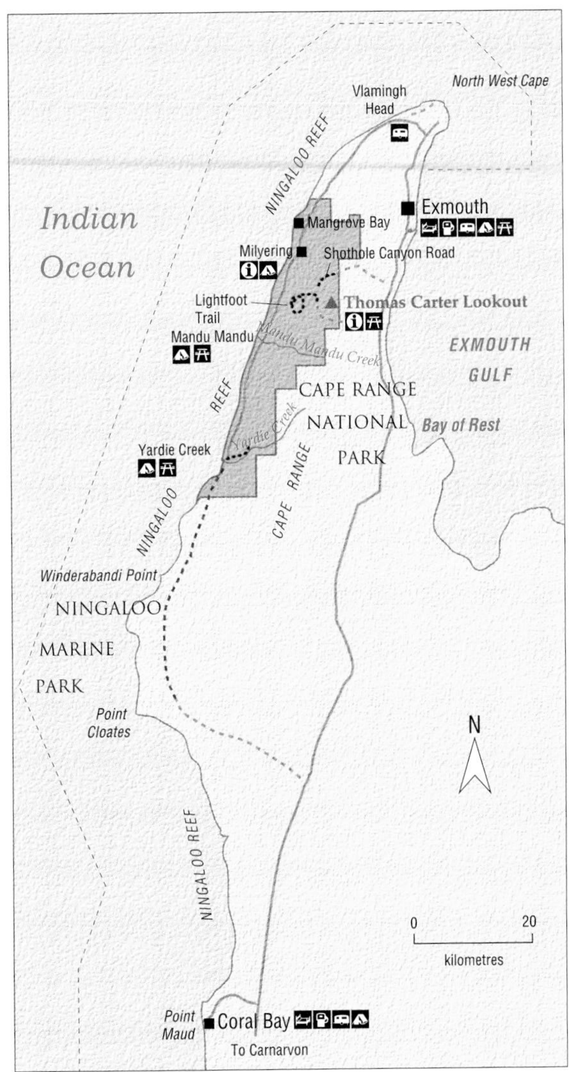

Above: *Ningaloo Reef has more than 180 species of coral—some of which is just 100 metres from shore—and is home to a multitude of colourful tropical fish. Non-divers can view the scene from the comfort of a glass-bottom boat.*

tourist info

Exmouth Tourist Bureau
(08) 9949 1176

Dive Shops: Coral Bay
(08) 9942 5940,
Exmouth (08) 9949 1201

Milyering Information
Centre (CALM)
(08) 9949 2808

Yardie Creek Tours
(08) 9949 2659

Purnululu National Park

Scientists tell us that this place is a geological masterpiece, with the unique Bungle Bungle Range rising from the flat, surrounding plain as a great bulk of weatherworn sandstone. Around the range's southern ramparts the beehive-shaped domes, for which the Bungles are renowned, dominate the landscape.

fact file

WHERE: 3000 km north of Perth via Broome, 110 km north of Halls Creek and 250 km south of Kununurra—4WD only Map: WA 2 F8

WHEN: May to September; the park is closed 1 January to 31 March

WHY: Spectacular ranges, beehive-shaped domes and magnificent gorges

SIZE: 209 000 ha

CONTACT: Halls Creek Visitor Information Centre (08) 9168 6262, or CALM Kununurra (08) 9168 4200

Australian Aboriginals know the area as Purnululu and have lived in the region and used its resources for generations.

The surrounding country was first opened up to European graziers in the late 1800s, while the national park was proclaimed in March 1987. It is managed by the Department of Conservation and Land Management (CALM) together with the local Australian Aboriginals, a number of whom are employed as rangers within the park.

Taking up a triangular-shaped piece of countryside, the national park and its adjoining conservation park covers 319 000 hectares.

Cathedral Gorge and Piccaninny Gorge

Located about 10 km east of the Walardi Camp is the car park and access track to Cathedral and Piccaninny Gorges. If there is any one gorge to go to while in Purnululu, it is Cathedral Gorge—it is a spectacular place, so take your time and enjoy it. You should allow about 2 hours for the return walk.

The walk to Piccaninny Gorge continues along Piccaninny Creek but is really an overnight walk of 30 km return. Make sure you let the ranger know before setting out on this one.

Echidna Chasm, Froghole and Mini Palms

The car park and access trails for these gorges are located about 15 km to the north of Kurrajong Camp. Echidna Chasm is an easy to moderate 2 km walk through a very narrow chasm with the walls towering upwards for over 100 metres. Froghole is an easy walk of 1.5 km but you should still allow about 1 hour, while the walk to Mini Palms is a harder 3-km jaunt, which could take 3 hours or more.

From the Air

To fully appreciate the stunning beauty of the unusual Bungles you really need to see the range from the air. Scenic flights are available in helicopters from either the Turkey Creek Roadhouse or from the Bellburn airstrip located in the park. Phone Heliwork on (08) 9168 1811 or (08) 9168 7335.

Light aircraft fly over the range from Halls Creek and Kununurra. While the flight is cheaper from

Right: *Keen eyes may spot the frill-necked lizard* (Chlamydosaurus kingii) *in the national park. The spectacular frill, sometimes as large as a dinner plate, is spread to intimidate predators.*

Distinctively striped, the Bungle Bungles are the eroded remnants of an ancient plateau. The orange bands are silica, while the darker bands are lichen; beneath is a core of white sandstone.

don't miss

Purnululu National Park has a wealth of wildlife. Over 130 species of birds live here, from rainbow bee-eaters to budgerigars, as well as animals such as euros, nail-tail wallabies and short-eared rock wallabies.

Halls Creek, you miss out on flying over delightful Lake Argyle and the amazing Argyle Diamond Mine.

Access and Camping

About 110 km north of Halls Creek, a rough 4WD route leads 53 km from the Northern Highway into the park and to the visitor centre and ranger station. The visitor centre has a public phone, soft drinks and souvenirs.

From this point it is just 5 km north to Kurrajong Camp or 16 km south to Walardi Camp. Both camps have facilities such as toilets, water and fireplaces with wood provided. There is a separate area for campers with their own generators. An entry fee and a camping fee per night is payable.

A number of tour operators based in either Kununurra or Halls Creek take visitors on a flight over the range and into the national park where camping

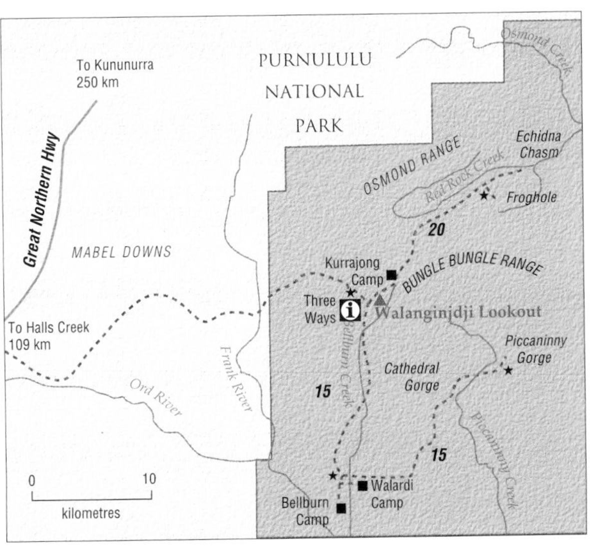

accommodation, transport and other amenities can be provided. Phone East Kimberley Tours on (08) 9168 2213, Oasis Air on (08) 9168 6462 or Alligator Airways on (08) 9168 1333.

Stirling Range National Park

The blue, many-peaked outline of the Stirling Range, when seen from a distance, stands tall, mysterious and alone. This truly dominant and intriguing landmark in the south-west corner of Western Australia looks for all the world like islands rising from a flat sea floor.

Above: *There are more than 13 species of banksias found in the Stirling Range. The flowers are rich in nectar and attract a variety of native birds.*

fact file

WHERE: 330 km south-east of Perth, and 75 km north of Albany
Map: WA 8 G9

WHEN: October and November for wildflowers, spring and autumn for bushwalking

WHY: Wildflowers, bush-walking, photography

SIZE: 115 920 ha

RANGER: CALM Albany (08) 9842 4500

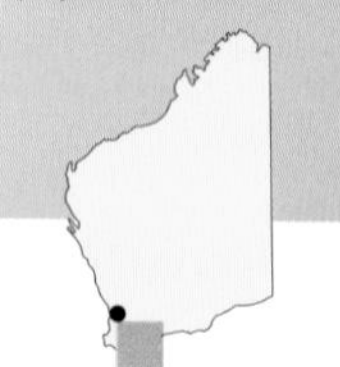

The Stirling Range is known for the concentration, diversity and beauty of its wildflowers.

Australian Aboriginals have lived around the Stirling Range for over 40 000 years.

Matthew Flinders had given the name of Mount Rugged to the eastern massif in 1802, but the real value of the Stirling was not realised until 1843, when botanist James Drummond began a study of the botanical riches that have lured visitors here ever since.

The bright red bracts (leaf-like parts) of mountain bells (Darwinia oxylepis) *give the impression of a single large flower, but they actually surround a cluster of smaller flowers.*

As early as the 1920s the recreational potential of the range was recognised, and today this area is one of Western Australia's premier national parks; its scenic and botanical attractions draw visitors in their thousands.

Surrounded by rolling farm land, the abrupt form of the Stirling Range has over a dozen summits reaching up over 750 metres, with Bluff Knoll standing supreme in the east at 1073 metres.

The general vegetation and terrain around the mountain range is thick, often prickly, with scrub covering much of the lower slopes. This gives way to rough stony sections with sparse growth in the higher parts.

Activities

The 42-km Stirling Range Drive runs through the centre of the park and is one of the best mountain drives to be found anywhere in Australia.

For those interested in wildflowers, the park and the Stirling Range Drive is magnificent with over 1500 species, 60 of which are endemic to the range.

The whole of the Stirling Range is a mecca for bushwalkers, with a variety of marked trails and harder routes ideal for exploring different sections of the park. Some of the formal walking trails include interesting routes to the crest of Mount Magog, Mount Talyuberlup, Mount Toolbrunup and Bluff Knoll. The Ridge Trail is a difficult and demanding route which climbs up to Ellen

Peak in the east and winds along the top of the ridge to Bluff Knoll.

There are also quite a number of much easier wildflower and scenic walks ranging from a few hundred metres to over 5 km.

Other activities in the park include abseiling, as well as photography and viewing the region's bountiful wildlife. Over 130 different species of birds have been recorded, while mammals include the often-seen western grey kangaroo.

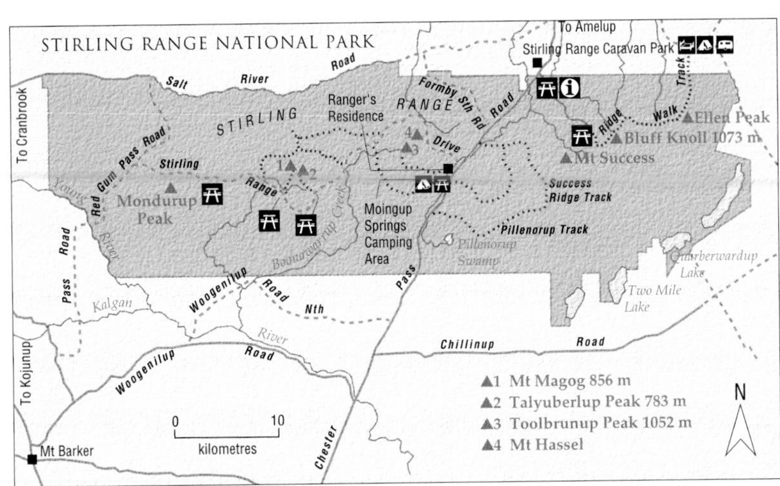

Access and Camping

All roads leading into the park, and the main tracks within, are either sealed or quite good gravel, suitable for conventional vehicles and caravans.

Throughout the park a number of picnic areas have been set up with barbecues, tables and toilet facilities. Camping is only allowed at the Moingup Springs camping area. A permit is required.

Overnight walkers should ensure they record their intended route and estimated time of return in the park's log books which are located at the Moingup Springs camp site and at the Bluff Knoll picnic site.

The Stirling Range Retreat Caravan Park, phone (08) 9827 9229, is found on the northern edge of the park on Chester Pass Road.

The summit of Bluff Knoll, the highest peak in the park, is the only place in Western Australia where snow is likely to fall in winter.

Cape Le Grand National Park

Long stretches of pristine, white, sandy beaches, clear aquamarine water and massive rocky outcrops are the outstanding features of this 32 000-hectare park just west of Esperance. An impressive chain of granite peaks, including Mount Le Grand and Frenchman Peak, rise above the surrounding undulating heath-covered sandplains.

fact file

WHERE: 50 km east of Esperance on the south coast of Western Australia Map: WA 9 D10

WHEN: September to May

WHY: Coastal and granite outcrop scenery, 4WD, swimming, bushwalking, fishing

SIZE: 32 000 ha

RANGER: (08) 9075 9022

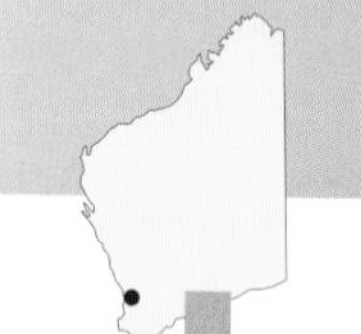

The plains support a wide variety of plant life, with wildflowers in spring making a colourful show. Almost tame kangaroos are another special attraction, as are the Australian sea lions and New Zealand fur seals that laze on the rocky foreshores or in the bays. In deeper water, southern right whales are often spotted.

Activities

Bushwalking is one of the national park's most popular activities. Numerous walking trails range from just a few hundred metres to a scenic 15-km coastal track from Le Grand Beach in the west to Rossiter Bay in the east.

Fishing is also popular. Salmon, blue groper and whiting are among the regular catches. Small boats can be launched off Le Grand Beach and at Lucky Bay.

New Zealand fur seals (Arctocephalus forsteri) *are found on the park's coast. They are smaller and have a more pointed snout than Australian seals.*

Swimming and snorkelling are a highlight of a visit here in summer.

Access and Camping

Access into the park is by sealed road from Esperance. Within the park most main roads are sealed or good gravel.

For those with 4WD vehicles there is a beach access route into the park from Esperance which leads from Wylie Bay to Le Grand Beach.

There are camping areas at Lucky Bay and at Le Grand Beach. Gas stoves should be used, as no wood fires are permitted. A camping fee applies.

Above: *The showy* Banksia speciosa, *notable for its long, serrated leaves, flowers through most of the year. It is one of many species found in the park.*

Left: *Heath-covered sandplains interspersed with swamps and freshwater pools are an ideal habitat for emus. They forage for fruits and insects.*

Kalbarri National Park

The Murchison River and the 80-km gorge it has cut, together with the spectacular coastal cliffs near the river's mouth, combine to form the magnificent centrepieces of Kalbarri National Park. The 186 000-hectare park has immense appeal to bushwalkers, photographers, anglers, canoeists and wildflower enthusiasts.

fact file

WHERE: 167 km north of Geraldton, 1 km from Kalbarri town
Map: WA 6 D5

WHEN: All year, although it can be hot in summer—the cool months are best for walking

WHY: Scenic gorges, bushwalking, photography, water sports

SIZE: 186 000 ha

RANGER: (08) 9937 1140

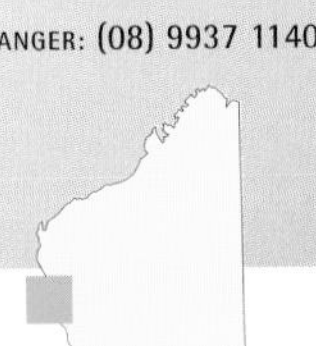

Top right: *The rich fishing grounds of the tidal Murchison River yield mulloway, tailor, sand whiting and the prized black bream. There is good fishing from both shore and dinghy.*

Above right: *Now compacted and weathered, the multicoloured layered sandstone of Kalbarri's cliffs and gorges began as sediment laid down on tidal flats more than 400 million years ago.*

The Coast and Gorge Country

Red Bluff, a rocky headland at the end of a surfing and swimming beach, is the beginning of a picturesque section of coastline. A sealed road leads along the clifftop with pull-ins to main points of interest, while a 12-km clifftop walking trail also leads south to Natural Bridge.

There's a beautiful beach at the foot of Eagle Gorge and colourful layered sands at Rainbow Valley; from Eagle Gorge an 8-km trek leads to Natural Bridge.

The Murchison River has carved some spectacular gorges and escarpments into the countryside. At each of the main vantage points of the Loop, Hawks Head, Z Bend and the Ross Graham Lookout there are stunning views as well as picnic facilities and walking trails.

Rafting and canoeing—for the experienced only—are popular, especially after heavy rains when the river is navigable.

Access and Camping

Access to the park is along gravel roads leading off the sealed road into Kalbarri.

As there are no formal camp sites in the park, most visitors use the thriving fishing and tourist township of nearby Kalbarri as a base.

More National Parks of Importance

Right: *The beach at Point Ann, in Fitzgerald River National Park, was the southern end of the rabbit-proof fence built in 1904 and stretching as far north as Meekatharra.*

Royal hakea (Hakea victoria) *is a feature of Fitzgerald River National Park's coastal heathland. The large, variegated and leathery leaves are long-lasting, with the colour becoming deeper each year.*

Fitzgerald River National Park

SIZE: 329 039 ha
MAP: WA 8 J8

This is one of Australia's most significant national parks and has been gazetted as a World Biosphere Reserve. It is rich in flora with 1784 different plant species recorded, of which 75 are endemic. A number of rare animals, including the dibbler–a small, speckled, marsupial mouse–live in the park. The birdlife is prolific, with 184 recorded species.

Fishing along the coast and in the rivers is popular, while keen photographers will appreciate the rugged coastline, which is also a good viewing place for southern right whales. There are also a number of walking trails within the park. Conventional vehicle access is available to many of the main attractions. A 4WD vehicle will give access to Fitzgerald Inlet, Trigelow Beach, Quoin Head and Whalebone Beach.

There are basic camping facilities at 4-Mile Beach, Quoin Head, Fitzgerald Inlet and Hamersley Inlet.

For more information contact the ranger on (08) 9835 5043.

With the removal of feral animals, Francois Peron National Park is now a sanctuary for the rare bandicoots and bettongs that once thrived along this arid coast.

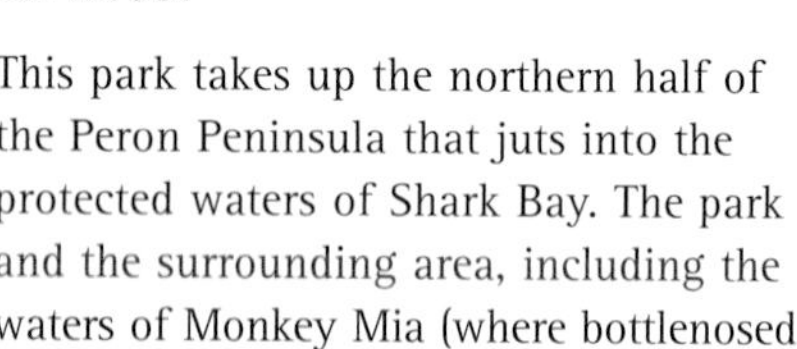

Francois Peron National Park

SIZE: 52 529 ha
MAP: WA 6 B1

This park takes up the northern half of the Peron Peninsula that juts into the protected waters of Shark Bay. The park and the surrounding area, including the waters of Monkey Mia (where bottlenosed dolphins mingle with people), are part of the Shark Bay World Heritage Area.

The old Peron homestead and outbuildings in the park have been restored and opened up to the public with a visitor centre in the old overseer's quarters.

Project Eden has seen the reintroduction of many native mammals previously extinct on the mainland, and the waters around the park are home to thousands of dugongs, turtles, dolphins and manta rays. There is good fishing by boat or from the beach all year round.

Access to the old homestead is along a well-maintained dirt road, while travelling further is 4WD only.

Camping is permitted in the park at Big Lagoon, Gregories, Bottle Bay, Cattle

Well, Herald Bight and South Gregories. Campers must be fully self-sufficient. Wood fires are banned. Camping and entry fees apply.

Contact the ranger in Denham on (08) 9948 1208, or at Monkey Mia on (08) 9948 1366.

John Forrest National Park

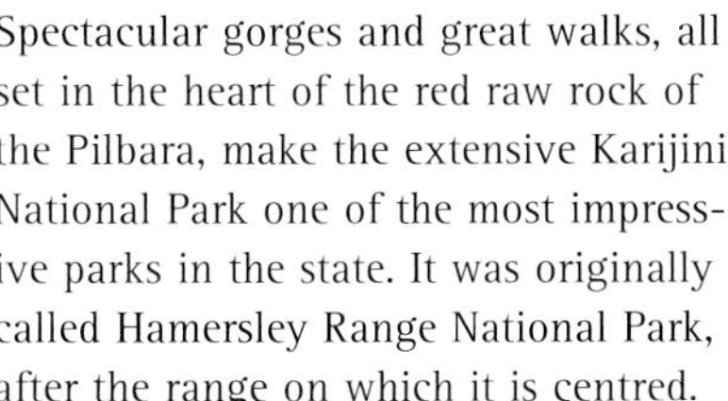

SIZE: 2676 hectares
MAP: WA 8 C4

Sheltered in the Darling Range Escarpment, this is the state's second-oldest park (established as a reserve in 1898), set in a jarrah forest that is still largely in its natural state. In the spring, thousands of tourists come just for the wide variety of wildflowers.

Another major feature of the park is the walking trails, which range in length from 200 metres to several kilometres, with most of the park's scenic attractions found along them. A favourite walk is the extensive John Forrest Heritage Trail.

Bike riding, particularly mountain biking, is also extremely popular in the park, and special trails have been established for horse riders.

Throughout the park there are a number of pleasant picnic spots, with barbecues, tables, and toilets, including disabled access.

Access to the park is by a good sealed road 10 km from the Perth suburb of Midland.

Bush camping is permitted within the park, but an application must be made to the park ranger, phone (08) 9298 8344.

Cycads, grass trees and a range of wildflowers—from orchids and kangaroo paws to wattles and banksias—form the lush understorey of the jarrah forest in John Forrest National Park.

Karijini National Park

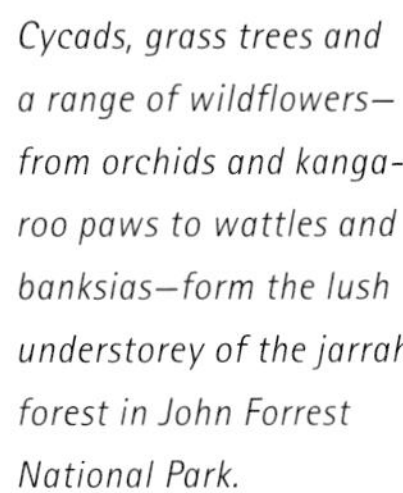

SIZE: 627 445 ha
MAP: WA 5 K5

Spectacular gorges and great walks, all set in the heart of the red raw rock of the Pilbara, make the extensive Karijini National Park one of the most impressive parks in the state. It was originally called Hamersley Range National Park, after the range on which it is centred.

Some of the most enjoyable walks in the park include Oxers Lookout, Joffre Falls, the Gorge Rim Walk as well as the Fortescue Falls and the nearby Fern Pool walk, the latter spot perfect for a swim. There are more extensive walking trails that range from just an hour or two to full-day ventures.

All the roads in the national park are either bitumen or gravel and are suitable for conventional vehicles.

The only camp sites located in the national park are Joffre, Weano and Fortescue. Entry and camping fees apply. A visitor centre is located not far from the Fortescue camping area. Phone (08) 9189 8121.

To contact a ranger (at Tom Price), phone (08) 9189 8157.

Waterways have carved spectacular gorges into the ancient plateau of Karijini National Park. The banded rock exposed here was laid down as sediment on the seafloor 2500 million years ago.

Covered with scattered shrubby trees, grasses and spinifex, Mount Augustus rises 717 metres above the stony sandplain. Springs and waterholes around its base make it an oasis for wildlife.

Right: *Variegated fairy-wrens* (Malurus lamberti) *thrive in the vegetation fringing waterholes in Millstream-Chichester National Park.*

don't miss

The Homestead Walk, which starts at the visitor centre in Millstream–Chichester National Park, is a delightful trail through an ancient ecosystem of tall palms and paperbarks, winding past Chinderwarriner Pool.

Millstream–Chichester National Park

SIZE: 199 736 ha
MAP: WA 5 J3

This park, straddling the Fortescue River, has natural freshwater springs fed from deep underground. Ivory-coloured waterlilies and clear pools surrounded by tall palms add to the beauty of this oasis.

In the northern section of the park is Python Pool, a permanent waterhole at the base of a tall cliff in the Chichester escarpment. There are a number of popular walking trails, while the two drives around the park take in Deep Reach Pool, Crossing Pool and the Cliff Lookout. Swimming, boating, canoeing and windsurfing are great ways to enjoy the waterways.

All roads are gravel and suitable for conventional vehicles. Camping areas are provided at Crossing Pool, Deep Reach Pool, and in the north at Snake Creek near Python Pool. The Millstream Homestead Visitor Centre is the best spot for more information, phone (08) 9184 5144. Entry and camping fees are charged.

Mount Augustus National Park

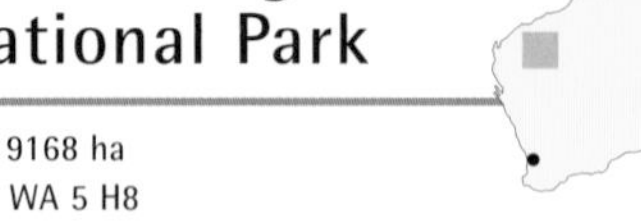

SIZE: 9168 ha
MAP: WA 5 H8

Located some 450 km east of Carnarvon, Mount Augustus is the world's largest rock. It is more than twice as big as Uluru (Ayers Rock) and millions of years older.

One of the main attractions at Burringurrah, as the peak is called by the local Wadjari people, is the climb to the top of the mount. Be warned, however, that this is a strenuous walk of 6 km each way. Other walking trails lead to Edneys Lookout, several Australian Aboriginal art sites and waterfalls.

A delightful picnic spot is found at nearby Cattle Pool—a permanent waterhole on the Lyons River lined by large, white river gums.

Access to and around the park is by gravel roads. Camping is not allowed, but a full range of accommodation is available at the Mount Augustus Outback Tourist Resort which is located just outside the park, phone (08) 9943 0527.

Rangers are based here from April to October, or phone CALM, Denham, on (08) 9948 1208.

Torndirrup National Park

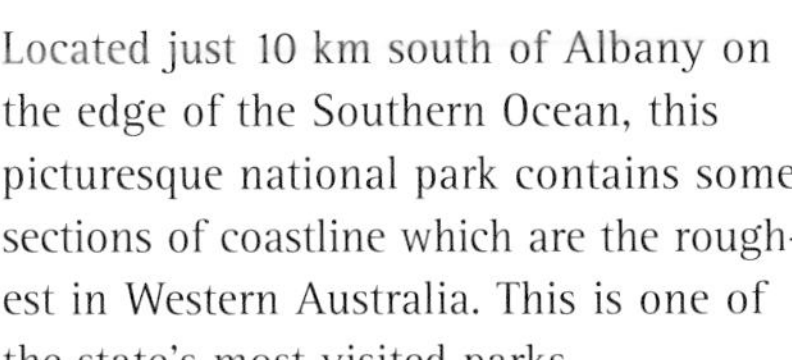

SIZE: 973 ha
MAP: WA 8 F10

Located just 10 km south of Albany on the edge of the Southern Ocean, this picturesque national park contains some sections of coastline which are the roughest in Western Australia. This is one of the state's most visited parks.

The area is a delight for bushwalking, both cross-country and around the park's many spectacular bays and headlands. There are both short and long walks with well laid-out trails available. Places not to be missed by visitors include the Gap, Natural Bridge, the Blowholes, Stony Hill and Salmon Holes—all are extremely dramatic and very scenic places.

Other activities include fishing, rock climbing (in designated areas), whale-watching in winter and wildflower viewing in spring.

With sealed roads leading to all main areas, access is suitable for conventional vehicles. There is no camping or facilities in this park, but there are barbecues, tables, a shop and toilets nearby.

Contact the CALM office at Albany on (08) 9842 4500 for more information.

Walpole–Nornalup National Park

SIZE: 18 000 ha
MAP: WA 8 D10

This park, situated 430 km south of Perth, is well known for its magnificent tall-timber country, featuring huge karri and tingle trees. Other superb scenic attractions include pristine rivers, waterfalls and long expanses of unspoilt coastline.

Popular activities include bushwalking, scenic drives, beach fishing, canoeing and sailing. The Valley of the Giants, featuring huge karri and red tingle trees, some several hundred years old, is the park's most popular attraction. It is also known for its wildflowers.

A conventional vehicle will get you around the park. There is also a 4WD access track that heads west from pretty Peaceful Bay, and to Bellanger Beach and the Blue Holes.

There are well-organised camping areas with toilets, barbecues and tables. Bush camping is allowed in designated areas. There are also four caravan parks, at Coalmine Beach, Rest Point, Peaceful Bay and on the South Coast Highway.

For more information contact CALM, Walpole, on (08) 9840 1027.

Below: *The massive, granite span known as Natural Bridge, located in Torndirrup National Park, was carved out by the pounding action of powerful Southern Ocean swells.*

Below: *The wheelchair-accessible Tree Top Walk spans a 40-metre gully in Walpole-Nornalup's Valley of the Giants. Visitors can stroll through a canopy of red tingle.*

Popular Parks at a Glance

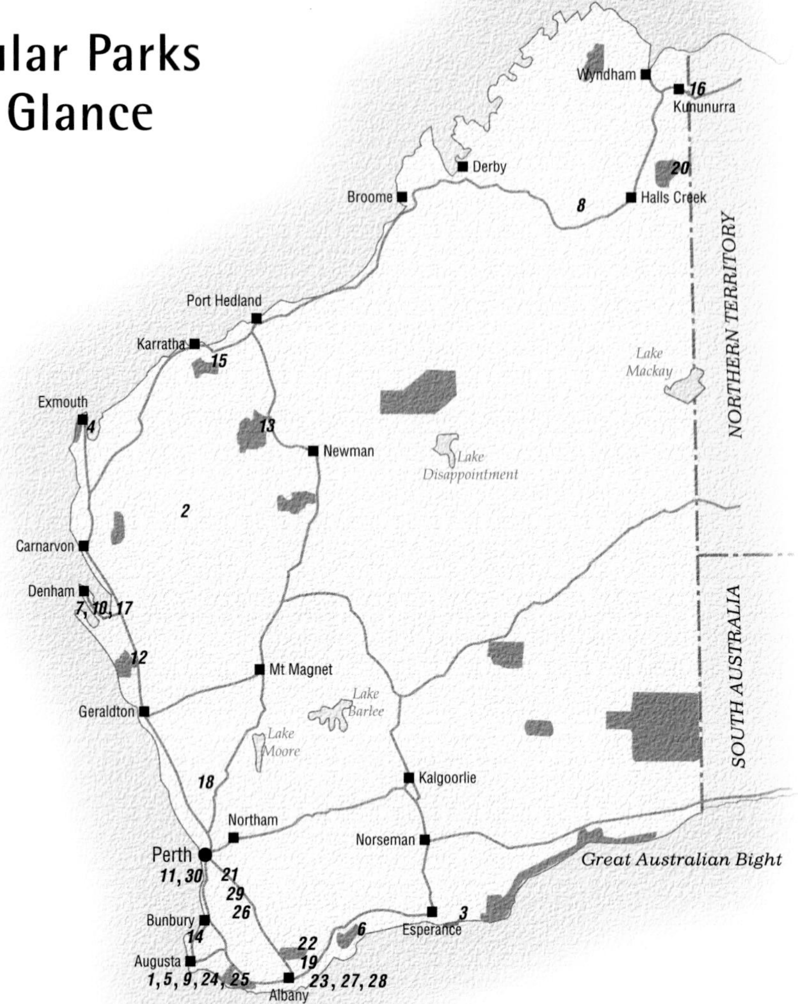

	Park	Camping	Caravan Access	Disabled Access	4WD Access	Picnic Areas	Toilets	Walking Tracks	Kiosk	Information
1	Beedelup NP					●	●	●		
2	Burringurrah (Mount Augustus) NP					●	●	●		
3	Cape Le Grand NP	●	●		●	●	●	●		●
4	Cape Range NP	●				●	●	●		
5	D'Entrecasteaux NP	●			●	●	●	●		
6	Fitzgerald River NP	●				●	●	●		
7	Francois Peron NP	●			●	●	●	●		●
8	Geikie Gorge NP			●		●	●	●		●
9	Gloucester NP					●	●	●		
10	Hamelin Pool Marine NR				●			●	●	●
11	John Forrest NP	●		●		●	●	●		
12	Kalbarri NP					●	●	●		
13	Karijini NP	●	●	●		●	●	●	●	●
14	Leeuwin–Naturaliste NP					●	●	●		
15	Millstream–Chichester NP	●	●			●	●	●		●
16	Mirima NP					●	●	●		
17	Monkey Mia Reserve					●	●	●	●	●
18	Nambung NP					●	●	●		
19	Porongurup NP					●	●	●		
20	Purnululu NP	●			●	●	●	●		
21	Serpentine NP			●		●	●	●		
22	Stirling Range NP	●				●	●	●		
23	Torndirrup NP							●		
24	Walpole–Nornalup NP	●	●		●	●	●	●		
25	Warren NP	●				●	●	●		
26	Wellington Forest NP	●	●			●	●	●		
27	West Cape Howe NP	●			●	●	●	●		
28	William Bay NP					●	●	●		
29	Yalgorup NP	●				●	●	●		
30	Yanchep NP	●		●		●	●	●	●	●

Map 1

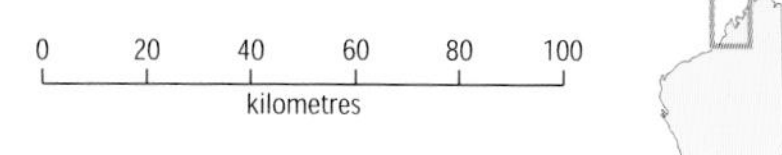

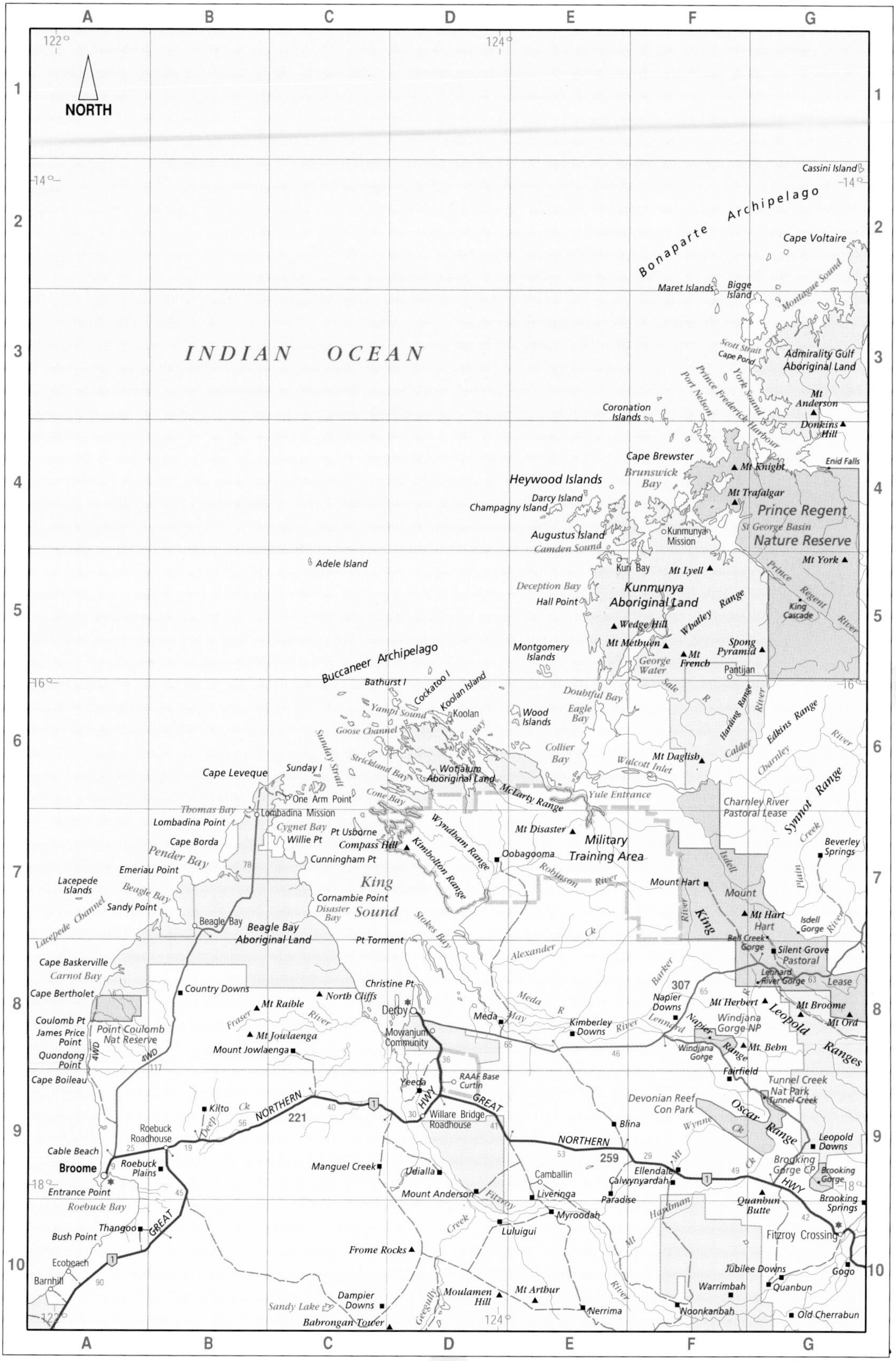

A B C D E F G

1 2 3 4 5 6 7 8 9 10

122° 124° 14° 16° 18°

NORTH

INDIAN OCEAN

Cassini Island
Bonaparte Archipelago
Cape Voltaire
Maret Islands
Bigge Island
Montague Sound
Scott Strait
Cape Pond
York Sound
Admiralty Gulf Aboriginal Land
Prince Frederick Harbour
Port Nelson
Mt Anderson
Coronation Islands
Donkins Hill
Cape Brewster
Enid Falls
Brunswick Bay
Mt Knight
Heywood Islands
Mt Trafalgar
Darcy Island
Champagny Island
Prince Regent Nature Reserve
St George Basin
Augustus Island
Kunmunya Mission
Camden Sound
Mt York
Adele Island
Kuri Bay
Mt Lyell
Deception Bay
Kunmunya Aboriginal Land
Hall Point
Whatley Range
Prince Regent River
King Cascade
Wedge Hill
Mt Methuen
Montgomery Islands
Spong Pyramid
Mt French
George Water
Pantijan
Buccaneer Archipelago
Bathurst I
Cockatoo I
Koolan Island
Koolan
Yampi Sound
Doubtful Bay
Sale R
Harding Range
Calder River
Edkins Range
Wood Islands
Eagle Bay
Goose Channel
Talbot Bay
Collier Bay
Sunday Strait
Mt Daglish
Walcott Inlet
Charnley River
Strickland Bay
Wotjalum Aboriginal Land
McLarty Range
Cape Leveque
Sunday I
Cone Bay
Yule Entrance
One Arm Point
Synnot Range
Thomas Bay
Lombadina Mission
Charnley River Pastoral Lease
Lombadina Point
Cygnet Bay
Wyndham Range
Mt Disaster
Willie Pt
Pt Usborne
Military Training Area
Cape Borda
Compass Hill
Plain Creek
Beverley Springs
Pender Bay
Kimbolton Range
Oobagooma
Cunningham Pt
Robinson River
Isdell
Emeriau Point
Lacepede Islands
King Sound
Mount Hart
Beagle Bay
Cornambie Point
Mount
Sandy Point
Disaster Bay
King River
Mt Hart
Lacepede Channel
Beagle Bay
Beagle Bay Aboriginal Land
Stokes Bay
Isdell Gorge
Isdell River
Pt Torment
Alexander Ck
Bell Creek Gorge
Silent Grove Pastoral
Cape Baskerville
Barker
Carnot Bay
307
Lennard River Gorge
Lease
Cape Bertholet
Country Downs
Christine Pt
Meda R
Napier Downs
Mt Herbert
Leopold Ranges
Mt Broome
North Cliffs
Mt Raible
Coulomb Pt
Fraser River
Derby
Meda
May
Kimberley Downs
Lennard River
Windjana Gorge NP
Mt Ord
James Price Point
Point Coulomb Nat Reserve
Mt Jowlaenga
Mowanjum Community
Napier Range
Quondong Point
4WD
Mount Jowlaenga
Windjana Gorge
Mt Behn
Fairfield
Tunnel Creek Nat Park
Cape Boileau
RAAF Base Curtin
Yeeda
Devonian Reef Con Park
Tunnel Creek
Oscar Range
Kilto
Deep Ck
NORTHERN
221
HWY
GREAT
Willare Bridge Roadhouse
Blina
Wynne Ck
Roebuck Roadhouse
Leopold Downs
NORTHERN
259
Cable Beach
Broome
Roebuck Plains
Manguel Creek
Udialla
Camballin
Ellendale
Calwynyardah
Brooking Gorge CP
Brooking Gorge
Entrance Point
Mount Anderson
Liveringa
Paradise
Quanbun Butte
Brooking Springs
Roebuck Bay
Fitzroy
Hardman
Myroodah
Thangoo
Luluigui
Bush Point
GREAT
Creek
Fitzroy Crossing
Mt
Ecobeach
Frome Rocks
Barnhill
Jubilee Downs
Gogo
Dampier Downs
Moulamen Hill
Mt Arthur
Warrimbah
Quanbun
Sandy Lake
Geegully
River
Nerrima
Noonkanbah
Old Cherrabun
Babrongan Tower

WA 2

WA

WA 4

Map 2

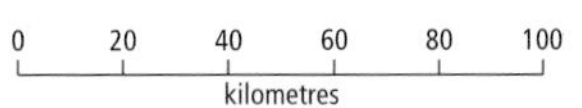

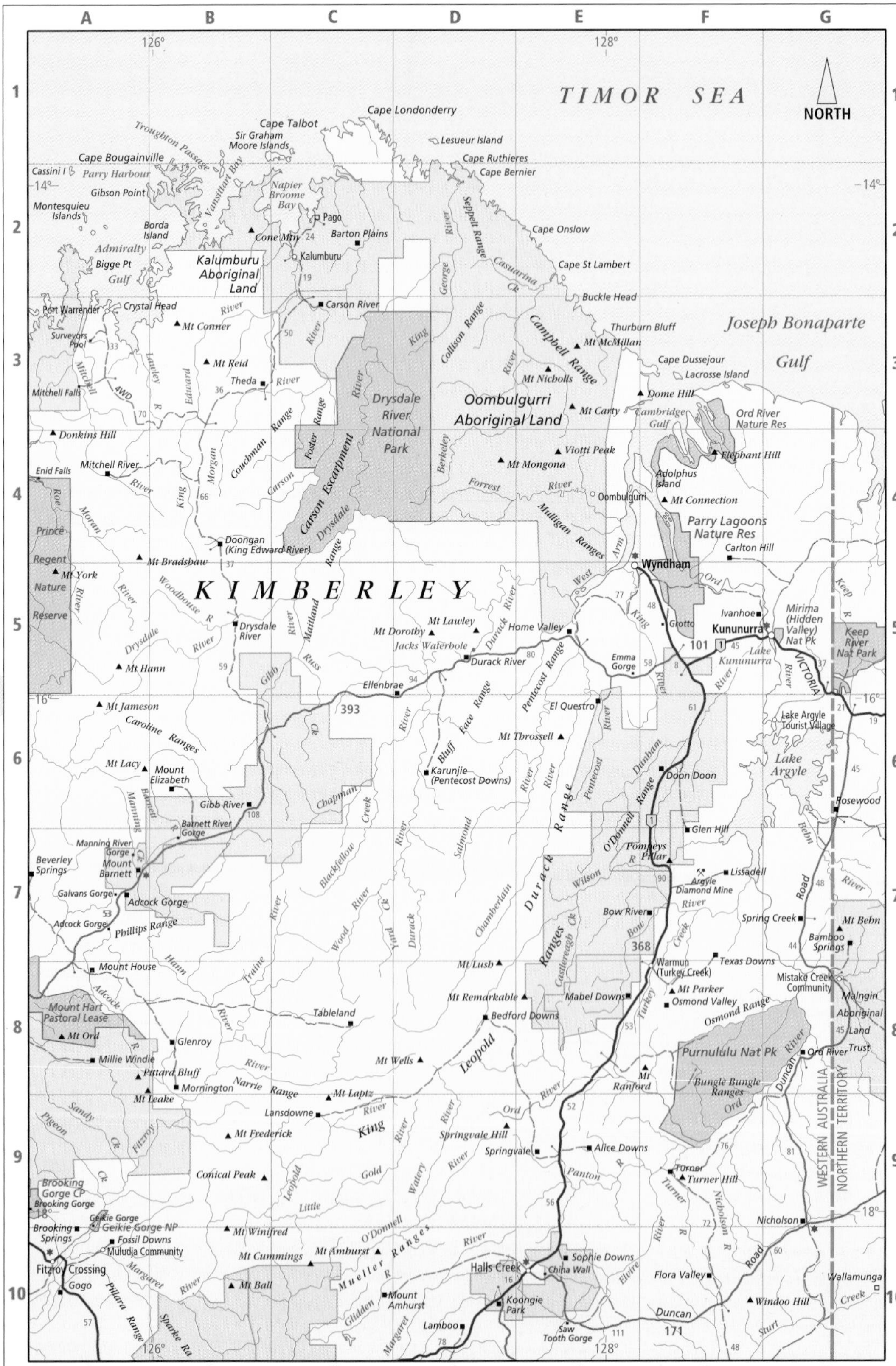

A B C D E F G

126° 128°

1 2 3 4 5 6 7 8 9 10

TIMOR SEA
NORTH
Cape Londonderry
Cape Talbot
Sir Graham Moore Islands
Troughton Passage
Lesueur Island
Cape Bougainville
Cape Ruthieres
Cape Bernier
Cassini I
Parry Harbour
Vansittart Bay
Gibson Point
Napier Broome Bay
-14°
Montesquieu Islands
Pago
Borda Island
Cone Mtn
Barton Plains
Seppelt Range
Cape Onslow
Admiralty Gulf
Bigge Pt
Kalumburu
Kalumburu Aboriginal Land
George River
Casuarina Ck
Cape St Lambert
Carson River
Buckle Head
Port Warrender
Crystal Head
Mt Connor
Surveyors Pool
King
Collison Range
Campbell Range
Thurburn Bluff
Joseph Bonaparte Gulf
Mt McMillan
Cape Dussejour
Mitchell
Mt Reid
Lacrosse Island
Mitchell Falls
4WD
Laurie R
Edward
Theda
River
Drysdale River National Park
Mt Nicholls
Oombulgurri Aboriginal Land
Dome Hill
Mt Carty
Cambridge Gulf
Ord River Nature Res
Donkins Hill
Couchman Range
Foster Range
Carson Escarpment
Berkeley
Viotti Peak
Elephant Hill
Enid Falls
Mitchell River
Morgan
Mt Mongona
Adolphus Island
Forrest River
Oombulgurri
Mt Connection
Prince Regent Nature Reserve
Roe River
Moran
Drysdale
Mulligan Ranges
Parry Lagoons Nature Res
Doongan (King Edward River)
Carlton Hill
Mt Bradshaw
Maitland Range
West Arm
Wyndham
Mt York
KIMBERLEY
Ord
Keep R
Woodhouse R
Durack River
Mt Lawley
Home Valley
Ivanhoe
Drysdale River
Mt Dorothy
Grotto
Kununurra
Mirima (Hidden Valley) Nat Pk
Keep River Nat Park
Jacks Waterbole
Durack River
Emma Gorge
Lake Kununurra
VICTORIA
Mt Hann
Gibb
Russ
Pentecost Range
Ellenbrae
El Questro
-16°
Mt Jameson
393
Bluff Face Range
Lake Argyle Tourist Village
Caroline Ranges
Mt Tbrossell
Mt Lacy
Mount Elizabeth
Karunjie (Pentecost Downs)
Dunham
Doon Doon
Lake Argyle
Chapman
Manning
Barnett
Gibb River
Durack Range
O'Donnell Range
Rosewood
Barnett River Gorge
Glen Hill
Blackfellow Creek
Salmond
Behn
Manning River Gorge
Pompeys Pillar
Beverley Springs
Mount Barnett
Wilson
Lissadell
Argyle Diamond Mine
Road
Galvans Gorge
Adcock Gorge
Chamberlain
Bow River
Spring Creek
Mt Behn
Adcock Gorge
Phillips Range
Wood River
Yard Ck
Durack
Castlereagh Ck
Ranges
Bow
368
Bamboo Springs
Mount House
Hann
Traine
Mt Lush
Warmun (Turkey Creek)
Texas Downs
Mistake Creek Community
Adcock
Mt Parker
Malngin Aboriginal Land Trust
Mount Hart Pastoral Lease
Tableland
Mt Remarkable
Mabel Downs
Osmond Valley
Osmond Range
Bedford Downs
Turkey
Mt Ord
Glenroy
Leopold
Purnululu Nat Pk
Ord River
Millie Windie
Mt Wells
Mt Ranford
Duncan
Pittard Bluff
Narrie Range
Mornington
Bungle Bungle Ranges
Mt Leake
Mt Laptz
Sandy Ck
Lansdowne
King
Ord River
WESTERN AUSTRALIA
NORTHERN TERRITORY
Pigeon
Fitzroy
Mt Frederick
Springvale Hill
Springvale
Alice Downs
Panton R
Conical Peak
Gold
Watery
Turner
Turner Hill
Brooking Gorge CP
Brooking Gorge
Leopold
Little
Nicholson R
-18°
Geikie Gorge
Geikie Gorge NP
Brooking Springs
Mt Winifred
O'Donnell
Nicholson
Fossil Downs
Muludja Community
Mt Cummings
Mt Amburst
Mueller Ranges
Sophie Downs
Fitzroy Crossing
Margaret
China Wall
Elvire
Gogo
Mt Ball
Halls Creek
Flora Valley
Wallamunga
Pillara Range
Glidden R
Mount Amburst
Koongie Park
Windoo Hill
Creek
Sparke Ra
Lamboo
Saw Tooth Gorge
Duncan
171
Sturt
Margaret

WA 1
NT 4
WA 3

Map 3

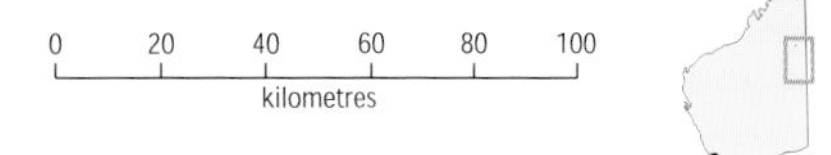
0
20
40
60
80
100
kilometres

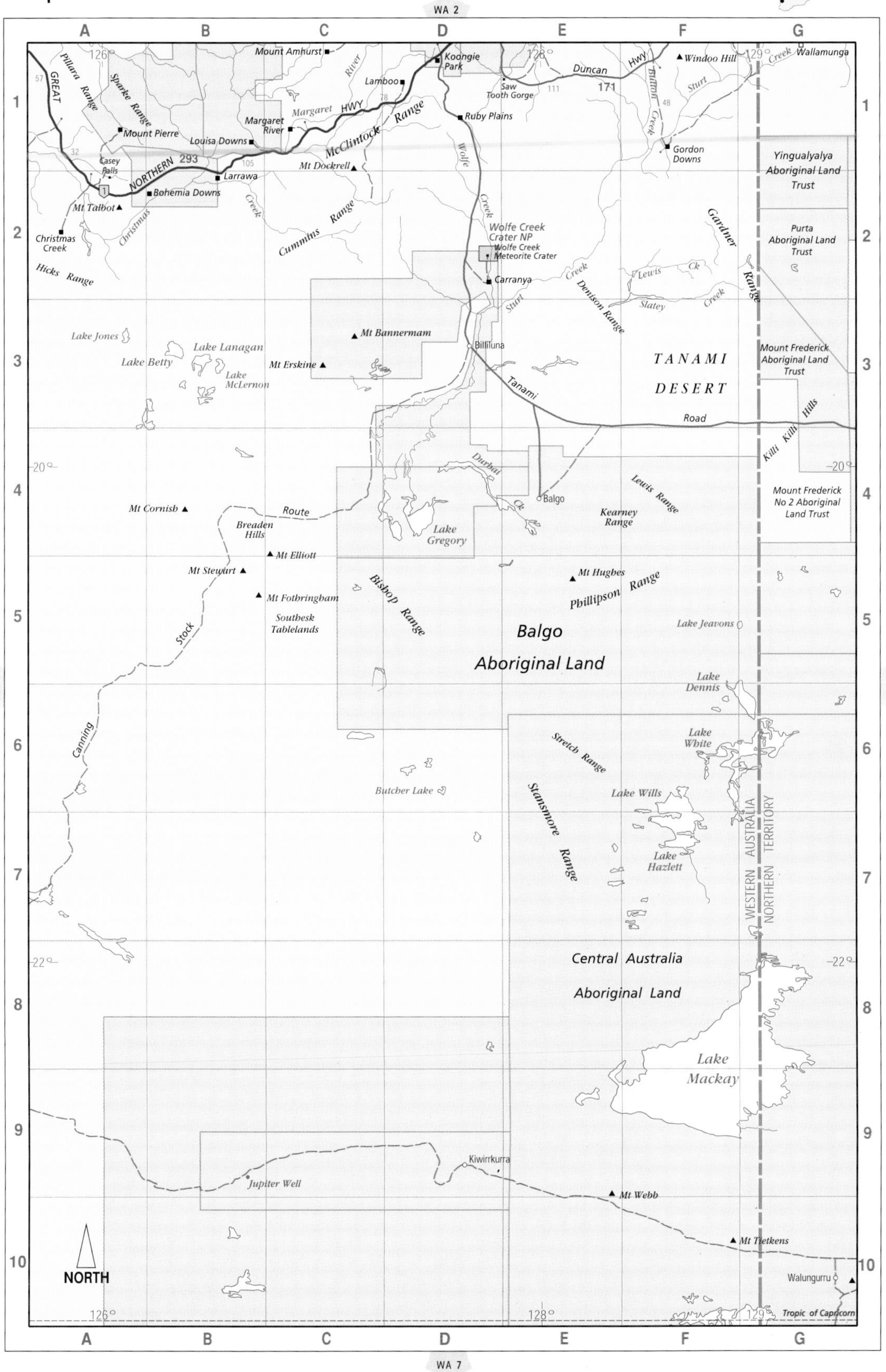

WA 2
Mount Amhurst
Koongie Park
Lamboo
Margaret River
Mount Pierre
Louisa Downs
Casey Falls
NORTHERN 293
Larrawa
Bohemia Downs
Mt Talbot
Christmas Creek
Mt Dockrell
McClintock Range
Ruby Plains
Saw Tooth Gorge
Duncan 171 Hwy
Windoo Hill
Wallamunga
Gordon Downs
Yingualyalya Aboriginal Land Trust
Purta Aboriginal Land Trust
Cummins Range
Hicks Range
Wolfe Creek Crater NP
Wolfe Creek Meteorite Crater
Carranya
Denison Range
Gardner Range
Mt Bannermam
Billiluna
Lake Jones
Lake Lanagan
Lake Betty
Lake McLernon
Mt Erskine
TANAMI DESERT
Mount Frederick Aboriginal Land Trust
Tanami Road
Killi Killi Hills
Mount Frederick No 2 Aboriginal Land Trust
Mt Cornish
Breaden Hills
Route
Balgo
Lewis Range
Kearney Range
Lake Gregory
Mt Elliott
Mt Stewart
Mt Fothringham
Southesk Tablelands
Bishop Range
Mt Hughes
Phillipson Range
Balgo Aboriginal Land
Lake Jeavons
Lake Dennis
Canning Stock
Lake White
Stretch Range
Stansmore Range
Butcher Lake
Lake Wills
Lake Hazlett
WESTERN AUSTRALIA
NORTHERN TERRITORY
Central Australia Aboriginal Land
Lake Mackay
Kiwirrkurra
Jupiter Well
Mt Webb
Mt Tietkens
Walungurru
NORTH
Tropic of Capricorn
WA 4
NT 5
WA 7

Map 4

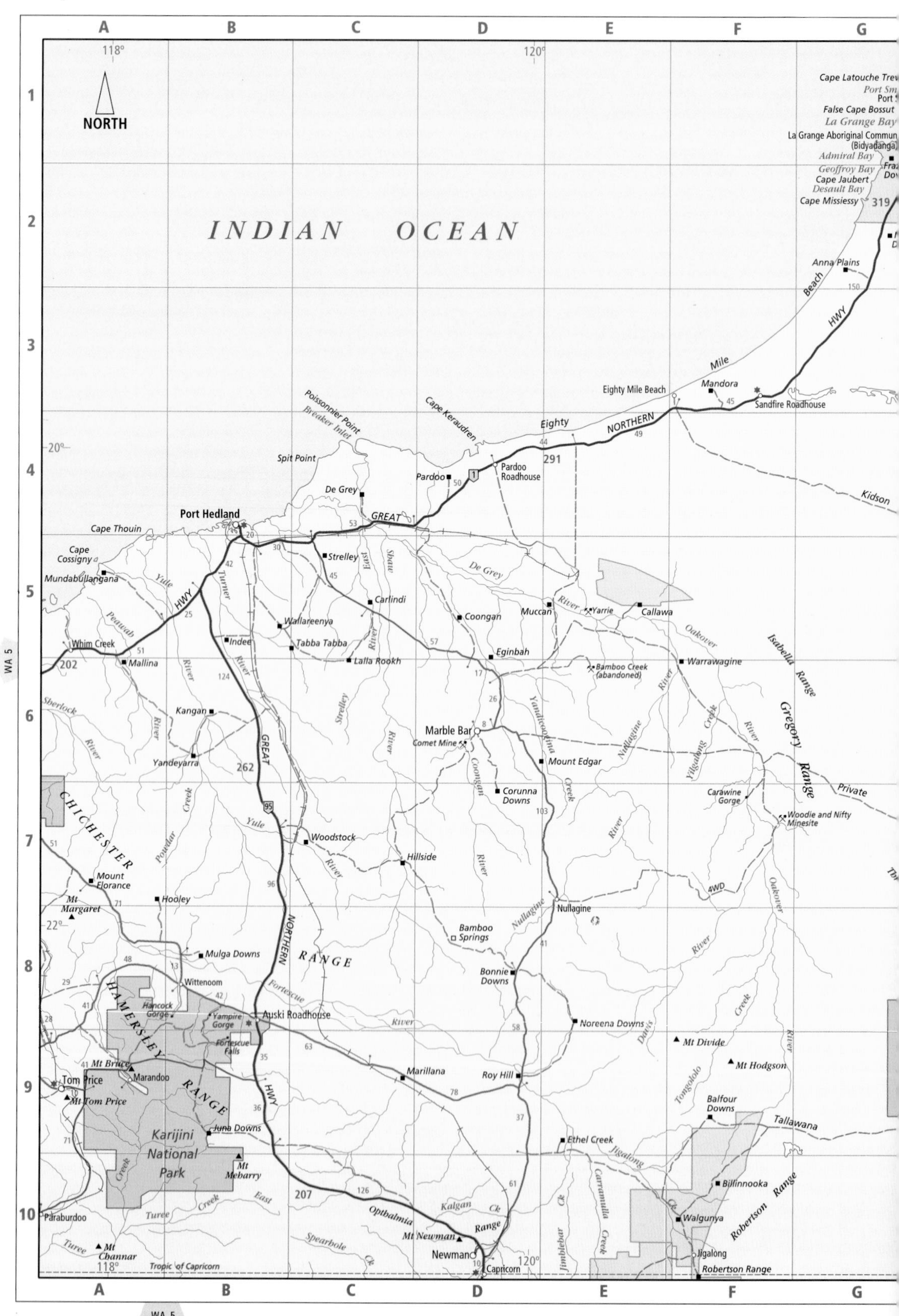
INDIAN OCEAN
NORTH
Port Hedland
Cape Thouin
Cape Cossigny
Mundabullangana
Whim Creek
Mallina
Spit Point
De Grey
Pardoo
Pardoo Roadhouse
Poissonnier Point
Breaker Inlet
Cape Keraudren
Eighty Mile Beach
Mandora
Sandfire Roadhouse
Anna Plains
Cape Latouche Treville
False Cape Bossut
La Grange Bay
La Grange Aboriginal Community (Bidyadanga)
Admiral Bay
Geoffroy Bay
Cape Jaubert
Desault Bay
Cape Missiessy
GREAT NORTHERN HWY
Strelley
Carlindi
Wallareenya
Tabba Tabba
Lalla Rookh
Indee
Coongan
Muccan
Yarrie
Callawa
Eginbah
Bamboo Creek (abandoned)
Warrawagine
Kangan
Yandeyarra
Marble Bar
Comet Mine
Mount Edgar
Corunna Downs
Carawine Gorge
Woodie and Nifty Minesite
Woodstock
Hillside
Mount Florance
Mt Margaret
Hooley
Nullagine
Bamboo Springs
Mulga Downs
Bonnie Downs
Wittenoom
Hancock Gorge
Yampire Gorge
Fortescue Falls
Auski Roadhouse
Noreena Downs
Mt Divide
Mt Hodgson
Mt Bruce
Marandoo
Tom Price
Mt Tom Price
Marillana
Roy Hill
Balfour Downs
Juna Downs
Karijini National Park
Mt Mebarry
Ethel Creek
Billinnooka
Walgunya
Jigalong
Robertson Range
Paraburdoo
Mt Channar
Mt Newman
Newman
Capricorn
Tropic of Capricorn
CHICHESTER RANGE
HAMERSLEY RANGE
Gregory Range
Isabella Range
Ophthalmia Range
Robertson Range
Kidson Track
Private
4WD
Tallawana
Yule River
Turner River
Peawah River
Sherlock River
Strelley River
Shaw River
East Strelley River
De Grey River
Oakover River
Nullagine River
Yilgalong Creek
Coongan River
Yandicoogina Creek
Powdar Creek
Fortescue River
Davis River
Tongololo Creek
Jigalong Creek
Carramulla Creek
Jimblebar Ck
Kalgan Ck
Spearhole Ck
Turee Creek
East Turee Creek
WA 5

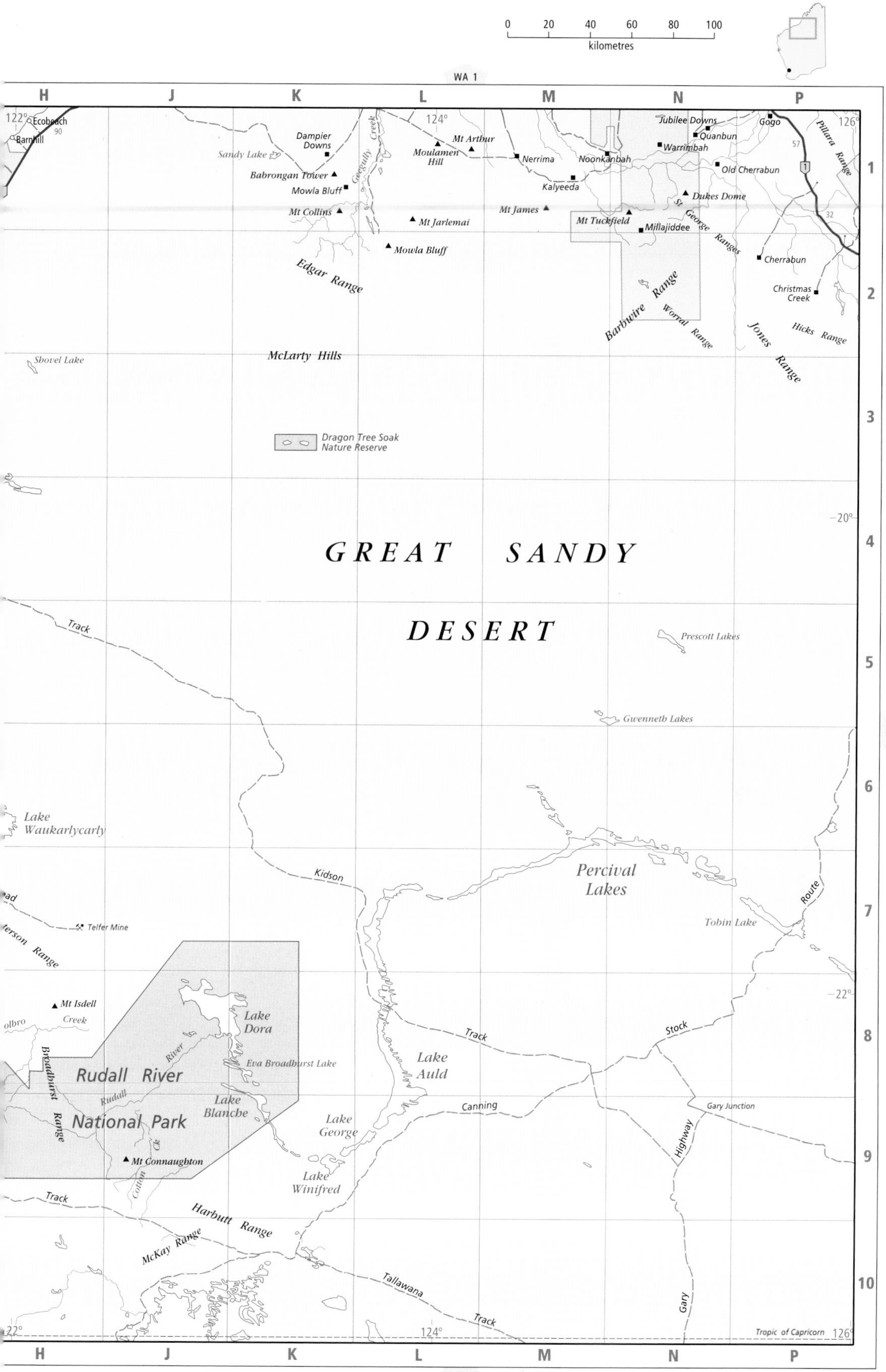

0 20 40 60 80 100
kilometres
H J K L M N P
1 2 3 4 5 6 7 8 9 10
122° 124° 126°
Ecobeach
Barnhill
Dampier Downs
Sandy Lake
Babrongan Tower
Mowla Bluff
Mt Collins
Geegully Creek
Moulamen Hill
Mt Arthur
Nerrima
Noonkanbah
Kalyeeda
Jubilee Downs
Quanbun
Warrimbah
Gogo
Old Cherrabun
Dukes Dome
Pillara Range
Mt James
Mt Jarlemai
Mt Tuckfield
Millajiddee
St George Ranges
Mowla Bluff
Edgar Range
Cherrabun
Christmas Creek
Barbwire Range
Worral Range
Jones Range
Hicks Range
Shovel Lake
McLarty Hills
Dragon Tree Soak Nature Reserve
20°
GREAT SANDY DESERT
Track
Prescott Lakes
Gwenneth Lakes
Lake Waukarlycarly
Kidson
Percival Lakes
Route
Tobin Lake
Telfer Mine
Paterson Range
Mt Isdell
Creek
Lake Dora
Broadhurst Range
River
Eva Broadhurst Lake
Rudall River National Park
Rudall
Lake Blanche
Track
Stock
Lake Auld
Canning
Gary Junction
Lake George
Highway
Mt Connaughton
Cotton Ck
Lake Winifred
Track
Harbutt Range
McKay Range
Tallawana
Track
Gary
22°
Tropic of Capricorn
WA 3
WA

Map 5

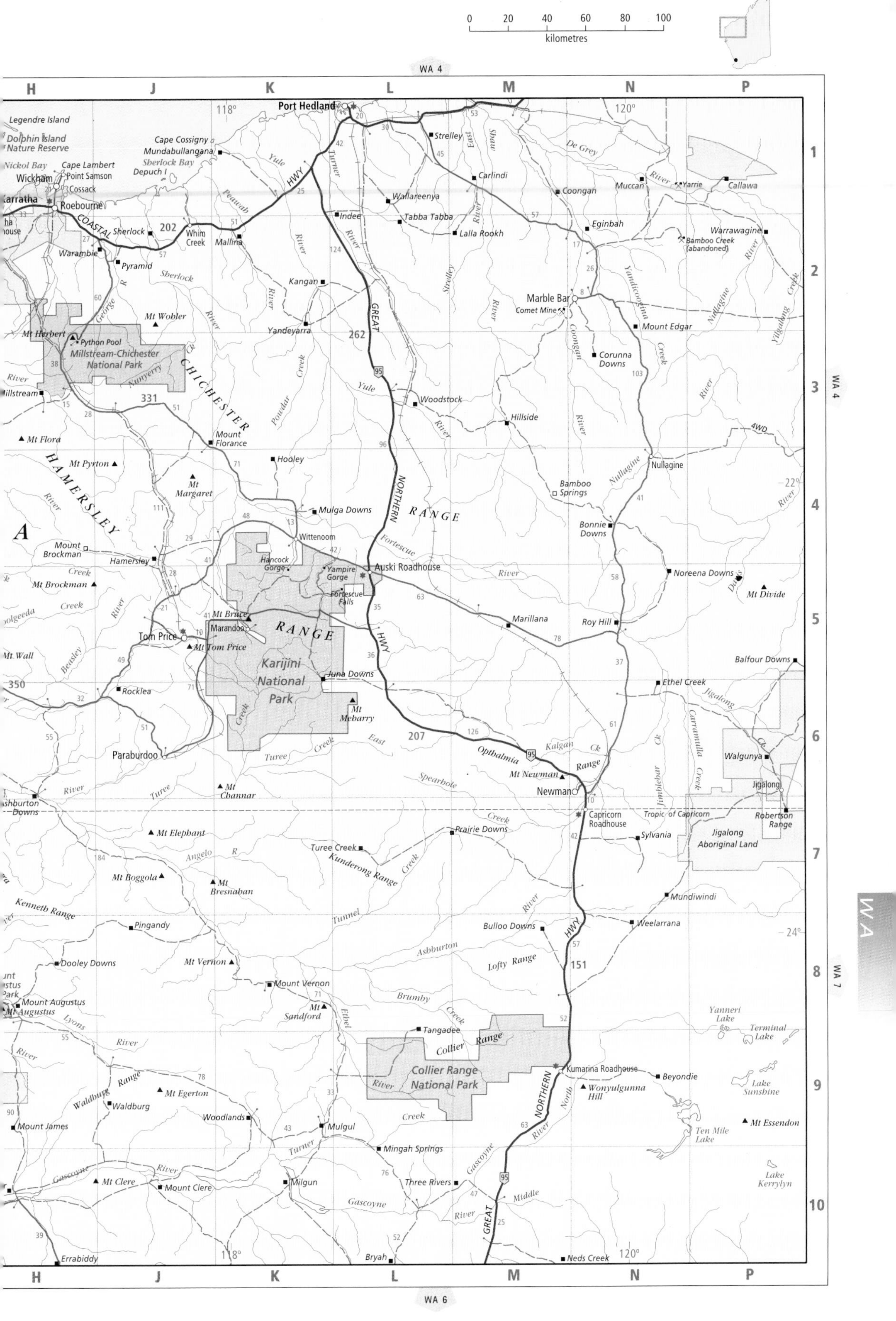

0 20 40 60 80 100
kilometres

WA 4

H J K L M N P

118° Port Hedland 120°
Legendre Island
Dolphin Island Nature Reserve
Cape Cossigny
Mundabullangana
Sherlock Bay
Depuch I
Nickol Bay
Cape Lambert
Point Samson
Wickham
Cossack
Karratha
Roebourne
COASTAL
Sherlock
202
Whim Creek
Mallina
Warambie
Pyramid
Sherlock
George R
Yule River
HWY
Peawah River
Turner River
Strelley
East
Shaw
De Grey
Carlindi
Coongan
Muccan
River
Yarrie
Callawa
Wallareenya
Indee
Tabba Tabba
Lalla Rookh
River
Eginbah
Warrawagine
Bamboo Creek (abandoned)
River
Kangan
Strelley
GREAT
River
Marble Bar
Comet Mine
Yandicoogina
Nullagine
Creek
Yilgalong Creek
Mt Wohler
Yandeyarra
262
Mount Edgar
Mt Herbert
Python Pool
Millstream-Chichester National Park
Nunyerry
Ck
CHICHESTER
Coongan
Corunna Downs
Creek
River
Millstream
Powdar Creek
Yule
Woodstock
River
Hillside
River
River
331
4WD
Mt Flora
Mount Florance
Hooley
NORTHERN
Nullagine
Mt Pyrton
HAMERSLEY
Mt Margaret
Bamboo Springs
River
Mulga Downs
RANGE
Bonnie Downs
A
Mount Brockman
Hamersley
Wittenoom
Fortescue
Hancock Gorge
Yampire Gorge
Auski Roadhouse
River
Noreena Downs
Mt Divide
Creek
Mt Brockman
Fortescue Falls
Creek
River
Mt Bruce
RANGE
Marandoo
Tom Price
Mt Tom Price
HWY
Marillana
Roy Hill
Mt Wall
Beasley
Karijini National Park
Balfour Downs
350
Rocklea
Juna Downs
Ethel Creek
Jigalong
Creek
Mt Mebarry
Carramulla Creek
207
East
Kalgan
Ck
Paraburdoo
Turee
Creek
Ophthalmia
Range
Walgunya
Mt Newman
Jimblebar Ck
Spearhole
Ashburton Downs
River
Turee
Mt Channar
Newman
Jigalong
Capricorn Roadhouse
Tropic of Capricorn
Robertson Range
Creek
Prairie Downs
Mt Elephant
Sylvania
Jigalong Aboriginal Land
Angelo R
Turee Creek
Kunderong Range
Creek
Mt Boggola
Mt Bresnahan
Kenneth Range
River
Mundiwindi
Tunnel
Pingandy
Bulloo Downs
Weelarrana
HWY
Ashburton
Lofty Range
Dooley Downs
Mt Vernon
151
Mount Vernon
Brumby
Mount Augustus National Park
Mount Augustus
Mt Augustus
Mt Sandford
Ethel
Creek
Yanneri Lake
Lyons
Terminal Lake
River
Tangadee
Collier Range
River
Collier Range National Park
Kumarina Roadhouse
Beyondie
Waldburg Range
Mt Egerton
River
Wonyulgunna Hill
Lake Sunshine
Waldburg
North
Mount James
Woodlands
Mulgul
Creek
NORTHERN
River
Mt Essendon
Ten Mile Lake
Turner
Mingah Springs
Gascoyne River
Mt Clere
Mount Clere
Milgun
Three Rivers
Gascoyne
Lake Kerrylyn
Gascoyne
River
Middle
GREAT
Bryah
Erabiddy
118°
Neds Creek
120°
-22°
-24°

1 2 3 4 5 6 7 8 9 10

H J K L M N P

WA 4
WA 7

WA 6

Map 6

WA 5
Shark Bay Marine Park
SHARK BAY
Cape Inscription
Cape Levillain
Dirk Hartog Island
Cape Peron North
Herald Bight
Herald Bluff
Francois Peron Nat Park
Cape Lesueur
Peron Homestead (Historic Site)
Monkey Mia
Quoin Head
Denham Sound
Denham
Faure Island
Dubaut Point
Petit Pt
Gladstone
Cape Bellefin
L'Haridon Bight
Hamelin Pool Marine Nature Reserve
Westernmost point of Australian mainland
Steep Point
Useless Loop (No access)
Goulet Bluff
Mt Direction
Nanga Bay
Cararang Pen
Garden Pt
Zuytdorp Point
Henri Freycinet Harbour
Carrarang
Hamelin
Overlander Roadhouse
Carbla
Tamala
Zuytdorp Cliffs
Coburn
Billabong Roadhouse
Zuytdorp Nature Reserve
Toolonga Nature Reserve
Nerren Nerren
Edaggee
Marron
Long Point
Wahroonga
Meedo
Wooramel
Wooramel Roadhouse
Carlaweelban Hill
Yaringa
NORTH WEST COASTAL HWY
Winderie
Towrana
Pimbee
Carey Downs
Gilroyd
Callytharra Springs
Woodleigh
Yalardy
Talisker
Dairy Creek
Dalgety Downs
Glenburgh
Erong Springs
Coordewandy
Yalbra
Innouendy
Mt Nairn
Byro
Breberle Lake
Curbur
Manfred
Mount Narryer
Muggon
Mt Murchison
Murchison Roadhouse
Meeberrie
Wooleen
Roderick
Boola
Mt Lt
New Forest
Twin Peaks
Murgoo
Sanford River
Yallalong
Billabalong
Burardy
Coolcalalaya
Kalbarri National Park
Ganthéaume Bay
Murchison House
Kalbarri
Red Bluff
Eagle Gorge
Hawks Head Lookout
Shell House
Natural Bridge
Bluff Point
Mary Springs
Yandi
Galena
Woolgorong
Pinegrove
Bullardoo
Wandina
Narloo
Mallee
Wagoe Beach
Kulla Kulla Hill
Ajana
Yuin
Tardie
Half Way Bay
Binnu
Shoal Point
Hutt Lagoon
Wandana Nature Res
Tallering Peak
Marlandy Hill
Gregory
Broken Anchor Bay
Pindaring Rocks
Urawa Nat Res
Gabyon
North Island
Whaleboat Cove
Horrocks
Bowes Hill
Northampton
Yuna
Naraling
East Yuna Nature Res
Tallering
Wurarga
Houtman Abrolhos
Geelvink Channel
Wallabi Group
Nabawa
Nanson
Mullewa
Pindar
Coronation Beach
Drummond Cove
Champion Bay
Greenough River
Barnong
Bunnawarra
Geraldton
Point Moore
Moonyoonooka
Burma Road NR
Sullivan
Tardun
Mellenbye
Easter Group
Cape Burney
Canna
Mangrove Group
Pelsaert Group
Greenough
Walkaway
Gutha
Flat Rocks
Yarragadee
Irwin
Pintharuka
Kadji Kadji
INDIAN OCEAN
Seven Mile Beach
BRAND HWY
Mingenew
Nullewa Lake
Morawa
Dongara
Port Denison
Strawberry Hill
Billeranga Hills
Koolanooka
Yardanogo Nature Res
White Point
Bowgada
Perenjori
Arrino
Cliff Head
Three Springs
Freshwater Point
Illawong
Beekeepers Nature Res
Wotto Nat Res
Yarra Yarra Lakes
Carnamah
Bunjil
Woodada Hill
Winchester
Latham
Coolimba
Eneabba
Tathra Nat Pk
Capamauro Nature Res
Coorow
Maya
Leeman
South Eneabba NR
Lake Logue NR
Alexander Morrison NP
Pinjarrega Nat Res
Green Head
Lesueur Nat Pk
Coomallo Nat Res
Marchagee
Wubin
North Head
Jurien Bay
Drovers Cave NP
Watheroo Nat Park
Salt Lakes
Jurien
Watheroo
Dalwallinu
Badgingarra
Pithara
NORTH
WA 8

0 20 40 60 80 100
kilometres

WA 5

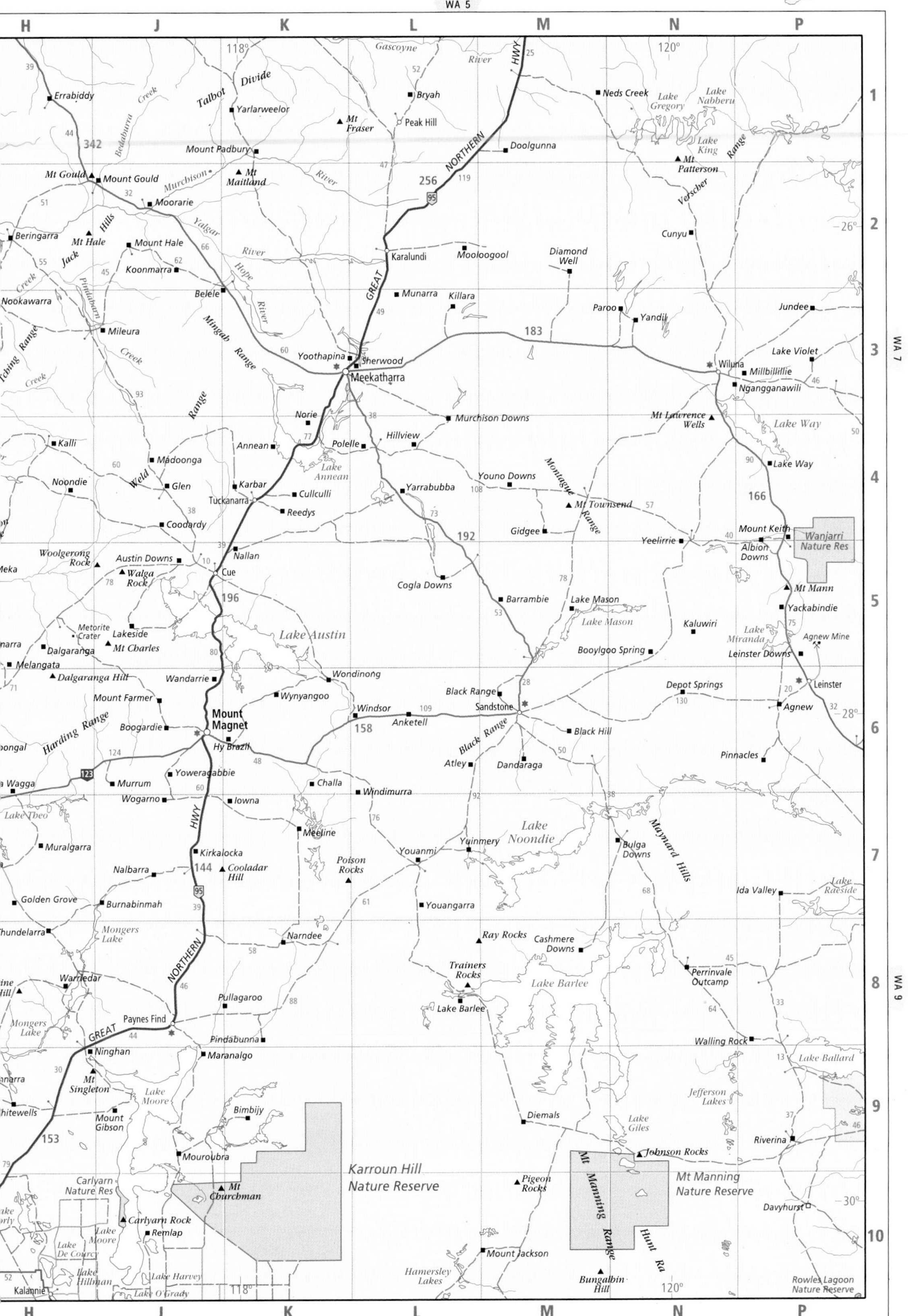

WA 7
WA 9

WA 8

Map 7

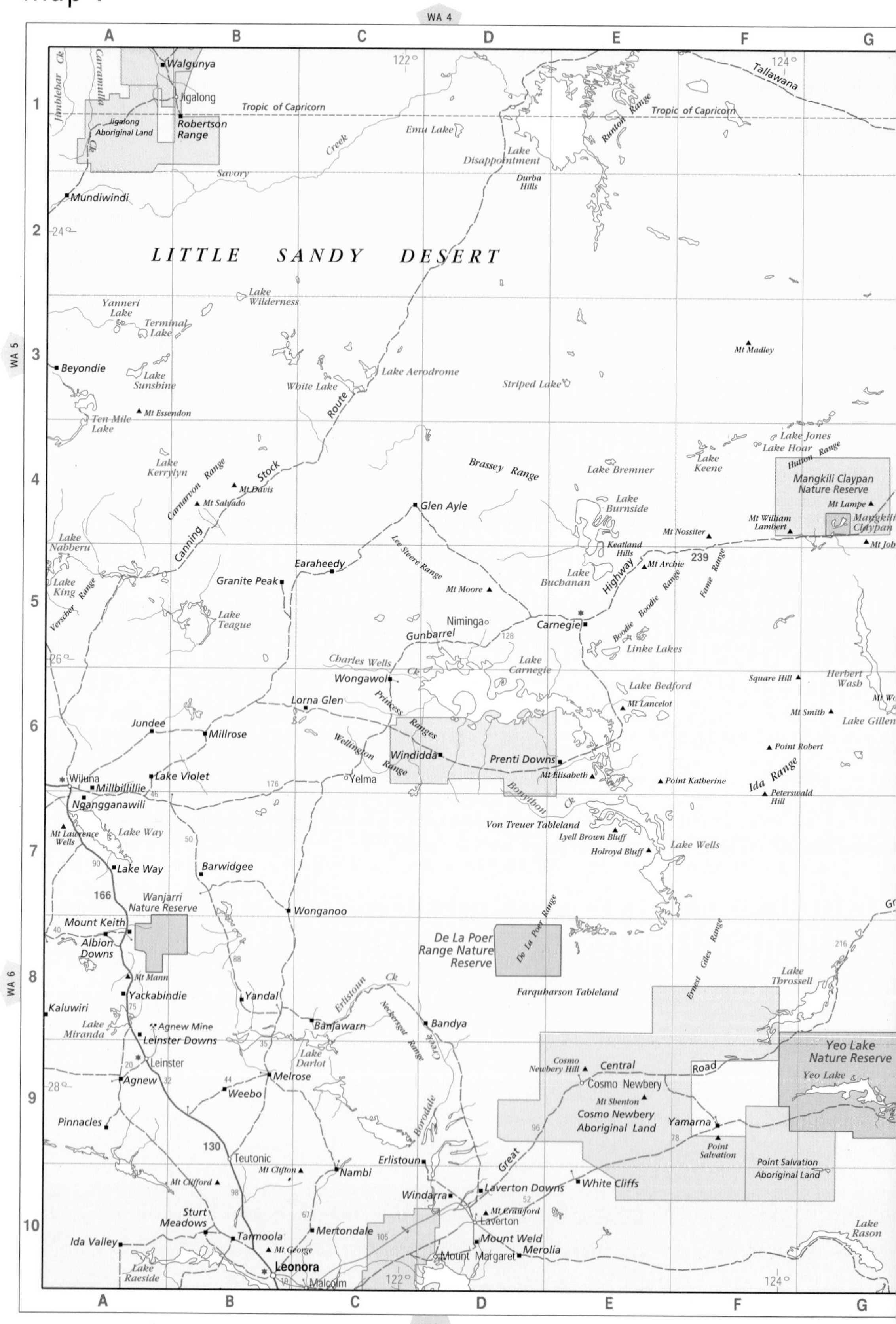

WA 3

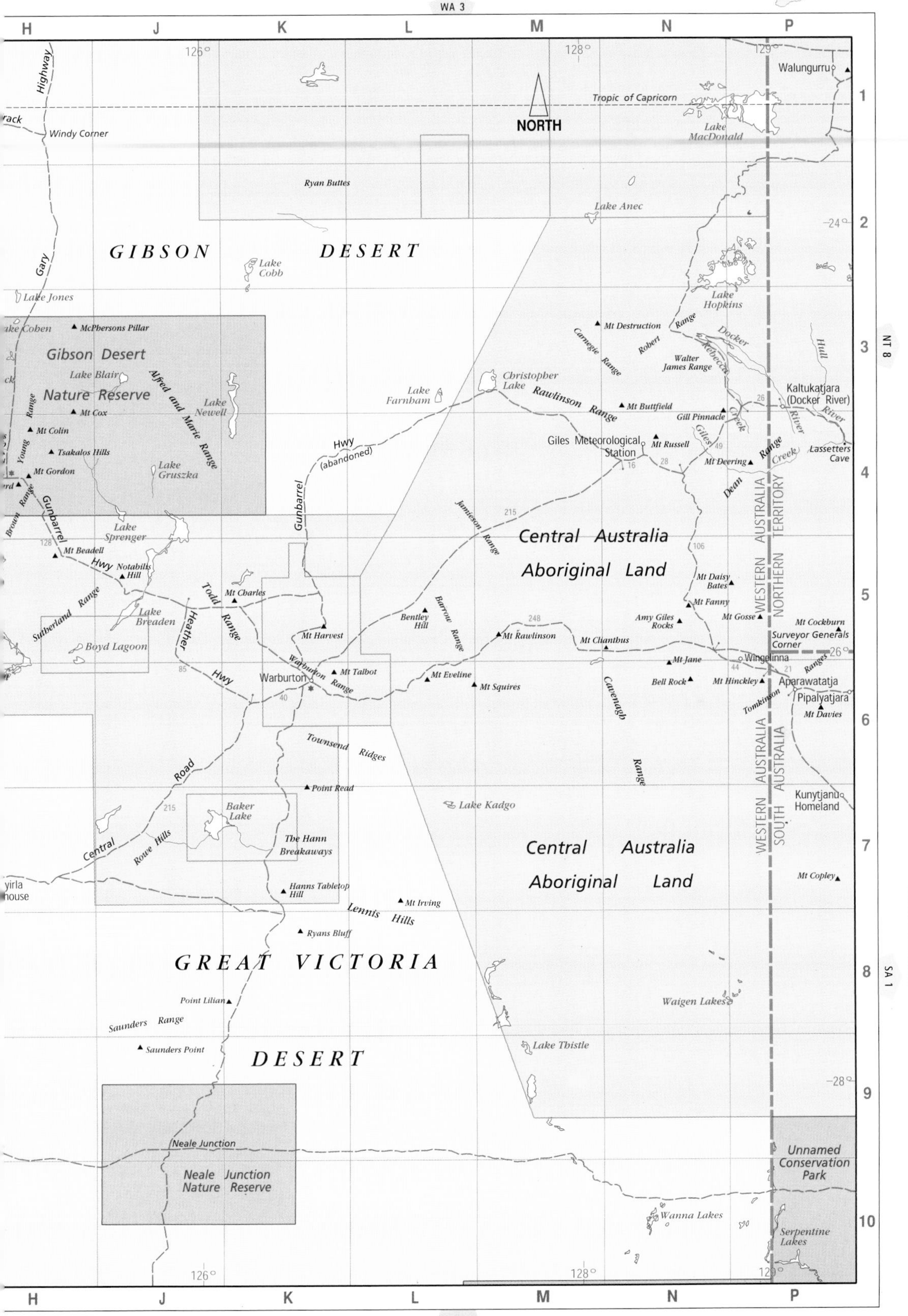

NT 8
SA 1

WA 9

Map 8

WA 6
A
B
C
D
E
F
G
INDIAN
OCEAN
North Head
Jurien Bay
Jurien
Drovers Cave NP
Watheroo Nat Park
Watheroo
Salt Lakes
Dalwallinu
Pithara
Kalannie
Lake De Courcy
Lake Hillman
Lake Moore
Lake Harvey
Lake O'Grady
Southern Beekeepers NR
Badgingarra Nat Park
Badgingarra
Jecundars Park
Bunketch
Beacon
Walki
Ronsard Bay
Thirsty Point
Cervantes
Miling
HWY
Damboring
Kulja
Mollerin Lake
Mollerin Nat Res
Nambung Nat Pk
Pinnacles
Grey
Berkshire Valley
Ballidu
Dandaragan
Moora
Bindi Bindi
Kokardine
Wanagarren Nature Res
Cataby
Walebing
Kondut
Wedge Island
Koojan
Waddington
Piawaning
Yerecoin
Cadoux
Manmanning
Koorda
Narkal
Gabbin
Bencubbin
Welbungin
Chiddarcooping Nature Res
Mukinbudin
Nilgen Nat Res
Namming NR
Gillingarra
Moore River
Wongan Hills
Cowcowing Lakes
Lake Wallambin
Lancelin
Moore River Nat Park
New Norcia
Ejanding
Nalkain
Lake Campion Nature Reserve
Lake Brown
Ledge Point
Karakin Lakes
Mogumber
Calingiri
Konnongorring
Amery
Minnivale
Benjaberring
Wyalkatchem
Trayning
Kununoppin
Nungarin
Lake Campion
Breton Bay
Wannamal
Dowerin
Korrelocking
Yelbeni
Seabird
Boonarring Nat Res
Bolgart
Goomalling
South Trayning
Nukarni
Guilderton
Yeal Nat Res
Gingin
Bindoon
Yorkrakine
Yorkrakine Hill
Burracoppin
Avon Valley Nat Park
Jennacubbine
Merredin
Two Rocks
Yanchep
Yanchep NP
Muchea
Toodyay
Hines Hill
Neerabup NP
Lake Pinjar
Bullsbrook
Northam
GREAT
EASTERN
Cunderdin
Quinns Rocks
Clackline
Grass Valley
Meckering
Tammin
Bungulla
Kellerberrin
Doodlakine
Korbel
Wanneroo
Wooroloo
Wundowie
Marmion Marine Park
Mullaloo
Upper Swan
Gidgegannup
Spencers Brook
Youndegin
Belka
Scarborough
Guildford
Midland
Chidlow
York
Bruce Rock
Rottnest Island
PERTH
Mundaring
The Lakes
Helena River Res
Green Hills
Kwolyin
Erikin
Yalbarrin
Pantapin
Badjaling
Mawson
Shackleton
Pickering Brook
Quairading
Dangin
Ardath
Narembeen
Fremantle
Gosnells
Kelmscott
Karragullen
Woodman Point
Cockburn Sound
Armadale
Mt Dale
BROOKTON
Beverley
Morbining
Babakin
Garden Island
Byford
Kwinana
Baldivis
Rockingham
Mundijong
Monadnocks Cons Park
Yenyening Lakes NR
Bilbarin
Corrigin
Lake Kurrenkutten
Bendering
Shoalwater Islands Marine Park
Warnbro Sound
Becher Point
Serpentine
Jarrahdale
Brookton
Aldersyde
Bulyee
Kunjin
Gorge Rock
Karlgarin
Karnup
Serpentine NP
Serpentine Dam
Mt Cooke
Keysbrook
Tutanning NR
Bullaring
Kondinin Lake
Kondinin
Mandurah
Peel Inlet
North Dandalup
Moorumbine
Pingelly
Newminster
Dawesville
Yunderup
Ravenswood
North Bannister
Cape Bouvard
Yalgorup NP
Pinjarra
Lake Banksiadale
Yealering
Kulin
Harvey Estuary
Bannister
Popanyinning
Yornaning
Cliffordville
Lake Clifton
Coolup
Dwellingup
Wandering
Boddington
Crossman
Wickepin
Jitarning
Preston Beach
Hamel
Waroona
Lane Poole Res
Marradong
Cuballing
Yilliminning
Dudinin
Harrismith
Yalgorup NP
Yarloop
Mt William
Mt Saddleback
Narrogin
Toolibin
Walyurin Rocks
Lake Preston
Quindanning
Williams
Taarblin Lake
Tarin Rock Nat Res
Lake Grace
Harvey
Highbury
Myalup Beach
Binningup Beach
Lane Poole Res
Harris Dam
Culbin
Piesseville
Kukerin
Australind
Koombana Bay
Brunswick Junction
Gundaring
Nippering
Moulyinning
Bunbury
Picton
Collie
Darkan
Arthur River
Wagin
Dumbleyung
Chinocup Nature Res
Dardanup
Wellington Dam
Bowelling
Dellyanine
Quanjallin
Dumbleyung Lake
Lake Chinocup
Geographe Bay
Stratham
Boyanup
Cordering
Norring Lake
Nyabing
Cape Naturaliste
Rocky Point
Tuart Forest NP
Capel
Donnybrook
Moodiarrup
Duranillin
Woodanilling
Moojebing
Kwobrup
Badgebup
Dunsborough
Yallingup
Busselton
Vasse
Kirup
Boscabel
Katanning
Coyrecup
Cape Clairault
Leeuwin-Naturaliste National Park
BUSSELL
VASSE
Balingup
Mardong
Gracetown
Cowaramup
Greenbushes
Boyup Brook
Muradup
Kojonup
Broomehill
Margaret River
Cape Mentelle
Rosa Brook
Gnowangerup
Ongerup
Prevelly
Nannup
Bridgetown
Witchcliffe
Blackwood
Tambellup
Leeuwin Naturaliste NP
Cape Freycinet
Donnelly
ALBANY
Tunney
Borden
Karridale
BROCKMAN
Gordon
Hamelin Bay
Kudardup
Scott Nat Park
Manjimup
Unicup Nature Res
Balicup Lake
Camel Lake NR
Amelup
Cape Hamelin
Hardy Inlet
Augusta
Flinders Bay
Cape Leeuwin
Beedelup Nat Park
Cranbrook
Lake Jasper
Black Pt
MUIRS
Quindinup Nat Res
Frankland
Tenterden
Toolbrunup Peak
Ellen Peak
Stirling Range Nat Park
Eastbrook
Quinninup
Rocky Gully
Kendenup
Yeagarup Beach
Pemberton
Warren Nat Park
Lake Muir
Lake Muir Nature Res
Callcup Hill
Shannon Nat Park
Table Hill
Mount Barker
Kamballup
Warren Beach
Northcliffe
Porongurup
Hassell Nat Pk
D'Entrecasteaux National Park
Mt Frankland National Park
Porongurup NP
Mt Frankland
Mt Lindsay
Narrikup
Point D'Entrecasteaux
Windy Harbour
Redmond
King River
Manypeaks
Quarram Nat Res
Bow Bridge
Walpole
Broke Inlet
Denmark
Wilson Inlet
Youngs
Albany
Two Peoples Bay
Two People Bay Nat Res
Cliffy Head
Nornalup
Frenchman Bay
King George Sound
Point Nuyts
Torbay
Bald Head
Walpole-Nornalup National Park
Point Irwin
Owingup NR
Point Hillier
William Bay
William Bay NP
West Cape Howe NP
West Cape Howe
Torndirrup Nat Pk
NORTH
32°
34°
116°
118°

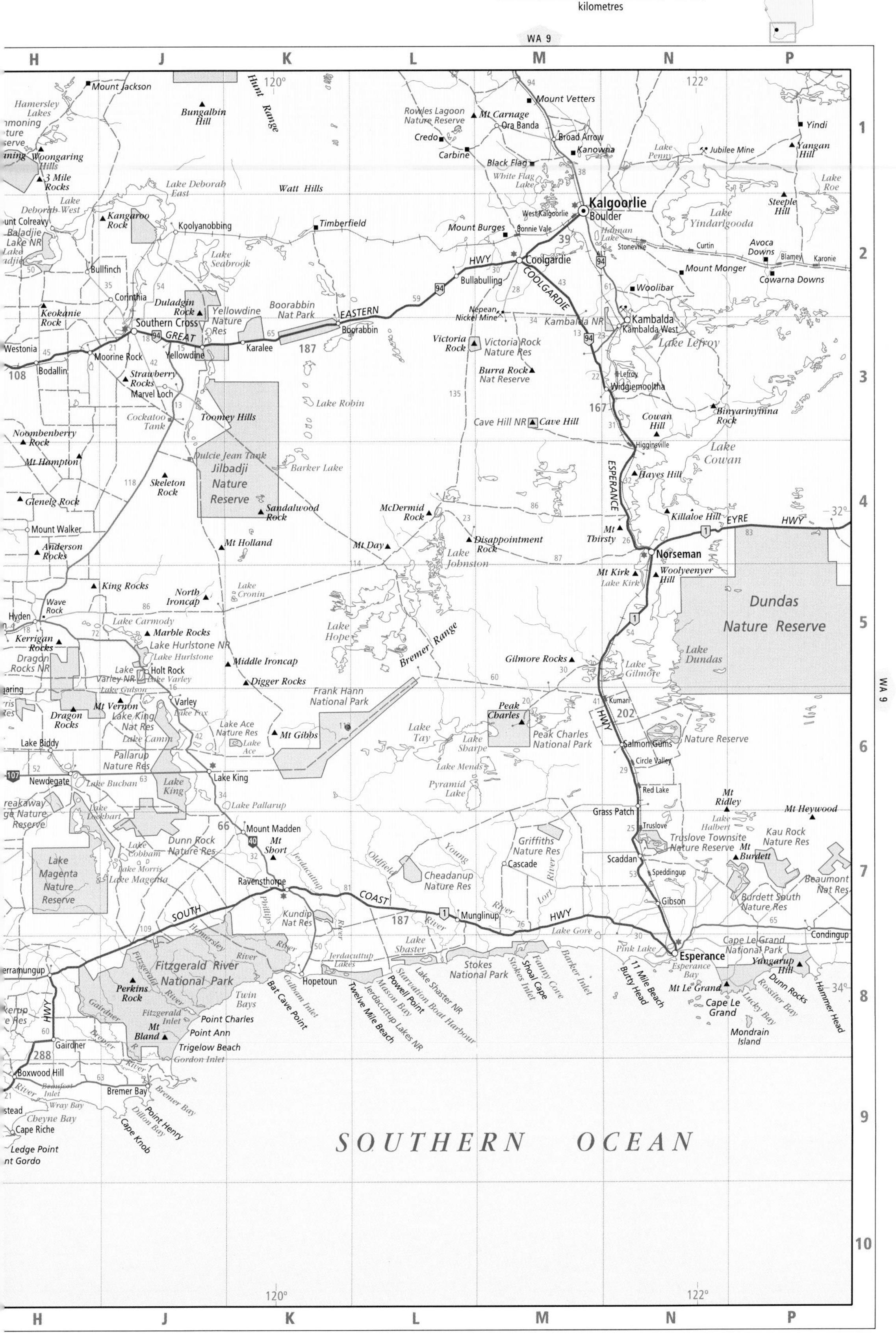

0 20 40 60 80 100
kilometres
WA 9
H J K L M N P
1 2 3 4 5 6 7 8 9 10
120°
122°
Mount Jackson
Hamersley Lakes
Bungalbin Hill
Hunt Range
Mount Vetters
Rowles Lagoon Nature Reserve
Mt Carnage
Ora Banda
Credo
Broad Arrow
Kanowna
Carbine
Black Flag
White Flag Lake
Yindi
Yangan Hill
Jubilee Mine
Lake Penny
Lake Roe
Woongaring Hills
3 Mile Rocks
Lake Deborah East
Watt Hills
Lake Deborah West
Kalgoorlie
Boulder
West Kalgoorlie
Steeple Hill
Lake Yindarlgooda
Kangaroo Rock
Koolyanobbing
Timberfield
Mount Burges
Bonnie Vale
Hannan Lake
Stoneville
Curtin
Avoca Downs
Blamey
Karonie
Baladjie Lake NR
Lake Seabrook
Coolgardie
Mount Monger
Cowarna Downs
Bullfinch
Bullabulling
Woolibar
Corinthia
Duladgin Rock
Yellowdine Nature Res
Boorabbin Nat Park
EASTERN
Nepean Nickel Mine
Kambalda
Kambalda West
Kambalda NR
Keokanie Rock
Southern Cross
GREAT
Boorabbin
Victoria Rock
Victoria Rock Nature Res
Lake Lefroy
Westonia
Moorine Rock
Yellowdine
Karalee
HWY
COOLGARDIE
Bodallin
Burra Rock Nat Res
Lefroy
Widgiemooltha
Strawberry Rocks
Marvel Loch
Lake Robin
Binyarinyinna Rock
Cockatoo Tank
Toomey Hills
Cave Hill NR
Cave Hill
Cowan Hill
Noombenberry Rock
Higginsville
Lake Cowan
Mt Hampton
Dulcie Jean Tank
Barker Lake
ESPERANCE
Hayes Hill
Jilbadji Nature Reserve
Skeleton Rock
Glenelg Rock
Sandalwood Rock
McDermid Rock
Killaloe Hill
EYRE
Mount Walker
Mt Holland
Disappointment Rock
Mt Thirsty
Norseman
Anderson Rocks
Mt Day
Lake Johnston
Mt Kirk
Lake Kirk
Woolyeenyer Hill
King Rocks
North Ironcap
Lake Cronin
Dundas Nature Reserve
Wave Rock
Hyden
Lake Carmody
Lake Hope
Bremer Range
Marble Rocks
Kerrigan Rocks
Lake Hurlstone NR
Lake Hurlstone
Lake Dundas
Dragon Rocks NR
Middle Ironcap
Gilmore Rocks
Lake Gilmore
Lake Varley NR
Holt Rock
Lake Varley
Digger Rocks
Lake Gulson
Frank Hann National Park
Varley
Mt Vernon
Lake Fox
Kumari
Dragon Rocks
Lake King Nat Res
Lake Ace Nature Res
Lake Ace
Mt Gibbs
Peak Charles
Lake Tay
Lake Sharpe
Peak Charles National Park
Lake Camm
Lake Biddy
Salmon Gums
Nature Reserve
Pallarup Nature Res
Circle Valley
Lake Mends
Newdegate
Lake Bucban
Lake King
Pyramid Lake
Red Lake
Mt Ridley
Breakaway Nature Reserve
Lake Lockhart
Lake Pallarup
Grass Patch
Mt Heywood
Lake Halbert
Mount Madden
Truslove
Truslove Townsite Nature Reserve
Kau Rock Nature Res
Dunn Rock Nature Res
Mt Short
Griffiths Nature Res
Lake Magenta Nature Reserve
Lake Cobham
Young
Mt Burdett
Lake Morris
Lake Magenta
Oldfield
Cascade
Scaddan
Jerdacuttup
Cheadanup Nature Res
Speddingup
Beaumont Nat Res
Ravensthorpe
Phillips
Lort
Gibson
Burdett South Nature Res
COAST
SOUTH
Kundip Nat Res
Munglinup
Condingup
Lake Gore
Hamersley
Lake Shaster
Pink Lake
Cape Le Grand National Park
Esperance
Esperance Bay
Yangarup Hill
Fitzgerald River National Park
Jerdacuttup Lakes
Stokes National Park
Ferramungup
Hopetoun
Perkins Rock
Twin Bays
Culham Inlet
Bat Cave Point
Lake Shaster NR
Starvation Boat Harbour
Shoal Cape
Stokes Inlet
Fanny Cove
Barker Inlet
11 Mile Beach
Butty Head
Mt Le Grand
Cape Le Grand
Dunn Rocks
Rossiter Bay
Lucky Bay
Hammer Head
Mondrain Island
Powell Point
Mason Bay
Jerdacuttup Lakes NR
Twelve Mile Beach
Gardner
Fitzgerald Inlet
Point Charles
Point Ann
Mt Bland
Trigelow Beach
Gordon Inlet
Gairdner
Boxwood Hill
Bremer Bay
Beaufort Inlet
Wray Bay
Stead
Cheyne Bay
Cape Riche
Point Henry
Dillon Bay
Cape Knob
Ledge Point
Point Gordo
SOUTHERN OCEAN
WA

Map 9

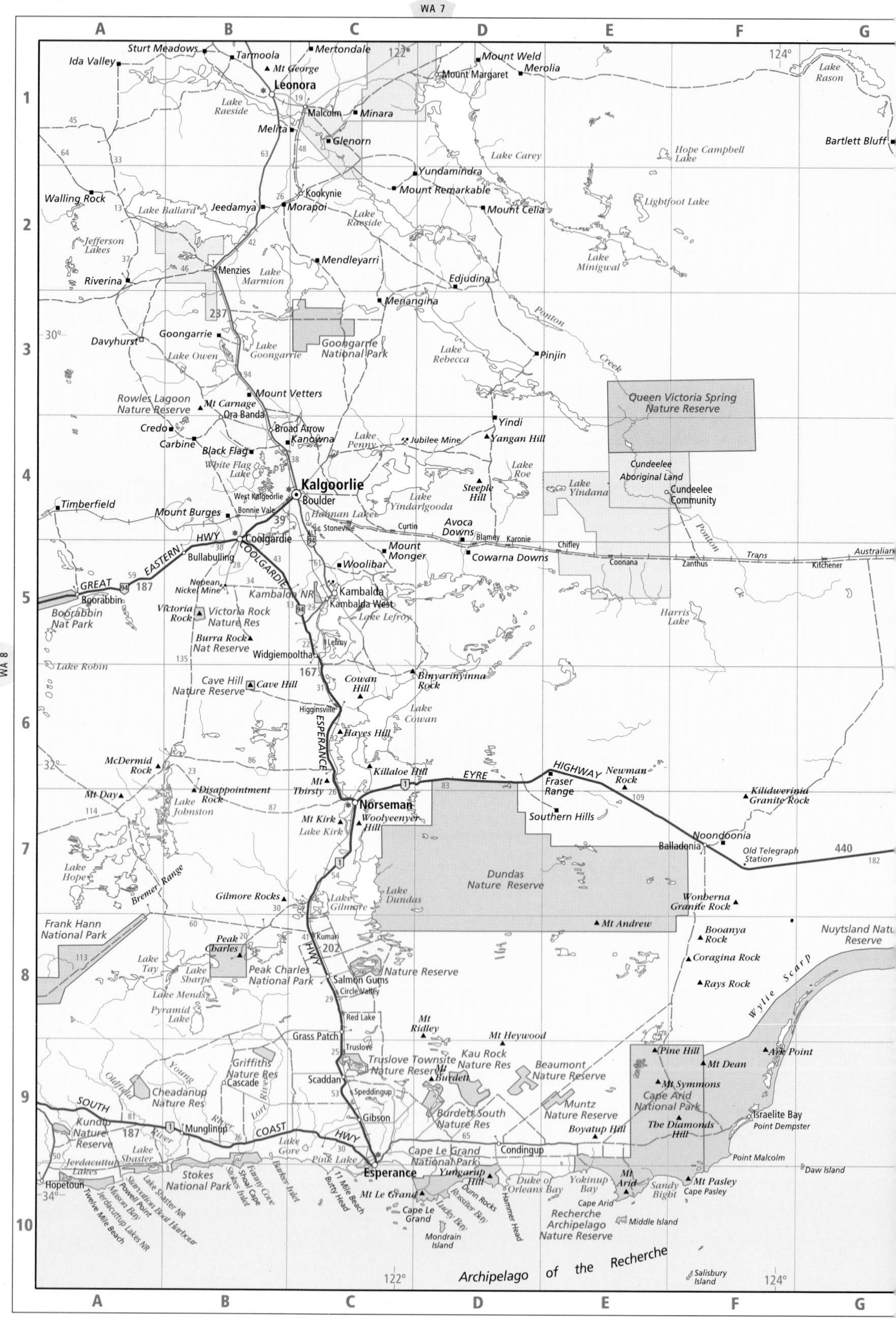
WA 7
WA 8
Leonora
Kalgoorlie
Boulder
Coolgardie
Norseman
Esperance
Menzies
Queen Victoria Spring Nature Reserve
Dundas Nature Reserve
Cape Arid National Park
Peak Charles National Park
Stokes National Park
Frank Hann National Park
Goongarrie National Park
Recherche Archipelago Nature Reserve
Archipelago of the Recherche
Lake Carey
Lake Rason
Lake Raeside
Lake Ballard
Lake Rebecca
Lake Cowan
Lake Lefroy
Lake Dundas
Wylie Scarp
Israelite Bay
Balladonia
Fraser Range
Eyre Highway
Great Eastern Hwy
Coolgardie Esperance Hwy
South Coast Hwy
Trans Australian

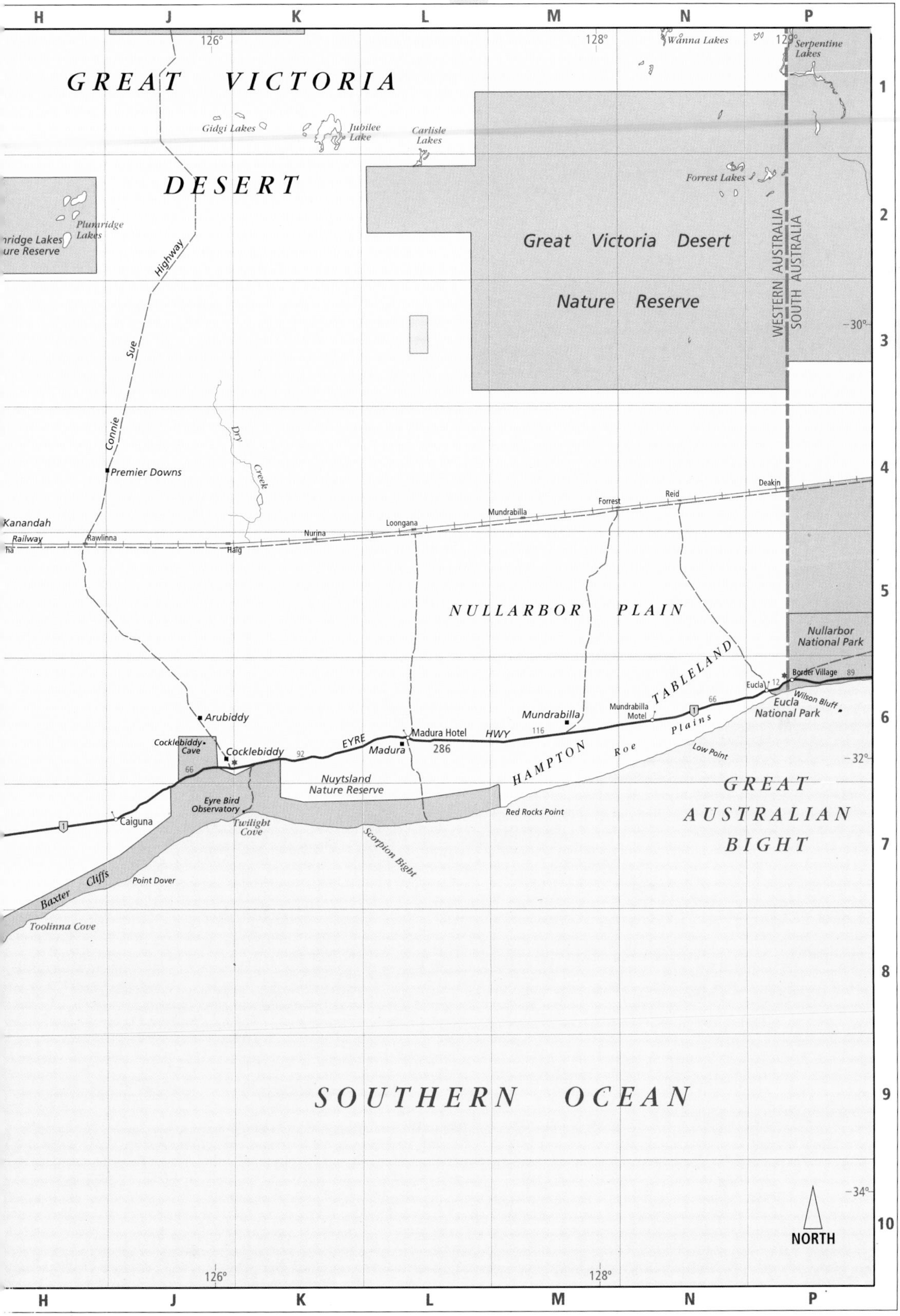

WA 7

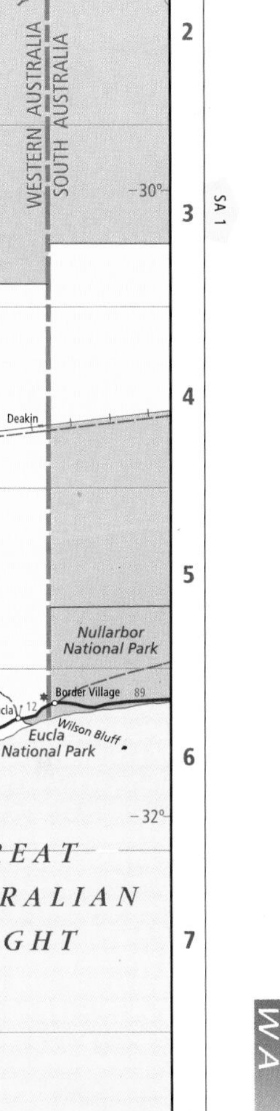
0 20 40 60 80 100
kilometres
H J K L M N P
126° 128° 129°
GREAT VICTORIA DESERT
Gidgi Lakes
Jubilee Lake
Carlisle Lakes
Wanna Lakes
Serpentine Lakes
Forrest Lakes
Plumridge Lakes
Great Victoria Desert Nature Reserve
WESTERN AUSTRALIA
SOUTH AUSTRALIA
30°
32°
34°
Connie Sue Highway
Dry Creek
Premier Downs
Kanandah
Railway
Rawlinna
Haig
Nurina
Loongana
Mundrabilla
Forrest
Reid
Deakin
NULLARBOR PLAIN
Nullarbor National Park
TABLELAND
Border Village
89
Eucla
12
Wilson Bluff
Eucla National Park
66
Mundrabilla Motel
Mundrabilla
Roe Plains
Low Point
Arubiddy
Cocklebiddy Cave
Cocklebiddy
92
EYRE HWY
Madura Hotel
Madura
286
116
HAMPTON
Nuytsland Nature Reserve
Red Rocks Point
GREAT AUSTRALIAN BIGHT
Eyre Bird Observatory
Twilight Cove
Caiguna
1
Scorpion Bight
Baxter Cliffs
Point Dover
Toolinna Cove
SOUTHERN OCEAN
NORTH
1 2 3 4 5 6 7 8 9 10

SA 1

Northern Territory

The Northern Territory, big and sparsely populated, is a region of many unique natural wonders, equally as spectacular as the world's best scenic locations. Still, barely 2 per cent of land within the 1 346 200 sq km of the Northern Territory is reserved as national parks. These protected areas reflect a vibrant diversity of landscape. There are the verdant wetlands of the far north, the semi-arid woodland forests and grassy plains of the Barkly Tableland and the dry arid zone of the south where the red sand dunes are interspersed with mountain ranges and rocky outcrops. Take time to explore and enjoy this ancient land. It will be impossible to see it all on one holiday, so choose your destinations carefully and make the most of your time in the magnificent north.

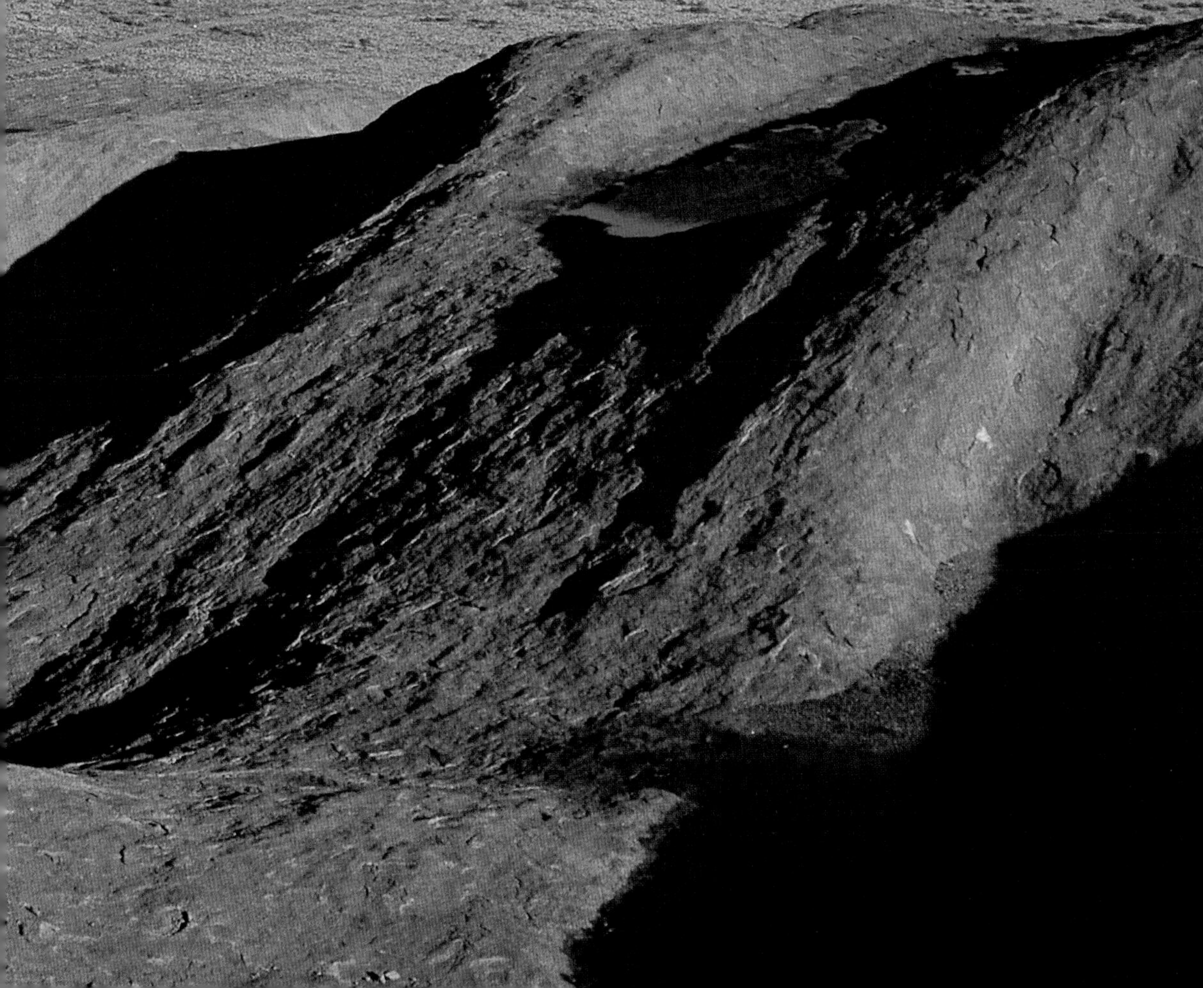

Kakadu National Park

One of this country's finest national and natural treasures is Kakadu National Park, which is also Australia's biggest national park. Towering over the park's wetlands is the huge 500-km long Arnhem Land escarpment, and everywhere you look in this ancient landscape you are left with a feeling of majesty and awe. Its natural geological features include interesting rock formations, huge waterways, quiet and peaceful streams, towering cliffs, spectacular waterfalls and cool lagoons.

World-Heritage-Listed Kakadu National Park is the gateway to Arnhemland. Almost 20 000 square kilometres in size (the same size as Denmark or Ireland), the park is full of spectacular scenery including pristine waterfalls.

fact file

WHERE: 147 km south-east of Darwin along the Stuart and Arnhem Highways, and 149 km north-east of Katherine Map: NT 2 D6

WHEN: April to October

WHY: Scenic gorges, waterfalls, wetlands, bushwalking, fishing, photography, birdwatching, Aboriginal art, camping

SIZE: 19 804 sq km

RANGER: Bowali Visitor Centre, open daily 8 a.m. to 5 p.m., P.O. Box 71, Jabiru, NT 0886 (08) 8938 1121

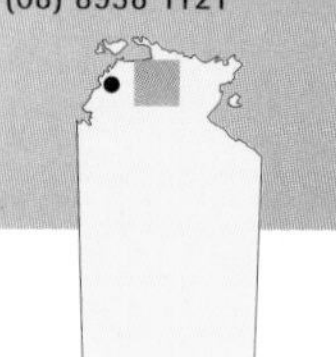

As well as Kakadu's unique geology, its diverse wildlife and extensive plant life all add up to a truly magnificent area. Kakadu also boasts some of the country's best Aboriginal rock art.

Proclaimed in 1979, the value of Kakadu's treasures is also reflected in the park's World Heritage listing, which occurred in 1981. The park was subsequently extended in various stages and now occupies 19 804 sq km.

A large portion of this wonderful park is owned by Australian Aboriginals (the Gagudju Association) who have maintained strong personal and spiritual links with these traditional lands for at least 60 000 years. The park is leased back to the Commonwealth and is managed by a specially selected board of management where the traditional owners are represented. Within the park boundaries are a couple of mineral leases and these have been the cause of quite a lot of controversy over recent times.

Today Kakadu National Park is drawing visitors from around Australia and, indeed, from all over the world, at a rate of well over 220 000 people every year, and the number is continually growing. Most come in the Top End's dry season, from April to October, when the climate is almost perfect for exploring and taking in all of the park's attractions.

For those few who come during the wet season, some of the rewards on offer are even more spectacular—the waterfalls are flowing at full strength, the many billabongs are full, and the area is lush and green everywhere. Roads to some of the more remote attractions may, however, be flooded and impassable during this time of year.

In contrast, by late in the dry season much of the bushland is tinder dry; grass fires, lit in the park as part of its management control system, have blackened much of the bushland area.

Activities

There are some splendid bushwalks leading off from car parks (as well as other cross-country treks) usually incorporating one of the park's many attractions, such as rock art, waterfalls, billabongs, fishing spots and swimming holes, to name a few.

The many indigenous art sites found in the park on cliffs, rock faces and in large natural rock shelters record Aboriginal history, culture and

Right: *The waterways in Kakadu, like this one near Jabiru, are lush and full during the wet season, when up to 1300 mm of rain falls on the region.*

beliefs. They also record the visits of Macassans who arrived from the north to fish, gather trepangs (sea cucumbers) and search for pearls. Visits by the Dutch, and later the British, are shown, and their ships, axes and firearms all feature in Kakadu's ochre art galleries.

Kakadu's Aboriginal rock art is of world significance and Ubirr Rock has been added in its own right to the World Heritage listing for its cultural, anthropological and archaeological value. Ubirr Rock, together with the other important rock art sites in the park at Nourlangie, Nanguluwur and Anbangbang, give the whole area a feeling of the ancestral power of the land unmatched anywhere else in the country.

Nature lovers will be enthralled by the 300 or more species of birds, including egrets, jabirus and brolgas, as well as many grass and bushland species. Wallabies, euros, wild black pigs, and even the occasional wild Timor pony are also found in the park, as are crocodiles.

To see and enjoy the park properly, allow at least 4 or 5 days (even more, depending on your personal interests). Insect repellent for flies and mosquitoes, a hat and good comfortable walking gear, fishing lines and lures are needed for your camping stay. The following are some of the park's most interesting and truly picturesque areas.

Some Aboriginal rock art sites in the Northern Territory are thought to be over 18 000 years old, and it is estimated that there are some 7000 art sites in Kakadu National Park alone.

Jabiru

This centre is Kakadu's residential hub. Fuel, supplies, a post office, supermarket, a wide range of services and accommodation, including the famous Gagudju Crocodile Hotel are all found here.

Scenic flights over Kakadu can also be arranged in Jabiru.

Ubirr Rock (on the left) is a popular site for day-trippers. It features rock art and living shelters, and from the top there is a great view of the surrounding floodplains and Arnhem Land.

Bowali Visitor Centre and Park Headquarters

Located on the edge of town on the Kakadu Highway, this is certainly worth a visit. Everything you need to know about the park is here, making this an ideal starting place for your Kakadu visit.

Ubirr

Ubirr is just 3 km north of the Border Store (which sells fuel and supplies) and some 40 km from Jabiru. This is one of the main accessible rock art sites in the park. A 1-km, easy walking circuit trail leads from the car park, while the main art site is also accessible by wheelchair.

There are various art styles, including the stick-like Mimi figures, some of which are estimated to be up to 20 000 years old, but the more recent, dramatic, x-ray style is the most striking.

Climb to the top of the rocky escarpment for splendid views over the Kakadu countryside, the nearby billabongs of the Arnhem wetlands and the huge Arnhem Land. The view from here, particularly around sunset, is quite stunning.

Nourlangie Rock

About 19 km south of the visitor centre is Nourlangie Rock, which is an art site of great significance to the traditional

owners. The main circuit trail of 1.5 km is a relatively easy stroll lasting about 1 hour—and most of it is accessible by wheelchair. The main galleries here include some excellent artwork, with signboards explaining the figures and the stories behind them. Namarrgon, the Lightning Man, is one of the gallery's most impressive figures.

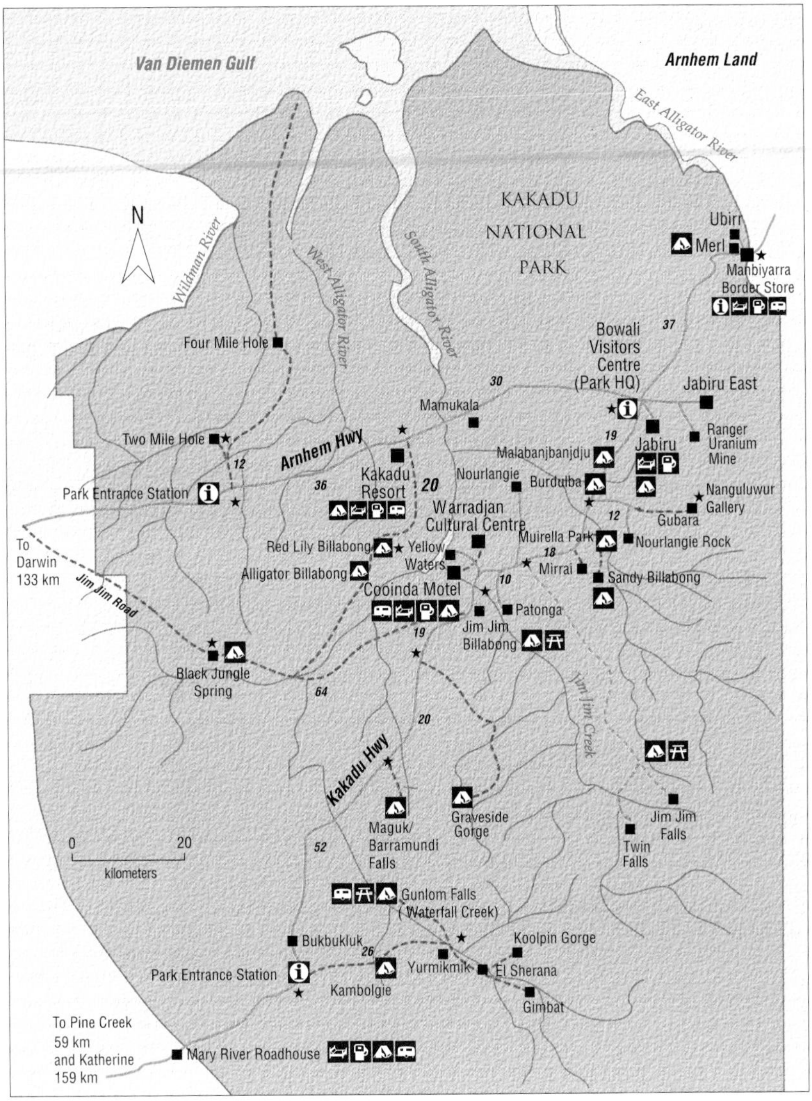

Nanguluwur Gallery Walk

This relatively easy, 3.4-km return walk (allow 2 hours) passes through flat and open woodlands on the western side of Nourlangie Rock and leads to one of the most interesting rock art sites in Kakadu. Its walls are like pages in a living history book, illustrating aspects of the lives of local Australian Aboriginal people from ancient times to the modern era.

Jim Jim Falls and Twin Falls

These falls are spectacular in the wet season when water thunders over the top of the Arnhem escarpment and plummets 200 m to the creek below. The falls are usually reduced to not much more than a trickle as the dry season progresses. Camping is allowed at Jim Jim where toilets, barbecues and tables are provided.

There are 300-plus native bird species that inhabit Kakadu National Park, including the coastal-dwelling rufous-banded honeyeater (Conopophila albogularis).

Commercial boat tours operate year-round on Yellow Waters; fishing and crocodile spotting are also popular in this wetland region.

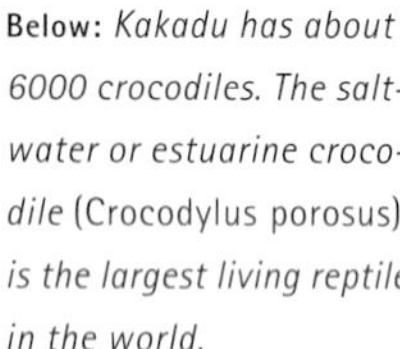

Below: *Kakadu has about 6000 crocodiles. The saltwater or estuarine crocodile* (Crocodylus porosus) *is the largest living reptile in the world.*

warning

Dangerous estuarine, or saltwater, crocodiles inhabit a number of the Kakadu waterways. Do not go into, and be very careful near, the water in these areas—look out for the crocodile warning signs. Many of the most popular swimming holes in the park are safe, but if in doubt, check with the local rangers.

For a great day trip only (as there is no camping allowed), a visit to the nearby Twin Falls is thoroughly recommended. On reaching the end of the trail at one of the creek's white sandy beaches, it's then into the water—take your inflatable mattress for a great paddle (about 1 km) towards the falls.

Yellow Waters

Located virtually in the centre of the park, Yellow Waters is a magnificent billabong on the South Alligator River. A boardwalk along the edge of this picturesque waterway is a must for birdwatchers, while boat cruises, especially at sunrise and sunset, are always popular. Crocodile spotting and fishing for prize barramundi are also highlights.

Camping is not allowed here, but situated just 1 km away is the Gagudju Cooinda Lodge which has a motel, caravan sites and camping facilities. Also located here is the Warradjan Aboriginal Cultural Centre, which provides a good insight into the local culture.

Barramundi Falls (Maguk)

Further south in Kakadu National Park, Barramundi Falls is reached by a 12-km 4WD track leading to a small waterfall, which tumbles down through the sandstone escarpment into a large, clear pool at the bottom. There are some beautiful swimming spots with sandy beaches along the walking track to the falls.

Gunlom Falls

Previously known as the UDP Falls, the Gunlom Falls are in the southern section of the park, 37 km off the main Kakadu Highway. The access road leads to a grassed picnic area, with the falls and the large, sandy-bottomed plunge pool only around 100 m away. The walking trail to the falls is suitable for wheelchair access. The Gunlom Falls are at their best when they are in flood.

Park Access

There's good access to Kakadu National Park, both from Darwin and from the south at Pine Creek. Both of the access routes are good, sealed, all-year-round roads which will only be closed in the most extreme weather conditions. An entry fee applies and your permit is valid for 14 days (or multiple entries to the park within the 14-day period).

Check with the rangers about road conditions within the park–some are accessible by 4WD only.

Camping

Kakadu offers some really superb camping experiences–often near waterfalls, billabongs, or with rocky escarpment outlooks. They range from caravan parks (including those at Jabiru, Cooinda and Kakadu Holiday Village), to several formal camping areas at Merl (near Ubirr), Muirella Park (between Jabiru and Yellow Waters), Mardugal (near Yellow Waters) and at Gunlom Falls. These areas are all equipped with showers, flushing toilets and water, and have adequate facilities for the disabled. Note that a camping fee is charged at these spots.

Throughout the park there are a number of other, less developed, tent camping areas, most with toilets and barbecues, but not showers. There are some in more remote locations with no facilities at all.

In addition to camp sites there are picnic areas located near many of the main attractions. Hotel or motel accommodation is available at Jabiru, Cooinda and at the Kakadu Holiday Village near the South Alligator River.

tourist info

Jabiru Tourist Centre
(08) 8979 2548 for tours

Aurora Kakadu Resort
(08) 8979 0166 for tours to all parts of the park

Twisted brown trunk of the tree Allosyncarpia ternata. *This tree occupies a variety of habitats including monsoon rainforest, upland savannah and rocky areas of the Arnhem Land Plateau.*

Below: *Great egrets* (Ardea alba) *were once hunted for the long plumes they develop in the breeding season, which were used to decorate ladies' hats.*

Gregory National Park

Measuring 1 050 000 ha, Gregory National Park is the Northern Territory's second-largest park after Kakadu. The Territory's largest waterway, the mighty Victoria River has, over millions of years, created a sweeping vista of towering red escarpments, majestic cliffs and hidden gorges with most of it protected within the park. The explorer Augustus Charles Gregory was the first European to explore the area during 1855 and his reports brought pioneer cattlemen into the Victoria River region.

fact file

WHERE: 160 km south-west of Katherine on the Victoria Highway
Map: NT 4 D5

WHEN: May to September

WHY: Rugged scenery, history, excellent bush-walks and camping, remote 4WD tracks

SIZE: 1 050 000 ha

RANGER: Timber Creek (08) 8975 0888, Bullita (08) 8975 0833 or Katherine Region Tourist Association (08) 8972 2650

Activities

Some of the best gorges and escarpments can be found off the main road near the Victoria River Crossing. The Escarpment Walk, and Joe's Creek Walk, the latter with hundreds of tall *Livistona* palms along the way, are particularly appealing. Australian Aboriginal art is also found on cliff faces along the trail. This is an easy to moderate walk, and you should allow 1 hour for the return trip.

The Kuwang Lookout, 57 km west of the crossing, is also worth visiting, and overlooks the surrounding countryside and Stokes Range.

An excellent boat ramp is easily accessible at Big Horse Creek and the river offers great fishing for barramundi. A well-established camping area with pit toilets is also located here.

Access further into the park to the old Bullita Homestead, which is 41 km off the highway from the turn-off 15 km from Timber Creek, is along a gravel track which, with care, can be covered in a conventional vehicle. The homestead has been restored and opened to visitors and is worth seeing.

Livistona humilis *is a small, single-trunked fan palm tree that grows to 4–6 metres tall. It is found only in the far north of the Northern Territory.*

Along the way a turn-off to the right leads to Limestone Gorge—an area of strange, grey dolomite towers and many fine examples of odd-looking boab trees. From the car park, there's an interesting 2-km circuit walk, the Limestone Ridge Trail, which leads through the limestone outcrops and flat savannah grasslands.

Camping areas with barbecues and toilets are located at Limestone Gorge and near the homestead.

Further into Gregory National Park is strictly 4WD country. There are three old stock routes—Bullita, Humbert and Wickham Tracks—that have an excellent set of trek notes and historic information available at the beginning of the tracks. It is necessary to sign an 'intentions book' detailing your vehicle, occupants and travel plans, and you also need to sign off at the end of the track. These old trails are particularly remote and

tourist info

Fishing and crocodile-spotting trips on the Victoria River are available by phoning:
Barra Fishing Safaris
(08) 8975 0688
Victoria River Roadhouse
(08) 8975 0744

quite rough and challenging in parts. For the adventurous they offer some great 4WD experiences, splendid scenery and lovely, remote camp sites beside rivers and waterholes along the way. There are no facilities at all along any of these 4WD tracks, so it is important to make sure you carry enough water and vehicle spares on these tracks.

Access

The best access to Gregory National Park is via the Victoria Highway from Katherine in the east or Kununurra in the west. A dirt road route from Top Springs and Victoria River Downs is a spectacular and little-used route that takes in Jasper Gorge.

All roads in the area, including the Victoria Highway, may be closed after heavy rains, particularly during the summer wet season.

Victoria River in Gregory National Park is the Northern Territory's largest waterway, and can easily be explored on a boat tour.

The nutwood tree (Terminalia arostrata) *is found only in the Top End. The Northern Territory national parks system nurtures many species of plants not seen elsewhere.*

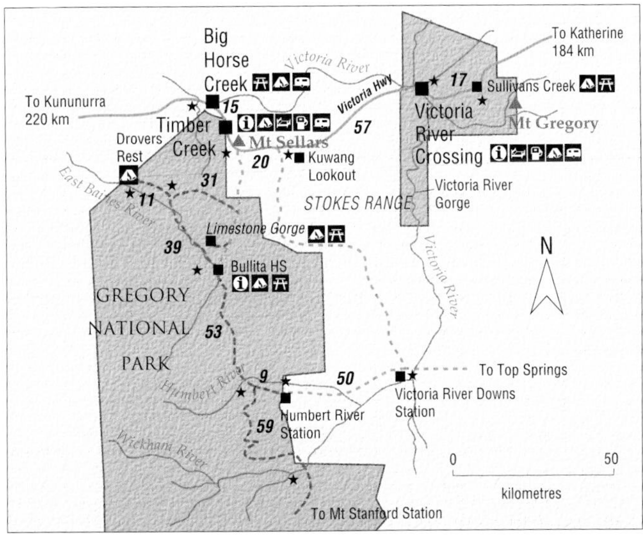

NT

Uluru–Kata Tjuta National Park

Uluru (Ayers Rock) and Kata Tjuta (the Olgas) are mystical, mysterious symbols in the heart of the Australian continent and are revered by both the Australian Aboriginal and European Australian cultures. While Uluru stands majestically some 340 metres above the surrounding plain, Kata Tjuta rises to 600 metres; both these land forms are remnants of a 100-million-year-old landscape.

fact file

WHERE: 465 km southwest of Alice Springs along the Stuart Highway and Lasseter Highway Map: NT 8 F8

WHEN: Beginning of April to end of October

WHY: Uluru (Ayers Rock): second largest monolith in the world, Australian Aboriginal culture, Kata Tjuta (the Olgas), stunning views, walking trails

SIZE: 132 566 ha

RANGER: National Park headquarters: (08) 8956 1100

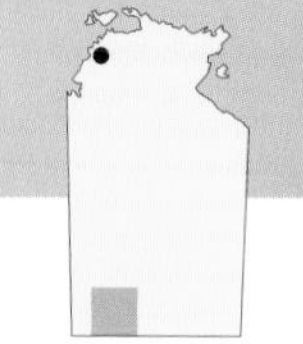

In the Past

The Australian Aboriginal people of this region, who have lived here for many generations, call themselves by the collective name of Anangu ('we people') and are made up of three main groups: the Yankunytjatjara, the Pitjantjatjara and the Ngaanyatjara.

The first European explorer to visit this area was Ernest Giles, who in 1872 named Mount Olga; W. E. Gosse arrived in 1873 and named Ayers Rock.

During the early part of the 1930s pastoral activity and mining exploration commenced, with tourism starting in the late 1940s. By the middle of the 1970s over 50 000 visitors a year were tramping over and around Uluru.

In 1985, after a long legal battle, the Anangu and the Uluru–Kata Tjuta Land Trust accepted the freehold title to their lands, which was then leased back to the Commonwealth Government as a national park. The park is now carefully managed on a co-operative basis with the traditional owners having a majority representation on the board.

In 1987 the United Nations inscribed Uluru–Kata Tjuta National Park onto the World Heritage List and it is now one of 12 Australian Biosphere Reserves.

Activities

It is important to note that both Uluru and Kata Tjuta are areas of special significance to Australian Aboriginal people and a number of sacred sites exist. When walking around both places the visitor will see signs which clearly mark where access is closed to the public.

For safety and cultural reasons the Anangu prefer that visitors do not climb up the rock, but those that do should remember that it is very steep and they should only climb along the route with the safety chain. The journey is 1.6 km return and should take about 2 hours.

Ernest Giles described Kata Tjuta's domes as 'round stones ... mixed as plums in a pudding and set in vast and rounded shapes upon the ground'.

Left: *Uluru is Australia's second-largest monolith and has long carried the status of a national icon. The Aboriginal people of this area prefer that visitors do not climb Uluru due to cultural reasons.*

Desert grevillea (Grevillea eriostachya) *has a wide geographic range across central and western Australia. Also known as yellow flame grevillea, it is in flower here, at the base of Uluru.*

Many of the geographic features of Uluru mark the ancient beliefs of the Australian Aboriginal people and these features may be seen by the visitor while walking along the circular path around Uluru. This walk is about 9-km long and should take around 4 hours. At Kata Tjuta, the Valley of the Winds Walk is 6 km (allow 3 hours return), while the Olga Gorge Walk is shorter, about 2 km and 1 hour return.

Over 400 species of plant life, 22 species of mammals, 150 different bird groups and many reptiles and frogs have been recorded, but visitors are likely to see only a fraction of these.

There are many tours departing from the Ayers Rock Resort. For more information contact the Visitor Centre. There are also more than 50 tour operators conducting business out of Alice Springs, so you should find something to suit you.

While the opportunity for photography is great, especially at sunrise and at sunset, the Anangu people do not like to be photographed. They ask that visitors do not film them or take photographs of their important spiritual areas.

Access and Accommodation

Major airlines offer flights to Yulara.

The 465-km drive from Alice Springs is along the sealed Stuart and Lasseter Highways and all the roads within the park are sealed.

There are no camping facilities or other accommodation within Uluru–Kata Tjuta National Park itself. The resort at Yulara has a range of accommodation from luxury to budget, as well as camping and supply facilities.

tourist info

Uluru–Kata Tjuta Cultural Centre
(08) 8956 1128

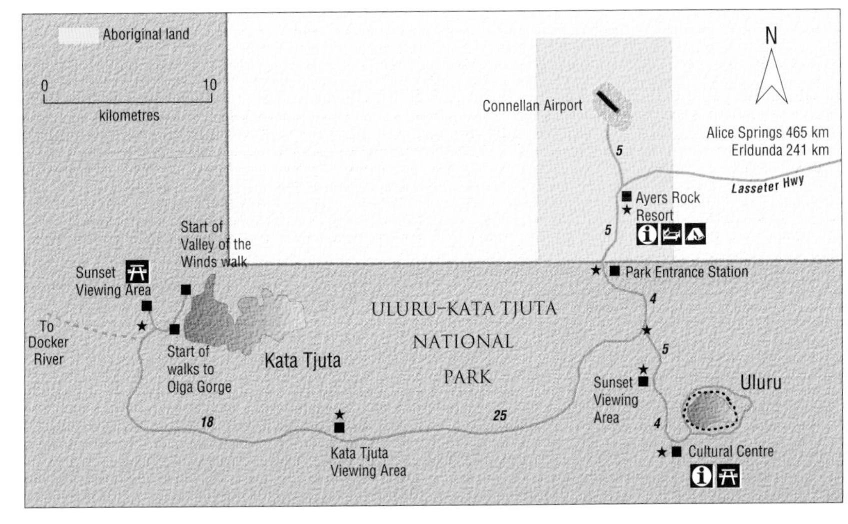

Litchfield National Park

Situated in the Top End, Litchfield National Park is thought by some people to be more spectacular than Kakadu! The park offers some of the most magnificent and diverse landscapes anywhere in the Northern Territory.

Some of the interesting features of Litchfield National Park include these intriguing magnetic termite mounds, as well as pockets of rainforest.

fact file

WHERE: 130 km from Darwin, about 2 hours drive, via Batchelor Map: NT 1 E6

WHEN: April to October

WHY: Tropical wilderness, waterfalls, bushwalks, natural mountain swimming pools, Lost City, large termite mounds, camping

SIZE: 143 000 ha

RANGER: Batchelor (08) 8976 0282

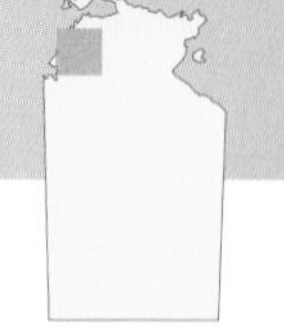

Dry woodlands and forests dominate the huge sandstone plateau which forms the heart of the park. Close to the plateau escarpment, springs give rise to creeks which tumble through rapids before cascading as waterfalls into deep pools in the rainforest valleys below. The most spectacular of these are Wangi, Florence, Tjaynera and Tolmer Falls.

Wangi Falls is a favourite of many visitors, as it allows camping within a 100-m stroll of a lovely, sandy pool set at the foot of the falls.

One of the most popular activities in Litchfield National Park is bushwalking. These walks range from flat and easy to some quite strenuous trails which often lead to crystal clear pools in which to cool off, refresh and relax.

Evidence of early pastoralist activity is found at the historic remains of the old Blyth Homestead, while the Lost City is a spectacular collection of free-standing sandstone formations.

For nature-lovers, brush-tailed possums and wallabies are regularly seen, along with blue-winged kookaburras and red-tailed black cockatoos.

Access and Camping

Today, most of the main sections of the park can be reached by sealed road. It is an easy 2-hour drive of 130 km from Darwin, via Batchelor. A 4WD track leads through the southern portion of the park to the Daly River Road.

Within the national park the main camping areas are at Wangi, Buley Rockholes and Florence Falls. There are several other bush camping areas scattered throughout the park. A camping fee applies at each of the main camping areas.

Sealed road access and short walking tracks in Litchfield National Park lead to refreshing swimming sites such as Buley Rockholes.

West MacDonnell National Park

The magnificent MacDonnell Ranges in central Australia reach heights of over 1500 metres above sea level and span some 400 km east to west across vibrant desert country not far from the town of Alice Springs.

fact file

WHERE: This park stretches from the fringe of Alice Springs township westwards for 220 km
Map: NT 7 D4

WHEN: April to September (Larapinta Trail may be closed between October and April)

WHY: Numerous scenic gorges and waterholes, walking trails, swimming, hiking, camping, cycling, scenic drives, Australian Aboriginal culture

SIZE: 206 973 ha

RANGER: Parks and Wildlife Commission, Park Visitor Information, Alice Springs
(08) 8951 8211

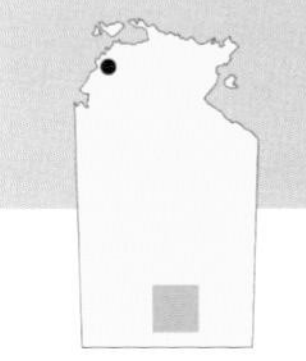

Early Aboriginal Australians lived and travelled throughout these lands pursuing their nomadic way of life until European explorers passed through the region in the 1860s. Then came the pastoralists, the telegraph line and the modern township we call Alice Springs.

The West MacDonnell National Park was established in 1994. The major natural features of the park are linked by the Larapinta Trail, a world-class bushwalking trail which follows the backbone of the ranges for about 220 km. This marvellous walking trail starts at the Alice Springs Telegraph Station and continues to Simpsons Gap. It then winds west via all the major attractions in the park—Standley Chasm, Serpentine Gorge, Glen Helen Gorge, Ormiston Gorge, Mount Sonder, Mount Giles, Redbank Gorge—to Mount Zeil.

Commercial tour operators offer many different scenic trips throughout West MacDonnell National Park; some of the best views are seen from the air.

All walkers must register with the nearest ranger station before setting off on a major walk. Most of the waterholes are extremely cold and will provide a very refreshing swim.

All these features are accessible by conventional vehicle and a short walk, with the exception of the mountain peaks and Roma Gorge which is 4WD access only. Namatjira Drive, which services the park, is sealed as far as Glen Helen Gorge, 130 km from Alice Springs. Beyond that point a formed gravel road runs west.

The variety to be found here is fantastic. There's early European history, rare wildlife, magnificent scenery, cool enjoyable swimming and walking trails, while the area is also an important refuge for a number of rare plant species and home to a special species of Central Australian fish.

Right: *Glen Helen Gorge is accessible and well worth visiting. The brilliant colours of this gorge are due to the dramatic red quartzite rock.*

tourist info

Commercial tour operators service the park from Alice Springs—for details contact the Visitor Information Centre (08) 8952 5800

More National Parks of Importance

Devils Marbles Conservation Reserve

SIZE: 1829 ha
MAP: NT 6 G6

The Devils Marbles are situated on either side of the Stuart Highway, 120 km south of Tennant Creek. These fascinating spherical and egg-shaped granite boulders, some balanced precariously on others, are a spectacular natural phenomenon that are well worth exploring, especially in the early morning or late evening light.

There are many informal walking tracks where the visitor may wander through the boulders and find great photo opportunities.

Bush camping facilities are provided which include shaded picnic tables, as well as fireplaces and toilets. A nominal camping fee applies.

The Devils Marbles is a registered Aboriginal sacred site and visitors are asked to respect the cultural heritage of the area.

For more details, phone the Parks Office, Tennant Creek (08) 8962 4599.

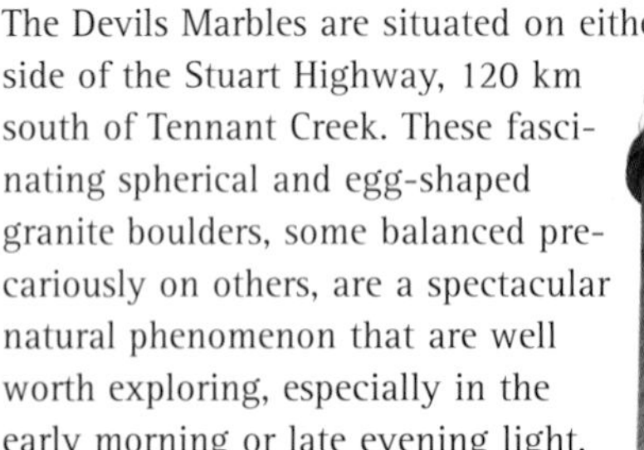

Right: *The historic lighthouse at Cape Don on the Cobourg Peninsula overlooks the remote and pristine beaches for which this area is famous.*

The rounded rocks that make up the unusual Devils Marbles formation are the eroded remains of a 1.5-billion-year-old granite intrusion.

Garig Gunak Barlu National Park

SIZE: 450 000 ha
MAP: NT 2 C2

The Cobourg Peninsula protrudes out into the Arafura Sea. This small peninsula contains the Garig Gunak Barlu National Park. The park is home to four main groups of Australian Aboriginals who now own and help manage the area.

During the 1500s, Macassans came from the north–collecting trepang, fishing and looking for pearls. In 1838 the British founded the Victoria Settlement in the seemingly idyllic setting of Port Essington, but it was abandoned little more than a decade later in 1849.

The park's main attractions are its remoteness, its pristine white sandy beaches and the superb fishing from the nearby coral reefs and offshore islands. The old Victoria Settlement, with its eerie crumbling ruins, is well worth a visit.

The park is 570 km by road from Darwin. Currently only 20 vehicles at any one time are allowed, and an access permit from the Parks Permits Officer is required, phone (08) 8999 4814.

It is advisable to book well in advance.

Camping is allowed at Smith Point. Accommodation is also available in well set-up beach huts or self-contained cabins. The Garig Store at Black Point, phone (08) 8979 0455, can organise the accommodation, as well as supplying fuel and supplies. Phone the Black Point Ranger Station on (08) 8979 0244.

Nitmiluk (Katherine Gorge) National Park

SIZE: 292 008 ha
MAP: NT 2 C8

Katherine Gorge, with its high cliffs of grey and orange sandstone towering over deep waterholes and lush pockets of rainforest, is one of the Territory's major natural attractions.

Now set within Nitmiluk National Park, much of the area included within the park is the traditional home of the

The distinctive red, rocky escarpment in Watarrka (Kings Canyon) National Park looks all the more spectacular against the stark white trunk of this eucalyptus tree.

Jawoyn people who help manage the park. The park has two main sections: the Katherine Gorge section in the south, and the Edith Falls section in the northwest. Both parts have sealed road access available all year round.

Wildlife found in the park includes kingfishers, butcherbirds and bowerbirds, wallabies, bandicoots and freshwater crocodiles.

Tour boat cruises operate from a base near the entrance to the majestic Katherine Gorge, where canoes are also available for hire. Barramundi fishing is a popular pastime on the river as well.

Bushwalking is another favourite activity, with both short and long walks available. Another way to see the gorge is by helicopter, which offers an exhilarating ride through the gorge system.

To contact rangers at Katherine Gorge, phone (08) 8972 1886, or at Edith Falls, phone (08) 8975 4852.

Watarrka (Kings Canyon) National Park

SIZE: 105 717 ha
MAP: NT 8 F6

Set in the George Gill Range and forming part of the Watarrka National Park, the geological masterpiece known as Kings Canyon has evolved over millions of years. The moist crevices of the canyon act as a refuge for many different animals as well as more than 600 plant species, of which over 60 are rare or relicts from a bygone era.

The national park was declared in 1983 and the land was handed back to the local Luritja people who are now involved in its management.

There are some magnificent walks in the area including the Kings Creek Walk and the longer Kings Canyon Walk, both of which should not be missed.

The shortest route to the national park from Alice Springs is along the Stuart and Ernest Giles Highways, while the Mereenie Loop Road via Hermannsburg is a slightly longer route of 327 km and will soon be sealed all the way. Access from Uluru is 279 km on a sealed road.

Kings Canyon Resort (08 8956 7422), located 7 km from the canyon and within the national park, has hotel rooms, serviced caravan sites and grassed camping grounds. You can phone the ranger on (08) 8956 7488.

Canoeing is a popular adventure activity and a great way to get close to the huge sandstone cliffs of Katherine Gorge in Nitmiluk National Park.

Popular Parks at a Glance

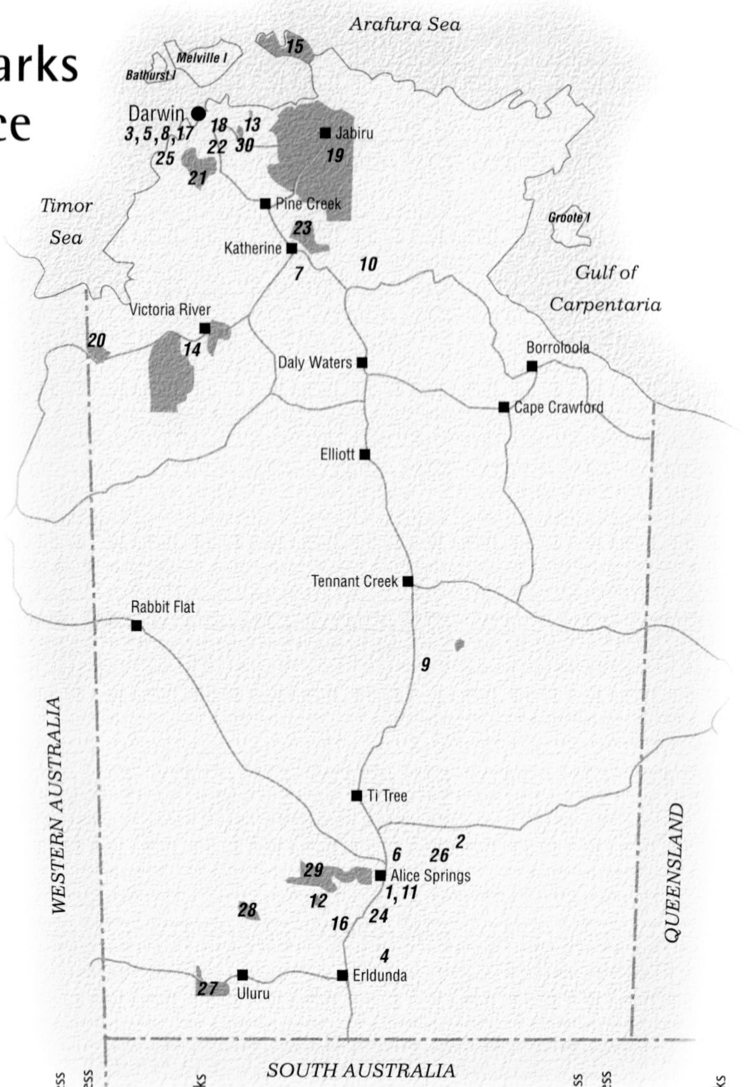

	Camping	Caravan Access	Disabled Access	4WD Access	Picnic Areas	Toilets	Walking Tracks	Kiosk	Information
1 Alice Springs DP			●		●	●	●	●	●
2 Arltunga HR			●	●	●	●	●		●
3 Casuarina CR					●	●	●		
4 Chambers Pillar HR	●			●	●	●	●	●	
5 Charles Darwin NP					●	●	●		
6 Corroboree Rock CR					●	●	●		●
7 Cutta Cutta Caves NP		●			●	●	●	●	●
8 Darwin Botanic Gardens			●		●	●	●		●
9 Devils Marbles CR	●	●			●	●	●		●
10 Elsey NP	●	●			●	●	●	●	
11 Emily and Jessie Gaps NP					●	●	●		
12 Finke Gorge NP	●			●	●	●	●		
13 Fogg Dam CR			●		●	●	●		
14 Gregory NP	●	●		●	●	●	●		
15 Garig Gunak Barlu NP	●			●	●	●	●	●	●

	Camping	Caravan Access	Disabled Access	4WD Access	Picnic Areas	Toilets	Walking Tracks	Kiosk	Information
16 Henbury Meteorite Craters CR	●				●	●	●		
17 Holmes Jungle NP					●	●	●		
18 Howard Springs NP			●		●	●	●		●
19 Kakadu NP	●	●	●	●	●	●	●	●	●
20 Keep River NP	●	●		●	●	●	●		●
21 Litchfield NP	●	●	●	●	●	●	●	●	●
22 Manton Dam RA					●	●	●		
23 Nitmiluk NP	●	●			●	●	●	●	●
24 Rainbow Valley CR	●			●	●	●	●		
25 Territory Wildlife Park			●		●	●	●		●
26 Trephina Gorge Nature Park	●	●		●	●	●	●		
27 Uluru–Kata Tjuta NP			●		●	●	●	●	●
28 Watarrka (Kings Canyon) NP			●		●	●	●	●	●
29 West Macdonnell NP	●	●		●	●	●	●	●	●
30 Window on the Wetlands VC			●		●	●			●

Map 1

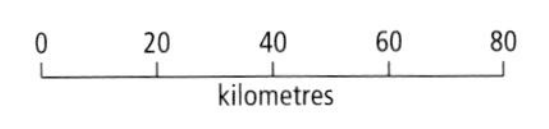

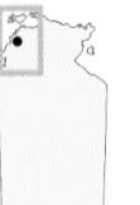

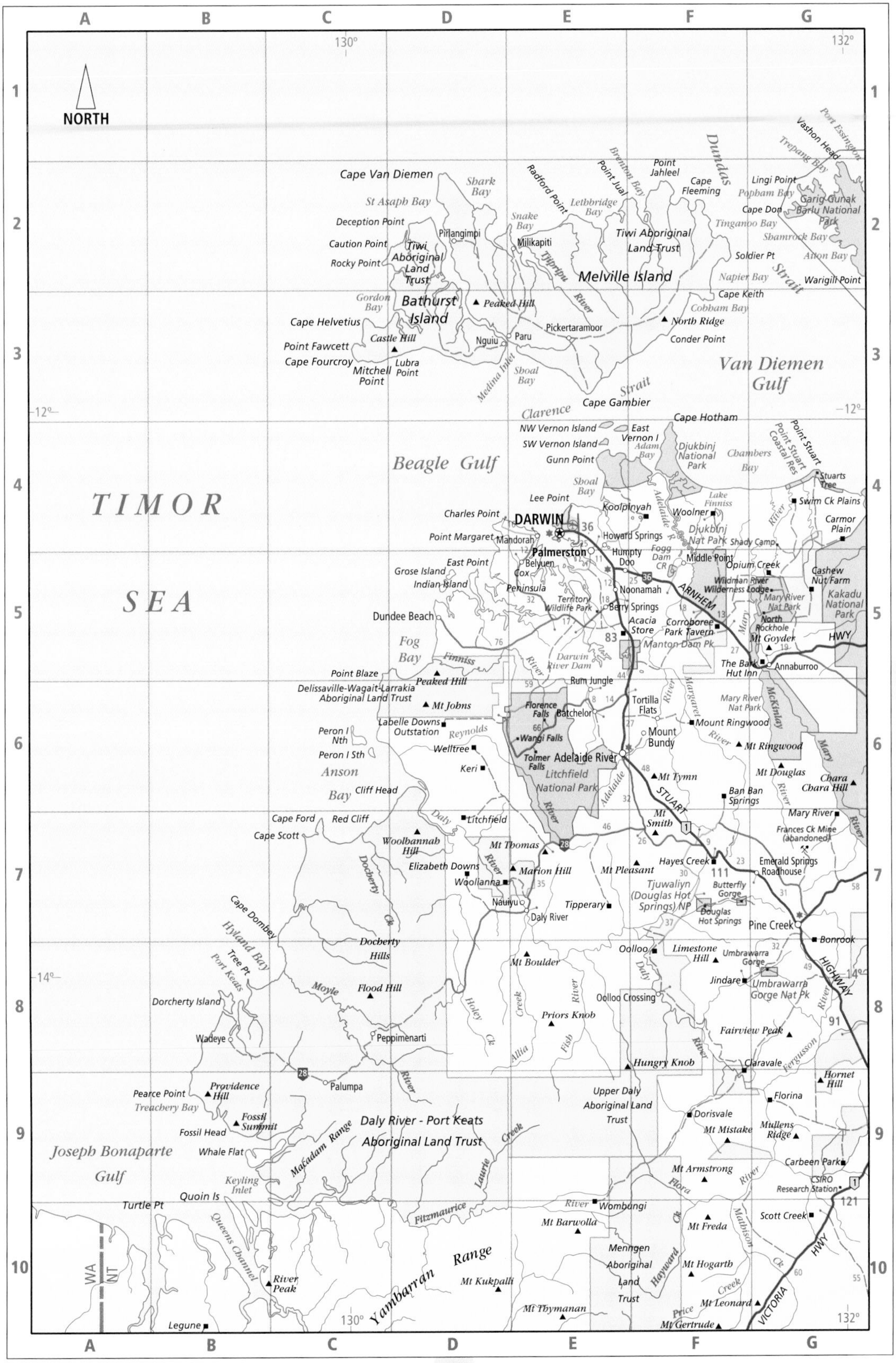

A B C D E F G

130° 132°

NORTH

TIMOR

SEA

Cape Van Diemen
St Asaph Bay
Deception Point
Caution Point
Rocky Point
Pirlangimpi
Tiwi Aboriginal Land Trust
Gordon Bay
Bathurst Island
Peaked Hill
Cape Helvetius
Castle Hill
Point Fawcett
Cape Fourcroy
Mitchell Point
Lubra Point
Nguiu
Paru
Medina Inlet
Shoal Bay
Shark Bay
Snake Bay
Milikapiti
Radford Point
Tjipripu River
Pickertaramoor
Lethbridge Bay
Brenton Bay
Point Jual
Point Jahleel
Cape Fleeming
Dundas
Tiwi Aboriginal Land Trust
Melville Island
North Ridge
Conder Point
Lingi Point
Popham Bay
Cape Don
Garig Gunak Barlu National Park
Tinganoo Bay
Shamrock Bay
Soldier Pt
Alton Bay
Strait
Napier Bay
Warigill Point
Cape Keith
Cobbam Bay
Vashon Head
Trepang Bay
Port Essington
Van Diemen Gulf
Clarence Strait
Cape Gambier
Cape Hotham
NW Vernon Island
SW Vernon Island
East Vernon I
Adam Bay
Gunn Point
Djukbinj National Park
Chambers Bay
Point Stuart
Point Stuart Coastal Res
Stuarts Tree
Beagle Gulf
Shoal Bay
Lee Point
Lake Finniss
Swim Ck Plains
Carmor Plain
Charles Point
DARWIN
36
Koolpinyah
Woolner
Point Margaret
Mandorah
Howard Springs
Djukbinj Nat Park
Shady Camp
Palmerston
Humpty Doo
Fogg Dam CR
Middle Point
Opium Creek
Cashew Nut Farm
Grose Island
East Point
Belyuen
Cox Peninsula
Indian Island
Noonamah
Wildman River Wilderness Lodge
ARNHEM
Mary River Nat Park
Kakadu National Park
Territory Wildlife Park
Berry Springs
Dundee Beach
Acacia Store
Corroboree Park Tavern
North Rockhole
Mt Goyder
HWY
Fog Bay
Finniss
Manton Dam Pk
83
Darwin River Dam
The Bark Hut Inn
Annaburroo
Point Blaze
Peaked Hill
Delissaville-Wagait-Larrakia Aboriginal Land Trust
Rum Jungle
Mt Johns
Florence Falls
Batchelor
Tortilla Flats
Margaret River
Mary River Nat Park
McKinlay
Labelle Downs Outstation
Reynolds
Wangi Falls
Mount Bundy
Mount Ringwood
Peron I Nth
Peron I Sth
Welltree
Tolmer Falls
Adelaide River
Mt Ringwood
Mary
Anson Bay
Keri
Litchfield National Park
Mt Tymn
Mt Douglas
Chara Chara Hill
Cliff Head
Adelaide
STUART
Ban Ban Springs
Mary River
Cape Ford
Red Cliff
Daly
Litchfield
Mt Smith
1
Frances Ck Mine (abandoned)
Cape Scott
Woolbannah Hill
Mt Thomas
28
Hayes Creek
Emerald Springs Roadhouse
Docherty
Elizabeth Downs
Marion Hill
Mt Pleasant
111
Woolianna
Tjuwaliyn (Douglas Hot Springs) NP
Butterfly Gorge
Nauiyu
Daly River
Tipperary
Douglas Hot Springs
Pine Creek
Cape Dombey
Hyland Bay
Tree Pt
Port Keats
Docherty Hills
Oolloo
Limestone Hill
Bonrook
Umbrawarra Gorge
Mt Boulder
Moyle
Flood Hill
Jindare
Umbrawarra Gorge Nat Pk
HIGHWAY
Dorcherty Island
Holey Ck
Creek
Fish River
Oolloo Crossing
Priors Knob
Fairview Peak
Wadeye
Peppimenarti
Allia
Hungry Knob
Claravale
Fergusson
River
Hornet Hill
Pearce Point
Providence Hill
Palumpa
Upper Daly Aboriginal Land Trust
Florina
Treachery Bay
Fossil Summit
Dorisvale
Mullens Ridge
Fossil Head
Daly River - Port Keats Aboriginal Land Trust
Mt Mistake
Joseph Bonaparte Gulf
Whale Flat
Macadam Range
Laurie Creek
Carbeen Park
Keyling Inlet
Mt Armstrong
Flora River
CSIRO Research Station
Quoin Is
Turtle Pt
Fitzmaurice River
Wombungi
121
Scott Creek
Queens Channel
Mt Barwolla
Mt Freda
Matbison Ck
HWY
WA NT
Range
Mennigen Aboriginal Land Trust
Hayward Ck
Mt Hogarth
River Peak
Yambarran
Mt Kukpalli
Creek
VICTORIA
Mt Thymanan
Mt Leonard
Price
Legune
Mt Gertrude

NT 2

NT 4

Map 2

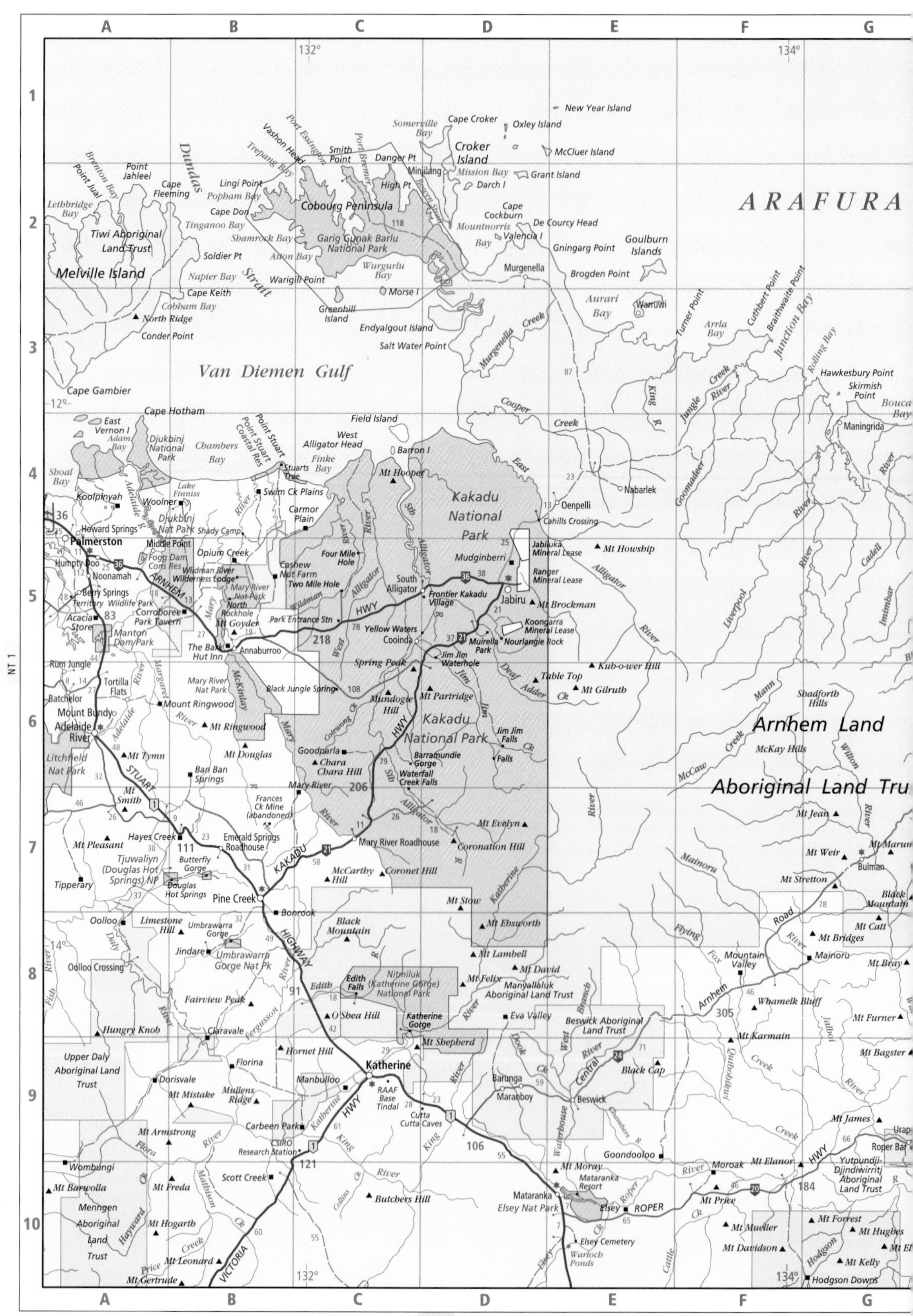
A
B
C
D
E
F
G
1
2
3
4
5
6
7
8
9
10
132°
134°
12°
14°
New Year Island
Cape Croker
Oxley Island
Somerville Bay
Croker Island
McCluer Island
Port Essington
Vashon Head
Smith Point
Port Bremer
Danger Pt
Minjilang
Mission Bay
Grant Island
Darch I
Trepang Bay
High Pt
Bowen Strait
Brenton Bay
Point Jual
Point Jahleel
Cape Fleeming
Dundas
Lingi Point
Popham Bay
Lethbridge Bay
Cape Don
Cobourg Peninsula
Cape Cockburn
De Courcy Head
Mountnorris Bay
Valencia I
Tinganoo Bay
Shamrock Bay
Garig Gunak Barlu National Park
118
Tiwi Aboriginal Land Trust
Gningarg Point
Goulburn Islands
ARAFURA
Soldier Pt
Alton Bay
Wurgurlu Bay
Murgenella
Brogden Point
Melville Island
Napier Bay
Strait
Warigill Point
Morse I
Cape Keith
Aurari Bay
Warruwi
Cobbam Bay
Greenhill Island
North Ridge
Endyalgout Island
Conder Point
Salt Water Point
Murgenella Creek
Turner Point
Arrla Bay
Cuthbert Point
Braithwaite Point
Junction Bay
Rolling Bay
Van Diemen Gulf
87
King R
Jungle Creek
River
Hawkesbury Point
Skirmish Point
Cape Gambier
Bouca Bay
Cooper Creek
Cape Hotham
East Vernon I
Adam Bay
Djukbinj National Park
Chambers Bay
Point Stuart
Point Stuart Coastal Res
Field Island
West Alligator Head
Finke Bay
Barron I
Maningrida
Shoal Bay
Stuarts Tree
Mt Hooper
East
Goomadeer
Lake Finniss
Swim Ck Plains
Kakadu National Park
23
Nabarlek
Koolpinyah
Woolner
Djukbinj Nat Park
Carmor Plain
13
Oenpelli
Cahills Crossing
36
Howard Springs
Shady Camp
Palmerston
Middle Point
25
Jabiluka Mineral Lease
Mt Howship
Fogg Dam Cons Res
Opium Creek
Four Mile Hole
Mudginberri
Humpty Doo
Wildman River Wilderness Lodge
Cashew Nut Farm
Noonamah
ARNHEM
South Alligator
38
Ranger Mineral Lease
Berry Springs
Mary River Nat Park
Two Mile Hole
Frontier Kakadu Village
Jabiru
Mt Brockman
Territory Wildlife Park
North Rockhole
Wildman
HWY
21
Acacia Store
83
Corroboree Park Tavern
Mt Goyder
Park Entrance Stn
78
Yellow Waters
Koongarra Mineral Lease
Manton Dam Park
Cooinda
37
Muirella Park
Nourlangie Rock
218
The Bark Hut Inn
Annaburroo
Rum Jungle
Spring Peak
Jim Jim Waterhole
Kub-o-wer Hill
Deaf Adder Ck
Table Top
Mt Gilruth
Tortilla Flats
Mary River Nat Park
Black Jungle Spring
108
Batchelor
Mundogie Hill
Mt Partridge
Shadforth Hills
Mount Bundy
Mount Ringwood
McKinlay
Mt Ringwood
Adelaide River
Cotwong Ck
Kakadu National Park
Jim Jim Falls
Arnhem Land
Litchfield Nat Park
Mt Tymn
Mt Douglas
Goodparla
Chara Chara Hill
Barramundie Gorge
Falls
McKay Hills
McCaw Creek
Wilton
Ban Ban Springs
Waterfall Creek Falls
Aboriginal Land Tru
STUART
Mt Smith
Mary River
206
Frances Ck Mine (abandoned)
Mt Jean
Mt Evelyn
Mt Pleasant
Hayes Creek
111
Emerald Springs Roadhouse
Mary River Roadhouse
Coronation Hill
Mt Weir
Mt Marun
Tjuwaliyn (Douglas Hot Springs) NP
Butterfly Gorge
KAKADU
McCarthy Hill
Coronet Hill
Mainoru
Bulman
Tipperary
Douglas Hot Springs
Pine Creek
Mt Stretton
Mt Stow
Katherine
Bonrook
Black Mountain
Oolloo
Limestone Hill
Umbrawarra Gorge
Black Mountain
Mt Ebsworth
Road
Mt Catt
Mt Bridges
Jindare
Umbrawarra Gorge Nat Pk
HIGHWAY
Flying Fox
Mountain Valley
Mainoru
Oolloo Crossing
Mt Lambell
Mt David
Mt Bray
Fish River
Daly
Edith Falls
Nitmiluk (Katherine Gorge) National Park
Mt Felix
Manyallaluk Aboriginal Land Trust
Arnhem
Whamelk Bluff
Fairview Peak
91
305
O'Shea Hill
Katherine Gorge
Eva Valley
Beswick Aboriginal Land Trust
Mt Furner
Hungry Knob
Claravale
Fergusson
Mt Shepherd
Mt Karmain
Upper Daly Aboriginal Land Trust
Florina
Hornet Hill
West Branch
Central River
Black Cap
Mt Bagster
Dorisvale
Manbulloo
RAAF Base Tindal
Barunga
Maranboy
Beswick
Quilbobiduri
Hodgson
Mt Mistake
Mullens Ridge
Cutta Cutta Caves
Dook Ck
Chambers
Mt James
Mt Armstrong
Carbeen Park
Waterhouse
Urap
Flora
King
River
CSIRO Research Station
106
Goondooloo
Roper Bar
Wombungi
121
Mt Moray
Moroak
Mt Elanor
HWY
Mt Barwolla
Mt Freda
Scott Creek
Mataranka Resort
Yutpundji-Djindiwirritj Aboriginal Land Trust
Mathison
Collins Ck
Butchers Hill
Mataranka
Elsey Nat Park
Elsey
ROPER
Mt Price
184
Mennen Aboriginal Land Trust
Hayward
Mt Hogarth
Mt Mueller
Mt Forrest
Mt Hughes
Elsey Cemetery
Warloch Ponds
Mt Davidson
Mt Kelly
Price Creek
Mt Leonard
VICTORIA
Cattle Ck
Mt Gertrude
Hodgson Downs

NT 1

NT 3

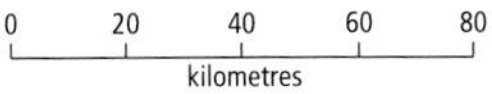

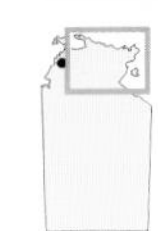

0 20 40 60 80
kilometres

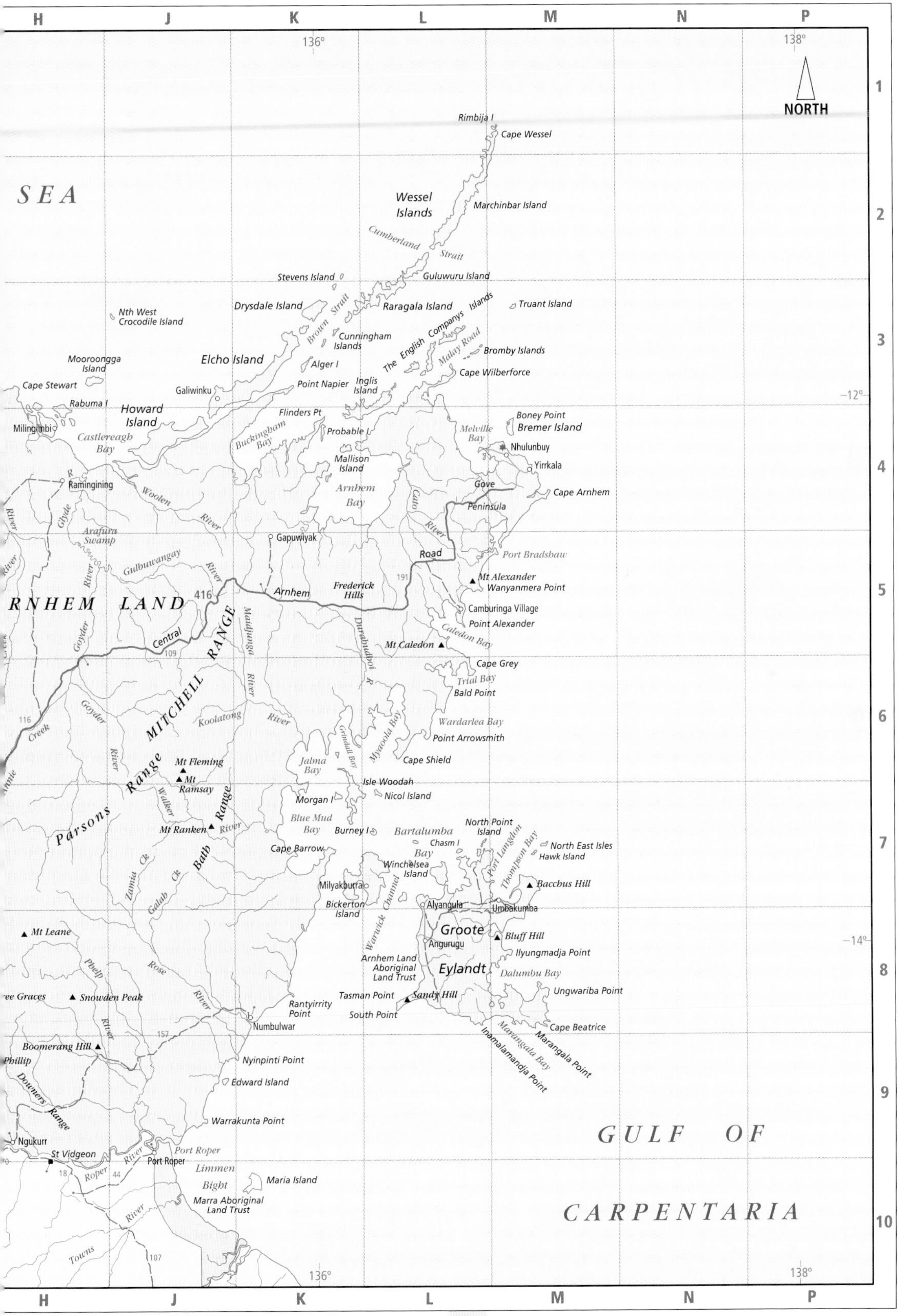

H J K L M N P

136° 138°

NORTH

1 2 3 4 5 6 7 8 9 10

SEA

Rimbija I
Cape Wessel
Wessel Islands
Marchinbar Island
Cumberland Strait
Stevens Island
Guluwuru Island
Drysdale Island
Brown Strait
Raragala Island
Truant Island
Nth West Crocodile Island
Cunningham Islands
The English Companys Islands
Malay Road
Bromby Islands
Mooroongga Island
Elcho Island
Alger I
Cape Wilberforce
Cape Stewart
Galiwinku
Point Napier
Inglis Island
Rabuma I
Howard Island
Flinders Pt
Boney Point
Bremer Island
Milingimbi
Castlereagh Bay
Buckingham Bay
Probable I
Melville Bay
Nhulunbuy
Mallison Island
Yirrkala
Ramingining
Woolen River
Arnhem Bay
Gove Peninsula
Cape Arnhem
Glyde
Cato River
Arafura Swamp
Gapuwiyak
Road
Port Bradshaw
Gulbuwangay
River
Mt Alexander
Wanyanmera Point
ARNHEM LAND
416
Arnhem
Frederick Hills
191
Camburinga Village
Point Alexander
Goyder
Central
109
MITCHELL RANGE
Mainjunga River
Durabudboi R
Caledon Bay
Mt Caledon
Cape Grey
Trial Bay
Bald Point
116
Creek
Goyder
Koolatong River
Wardarlea Bay
Point Arrowsmith
Grindall Bay
Myaoola Bay
Cape Shield
Mt Fleming
Mt Ramsay
Range
Jalma Bay
Isle Woodah
Nicol Island
Walker
Morgan I
Parsons
Bath Range
Blue Mud Bay
Mt Ranken
Burney I
Bartalumba Bay
North Point Island
Chasm I
Port Langdon
Thompson Bay
North East Isles
Hawk Island
Cape Barrow
Winchelsea Island
Zamia Ck
Galab Ck
Milyakburra
Channel
Bacchus Hill
Bickerton Island
Warwick
Alyangula
Umbakumba
Mt Leane
Groote Eylandt
Bluff Hill
Angurugu
Ilyungmadja Point
Phelp
Rose
Arnhem Land Aboriginal Land Trust
Dalumbu Bay
Ungwariba Point
ee Graces
Snowden Peak
River
Rantyirrity Point
Tasman Point
Sandy Hill
South Point
Cape Beatrice
Numbulwar
157
Marangala Bay
Marangala Point
Inamalamandja Point
Boomerang Hill
Phillip
Nyinpinti Point
Downers Range
Edward Island
Warrakunta Point
GULF OF CARPENTARIA
Ngukurr
St Vidgeon
Port Roper
Port Roper
River
18
Roper
44
Limmen Bight
Maria Island
Marra Aboriginal Land Trust
River
Towns
107
12°
14°

Map 3

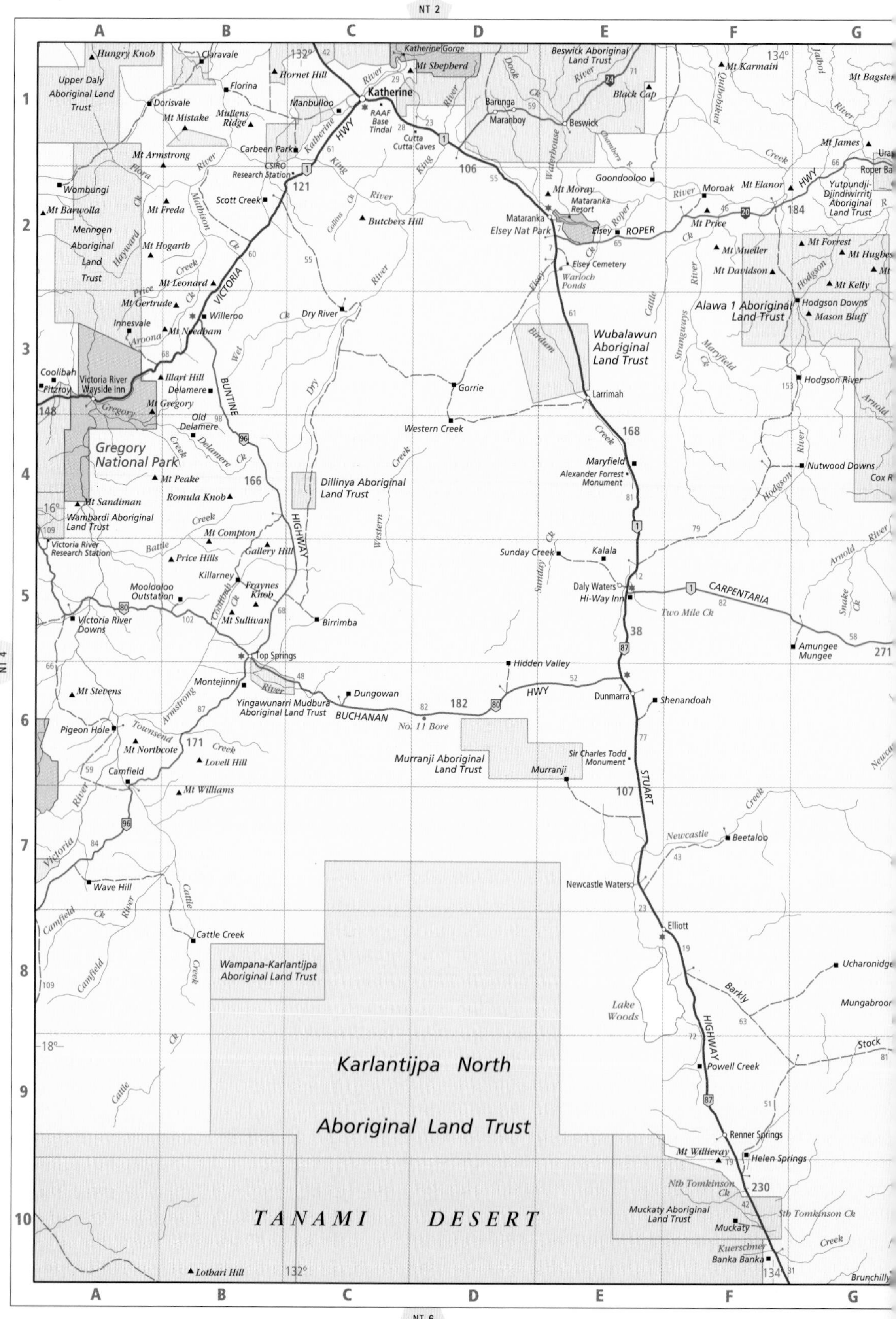
NT 2
NT 4
NT 6
A
B
C
D
E
F
G
1
2
3
4
5
6
7
8
9
10
132°
134°
16°
18°
Hungry Knob
Claravale
Hornet Hill
Katherine Gorge
Mt Shepherd
Beswick Aboriginal Land Trust
Mt Karmain
Mt Bagster
Upper Daly Aboriginal Land Trust
Florina
Katherine
Black Cap
Dorisvale
Mt Mistake
Mullens Ridge
Manbulloo
RAAF Base Tindal
Barunga
Maranboy
Beswick
Cutta Cutta Caves
Mt Armstrong
Carbeen Park
CSIRO Research Station
Mt James
Roper Ba
Wombungi
Goondooloo
Scott Creek
Mt Moray
Mataranka Resort
Moroak
Mt Elanor
Yutpundji-Djindiwirritj Aboriginal Land Trust
Mt Barwolla
Mt Freda
Butchers Hill
Mataranka
Elsey Nat Park
Elsey
ROPER
Mt Price
HWY
Menngen Aboriginal Land Trust
Mt Hogarth
Mt Mueller
Mt Forrest
Mt Hughes
Mt Davidson
Elsey Cemetery
Warloch Ponds
Mt Kelly
Mt Leonard
Mt Gertrude
VICTORIA
Dry River
Alawa 1 Aboriginal Land Trust
Hodgson Downs
Mason Bluff
Innesvale
Willeroo
Mt Needham
Wubalawun Aboriginal Land Trust
Coolibah
Fitzroy
Victoria River Wayside Inn
Illari Hill
Delamere
Gorrie
Hodgson River
Larrimah
Mt Gregory
BUNTINE
Old Delamere
Western Creek
Gregory National Park
Maryfield
Alexander Forrest Monument
Nutwood Downs
Mt Peake
Dillinya Aboriginal Land Trust
Cox R
Mt Sandiman
Romula Knob
Wambardi Aboriginal Land Trust
Mt Compton
HIGHWAY
Victoria River Research Station
Gallery Hill
Price Hills
Sunday Creek
Kalala
Killarney
Fraynes Knob
Daly Waters
Hi-Way Inn
CARPENTARIA
Mooloolooo Outstation
Two Mile Ck
Victoria River Downs
Mt Sullivan
Birrimba
Amungee Mungee
Top Springs
Hidden Valley
Mt Stevens
Montejinni
Yingawunarri Mudbura Aboriginal Land Trust
Dungowan
Dunmarra
Shenandoah
BUCHANAN
No. 11 Bore
Pigeon Hole
Mt Northcote
Lovell Hill
Murranji Aboriginal Land Trust
Sir Charles Todd Monument
Camfield
Murranji
STUART
Mt Williams
Beetaloo
Wave Hill
Newcastle Waters
Elliott
Cattle Creek
Wampana-Karlantijpa Aboriginal Land Trust
Ucharonidge
Barkly
Lake Woods
Mungabroom
Stock
Powell Creek
Karlantijpa North Aboriginal Land Trust
Renner Springs
Mt Willieray
Helen Springs
Nth Tomkinson Ck
Muckaty Aboriginal Land Trust
Sth Tomkinson Ck
TANAMI DESERT
Muckaty
Kuerschner
Banka Banka
Lotbari Hill
Brunchilly

0 20 40 60 80
kilometres

NT 2

QLD 3

NT 6

Map 4

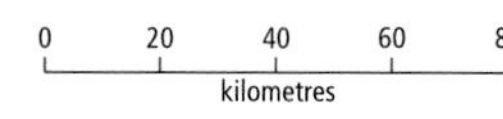

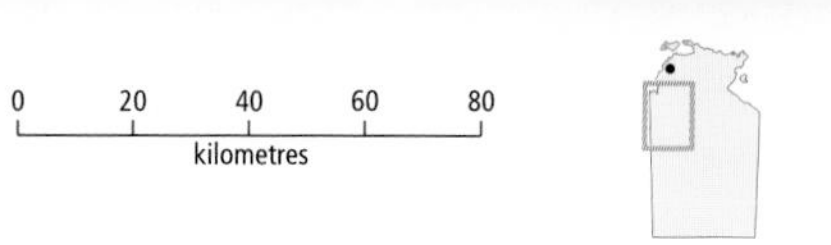

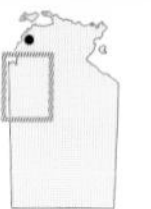

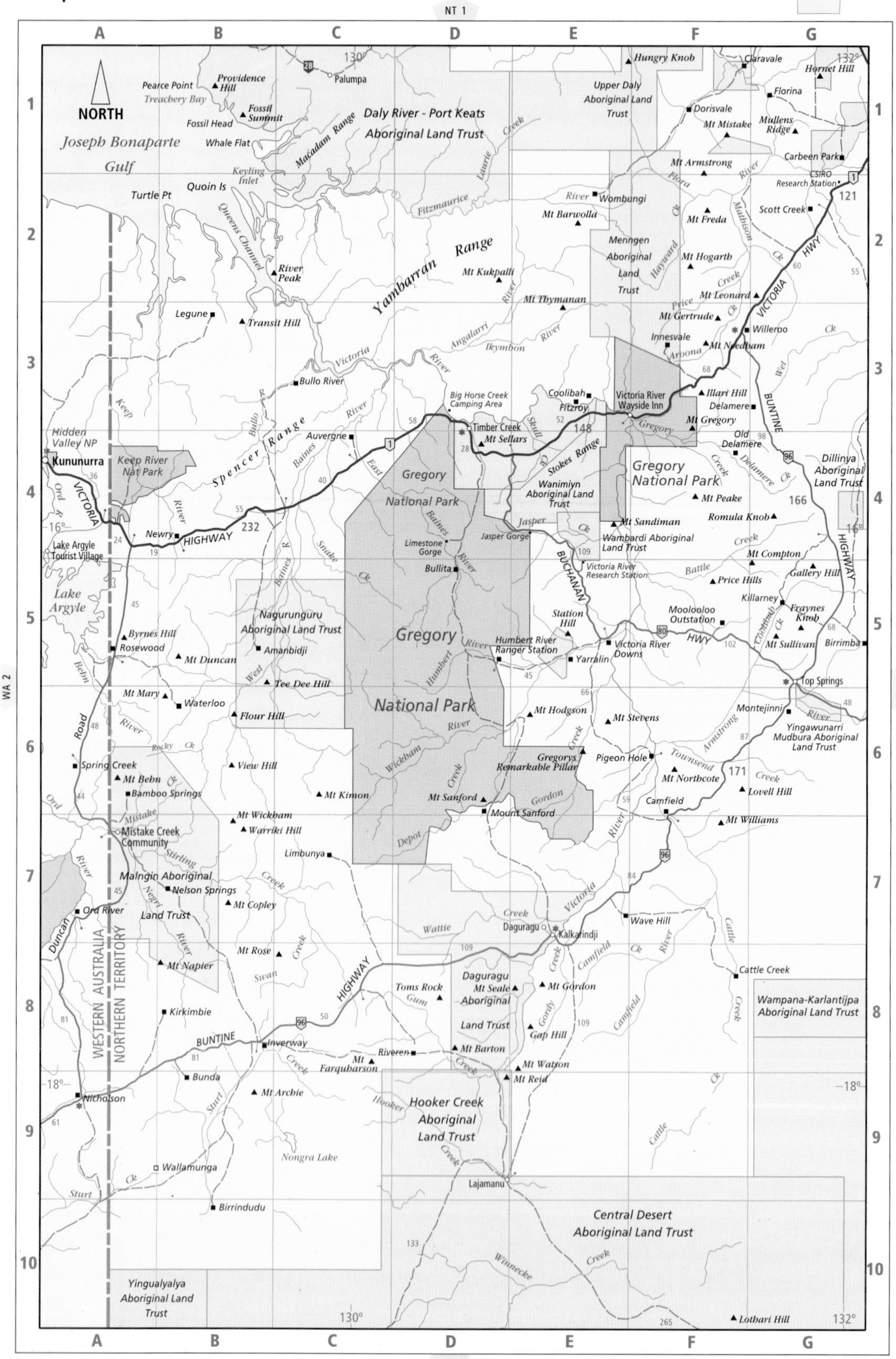

NT 1

A B C D E F G

1 2 3 4 5 6 7 8 9 10

NORTH
Pearce Point
Providence Hill
Treachery Bay
Fossil Summit
Fossil Head
Joseph Bonaparte Gulf
Whale Flat
Palumpa
130°
Macadam Range
Daly River - Port Keats Aboriginal Land Trust
Laurie Creek
Hungry Knob
Upper Daly Aboriginal Land Trust
Claravale
Hornet Hill
132°
Florina
Dorisvale
Mt Mistake
Mullens Ridge
Carbeen Park
Mt Armstrong
Flora River
CSIRO Research Station
Keyling Inlet
Quoin Is
Turtle Pt
Fitzmaurice River
Wombungi
Mt Barwolla
Mt Freda
Scott Creek
Mathison Ck
121
Queens Channel
Yambarran Range
Menngen Aboriginal Land Trust
Hayward Ck
Mt Hogarth
HWY
River Peak
Mt Kukpalli
Mt Thymanan
Price Creek
Mt Leonard
Mt Gertrude
VICTORIA
60
55
Legune
Transit Hill
Angalarri River
Willeroo
Innesvale
Aroona Ck
Mt Needham
Ikymbon River
Victoria River
Bullo River
Big Horse Creek Camping Area
Coolibah
Fitzroy
Victoria River Wayside Inn
Illari Hill
Delamere
BUNTINE
Wet Ck
68
Keep River
Bullo R
Spencer Range
Auvergne
58
Timber Creek
Mt Sellars
Skull Ck
52
148
Gregory
Mt Gregory
Old Delamere
98
Hidden Valley NP
Kununurra
Keep River Nat Park
Baines River
East
1
28
Stokes Range
Gregory National Park
Creek
Delamere Ck
96
Dillinya Aboriginal Land Trust
36
40
Wanimiyn Aboriginal Land Trust
Mt Peake
166
Ord R
VICTORIA
River
55
Romula Knob
16°
Jasper
Mt Sandiman
Newry
HIGHWAY
232
Jasper Gorge
Ck
Wambardi Aboriginal Land Trust
Creek
HIGHWAY
Lake Argyle Tourist Village
24
19
Limestone Gorge
Snake Ck
BUCHANAN
109
Mt Compton
Bullita
Victoria River Research Station
Battle
Gallery Hill
Lake Argyle
45
Nagurunguru Aboriginal Land Trust
Price Hills
Killarney
Station Hill
Mooloolooo Outstation
Fraynes Knob
Byrnes Hill
Gregory
Humbert River Ranger Station
80
HWY
Rosewood
Amanbidji
Victoria River Downs
Coolibah Ck
Mt Sullivan
Birrimba
Mt Duncan
Yarralin
102
Behn
West
Humbert
45
Tee Dee Hill
Top Springs
Mt Mary
Waterloo
66
48
National Park
Mt Hodgson
Montejinni
Flour Hill
Mt Stevens
River
Yingawunarri Mudbura Aboriginal Land Trust
Road
48
River
Armstrong
87
Rocky Ck
Wickham
Creek
Spring Creek
View Hill
Gregorys Remarkable Pillar
Pigeon Hole
Townsend
Mt Behn
171
Creek
Mt Northcote
Bamboo Springs
Mt Kimon
Mt Sanford
Lovell Hill
Gordon
Ord
44
59
Camfield
Mt Wickham
Mount Sanford
Mt Williams
Mistake Creek Community
Warriki Hill
Depot
River
Stirling
Limbunya
96
River
Malngin Aboriginal Land Trust
Nelson Springs
Creek
84
Negri River
45
Victoria
Ord River
Mt Copley
Creek
Wave Hill
Cattle
Duncan
Daguragu
Kalkarindji
Wattie
Mt Rose
Creek
109
Creek
Camfield
Ck
River
Mt Napier
Swan
HIGHWAY
Cattle Creek
WESTERN AUSTRALIA
NORTHERN TERRITORY
Toms Rock
Gum
Daguragu Aboriginal Land Trust
Mt Seale
Mt Gordon
Gordy
Camfield
Wampana-Karlantijpa Aboriginal Land Trust
Creek
Kirkimbie
50
96
81
109
Gap Hill
BUNTINE
Inverway
Riveren
Mt Barton
Mt Farquharson
81
Creek
Mt Watson
Bunda
Mt Reid
18°
Hooker Creek Aboriginal Land Trust
Mt Archie
Nicholson
Sturt
Hooker
Ck
61
Cattle
Creek
Nongra Lake
Wallamunga
Lajamanu
Sturt
Ck
Birrindudu
Central Desert Aboriginal Land Trust
133
Winnecke
Creek
Yingualyalya Aboriginal Land Trust
130°
265
Lothari Hill
132°

WA 2

NT 3

NT 5

Map 5

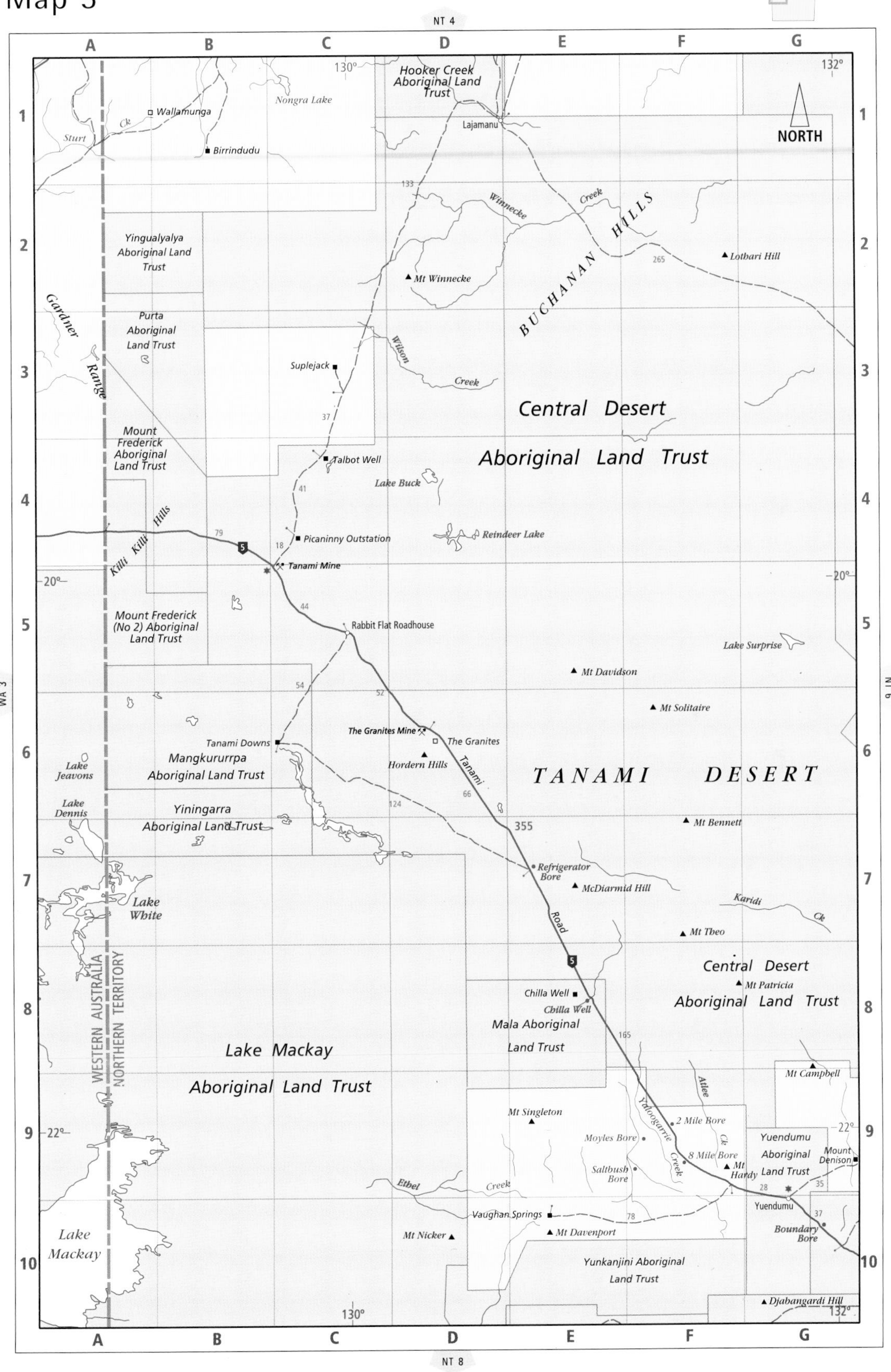

NT 4
NT 8
WA 3
NT 6
NORTH
kilometres
Hooker Creek Aboriginal Land Trust
Lajamanu
Wallamunga
Birrindudu
Nongra Lake
Sturt Ck
Yingualyalya Aboriginal Land Trust
Purta Aboriginal Land Trust
Gardner Range
Mount Frederick Aboriginal Land Trust
Killi Killi Hills
Mount Frederick (No 2) Aboriginal Land Trust
Winnecke Creek
BUCHANAN HILLS
Lotbari Hill
Mt Winnecke
Wilson Creek
Suplejack
Central Desert Aboriginal Land Trust
Talbot Well
Lake Buck
Picaninny Outstation
Reindeer Lake
Tanami Mine
Rabbit Flat Roadhouse
Lake Surprise
Mt Davidson
Mt Solitaire
The Granites Mine
The Granites
Hordern Hills
Tanami Downs
Mangkururrpa Aboriginal Land Trust
Lake Jeavons
Lake Dennis
Yiningarra Aboriginal Land Trust
TANAMI DESERT
Mt Bennett
Tanami Road
Refrigerator Bore
McDiarmid Hill
Karidi Ck
Lake White
Mt Theo
WESTERN AUSTRALIA
NORTHERN TERRITORY
Central Desert Aboriginal Land Trust
Mt Patricia
Chilla Well
Mala Aboriginal Land Trust
Lake Mackay Aboriginal Land Trust
Mt Campbell
Atlee Ck
Yaloogarrie Creek
Mt Singleton
2 Mile Bore
Moyles Bore
8 Mile Bore
Saltbush Bore
Mt Hardy
Yuendumu Aboriginal Land Trust
Mount Denison
Etbel Creek
Yuendumu
Vaughan Springs
Boundary Bore
Mt Nicker
Mt Davenport
Lake Mackay
Yunkanjini Aboriginal Land Trust
Djabangardi Hill
NT

Map 6

NT 3
TANAMI DESERT
Karlantijpa North
Aboriginal Land Trust
Central Desert
Aboriginal Land Trust
Karlantijpa South
Aboriginal Land Trust
TANAMI DESERT
Wirliyajarrayi
Aboriginal
Land Trust
Central Desert
Aboriginal Land Trust
Pawu Aboriginal
Land Trust
Yuendumu
Aboriginal
Land Trust
Yalpirakinu Aboriginal
Land Trust
Yunkanjini Aboriginal
Land Trust
Ahakeye Aboriginal
Land Trust
Mungkarta
Aboriginal
Land Trust
Tennant Creek
Renner Springs
Helen Springs
Muckaty
Banka Banka
Three Ways Roadhouse
Devils Marbles
Conservation Reserve
Wauchope
Wycliffe Well
Roadhouse
Barrow Creek
Ti-Tree
Central Mt Stuart
Historical Reserve
Yuendumu
Tanami Road
STUART HWY
SANDOVER HWY
NT 5
NT 7

NT 3

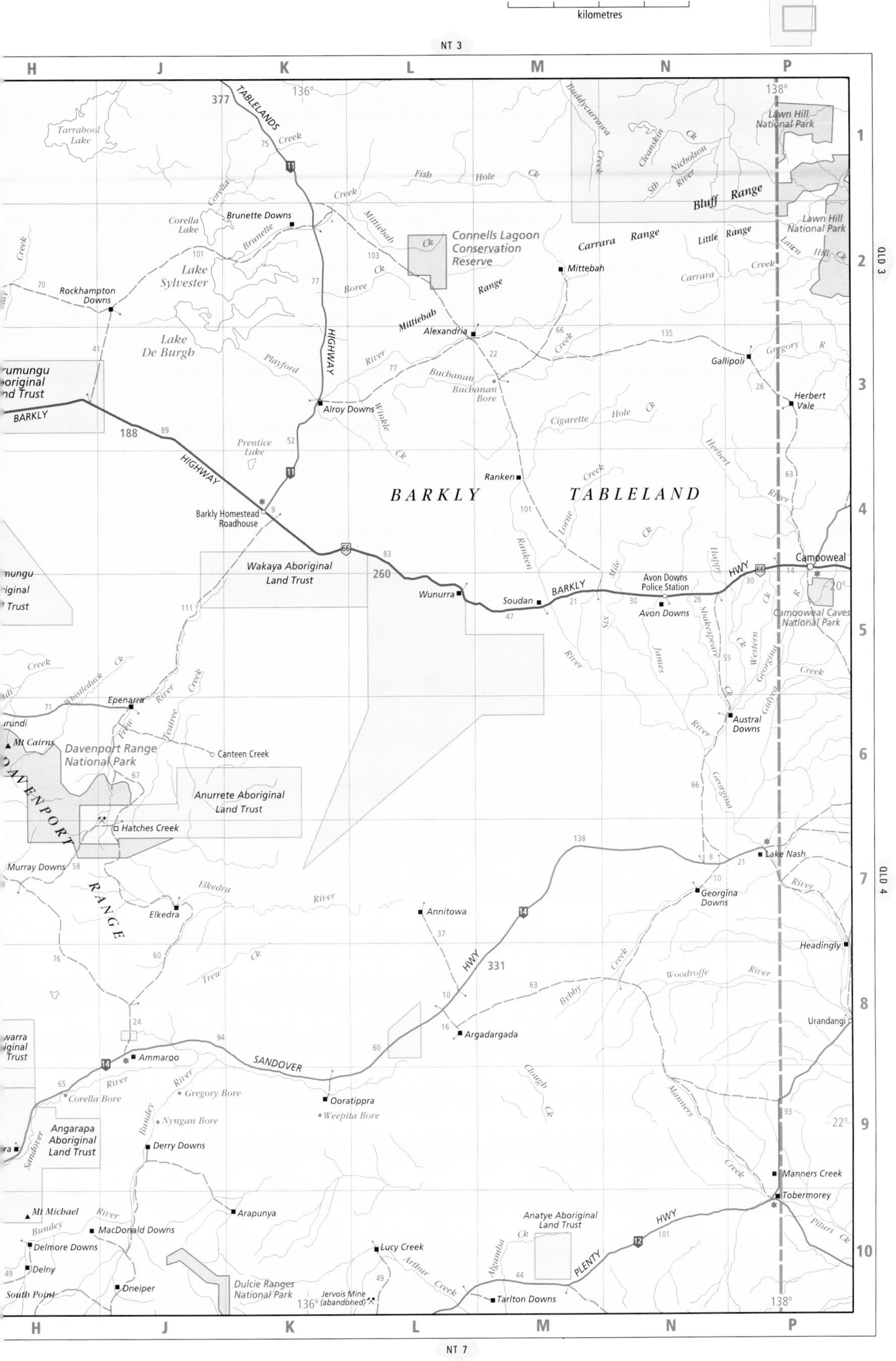

0 20 40 60 80
kilometres
BARKLY TABLELAND
TABLELANDS HIGHWAY
BARKLY HIGHWAY
SANDOVER HWY
PLENTY HWY
Lawn Hill National Park
Connells Lagoon Conservation Reserve
Bluff Range
Carrara Range
Little Range
Mittiebab Range
Brunette Downs
Corella Lake
Lake Sylvester
Lake De Burgh
Tarrabool Lake
Rockhampton Downs
Mittebah
Alexandria
Gallipoli
Herbert Vale
Buchanan Bore
Alroy Downs
Prentice Lake
Ranken
Barkly Homestead Roadhouse
Wakaya Aboriginal Land Trust
Wunurra
Soudan
Avon Downs Police Station
Avon Downs
Camooweal
Camooweal Caves National Park
Austral Downs
Epenarra
Canteen Creek
Davenport Range National Park
DAVENPORT RANGE
Mt Cairns
Anurrete Aboriginal Land Trust
Hatches Creek
Murray Downs
Elkedra
Lake Nash
Georgina Downs
Annitowa
Headingly
Urandangi
Argadargada
Ammaroo
Corella Bore
Gregory Bore
Ooratippra
Weepita Bore
Nyngan Bore
Angarapa Aboriginal Land Trust
Derry Downs
Manners Creek
Tobermorey
Arapunya
Mt Michael
MacDonald Downs
Delmore Downs
Delny
South Point
Dneiper
Dulcie Ranges National Park
Jervois Mine (abandoned)
Lucy Creek
Anatye Aboriginal Land Trust
Tarlton Downs
136°
138°
20°
22°
QLD 3
QLD 4
NT

NT 7

Map 7

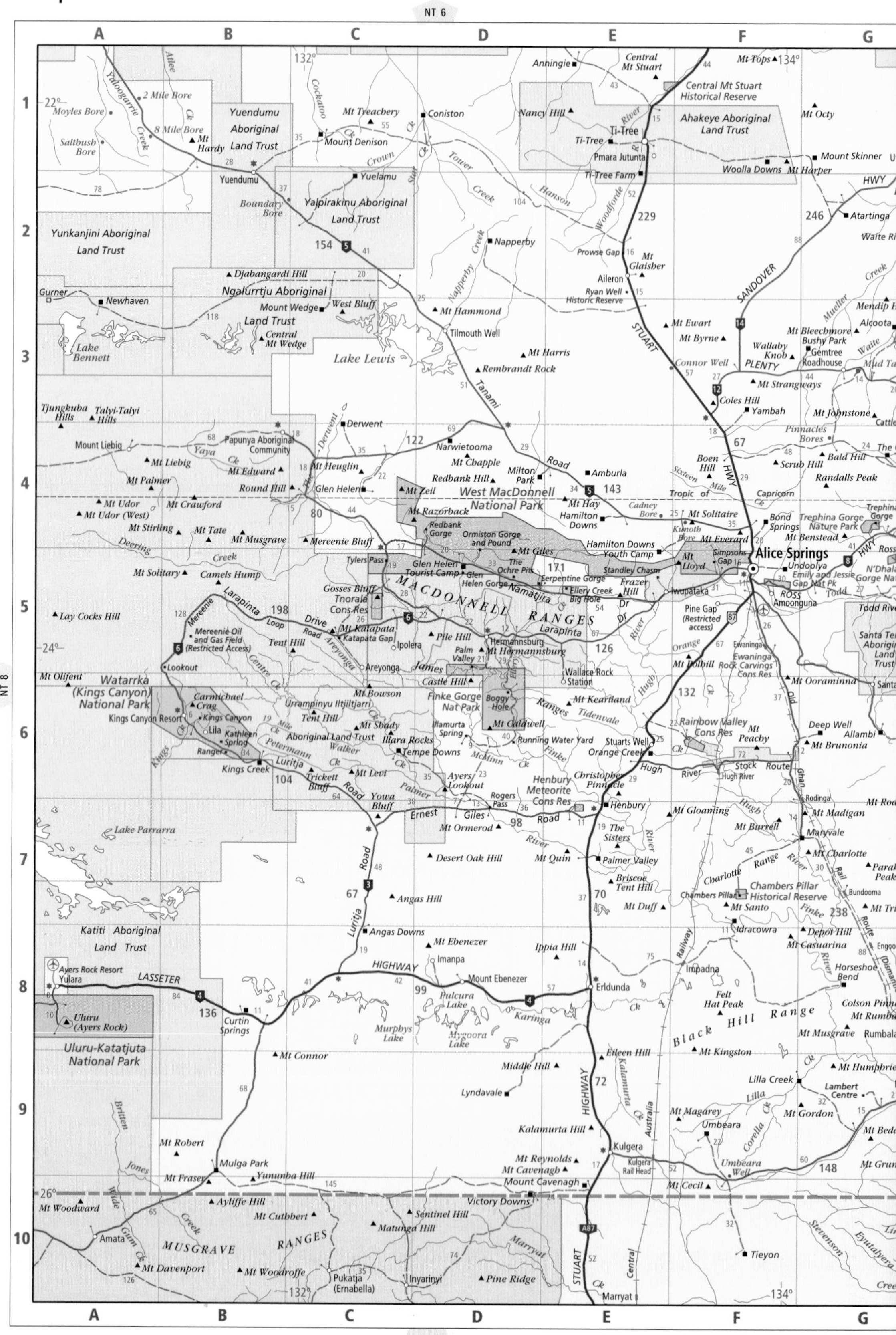
NT 6
NT 8
SA 1
A
B
C
D
E
F
G
1
2
3
4
5
6
7
8
9
10
132°
134°
22°
24°
26°
Anningie
Central Mt Stuart
Mt Tops
Central Mt Stuart Historical Reserve
Moyles Bore
2 Mile Bore
8 Mile Bore
Mt Hardy
Saltbush Bore
Yuendumu Aboriginal Land Trust
Mt Treachery
Coniston
Mount Denison
Nancy Hill
Ti-Tree
Pmara Jutunta
Ti-Tree Farm
Ahakeye Aboriginal Land Trust
Mt Octy
Mount Skinner
Woolla Downs
Mt Harper
Yuendumu
Boundary Bore
Yuelamu
Yalpirakinu Aboriginal Land Trust
Crown
Tower
Creek
Hanson
Woodforde
229
246
Atartinga
Waite River
Yunkanjini Aboriginal Land Trust
154
Napperby
Prowse Gap
Mt Glaisher
Aileron
Ryan Well Historic Reserve
SANDOVER
Creek
Djabangardi Hill
Gurner
Newhaven
Ngalurrtju Aboriginal Land Trust
Mount Wedge
West Bluff
Central Mt Wedge
Mt Hammond
Tilmouth Well
Lake Bennett
Lake Lewis
Mt Harris
Rembrandt Rock
STUART
Mt Ewart
Mt Byrne
Wallaby Knob
PLENTY
Mt Bleechmore
Bushy Park
Gemtree Roadhouse
Mendip Hills
Alcoota
Connor Well
Mt Strangways
Tanami
Coles Hill
Yambah
Mt Johnstone
Cattle
Tjungkuba Hills
Talyi-Talyi Hills
Derwent
122
Narwietooma
67
Pinnacles Bores
Mount Liebig
Papunya Aboriginal Community
Yaya Ck
Mt Heuglin
Mt Chapple
Road
Amburla
Boen Hill
Bald Hill
Mt Liebig
Mt Edward
Redbank Hill
Milton Park
Scrub Hill
Randalls Peak
Mt Palmer
Round Hill
Glen Helen
Mt Zeil
West MacDonnell National Park
143
Sixteen Mile
HWY
Tropic of Capricorn
Mt Udor
Mt Udor (West)
Mt Crawford
80
Mt Razorback
Mt Hay
Hamilton Downs
Cadney Bore
Mt Solitaire
Bond Springs
Trephina Gorge Nature Park
Trephina Gorge
Mt Stirling
Mt Tate
Mt Musgrave
Mereenie Bluff
Redbank Gorge
Ormiston Gorge and Pound
Mt Giles
Hamilton Downs Youth Camp
Kunoth Bore
Mt Everard
Mt Benstead
Deering
Creek
Tylers Pass
Glen Helen Tourist Camp
The Ochre Pits
171
Standley Chasm
Mt Lloyd
Simpsons Gap
Alice Springs
Undoolya
Emily and Jessie Gap Nat Pk
N'Dhala Gorge Nat Pk
Mt Solitary
Camels Hump
Glen Helen Gorge
Serpentine Gorge
Frazer Hill
Namatjira
Ellery Creek Big Hole
Iwupataka
ROSS
Amoonguna
Todd River
Gosses Bluff
Tnorala Cons Res
MACDONNELL RANGES
Larapinta
198
Loop
Drive
Lay Cocks Hill
Mereenie
Mereenie Oil and Gas Field (Restricted Access)
Road
Mt Katapata
Katapata Gap
Tent Hill
Ipolera
Pile Hill
Hermannsburg
Mt Hermannsburg
126
Pine Gap (Restricted access)
Santa Teresa Aboriginal Land Trust
Orange
Ewaninga
Ewaninga Rock Carvings Cons Res
Lookout
Centre Ck
Areyonga
Palm Valley
James
Castle Hill
Wallace Rock Station
Mt Polbill
Mt Olifent
Watarrka (Kings Canyon) National Park
Kings Canyon Resort
Carmichael Crag
Kings Canyon
Lila
Kathleen Spring
Ranger
Kings Creek
Mt Bowson
Urrampinyu Iltjiltjarri Aboriginal Land Trust
Finke Gorge Nat Park
Boggy Hole
Mt Kearnland
Tidenvale
132
Mt Ooraminna
Tent Hill
Mt Shady
Illamurta Spring
Mt Caldwell
Ranges
Rainbow Valley Cons Res
Mt Peachy
Deep Well
Allambi
Mt Brunonia
Illara Rocks
Tempe Downs
Running Water Yard
Stuarts Well
Orange Creek
Stock Route
Hugh River
Peterman
Walker
Luritja
104
Mt Levi
Trickett Bluff
Ayers Lookout
Christopher Pinnacle
Henbury Meteorite Cons Res
Henbury
Rodinga
Mt Rodinga
Yowa Bluff
Ernest Giles
Rogers Pass
98
Road
Mt Gloaming
Mt Madigan
Lake Parrarra
Mt Ormerod
The Sisters
Mt Burrell
Maryvale
Desert Oak Hill
Mt Quin
Palmer Valley
Mt Charlotte
Parak Peak
Briscoe Tent Hill
Charlotte Range
Chambers Pillar
Chambers Pillar Historical Reserve
Bundooma
Angas Hill
70
Mt Duff
Mt Santo
238
Katiti Aboriginal Land Trust
Angas Downs
Idracowra
Depot Hill
Mt Casuarina
Mt Ebenezer
Ippia Hill
Railway
Ayers Rock Resort
Yulara
LASSETER
HIGHWAY
Imanpa
Mount Ebenezer
Impadna
Horseshoe Bend
99
Erldunda
Pulcura Lake
Karinga
Felt Hat Peak
Colson Pinnacle
Mt Rumbalara
Rumbalara
Uluru (Ayers Rock)
136
Curtin Springs
Murphys Lake
Mygoora Lake
Black Hill Range
Mt Musgrave
Uluru-Katatjuta National Park
Mt Connor
Middle Hill
Eileen Hill
Mt Kingston
Mt Humphries
Lyndavale
72
Kalamurta Ck
Lilla Creek
Lambert Centre
Britten
Mt Magarey
Mt Gordon
HIGHWAY
Umbeara
Kalamurta Hill
Corella Ck
Australia
Mt Bedford
Mt Robert
Mt Reynolds
Kulgera
Mt Cavenagh
Kulgera Rail Head
Umbeara Well
148
Mt Grun
Jones
Mulga Park
Yununba Hill
Mt Fraser
Mount Cavenagh
Mt Cecil
Mt Woodward
Ayliffe Hill
Mt Cuthbert
Victory Downs
Sentinel Hill
Matunga Hill
Wide Gum Ck
Amata
MUSGRAVE RANGES
Marryat
Tieyon
Stevenson
Mt Davenport
Mt Woodroffe
Pukatja (Ernabella)
Inyarinyi
Pine Ridge
STUART
Central
Marryat

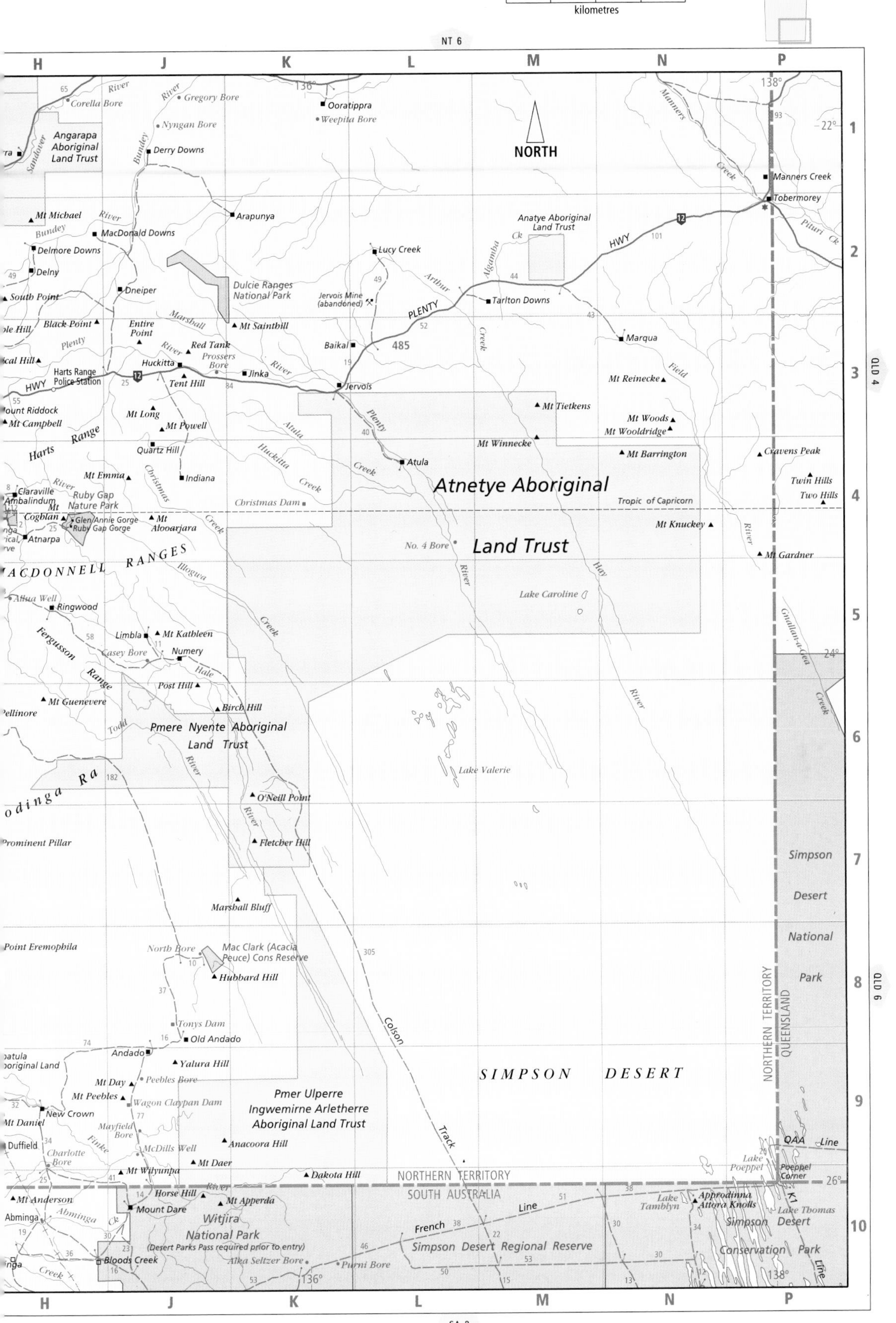
0 20 40 60 80
kilometres
NORTH
Angarapa Aboriginal Land Trust
Corella Bore
Gregory Bore
Nyngan Bore
Ooratippra
Weepita Bore
Derry Downs
Manners Creek
Tobermorey
Arapunya
Mt Michael
MacDonald Downs
Delmore Downs
Delny
Anatye Aboriginal Land Trust
Lucy Creek
HWY
Dneiper
South Point
Dulcie Ranges National Park
Jervois Mine (abandoned)
Tarlton Downs
PLENTY
Black Point
Entire Point
Mt Saintbill
Marqua
Red Tank
Prossers Bore
Baikal
485
Huckitta
Jinka
Harts Range Police Station
Tent Hill
Jervois
Mt Reinecke
Mt Tietkens
Mt Long
Mt Powell
Mt Campbell
Mt Woods
Mt Wooldridge
Mt Winnecke
Quartz Hill
Mt Barrington
Cravens Peak
Harts Range
Atula
Mt Emma
Indiana
Atnetye Aboriginal Land Trust
Twin Hills
Two Hills
Claraville
Ambalindum
Ruby Gap Nature Park
Christmas Dam
Tropic of Capricorn
Mt Cogblan
Glen Annie Gorge
Ruby Gap Gorge
Mt Alooarjara
Mt Knuckey
Atnarpa
No. 4 Bore
MACDONNELL RANGES
Mt Gardner
Lake Caroline
Allua Well
Ringwood
Limbla
Mt Kathleen
Fergusson Range
Casey Bore
Numery
Post Hill
Mt Guenevere
Birch Hill
Pellinore
Pmere Nyente Aboriginal Land Trust
Lake Valerie
O'Neill Point
Prominent Pillar
Fletcher Hill
Simpson Desert National Park
Marshall Bluff
Point Eremophila
North Bore
Mac Clark (Acacia Peuce) Cons Reserve
Hubbard Hill
Tonys Dam
Old Andado
Andado
Yalura Hill
SIMPSON DESERT
Mt Day
Peebles Bore
Mt Peebles
Wagon Claypan Dam
Pmer Ulperre Ingwemirne Arletherre Aboriginal Land Trust
New Crown
Mt Daniel
Mayfield Bore
Colson Track
Duffield
Charlotte Bore
McDills Well
Anacoora Hill
Mt Daer
QAA Line
Mt Wilyunpa
Dakota Hill
Lake Poeppel
Poeppel Corner
NORTHERN TERRITORY
QUEENSLAND
SOUTH AUSTRALIA
Mt Anderson
Horse Hill
Mt Apperda
Lake Tamblyn
Approdinna Attora Knolls
Lake Thomas
Abminga
Mount Dare
Witjira National Park
(Desert Parks Pass required prior to entry)
French Line
Simpson Desert Regional Reserve
Simpson Desert Conservation Park
Bloods Creek
Alka Seltzer Bore
Purni Bore
QLD 4
QLD 6
NT

Map 8

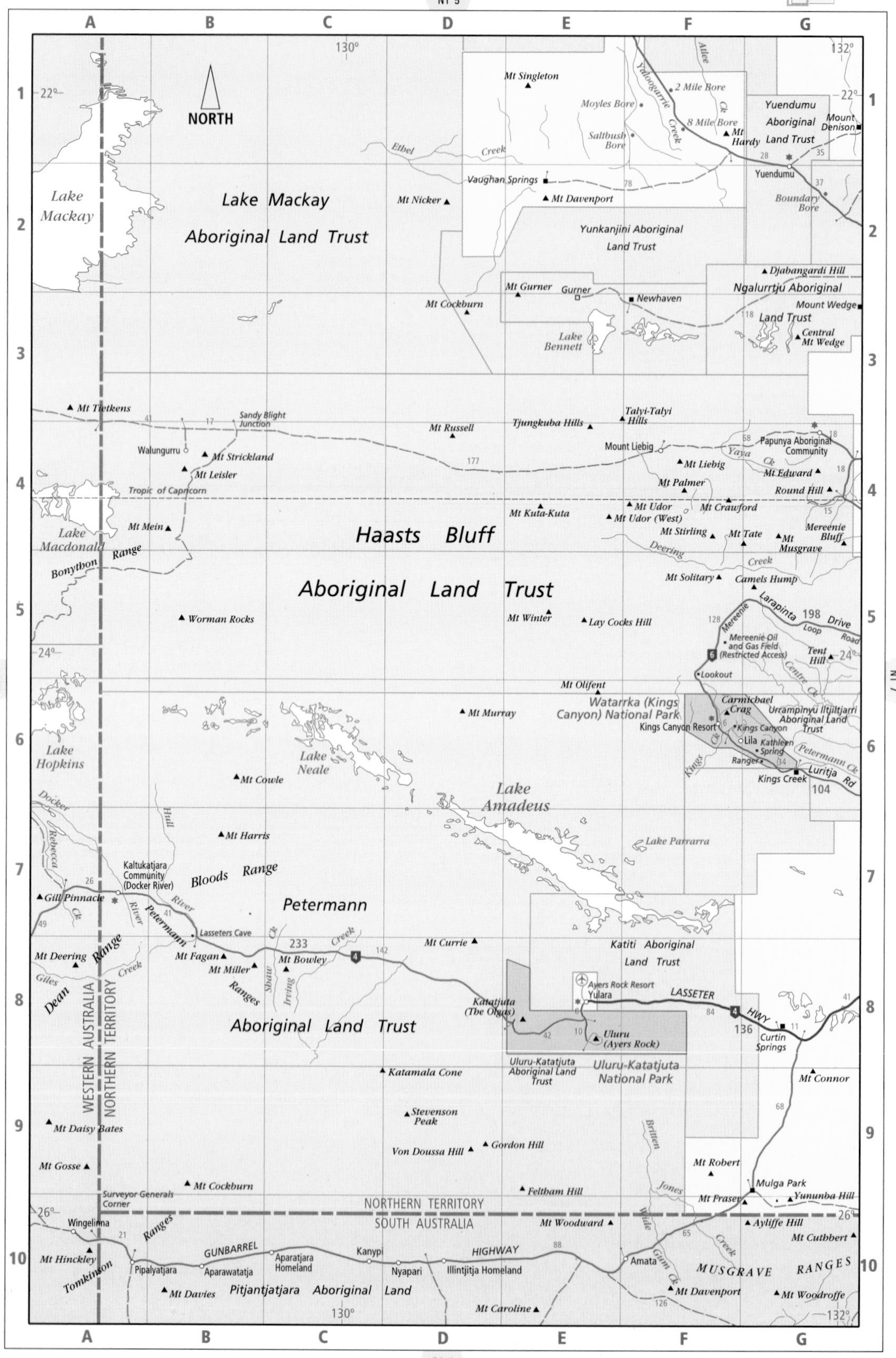
0 20 40 60 80
kilometres
NT 5
NORTH
Lake Mackay
Lake Mackay Aboriginal Land Trust
Mt Singleton
Moyles Bore
2 Mile Bore
8 Mile Bore
Mt Hardy
Saltbush Bore
Yalooguarrie Creek
Atlee Ck
Yuendumu Aboriginal Land Trust
Mount Denison
Yuendumu
Boundary Bore
Etbel Creek
Vaughan Springs
Mt Nicker
Mt Davenport
Yunkanjini Aboriginal Land Trust
Djabangardi Hill
Ngalurrtju Aboriginal Land Trust
Mount Wedge
Central Mt Wedge
Mt Gurner
Gurner
Newhaven
Mt Cockburn
Lake Bennett
Mt Tietkens
Sandy Blight Junction
Walungurru
Mt Strickland
Mt Leisler
Tropic of Capricorn
Mt Russell
Tjungkuba Hills
Talyi-Talyi Hills
Mount Liebig
Papunya Aboriginal Community
Yaya Ck
Mt Liebig
Mt Edward
Mt Palmer
Round Hill
Mt Udor
Mt Udor (West)
Mt Crawford
Mt Kuta-Kuta
Mt Mein
Lake Macdonald
Bonytbon Range
Haasts Bluff Aboriginal Land Trust
Mt Stirling
Mt Tate
Mt Musgrave
Mereenie Bluff
Deering Creek
Mt Solitary
Camels Hump
Larapinta Drive
Mereenie Loop Road
Worman Rocks
Mt Winter
Lay Cocks Hill
Mereenie Oil and Gas Field (Restricted Access)
Tent Hill
Lookout
Centre Ck
Mt Olifent
Watarrka (Kings Canyon) National Park
Carmichael Crag
Urrampinyu Iltjiltjarri Aboriginal Land Trust
Kings Canyon Resort
Kings Canyon
Lila
Kathleen Spring
Ranger
Kings Creek
Petermann Ck
Luritja Rd
Kings Ck
Mt Murray
Lake Neale
Lake Hopkins
Mt Cowle
Lake Amadeus
Lake Parrarra
Docker
Rebecca
Hull
Mt Harris
Kaltukatjara Community (Docker River)
Bloods Range
Gill Pinnacle
Petermann
Petermann River
Lasseters Cave
Shaw Ck
Creek
Mt Currie
Katiti Aboriginal Land Trust
Mt Deering
Dean Range
Giles Creek
Mt Fagan
Mt Miller
Mt Bowley
Irving
Ranges
Ayers Rock Resort
Yulara
LASSETER HWY
Katatjuta (The Olgas)
Uluru (Ayers Rock)
Curtin Springs
Aboriginal Land Trust
WESTERN AUSTRALIA
NORTHERN TERRITORY
Uluru-Katatjuta Aboriginal Land Trust
Uluru-Katatjuta National Park
Katamala Cone
Mt Connor
Stevenson Peak
Britten
Mt Daisy Bates
Von Doussa Hill
Gordon Hill
Mt Gosse
Mt Robert
Mt Cockburn
Feltham Hill
Jones
Mulga Park
Surveyor Generals Corner
Mt Fraser
Yunumba Hill
NORTHERN TERRITORY
SOUTH AUSTRALIA
Wingelinna
Mt Woodward
Ayliffe Hill
Wide Gum Ck
Creek
Mt Cuthbert
Ranges
GUNBARREL
HIGHWAY
Mt Hinckley
Tomkinson
Pipalyatjara
Aparawatatja
Aparatjara Homeland
Kanypi
Nyapari
Illintjitja Homeland
Amata
MUSGRAVE RANGES
Mt Davies
Pitjantjatjara Aboriginal Land
Mt Davenport
Mt Woodroffe
Mt Caroline
WA 7
NT 7
SA 1

Index and Gazetteer

Text entries for National Parks are shown in **bold**. Map references appear in the form of map title and grid reference, eg. WA 6 F2.

Acknowledgements

The Publisher believes that permission for use of all images has been obtained from the copyright owners, however, if any errors or omissions have occurred Global Book Publishing would be pleased to hear from copyright owners.

Back cover, bottom: © Alex Hinds; image from BigStockPhoto.com
p. 1: © Holger Leue; Image courtesy of Tourism Victoria
p. 2: Image courtesy of South Australian Tourism Commission
p. 3: Image courtesy of Tourism New South Wales
p. 6: © David Freund; image from iStockphoto.com
pp. 8–9, centre top; p. 17, right: Images courtesy of Tourism Queensland Image Library
pp. 18–19, bottom: Image courtesy of P&O Australian Resorts
p. 19, top; p. 23, top: Images courtesy of Tourism Queensland
p. 25; p. 31: Images courtesy of Tourism Queensland Image Library
p. 32: © Henry Price; image from iStockphoto.com
p. 34, bottom; p. 37, centre: Images courtesy of Tourism Queensland
p. 38, top; p. 39, bottom: Images courtesy of Tourism Queensland
p. 51: Table information reproduced with permission of Queensland EPA
p. 55, bottom left; p. 60, top: Images courtesy of Tourism New South Wales
p. 74, bottom: Image courtesy of John Hancock
p. 76, top; p. 78; p. 79, bottom: Images courtesy of Tourism New South Wales
p. 100, top; p. 103, centre; p. 106, top right: Courtesy of Tourism Victoria
p. 108: © Hank Shiffman; image from BigStockPhoto.com
p. 109, bottom: © David Scaletti; image from Tourism Victoria
p. 126, top: © Peter Dunphy; image from Tourism Victoria
p. 144, bottom left: Image courtesy of P&O Australian Resorts
pp 144-145: © Joel Grant; image from iStockphoto.com
p. 146, bottom left: Image courtesy of P&O Australian Resorts
p. 168 top: Image courtesy of South Australian Tourism Commission
p. 197, bottom: © Robert Dao; image from iStockphoto.com
p. 230, top; p. 234, top; Images courtesy of Northern Territory Tourist Commission
p. 238, bottom; p. 243, bottom: Images courtesy of Northern Territory Tourist Commission